Worlds of Difference

Worlds of Difference

Rethinking the Ethics of Global Education for the 21st Century

edited by Peter Pericles Trifonas

Routledge
Taylor & Francis Group
LONDON AND NEW YORK

First published 2008 by Paradigm Publishers

Published 2016 by Routledge
2 Park Square, Milton Park, Abingdon, Oxon OX14 4RN
711 Third Avenue, New York, NY 10017, USA

Routledge is an imprint of the Taylor & Francis Group, an informa business

Library of Congress Cataloging-in-Publication Data
Worlds of difference : rethinking the ethics of global education for the 21st century / edited by Peter Pericles Trifonas.
p. cm.
Includes bibliographical references and index.
ISBN-13: 978-1-59451-387-9 (hc : alk. paper)
ISBN: 978-1-59451-388-6 (pbk : alk. paper) 1. Educational anthropology. 2. Educational equalization. 3. Postmodernism and education. I. Trifonas, Peter Pericles, 1960-
LB45.W67 2007
306.43—dc22

2007016429

Designed and typeset by Straight Creek Bookmakers.

ISBN 13: 978-1-59451-387-9 (hbk)
ISBN 13: 978-1-59451-388-6 (pbk)

Editor's Dedication

For my father, Panayiotis

Contents

Introduction

Worlds of Difference engages the social constellations of education and what it means to actualize a public sphere for pedagogy that depends on the political conditions of an incessant globalization of cultures. Its chapters aim to elucidate the philosophical and ethical implications of arguments that slide across the continua of theoretical and political thought from the neo-liberal right to the democratic left. Questions of citizenship and democracy always arise in relation to problems of achieving "unity in diversity" and what that means for principles of equity, sovereignty, and the right of subjective agency. Each contribution to this collection leads us into the complex pathways of these burning issues and navigates a way for us to think about them as sites of praxis through which faith and hope in the power of subjective agency can be restored. The collection looks forward to the possibility of enacting new horizons of theory and practice for social reconstruction via the forum of an open, inclusive, and public discourse on the ethics of education in the twenty-first century. Only by opening up the contested spaces of meaning-making within the public sphere of education can we begin on the quest for social justice with a responsibility to a future yet to come, with a vision of individual and communal empowerment through education, and a pedagogy of critical democratic praxis amid worlds of difference.

Michael Apple takes to task the world of educational policy. He highlights the fact that there have been very few periods when education has taken such a central place in public debates, but laments the narrow ideological range of the conceptual and political forms in which this debate is carried out. According to Apple, these debates that were formerly seen as rightist policies have now become accepted as "common sense." Conservative policies are now often seen as "radical" but necessary solutions to an educational system that is out of control and is no longer responsive to the needs of "the people." Thus, a new kind of conservatism has evolved and has taken center stage in many nations, one that is best seen as the "conservative modernization" of the New Right. Apple shows how these ideas have been taken up by a much larger segment of government and policy makers and have even been appropriated by groups who one would least expect to do so, such as African American activists.

Jonathan Arendt presents a critical narrative of the U.S. government's reaction to the effects of Hurricane Katrina on New Orleans. While driving a U-Haul, alone, from Houston to Toronto with no company other than an AM/FM radio during the last week of August 2005, Arendt listened to a great deal of talk radio. He analyzes and reflects on the radio discussions of the disaster. As a recent elective cultural expatriate of Louisiana, he was interminably attached to the radio and television sets in hotel rooms and a friend's house, trying to gather as much information as possible about the fate of family and friends and dealing with his personal trauma and the incredible guilt of being far away from the wake of Katrina, unable to help. Arendt explains, "I am from Louisiana, but I felt that that fact didn't legitimate the horror I was feeling, because I was safe on the road, every minute taking me farther away from 'home' so I had no business claiming any sort of personal trauma." Even though he could not imagine the misery of the people who had to live amid the destruction, he listened to those, who like him could only witness the horror through the media, calling their local radio stations to voice their opinions, completely unaware of their privileged ability to make a phone call and watch on television those whose lives were irreparably changed. Arendt examines the reasons for his shock at hearing many of the phone calls lacking any modicum of sympathy. He tries to understand what caused these people, blissfully blessed with an air-conditioned ignorance and indifference, to abandon their "fellow Americans" in a tremendous time of need. He analyzes this indicative and troubling trend in United States today, where there is a growing middle-class resentment toward the poor and needy, especially when they are non-white. For Arendt, the reactions to the effects of Hurricane Katrina on the fate of the New Orleans population provides an exemplary case study for examining the hardening attitude of the middle class toward the dependent poor and the extent of the racial divide between the black and Latino urban poor and the white suburban middle class.

Douglas Kellner argues that educators need to cultivate multiple literacies for contemporary technological and multicultural societies, that teachers need to develop new literacies of diverse sorts, including a more fundamental importance for print literacy, to meet the challenge of restructuring education for a hi-tech, multicultural society and global culture. In a period of dramatic technological and social change, education needs to help produce a variety of types of literacies to make current pedagogy relevant to the demands of the contemporary era. As new technologies are altering every aspect of our society and culture, we need to comprehend and make use of them both to understand and transform our worlds. In particular, by introducing multiple literacies to empower individuals and groups traditionally excluded, education could be reconstructed to make it more responsive to the challenges of a democratic and multicultural society.

Brenda Trofanenko discusses one of the most powerful institutions that defines identity: the museum. The museum is a place where "culture" is often embodied as a shared descent, or, at least, as the educational institution of a "people" with a historically stable and unchanging identity. Trofanenko makes us aware that what comes to be understood as culture in a museum is often a curator's authority to label and display an artifact with an interpretation projected onto an object then identified and named as culture. As modern educational institutions, broadly defined, museums have fashioned the concepts of culture and of cultural identity during the last century, in an effort to naturalize their educational imperative. Yet, this subscribed culture and cultural identity is not without question, both from within and beyond the institutional realms. What has operated as the museum's imperative of defining an unquestioned representation of culture comes up against resistance, where museums have also had to struggle to keep how they define culture and cultural identity from becoming the source of their own educational undoing. Trofanenko points out that postcolonial scholarship has engaged the universals that define identity across a range of sites including museums, with a purpose of distinguishing shared principles and problems in the ways that culturally diverse groups are being represented, or named, today. Ethnology museums, those museums whose collections and intent focus on culture, reflect how cultural identity is defined by its imperial imperative, by the ability to define cultural identity through the circulation of certain representations. Yet, both partial and situated identities are constructed through the historically defined privileges and rights granted by the public and the museums' own professional organizations. While each museum reflects its institutional norms and values by way of its collection and display mandates, the debate concerning museums and First Nations objects and exhibitions has prompted extending and encouraging expressions of resistance. Calls for self-representation and repatriation of objects from Native and non-Native groups both within and beyond the museum indicate that this display of identity is imbued with political and ideological questions. The museum is also about how the legacy of imperialism to name and define cultural difference is to be challenged, in order to consider the conditions of possibility made available by understanding how identity is framed within difference and how employing difference serves as an educational starting point. Museums maintain a sense of knowing about the other while, as many critics have made clear, continuing to question how they work against their historically defined exclusion and how they contribute to the alienation of various cultural and ethnic groups they purport to represent.

Neil Harrison critiques two common discourses in Australia about Aboriginal people. The first is a discourse of enlightenment in which Aboriginal people are positioned between the two poles of deficit and enlightenment. The second is a romantic discourse where the speaker marvels at the order of Aboriginal society. An example of the first discourse appeals to the poor academic performance of Aboriginal students on basic skills tests and positions students against an image of deficit that reifies a "merry-go-round of misery." But it also invokes a competitive relation between Aboriginal and migrant children to suggest that if Aboriginal students work hard, they too can do as well as the latter group. Harrison details how speakers of "Aboriginal English" are usually positioned within the discourse of enlightenment where Aboriginal students in schools, for example, are considered to speak bad English, but they are also positioned in relation to a promise that "Standard Australian English" (SE) will deliver them from the powerlessness of their Aboriginal lives to get a job in white society. He questions the logic of a discourse and educational policy that endows "Standard Australian English" with the power to provide people with a better life. But better than what? A better life for Aboriginal people is often produced in discourse in relation to an Aboriginal past or a non-Aboriginal future. Harrison shows how students in schools and universities replicate these discourses by talking about Aboriginal people as being able to make a choice between the poles of disadvantage and opportunity. Given the pervasiveness of these dichotomies and the discourses that reproduce them in western society, it is almost impossible for students as speakers of "Standard English" to talk and think about people, including themselves, in any other way.

Lisa Taylor argues that any understanding of the contemporary context of globalization needs to be contextualized within an analysis of earlier colonial processes of global circulation, specifically universalist modernity's incorporation/configuration and deployment of difference. In the current era, at least two forms or configurations of globalization coexist. The first is organized by imperial grand narratives and raced, ethnicized, gendered, and classed discourses of national identity that depend upon the absolute separation and binary opposition of difference. This older, more unitary, and seemingly more homogenous system of globalization is challenged by a newer "global postmodern" that caters to and promotes an Americanized, anglophone mass culture. Its façade presents itself as a celebration of difference and the endless pleasure of its proliferation. In the consumption and commodification of diversity and "exotica," this system capitalizes upon cultural, gendered, and classed difference in order to enhance global marketing and exploit divisions of labor. Taylor asks: What visions of difference are being naturalized in these two co-existing forms of globalization? In both forms of globalization in which we are living today, the figure of difference is pivotal to social, cultural, political, and economic relations of power, value, and access to resources, opportunity, and security. Consequently, it remains crucial to the many long traditions of education for social justice addressed in this anthology, as the political and conceptual terrain of our transformative work.

Taylor deconstructs the logic of these two conceptualizations of difference outlined above and how they prove highly dangerous as they inform educational projects: the first has fueled assimilationist pedagogies (such as English-only approaches to the education of ESL students) and essentialist identity-based politics within critical education. The second can be associated with reductive forms of multicultural education that celebrate a show-and-tell ethnotourism approach to difference and are silent on issues of discrimination. For Taylor a question remains: Which imaginings of difference might ground an integrative, radically equitable project for social change? She explores this question with reference to feminist and postcolonial translation theory. I ground my discussion in ethnographic material excerpted from a qualitative case study of the experiences of discrimination shared and collectively explored by thirty English as a Second Language (ESL) high school students within the context of a Freirean-style, integrative antiracism leadership program in Toronto, Canada. In order to understand the ways their difference was framed in their experiences and the ways they reconstituted it as a strategic, relational standpoint and speaking position, she reframes these as translational negotiations of identity, meaning, and value that strive to articulate what Homi Bhabha has described as "an intercultural ethic of contiguity." Taylor poses urgent questions facing us as educators for social change, sketching an initial proposal for a pedagogy of critical cultural translation.

Peter McLaren and Valerie Scatamburlo-D'Annibale argue for the importance of resuscitating the concepts of class, class analysis, and class struggle in this age of globalized capitalism. The "discourse radicalism" of contemporary left poseurs in the academy has led to a fashionable apostasy that has severed the critical links between theory and revolutionary praxis. Taking a cue from Marx, McLaren and Scatamburlo-D'Annibale contend that much of what falls under the rubric of "post-al" theory and politics is rather superficial and esoteric; little more than an academic exercise of nominalism and excessive discursivism. They show how the fetishization of language has led us willy-nilly down a path where politics takes a back seat to aesthetics, where form takes precedence over substance, and where pseudo-radicalism replaces genuine political engagement with inequitable social and economic arrangements. Today, equal amounts of busy work are carried out by many "left" intellectuals in the form of a flighty theoreticism that bears little connection to the realities of our contemporary world. They no longer ask nor explore the "big" questions because they've painted themselves into a corner of particularisms, fetishized conceptions of "difference," tropicity, and the rhetoricity of discourse. More starkly for McLaren and Scatamburlo-D'Annibale, they have also expunged questions of class and the interrogation of capitalism from the theoretical and political canvas. What, then, must be done, both theoretically and politically? To these questions there are no easy answers or prescriptions, and McLaren and Scatamburlo-D'Annibale do not purport to offer simple solutions nor to exhaust all political possibilities. But they believe that if social change is the aim for the "left"—as it has traditionally been—it must resuscitate a sustained and unrelenting interrogation of capitalism, and it must overcome the corrosive skepticism of those narratives that have rendered visions of social transformation as hopelessly obsolete. Indeed, transcending the debilitating political pessimism that characterizes whatever remains of the left is the most important issue anyone seriously interested in social change must confront. The criticisms are not advocating an anti-theory stance. Rather, McLaren and Scatamburlo-D'Annibale are concerned with the kinds of theoretical discourses that have become so common in Leftist circles—those that have become so trapped in the prison house of discursivity and textuality that they have contributed little to understanding the actual complexion of contemporary capitalism, those that revel in theorizing endlessly about gender, race, ethnicity, and class but which tend to say very little about the latter and which have even less to say about the material conditions of actual people. To this end, McLaren and Scatamburlo-D'Annibale call for a serious reconsideration of the enduring relevance of Marx and the tradition of historical materialism.

Peter Trifonas and Paulo Ghiraldelli, Jr. examine how the phenomena of virtual learning and its environments are characterized when we look at the theoretical presuppositions supporting the pragmatics of new digital technologies through a contemporary philosophical perspective on experience and education. Postmodern epistemological doubt settles in between the apparatus used for the technical manipulation of information and its archival containment of data as virtual signs of understanding. Trifonas and Ghiraldelli analyze the need for a techno-epistemology—or a view of virtual knowledge that takes into account the influences of technological mediation upon the sources of its production and perception. Representation deforms, denatures, and supplements the originary eidetic structures of conceptual formations. Technology redeems a postmodern epistemological doubt by quelling it in the practice of facilitating pragmatic ends through the supplementation of human weakness. Trifonas and Ghiraldelli argue that the origins of technology can be thought of as the supplementation of experience. Technology is a prosthetic of and for the deficiency of reason. Such a post-Darwinian supplementation of nature readily follows the "principle of optimal performance." Technology presupposes the need for the proof of the efficacy of research and scientific knowledge. The concreteness of its manifest structures and operations objectify the union of thought and action. Trifonas and Ghiraldelli show how the foundation for the instrumental reason of education is born when the root of technology becomes competence rather than invention or *poiesis,* utility rather than creativity or art. The economizing of reason as "instrumental" has serious implications for the production of knowledge in educational contexts by promoting the logic of end-oriented practice. The point is to add to the cultural archive of information for social profit. Trifonas and Ghiraldelli warn that a lack of ecological and intellectual altruism that directs the reason of technology toward the practical incentives of a marketable and reproducible knowledge is dangerous to the imperatives of education for the public good.

Henry Giroux takes a stand on the ill-fated war in Iraq, its reckless free-market triumphalism that is deciding the fate of most nations of the world. He criticizes the disregard for human rights of United States citizens and the increasing support at the highest levels of government for radical Christian religious groups. Giroux shows what is often ignored by many critics: the war being waged on the "home front." This war can be seen not only in the crushing assault on unions and civil liberties, but also in the restructuring of the tax system to benefit the rich and drain resources from the poor and the middle class. The war at home has been exacerbated by the ascendancy of neoliberal corporate culture into every aspect of American life. For Giroux, neoliberalism consolidates economic power in the hands of the few, aggressively attempts to destroy the welfare state, subordinates the needs of society to the dictates of corporate power, views misfortune as a weakness, and deems public services and goods an unconscionable luxury. Giroux contends that, with few exceptions, the project of democratizing public goods, redistributing resources, and addressing important social problems has fallen into disrepute in the popular imagination as the logic of the market undermines the most basic social solidarities. The consequences include not only a weakened social state, but a growing sense of insecurity, cynicism, and political retreat on the part of the general public. With the reconfiguration of the state, Giroux examines how democracy increasingly appears damaged, if not fatally wounded, as those who are young, poor, immigrants, or people of color are excluded from the operations of power, the realm of politics, and crucial social provisions. Americans have embraced as a defining feature of politics the idea that all levels of government would assume a large measure of responsibility for providing the resources, social provisions, security, and modes of education which enable young people to be prepared for the present while offering them a better future as the meaning and depth of an inclusive democracy are simultaneously expanded. But just as education has been separated from any viable notion of politics, Giroux traces how youth have been separated from the discourse of either the social contract or any ethical notion of what it might mean for society to provide young people with the prospects of a decent and democratic future. In America, youth increasingly have come to be seen as a problem rather than as a resource for investing in the future. Framed largely as a generation of suspects, they are now treated as either a disposable population, fodder for a barbaric war in Iraq, or the source of most of society's problems. Giroux maintains that youth now constitute a crisis that has less to do with improving the future than with denying it. He shows how the logic of punishment and fear have replaced compassion and social investment as the most important modalities mediating the relationship of youth to the larger social order.

Mario Di Paolantonio traces the particular paradox that entangles us when we work to transmit the past. Because the historian works with the texts of an other who cannot speak, the historian must pledge a *promise* to remain loyal to the words of a witness, in a gesture of pure *affiliation* to restore the past in its own terms, guarding its summons against any present condensation or reduction. Di Paolantonio nods to the impossibility of ever fully realizing this promise and affiliation. If the historian's pledge to the past merely transmits a negative protocol for policing our fidelity to the text, it surely falls short of registering a "living narration" that can evoke, in this present and in subsequent generations, the task of giving countenance, of meeting, responding, and passing on the past. Moreover, for Di Paolantonio, there is a risk of this pledge to fidelity becoming a relentlessly insistent and restrictive demand, perhaps even a form of necrophilia, which would foreclose the creativity required by those in the present to reanimate the past as one of "our" concerns. The problem of the truth of historical witness is framed by a series of interconnected questions: In the narrow confines of such a restrictive injunction for historical transmission, what could possibly motivate and engage us to grapple with the words of an absent other, with an alien way of speaking? For in order to engage with this task, in order to meet with and so feel obligated to stories from other times and places, do we not need to begin our response in our immediate discursive reality? Surely we cannot become obligated to represent/engage with the past through an unmediated form. Unquestionably then, the past requires a "contact point," an "annotation," a thorough reworking through our present modes of reception and dissemination in order for it to be re-presentable and meaningful to us. But once this past becomes expressed as one of our concerns, through our present forms of mediation and terms, what preserves its difference from being wholly subsumed? What prevents its otherness from being compressed and revised within the exigencies of the moment, within a form that fits the present model of circulation? What guards the past from becoming a mere footnote that authorizes our terms and legitimizes our desires? How can it be annotated, brought into our present terms, so that it engages and motivates us to honor its words, so that we may respect and respond to its difference? Di Paolantonio shows us the solecism of a historiography that seeks to transmit the past into the present in order to preserve the difference of the past while simultaneously generating an understanding that conforms and expands our present vocabulary. Hermeneutics appears to offer a thorough lesson and means of resolving the paradox of historical transmission. But what are the ethical consequences of this hermeneutical way of working with the past? Engaging the double binds that Jacques Derrida sets up in his essay "This Is Not An Oral Footnote" and also drawing on Walter Benjamin's "The Task of the Translator," Di Paolantonio traces the indelible entanglements and limits of the hermeneutical endeavour to transmit what is other to our present terms.

Peter Pericles Trifonas and Greg O'Leary begin from the premise that we have lived within the divide of conceptual locations of so-called modernist and postmodernist perspectives for so long that we have constructed paradigms of exclusion with respect to understanding how to overcome difference within pedagogical formations and what it means to know. They believe there is a current need to readdress the conceptual grounds of the divide, to clarify some of the ideological presuppositions, and to reach a synthesis between paradigmatic positions in terms of where curriculum theory currently stands. Within this chapter, Trifonas and O'Leary trace the historical reintroduction of a modernist view of education through a seminal article written by Paul Hirst some forty years ago. As a corrective to overly generalized depictions of modernist educational theory,. which sometimes reduce all modernist pedagogy to a series of vague all-inclusive descriptors, they engage with this specific and "famous" article on liberal education from the academic right. By juxtaposing Hirst's conception of a liberal education (which is both situated within and differentiated from the classical principles that preceded it) with some of the postmodern and poststructural ideas around education and knowledge that have since followed, they begin to map out future trajectories and pathways for education and curriculum theory. To simply ask what knowledge is worth most is no longer enough. It reveals the limitations of a pseudo-, unproductive schism that has stunted the growth and progress of educational thinking. Rather than providing yet another tug in a war of positions, Trifonas and O'Leary explain why it is time to direct our efforts toward responsibly engaging others in education for a new ethical "turn" in educational thinking and our conception of academic responsibility.

CHAPTER 1

Strategic Alliance or Hegemonic Strategy?

Multicultural Conservatism in America

Michael W. Apple

Mapping Conservative Modernization

This is both a good and bad time in the world of educational policy. On the one hand, there have been very few periods when education has taken such a central place in public debates about our present and future. On the other hand, an increasingly limited range of ideological and discursive resources dominates the conceptual and political forms in which this debate is carried out. These debates are occurring on an uneven playing field, one in which what were formerly seen as rightist policies have now become "common-sense" (Apple 2000, 2006). Yet, such conservative policies have a different kind of cachet today. There is a sense that these are not only things that will protect a romantic past; these policies are now often seen as "radical" but necessary solutions to an educational system that is out of control and is no longer responsive to the needs of "the people."

Thus, a new kind of conservatism has evolved and has taken center stage in many nations, one that is best seen as "conservative modernization" (Dale 1989/1990, Apple 2006, Apple and Buras 2006). Although parts of these positions may have originated within the New Right, they are now not limited to what has traditionally been called the Right, however. They have been taken up by a much larger segment of government and policy makers and, as we shall see in this chapter, have even been appropriated by groups who one would least expect to do so, such as African American activists. How are we to understand this? In answering this question, while my focus here shall largely be on the United States, the tendencies I describe have implications well beyond one nation.

The concepts we use to try to understand and act on the world in which we live do not by themselves determine the answers we may find. Answers are not determined by words, but by the power relations that impose their interpretations of these concepts. Yet, there are key words that continually surface in the debates over education. These key words have complicated histories, histories that are connected to the social movements out of which they arose and in which they are struggled over today. These words have their own histories, but they are increasingly interrelated. The concepts are simple to list: markets, standards, accountability, tradition, God, and a number of others. Behind each of these topics is an assemblage of other words that have an emotional valence and that provide the support for the ways in which differential power works in our daily lives. These concepts include democracy, freedom, choice, morality, family, culture, and a number of other key concepts. And each of these in turn is intertextual. Each and every one of these is connected to an entire set of assumptions about "appropriate" institutions, values, social relationships, and policies.

Think of this situation as something of a road map. Using one key word—*markets*—sends you onto a highway that is going in one direction and that has exits in some places but not others. If you are on a highway labeled Market, your general direction is toward a section of the country named The Economy. You take the exit named Individualism that goes by way of another road called Consumer Choice. Exits with words such as Unions, Collective Freedom, The Common Good, Politics, and similar destinations are to be avoided if they are on the map at all. The first road is a simple route with one goal—deciding where one wants to go without a lot of time-wasting discussion and getting there by the fastest and cheapest method possible. There is a second route, however, and this one involves a good deal of collective deliberation about where we might want to go. It assumes that there may be some continuing deliberation about not only the goal, but also even the route itself. Its exits are the ones that were avoided on the first route.

There are powerful interests that have made the road map and the roads. Some want only the road labeled Market, because this supposedly leads to Individual Choice. Others will go down that road, but only if the exits are those that have a long history of "real culture" and "real knowledge." Still others will take the market road because for them God has said that this is "his" road. And finally, another group will sign on to this tour because they have skills in mapmaking and in determining how far we are from our goal. There's some discussion and some compromise—and perhaps even some lingering tension—among these various groups about which exits will ultimately be stopped at, but by and large they all head off in that direction.

This exercise in storytelling maps on to reality in important ways. The first group is what is appropriately called *neoliberals*. They are deeply committed to markets and to freedom as "individual choice." The second group, *neoconservatives*, has a vision of an Edenic past and wants a return to discipline and traditional knowledge. The third, one that is increasingly powerful in the United States and elsewhere, is what I call *authoritarian populists*—religious fundamentalists and conservative evangelicals who want a return to (their) God in all of our institutions.[1] And finally, the mapmakers and experts on whether we got there are members of a particular fraction of the managerial and professional *new middle class*.

In analyzing this complex configuration of interests around conservative modernization, I have argued that we need to act in a way similar to what Eric Hobsbawm described as the historian's and social critic's duty. For Hobsbawm, the task is to be the "professional remembrancers of what [our] fellow citizens wish to forget" (Hobsbawm 1994, p. 3). That is, it requires us to detail the absent presences, the there that is not there, in most rightist policies in education. How does their language work to highlight certain things as "real" problems, while marginalizing others? What are the effects of the policies that they have promoted? How do the seemingly contradictory policies that have emerged from the various fractions of the Right, aspects of which have now taken on a life of their own at times—such as the marketization of education through voucher plans, the pressure to "return" to the Western tradition and to a supposedly common culture, the commitment to get God back into the schools and classrooms of America, and the growth of national and state curriculum and reductive national and state (and often "high-stakes") testing—actually get put together in creative ways to push many of the aspects of these rightist agendas forward?

In a number of recent books, I have critically analyzed why and how this has occurred. Along with others (see, e.g., Whitty, Power, and Halpin 1998; Gillborn and Youdell 2000; Power, Edwards, Whitty, and Wigfall 2003; Ball 2003), I have examined a range of proposals for educational "reform" such as marketization, standards, national/statewide curricula and national/statewide testing. This critical examination has demonstrated that, even with the often good intentions of the proponents of many of these kinds of proposals, in the long run they may actually exacerbate inequalities, especially around class and race. Furthermore, they may paradoxically cause us both to misrecognize what actually causes difficult social and educational problems and to miss some important democratic alternatives that may offer more hope in the long run (see, e.g., Apple 2006, Apple et al. 2003, Apple 2000, Apple and Beane 1999).

It is helpful to think of this as having been accomplished through the use of a vast socio-/pedagogic project, a project that has actively—and in large part successfully—sought to transform our very ideas about democracy. Democracy is no longer a political concept; rather it is wholly an economic concept in which unattached individuals—supposedly making "rational" choices on an unfettered market—will ultimately lead to a better society. As Foner (1998) reminds us, it has taken decades of creative ideological work to change our commonsense ideas about democracy. Not only does this change fly in the face of a very long tradition of collective understandings of democracy in the United States, but it has also led to the destruction of many communities, jobs, health care, and so many other institutions not only in the United States but also throughout the world (Katz 2001, Greider 1997). Hidden assumptions about class and a goodly portion of the politics of whiteness may make it hard for us to face this honestly (see Fine et al. 1997, Lipman 2004, Valenzuela 2005).

But let me stop myself here. I should have put two words in the last sentences of the preceding paragraph—*us* and *we*—in quotation marks. Who is the "we"? Does it include all those who have been hurt by that combination of neoliberal and neoconservative polices that now play such an important role in our discourse in education? If these policies have a disproportionate and negative effect on, say, the working class and on people of color—as they seem to do—should we assume that, for example, all persons of color will recognize this and will reject both the policies and their underlying ideologies? That this is not the case is the subject of the rest of this chapter.

Strange Allies

Given the history of their struggles for both redistribution and recognition, it would be very difficult to integrate historically disenfranchised social groups, especially people of color, under the umbrella of conservative modernization (Fraser 1997, Apple 2000). However, this does not make it impossible. One of the ways in which hegemonic alliances are built is through a process in which dominant groups creatively use the elements of "good sense" that disenfranchised groups possess and then attach their neoliberal and neoconservative agendas to these elements (Apple 2006, Apple and Buras 2006). Unfortunately, the partial success of such a strategy among those groups who are often counted as "despised others" (Fraser 1997) in our societies is a subject that many progressives would like to forget. Yet, there is increasing evidence that there are growing numbers of members of "minority" groups, conservative women, and gays and lesbians who are activists in neoliberal and neoconservative movements, and to a lesser extent in authoritarian populist religious movements. (Of course, given the crucial role that black churches have played in the historical struggles for justice [West 1982], it would be surprising if there were not elements of such sentiments within African American communities.)

There have been exceptions to this relative neglect. In a recent book, Dillard (2001), for example, critically examines a number of the key actors within conservative circles who themselves are members of historically oppressed groups, but who—for a variety of personal and political reasons—give vocal support to neoliberal and neoconservative causes. Aggressively "free" market policies, a rejection of affirmative action and the use of race and/or gender as a category in public decisions, mobilizing for public funding for religiously based schooling, welfare "reform," and a host of similar issues provide the centers of gravity for these individuals. Many of the figures on which she focuses will be familiar to those on the United States' side of the Atlantic: Dinesh D'Sousa, Thomas Sowell, Clarence Thomas, Linda Chavez, Glenn Loury, Richard Rodriguez, and similar national spokespersons of conservative causes. Each of these figures is a person of color. Among them are well-known academics, journalists, government officials, and a justice of the Supreme Court. Other figures may be familiar only to those readers who have closely followed the cultural and political debates on the Right in the United States over such things as educational policy, sexuality, affirmative action, and welfare reform: Star Parker, George Schuyler, Andrew Sullivan, Elizabeth Wright, Bruce Bawer, and Susan Au Allen, among others.[2]

There is of course a history of dominant groups using—or at least giving visibility to—"minority" voices to "say the unsayable" in the United States and elsewhere (Lewis 1993, 2000). Thus, for example, Ward Connerly, a prominent conservative African American businessman and a vocal member of the Board of Regents of the University of California, has taken a very visible stand against affirmative action. For him, government involvement is actually harmful to black Americans. "While others are assimilating, blacks are getting further and further away from one nation indivisible" (quoted in Dillard 2001, p. 50). His insistence on "individual merit" and his rejection of state intervention for the cause of equality has clearly been employed by the larger, and mostly white, conservative movement to legitimate its own policies. As a prominent conservative spokeswoman put it, "You can't have white guys saying you don't need affirmative action" (Dillard 2001, p. 15). Powerful neoliberal and neoconservative movements both inside and outside government circles, hence, can steadily expand the realm of what is in fact sayable by prefacing what would otherwise be seen as consistently racist positions with a quote from a well-known black spokesperson. One of the most articulate critics of such moves states that this enables dominant economic, cultural, and racial groups "to cannibalize the moral authority of minority voices by skirting responsibility" (Dillard 2001, p. 20).

Because of this very history of dominant groups employing the selective voice of the "other" to legitimize its actions (see Apple and Buras 2006), there has been a concomitant history of regarding those members of minority communities who openly affiliate with conservative movements as "pariahs." They have been dismissed as either "traitors" or "sell-outs," and even seen as "self-loathing reactionaries who are little more than dupes of powerful white . . . conservatives" (Dillard 2001, p. 4). While these labels are powerful indeed, many conservative persons of color see themselves very differently. In their self-perception, they are "crusading rebels" against a state and a liberal elite within the ranks of their own communities whose own self-understanding as "helping the people" actually mystifies policies that work to destroy the very moral and social foundations of their communities. Here they can also turn to a rich history of nationalist, self-help, and conservative moral principles within these communities as a source of "authenticity" and legitimacy (Dillard 2001, p. 13).

Of course, there *are* internally developed conservative traditions within, say, communities of color, many of which have made lasting contributions to the very existence and continuity of the cultures within these communities (see, e.g., Lewis 1993, 2000). However, given the fact that so much of the conservative tradition in the United States was explicitly shaped by racist and racializing discourses and practices,[3] and by a strongly anti-immigrant heritage as well (a powerful element that is very visible again), and given the fact that much of the current neoliberal and neoconservative attacks on the public sphere have had disproportionate effects on the gains of poor communities and on communities of color, the current existence and growth of such movement among dispossessed groups is more than a little striking.[4] This makes their current iterations all the more interesting.

As we shall see, neoliberal and neoconservative economic, political, and cultural movements *and* some of the African American groups that have been connected to them are both seeking to redefine the relations of power in particular social fields, with education being a prime site where these relations of power are being worked through (Bourdieu 1984). A complex process of discursive and positional disarticulation and rearticulation is going on here, as dominant groups attempt to pull dispossessed collectivities under their own leadership and dispossessed groups themselves attempt to employ the social, economic, and cultural capital usually possessed by dominant groups to gain collective power for themselves. As we shall also see, the label "conservative" cannot be employed easily in understanding the actions of all of the dispossessed groups who do ally themselves with conservative causes without at the same time reducing the complexity of the particular social fields of power on which they operate.

Perhaps the most interesting example of the processes of discursive and social disarticulation and rearticulation that one could find today involves the growing African American support for neoliberal policies such as voucher plans (see, e.g., Moe 2001). A key instance is the Black Alliance for Educational Options (BAEO), a group of African American parents and activists that is chaired by Howard Fuller, the former superintendent of Milwaukee public schools, one of the most racially segregated school systems in the United States (Apple and Pedroni 2005). BAEO provides vocal support for voucher plans, "choice" (a sliding signifier whose meaning has increasingly become fixed around issues of vouchers in the United States when it is used in political discourse), and similar conservative proposals. It has generated considerable support within black communities throughout the nation, particularly within poor inner-city areas, and has an identifiable presence in 27 cities within the United States.[5] The fact that the supreme court of Wisconsin has ruled that the Milwaukee voucher plan is constitutional and the United States Supreme Court ruled that the Cleveland voucher plan is also constitutional gives more legal and political legitimacy to BAEO's efforts, since both plans were officially aimed at providing the "right to exit" for inner-city and largely "minority" residents.

A sense of the language that underpins BAEO's commitment can be seen in the following quote:

> Our children are our most precious resource. It is our responsibility to love them, nurture them and protect them. It is also our responsibility to ensure that they are properly educated. Without a good education, they will [not] have a real chance to engage in the practice of freedom: the process of engaging in the fight to transform their world. (BAEO 2006a)

BAEO's mission is clear. "The Black Alliance for Educational Options is a national, nonpartisan member organization whose mission is to actively support parental choice to empower families and increase educational options for Black children" (BAEO 2006b). Its position is even clearer in its manifesto. The use of language here is striking. The language of neoliberalism (choice, parental empowerment, accountability, individual freedom) is reappropriated and sutured together with ideas of collective black freedom and a deep concern for the community's children. This creates something of a "hybrid" discourse that blends together meanings from multiple political sources and agendas. In some ways, this is similar to the long history of critical cultural analyses that demonstrate that people form bricolages in their daily lives and can employ language and commodities in ways undreamed of by the original producers of the language and products (see, e.g., Willis 1990).

While this process of rearticulation and use is important to note, it is equally essential to recognize something that makes the creative bricolage in which BAEO is engaged somewhat more problematic. A very large portion of the group's funding comes directly from conservative sources such as the Bradley

> BAEO Manifesto
>
> Current systems of K-12 education work well for many of America's children. But, for far too many children, the current systems do not work well at all. A high percentage of these children are poor children of color living in urban areas. For these children, the old educational strategies and institutional arrangements are not preparing them to be productive and socially responsible citizens. This requires that we dramatically change our teaching and learning strategies and create new governance and financial structures.
>
> BAEO believes we must develop new systems of learning opportunities to complement and expand existing systems. We need systems that truly empower parents, that allow dollars to follow students, that hold adults as well as students accountable for academic achievement, and that alter the power arrangements that are the foundation for existing systems.
>
> BAEO understands that there are no "silver bullets" or "magic wands" which will instantly make things better for our children. BAEO is also not anti-public school. However, we do believe that parent choice must be the centerpiece of strategies and tactics aimed at improving education for our children. We must empower parents, particularly low-income parents, to make the best choices for their children's education.
>
> Consider the potential impact of this power in the hands of families who previously have had little or no control over the flow and distribution of the money that drives the policies and procedures of the educational systems of this country. Consider how the absence of this power means that their children will remain trapped in schools that more affluent parents, some of whom oppose parental choice, would never tolerate for their own children. Consider how this power shift may change the shape of the future for their children.
>
> BAEO will bring together the ideas, aspirations, energies, and experiences of all generations in this struggle. (BAEO 2006c)

Foundation. The Bradley Foundation, a well-known sponsor of conservative causes, has not only been in the forefront of providing support for vouchers and privatization initiatives, but also is one of the groups that provided significant support for Herrnstein and Murray's book, *The Bell Curve* (1994), a volume that argued that African Americans were on average less intelligent than whites and that this was genetic in nature. Thus, it would be important to ask about the nature and effects of the connections being made between rightist ideological and financial sources and BAEO itself. It is not inconsequential that neoliberal and neoconservative foundations provide not only funding but media visibility for "minority" groups who support—even critically—their agendas.

The genesis of such funding is not inconsequential. Many of the strongest proponents of vouchers and similar plans may claim that their positions are based on a belief in the efficiency of markets, on the fear of a secularization of the sacred, or on the dangers of losing the values and beliefs that give meaning to their lives. However, historically, neither the economic nor the moral elements of this critique can be totally set apart from their partial genesis in the struggles over racial segregation, over busing to achieve integration, and in the loss of a federal tax exemption by conservative—and usually white only—religious academies. In short, the fear of the "racial other" has played a significant role in this discursive construction of the "problem of the public school" (Apple 2006). Does this mean that groups such as BAEO are simply being manipulated by neoliberal and neoconservative foundations and movements? An answer to this question is not easy, but even with my cautions stated above it is certainly not a simple yes.

Strategic Compromises?

It is important not to engage in reductive analyses here, ones, for example, that assume that simply because a group's funding comes from a specific source, therefore all of its own agendas will be fundamentally determined by where it gets its money. This is certainly not always the case. Indeed, in public forums and in discussions Tom Pedroni and I have had with some of the leaders of BAEO, they have argued that they will use any funding sources available so that they can follow their own specific program of action. They would accept money from more liberal sources; but Bradley and other conservative foundations have come forward much more readily.[6] In the minds of the leaders of BAEO, the African American activists are in control, not the conservative foundations. Thus, for BAEO, they see themselves as strategically positioning themselves in order to get funding from conservative sources. What they do with this funding, such as their strong (and well-advertised in the media) support for voucher plans (although this support too is contingent and sometimes depends on local power relations), is wholly their decision. For them, the space provided by educational markets can be reoccupied for black cultural and/or nationalist politics and can be employed to stop what seems to them (more than a little accurately in my opinion) to be the strikingly ineffective, and even damaging, education of black children.[7]

However, while I have a good deal of respect for a number of the leaders of BAEO, it is important to remember that they are not the only ones strategically organizing on this social field of power. Like BAEO, groups affiliated with, say, the Bradley Foundation also know exactly what they are doing and know very well how to employ the agendas of BAEO for their own purposes, purposes that in the long term often may run directly counter to the interests of the majority of those with less power at both the national and regional levels. Is it really in the long-term interests of people of color to be affiliated with the same groups who provided funding and support for books such as Herrnstein and Murray's (1994) *The Bell Curve*? I think not, although once again we need to recognize the complexities involved here.

I am certain that this kind of question is constantly raised about the conservative stances taken by the people of color who have made alliances with, say, neoliberals and neoconservatives—and by the activists within BAEO itself. When members of groups who are consistently "othered" in this society strategically take on identities that support dominant groups, such questioning is natural and I believe essential. However, it is also crucial to remember that members of historically oppressed and marginalized groups have *always* had to act on a terrain that is not of their choosing, have always had to act strategically and creatively to gain some measure of support from dominant groups to advance their causes (Lewis 1993, 2000; Omi and Winant 1994). It is also the case that more recently national and local leaders of the Democratic Party in the United States have too often assumed that black support is simply *there*, that it doesn't need to be worked for. Because of this, we may see the further development of "unusual alliances" over specific issues such as educational policies. When this is coupled with some of the tacit and/or overt support within some communities of color not only for voucher plans but for antigay, antiabortion, pro-school prayer, and similar initiatives, the suturing together of some black groups with larger conservative movements on particular issues is not totally surprising (see Dillard 2001).

The existence and growing power of committed movements such as BAEO, though, does point out that we need to be careful about stereotyping groups who may publicly support neoliberal and neoconservative policies. Their perspectives need to be examined carefully and taken seriously, not simply dismissed as totally misguided, as people who have been duped into unthinking acceptance of a harmful set of ideologies. There are complicated strategic moves being made on an equally complex social field of power. I may—and do—strongly disagree with a number of the positions that groups such as BAEO take. However, to assume that they are simply puppets of conservative forces is not only to be too dismissive of their own attempts at social maneuvering, but I also believe that it may be tacitly racist as well (Apple and Pedroni 2005, Pedroni in press).

Saying this doesn't mean that we need to weaken our arguments against marketization and privatization of schooling. Voucher and tax credit plans (the later ultimately may actually be more dangerous) will still have some extremely problematic effects in the long term. One of the most important effects could be a *demobilization* of social movements within communities of color. Schools have played central roles in the creation of movements for justice. In essence, rather than being peripheral reflections of larger battles and dynamics, struggles over schooling—over what should be taught, over the relationship between schools and local communities, over the very ends and means of the institution itself—have provided a crucible for the *formation* of larger social movements toward equality (Hogan 1982, Apple et al. 2003, Anyon 2005). These collective movements have transformed our definitions of rights, of who should have them, and of the role of the government in guaranteeing these rights. Absent organized, communitywide mobilizations, these transformations would not have occurred.

This is under threat currently. Definitions of democracy based on possessive individualism, on the citizen as only a "consumer," are inherently grounded in a process of de-racing, de-classing, and de-gendering (Ball 1994). These are the very groups who have employed struggles over educational access and outcomes to form themselves as self-conscious actors. If it is the case, as I strongly believe it is, that it is the organized efforts of social movements that ultimately have led to the transformation of our educational system in more democratic directions (Apple 2000), the long-term effects of neoliberal definitions of democracy may be truly tragic for communities of color, not "only" in increasing inequalities in schools (see, e.g., Apple 2006, Valenzuela 2005, Lipman 2004, McNeil 2000, Gillborn and Youdell 2000), but in leading to a very real loss of the impetus for *collective* solutions to pressing social problems (Anyon 2005). If all problems are simply "solved" by individual choices on a market, then collective mobilizations tend to wither and perhaps even disappear. If history is any guide here, the results will not be pleasant. Thus, although short-term support for neoliberal and neoconservative policies may seem strategically wise to some members of less powerful groups, and may in fact generate short-term mobilizations, I remain deeply worried about what will happen over time.[8] It is the long-term implications of individuating processes and ideologies, and their effects on the necessity of larger and constantly growing social mobilizations that aim toward substantive transformations within the public sphere, that need to be of concern as well.

A concern over the effects of individuation that such "choice" programs may ultimately bring is unfortunately actually mirrored in the (already limited) literature on black support for neoliberal and neoconservative policies. All too much of the critical literature on such "strategic alliances," even such work as Dillard's compelling book (2001), tends to focus on individuals, rather than on larger social movements. As I noted above, it is social movements that historically have had the power to transform social and educational policy and practice. An emphasis on individuals does humanize the issues that are in contention and it does allow us to see the people behind the rightist presence within marginalized communities. However, this very focus causes us to miss the dynamics that have led to the growth of groups such as BAEO and to the strategic moves that are being self-consciously made on the unequal social fields of power in which educational policy operates.

This doesn't vitiate the strength of what such analyses of the growing conservative tendencies among some "othered" communities have given us. However, the question is not whether it is possible to build a rightist-led coalition that will include elements of "multiculturalism." Indeed, as I have shown in this chapter, such a process is in part already being successfully attempted. Instead, the questions we must constantly ask are the following: At what cost? At whose expense?

We do know, for example, that the integration of some elements of communities that have historically been seen as "the other" has occurred, that certain elements have been brought under the umbrella of conservative modernization. For instance, some Latino/as, Asian Americans, gays and lesbians, and others have given their support to what are surprisingly conservative causes. Although perhaps overstating her arguments for political reasons, Dillard, for example, is at her most perceptive when she sees that the roots of the support of conservative positions among some members of oppressed groups may often be based in not wanting to "be black." It is worth quoting her at length here.

> [One] point on which Latino, Asian-American, women, and homosexual conservatives seem to agree is the desire, to restate the matter bluntly, not to be like blacks—members of a group that persists in pressing for collective redress from the government rather than pursuing the path of individualism, upward mobility, and assimilation. That some Latino and Asian-American conservatives have engaged in this narrative is troubling. If Toni Morrison is even partially correct in asserting that previous waves of immigrants have embraced (white, middle class) American identity "on the back of blacks," then there is reason to fear that new immigrants will seek to replicate this pattern. In the process, the already tense relationships among African Americans, Latinos, and Asian-Americans could degenerate. That some African American conservatives, a contingent that remains predominantly middle and upper-middle class, appear content to follow suit—to assimilate on the backs of the black poor—is doubly disturbing. (Dillard 2001, p. 182)

Although I do not think that her arguments are as applicable to groups such as BAEO, for many other persons and organizations with which she does deal Dillard's points need to be taken very seriously. For the implication of such arguments is that the major losers in the shifting discursive terrain surrounding race and identity may very well prove once again to be poor blacks. Once more, they will be pathologized. Their voices will be silenced. And they will continue to be "everybody's convenient and favorite scapegoat" (p. 182). Given the central place that race has played in the development of the neoconservative movement of "return" and the neoliberal movement of "choice" (Apple 2006, Apple and Buras 2006), we should not be surprised if rightist multiculturalism promises more of the same, but is covered in a new and seemingly more diverse discourse.

"Not wanting to be black" does not explain the support of vouchers by groups such as BAEO, however. Instead, it is the very fact of *being black*, of recognizing and fighting against their social and cultural positioning as the ultimate "other," that has caused them to seek out strategic—some might say heretical—alliances with some of the main tendencies that, paradoxically, have been in the forefront historically in supporting such positioning. In *Educating the "Right" Way* (Apple 2006), I call for thinking heretically about possible alliances that might subvert parts of the agendas involved in conservative modernization. Whether BAEO's "heretical actions" actually do subvert such agendas and the racial stratification of schools remains to be seen. I fear that they may not. But one must also ask what choices they in fact do have given the structures of inequality that currently exist.

Conclusion

In this chapter, I have examined a growing phenomenon—the growth of seemingly conservative sentiments among "despised others." At the core of my analysis is a concern about what is at stake for all of us if rightist multiculturalism succeeds in redefining what and whose knowledge is of most worth and what our social and educational policies are meant to do. Yet, no matter what one's position is on the wisdom of BAEO's strategic actions, the entire case provides a crucial example of the politics of disarticulation and rearticulation, on the ways in which social movements and alliances are formed and re-formed out of the material and ideological conditions of daily life, and of the politics of discursive reappropriation (Hall 1996, Apple and Pedroni 2005, Apple 2006).[9] Thus, an analysis of such movements is important both in terms of the balance of forces and power involved in specific educational reforms, but also in terms of more general issues concerning the processes of social transformation and agency. A critical but sympathetic understanding of groups such as BAEO may enable us to avoid the essentialism and reductionism that enters into critical sociological work on the role of struggles over the state. It can provide a more nuanced sense of social actors and the possibilities and limits of strategic alliances in a time of conservative modernization (see Apple and Pedroni 2005, Pedroni in press).

While I support the struggles of groups such as BAEO and have a good deal of sympathy with their critique of the current functioning of public (state-supported) schools, I have very real worries about whether they can control the uses to which their support of neoliberal policies will be put.

Yet, having said this, there may be some salutary effects of their efforts to mobilize around vouchers.

If the common school loses its legitimacy among significant numbers of people within communities of color—and there is some evidence that this may be happening within some communities (Moe 2001)—this may force a re-examination of the unequal ways in which schools are currently financed in the United States, where a school's funding is dependent on the local tax base and its very real inequalities. It also may create the conditions in which teachers and their unions may have to work much more closely with local communities than is the case now simply in order for teachers to maintain their legitimacy in the eyes of people of color (for examples, see Apple and Beane in press, Gutstein 2006). I say this knowing that, oddly enough, this might provide evidence for parts of the neoliberal case about school markets. Fear of competition among teachers and other educators then may have hidden effects that may, finally, lead to even more support among them for needed changes in schools.

Having said this, however, I predict the opposite. While these changes may occur, it is unfortunately just as likely that the effects will be less positive in their long-term consequences. Less funding will be given to public schools. A politics of blame will evolve in which parents who have no choice but to keep their children in underfunded and highly policed inner-city schools will be seen as the source of the problem of the common school (Andre-Bechely 2006, Anyon 2005, Lipman 2004). Much depends on the balance of forces at the time. Given what I and others have shown about the often negative results of the combination of neoconservative and neoliberal reforms in schools, I am not sanguine about what will happen. At the very least, though, we need to be aware that the complicated politics and strategic maneuverings that are occurring on the terrain of educational policy will have complicated, contradictory, and unforeseen results. The example of BAEO signifies the beginning, not the end, of this story.

Although I have focused on the growth of strategic alliances between "despised others" and conservative forces in the United States, I predict that such alliances may not be limited to this one nation.[10] This may be disturbing to many progressively inclined educators, and this leads to my final point. Any groups that disagree with BAEO about the wisdom of supporting vouchers and of making tactical alliances with the Right have a task that goes well beyond simply criticizing their position or their strategy. Critics of their positions and strategies must have a detailed and in-depth understanding both of what generates their anger at public schools and at the lack of responsiveness that all too many school systems have shown to communities of color and the poor and working class for decades. The conditions to which groups like BAEO are responding are *real* and immensely destructive on real children in real communities (see, example.g., Kozol 1991, 2005). Thus, those who worry about BAEO must ask what they themselves are for. They need to redouble their own efforts to end the racial contract that underpins "our" economic and political institutions (Mills 1997), to work even harder to provide the economic and cultural conditions that would make African American parents and so many other communities of color have faith in their schools, and to challenge the ways in which a politics of whiteness underpins so much of the daily life of this society. Simply saying no to BAEO, then, is not enough. Indeed, I would claim that it is a racializing act itself unless it is accompanied by powerful antiracist actions.

Acknowledgments

I would like to thank David Gillborn, Steven Selden, and in particular Tom Pedroni for their perceptive comments on the issues raised in this chapter. Tom Pedroni has offered important conceptual, historical, and empirical suggestions and criticisms. A number of my arguments are indebted to his own ongoing investigation of BAEO and the complexities of African American educational politics. See Pedroni (in press). An earlier version of this chapter appeared in the *London Review of Education*. More extensive treatments of these issues can be found in Apple (2006) and Apple and Pedroni (2005).

Notes

1. The term *authoritarian populism* originally comes from the compelling work of Stuart Hall. Unlike Hall, however, I would prefer to limit its use to a particular group of people who make up the "religious right." For more on this, see Hall (1980) and Apple (2006).

2. Although her analysis could be more detailed and subtle in certain places, Dillard (2001) does a good job of detailing the "structures of feeling" of conservative affiliations among a number of people who usually are not expected to take such positions. She deals with a wide range of different forms of conservative leanings: from the economy, the legitimacy of activist government, the politics of the body, and the role of religion in public affairs on the one hand, to questions dealing with what knowledge should and should not be taught as "legitimate" and, say, the place of race in university admissions on the other.

3. "Progressive" traditions in the United States were not free of such racializing and racist logics. See, for example, Selden (1999).

4. That, say, a number of African American groups, ones that are making alliances with distinctly conservative movements, exist and are growing says something very important about the fascination with identity politics among many progressive scholars and activists in education and elsewhere. Too often writing on identity (wrongly) assumes that identity politics is a "good thing," that people inexorably move in progressive directions as they pursue what Nancy Fraser would call a politics of

recognition (Fraser, 1997). Yet, any serious study of rightist movements demonstrates that identity politics is just as apt to take, say, angry and retrogressive forms—antigay, racist nativism, antiwomen, etc. For many such people, "we" are the new oppressed, with that "we" not including most people of color, feminists, "sexual deviants," immigrants, and so on (see, e.g., Kintz 1997, Blee 2002, Apple and Buras 2006). Yet, as I noted earlier, even people within these "despised" groups themselves may take on such retrogressive identities.

5. BAEO is a heterogeneous organization. Much, though not all, of BAEO's leadership is from the middle class, but it does have a good deal of grassroots support. Where it specifically meets and intersects with Rightist organizations, those who interact with such organizations tend not to be among the poor and working class. However, a class analysis is not sufficient here. Racial solidarity may come first; race fundamentally mediates class relations. Thus, the issue of the class position of BAEO's leadership needs to be thought about in complex and subtle ways. I wish to thank Tom Pedroni for this point. See Apple and Pedroni (2005) and Pedroni (in press).

6. In this regard, Tom Pedroni's research on BAEO is of considerable importance. See Pedroni (in press).

7. In this regard, the political issue they are facing is in some ways similar to the debates over "market socialism." Can economic and political forms developed under the auspices of less progressive tendencies and power relations be employed to further goals that are organized around a very different set of ideological sentiments? See, for example, Bardhan and Roemer (1993) and Ollman (1998).

8. Dillard (2001) herself is very fair in her assessment of what the implications of such support may be. She nicely shows the contradictions of the arguments and logic of the people she focuses upon. In doing so, she draws upon some of the more cogent analyses of the relationship between democracy and the maintenance of the public sphere on the one hand and an expansive and rich understanding of what it means to be a citizen on the other. Readers of her discussion would also be well served to connect her arguments to the historical struggles over the very meanings of our concepts of democracy, freedom, and citizenship such as that found in Eric Foner's illuminating book *The Story of American Freedom* (1998), but Dillard's discussion is substantive and useful. It also serves as a reminder of the continuing importance of a number of democratic and critical writers such as Hannah Arendt (1973, 1990), whose work, while not perfect by any means, unfortunately is no longer read as often as it should be.

9. An analysis of groups such as BAEO could enable us to extend the range of Basil Bernstein's work on *recontextualization* as well. See Bernstein (1990).

10. Heidi Safia Mirza's ongoing work on the role of schooling in communities of color in England is very interesting in this regard.

References

Andre-Bechely, L. (2006) *Could It Be Otherwise? Parents and the Inequities of Public School Choice.* New York: Routledge.

Anyon, J. (2005) *Radical Possibilities: Public Policy, Urban Education, and a New Social Movement.* New York: Routledge.

Apple, M.W. (2000) *Official Knowledge,* 2nd edition. New York: Routledge.

———. (2006) *Educating the "Right" Way: Markets, Standards, God, and Inequality,* 2nd edition. New York: Routledge.

Apple, M.W. and Beane, J.A. (1999) *Democratic Schools: Lessons from the Chalk Face.* Buckingham: Open University Press.

———. (in press) *Democratic Schools,* 2nd edition. Portsmouth, NH: Heinemann.

Apple, M.W. and Buras, K.L. (eds.) (2006) *The Subaltern Speak: Curriculum, Power, and Educational Struggles.* New York: Routledge.

Apple, M.W. and Pedroni, T. (2005) "Conservative Alliance Building and African American Support for Voucher Plans," *Teachers College Record* 107: 2068–2105.

Apple, M.W. et al. (2003). *State and the Politics of Knowledge.* New York: Routledge-Falmer.

Arendt, H. (1973) *The Human Condition.* Chicago: University of Chicago Press.

———. (1990) *On Revolution.* New York: Penguin Books.

Ball, S. (1994) *Education Reform.* Buckingham: Open University Press.

———. (2003) *Class Strategies and the Education Market.* New York: Routledge.

Bardhan, P. and Roemer, J. (eds.) (1993) *Market Socialism: The Current Debate.* New York: Oxford University Press.

Bernstein, B. (1990) *The Structuring of Pedagogic Discourse.* New York: Routledge.

Black Alliance for Educational Options (BAEO) (2006a) http://www.baeo.org.

———. (2006b) http://www.baeo.org/programs?program_id=7&program_category_secondary_page_id=27 (accessed DATE, 2006).

———. (2006c) http://www.baeo.org/about/manifesto/htm.

Blee, K. (2002) *Inside Organized Racism: Women in the Hate Movement.* Berkeley: University of California Press.

Bourdieu, P. (1984) *Distinction.* Cambridge: Harvard University Press.

Dale, R. (1989/1990) "The Thatcherite project in education," *Critical Social Policy* 9, 1: 4–19.

Dillard, A.D. (2001) *Guess Who's Coming to Dinner Now: Multicultural Conservatism in America.* New York: New York University Press.

Fine, M., Weis, L., Powell, L., and Wong, L.M. (eds.) (1997) *Off White.* New York: Routledge.

Foner, E. (1998) *The Story of American Freedom.* New York: Norton.

Fraser, N. (1997) *Justice Interruptus.* New York: Routledge.

Gillborn, D. and Youdell, D. (2000) *Rationing Education.* Philadelphia: Open University Press.

Greider, W. (1997) *One World, Ready or Not.* New York: Simon and Schuster.

Gutstein, E. (2006) *Reading and Writing the World with Mathematics.* New York: Routledge.

Hall, S. (1980) "Popular Democratic vs. Authoritarian Populism," in A. Hunt (ed.), *Marxism and Democracy.* London: Lawrence and Wishart.

———. (1996) "On Postmodernism and Articulation," in D. Morley and K-H. Chen (eds.), *Stuart Hall: Critical Dialogues in Cultural Studies.* New York: Routledge.

Herrnstein, R. and Murray, C. (1994) *The Bell Curve.* New York: Free Press.
Hobsbawm, E. (1994) *The Age of Extremes.* New York: Pantheon.
Hogan, D. (1982) "Education and class formation," in M.W. Apple (ed.), *Cultural and Economic Reproduction in Education.* Boston: Routledge and Kegan Paul.
Katz, M.B. (2001) *The Price of Citizenship.* New York: Metropolitan Books.
Kintz, L. (1997) *Between Jesus and the Market.* Durham, NC: Duke University Press.
Kozol, J. (1991) *Savage Inequalities.* New York: Crown.
———. (2005) *The Shame of the Nation: The Restoration of Apartheid Schooling in America.* New York: Crown.
Lewis, D.L. (1993) *W.E.B. DuBois: Biography of a Race, 1868–1919.* New York: Henry Holt.
———. (2000) *W.E.B. DuBois: The Fight for Equality and the American Century, 1919–1963.* New York: Henry Holt.
Lipman, P. (2004) *High Stakes Education.* New York: Routledge.
McNeil, L. (2000) *Contradictions of School Reform.* New York: Routledge.
Mills, C. (1997) *The Racial Contract.* Ithaca, NY: Cornell University Press.
Moe, T. (2001) *Schools, Vouchers, and the American Public.* Washington, DC: Brookings Institution.
Ollman, B. (ed.) (1998) *Market Socialism: The Debate among Socialists.* New York: Routledge.
Omi, M. and Winant, H. (1994) *Racial Formation in the United States,* 2nd edition. New York: Routledge.
Pedroni, T. (in press) *Market Movements: African American Involvement in School Voucher Reform.* New York: Routledge.
Power, S., Edwards, T., Whitty, G., and Wigfall, V. (2003) *Education and the Middle Class.* Philadelphia: Open University Press.
Selden, S. (1999) *Inheriting Shame.* New York: Teachers College Press.
Valenzuela, A. (ed.) (2005) *Leaving Children Behind.* Albany: State University of New York Press.
West, C. (1982) *Prophesy Deliverance!* Philadelphia: Westminster Press.
Whitty, G., Power, S., and Halpin, D. (1998) *Devolution and Choice in Education.* Buckingham: Open University Press.
Willis, P. (1990) *Common Culture.* Boulder, CO: Westview.

CHAPTER 2

The "Them" and the "I" of a Hurricane

Broadcast News Influences on the Reality and Attitudes of Its Viewers

Jonathan Arendt

> It was a cold-blooded lie that a god had lovingly made the world and set out the sun and moon as lights to land dwellers, that brothers had fought, that one of the races was saved, the other cursed. Yet he, the old Shaper, might make it true, by the sweetness of his harp, his cunning trickery. It came to me with a fierce jolt that I wanted it. As they did too, though with vicious animals, cunning, cracked with theories. I wanted it, yes! Even if I must be the outcast, cursed by the rules of his hideous fable.
>
> *Grendel, John Gardner*

Driving a U-Haul, alone, from Houston to Toronto with no company other than an AM/FM stereo avails one with the opportunity to listen to and reflect upon a great deal of talk radio. When this is the last week of August 2005, much of the airtime is dedicated to regular updates on the devastation coming out of New Orleans in the wake of Hurricane Katrina. As a recent elective cultural expatriate of Louisiana, I was interminably attached to the radio and television sets in hotel rooms and a friend's house trying to gather as much information as I possibly could about my family and friends. I couldn't believe the images I was seeing on television and I felt incredibly guilty. I am from Louisiana but I felt that that fact didn't legitimate the horror I was feeling because I was safe on the road, every minute taking me farther away from "home" so I had no business claiming any sort of personal trauma. I couldn't imagine the misery of the people who had to live amidst the destruction and

I would never presume to know what they must have been feeling. And yet, that didn't stop others, callers all over the United States, from calling their local radio stations and voicing their opinions, completely unaware of their privileged ability to make a phone call and watch on television those whose lives were irreparably changed.

I was shocked to hear many of the phone calls lacking any modicum of sympathy; some went so far as to lecture the New Orleanians as if they could actually hear. One caller in Ohio staunchly declared how his suburban neighborhood "would never act like that"; how can one make such a claim when no comparable crisis has been faced? I heard a New Yorker further disassociate himself from these "savages" but, through his generosity, still offered a solution: "Just start walking." The electricity went out in New York City a couple of years ago, after all, and the people were very civil and they simply walked home. Again, I was amazed at the ignorance and the wholly inadequate analogizing. The lights go out in New York City and people are able to walk down streets to get home a few miles away, whereas New Orleans is in complete disarray and there is *no home* for most people to return to and the farthest area of relative safety is dozens of miles away along routes rendered impassable by the storm. These are merely a couple of phone calls that represented the majority of callers I listened to.

I simply didn't understand what caused these people, blissfully blessed with an air-conditioned ignorance and indifference, to abandon their "fellow Americans" in a tremendous time of need. But it struck me as indicative of a troubling trend in the United States today, a growing middle-class resentment toward the poor and needy, especially when they are nonwhite. Jack Beatty wrote that "the crisis of the middle class is of commanding gravity.... The crisis is hardening the attitude of the middle class toward the dependent poor, and to the extent that the poor and urban and black and Latino and the middle class suburban and white, race relations are under a new exogenous strain" (McCarthy et al. 1997, p. 232). Hurricane Katrina provides an exemplary case study for the strain Beatty was addressing. Elsewhere, in two different *Time* magazine articles, the same issue was examined, this "new mood in political and social life in the United States: a mood articulated in suburban fear of encirclement by difference, and increasingly formulated in a language and politics of what James and Nietzsche called 'resentment.' The dangerous inner city and the world 'outside' are brought into the suburban home through television" (McCarthy et al. 1997, p.232–233). What results is a strain on a conflict between social classes and this conflict intensifies as "the dual model of the rich-versus-poor city splinters into fragmentary communities signified by images of the roaming homeless on network television" (McCarthy et al. 1997, p. 233). Research has established that television can (in)form attitudes and awareness of the "Other," a point I'll return to later in the piece.

What I find most disturbing, here, though, is the manner in which this resentment manifests itself in the opinions I heard on the radio and have since seen elsewhere. As pundits debated the manner and merits of aid for hurricane victims, I was amazed to hear the number of people who, over and over again, exhibited the belief that "the needs of the inner city are ... a wasteful 'social agenda'" (McCarthy et al. 1997, p. 233). It's not just talk-show callers and media personalities where this view of dependence is perpetuated. A multicultural education professor at a prominent university in the United States has written, "Minorities tend to confirm their status as victims by remaining dependent upon whites and the perpetuation of white guilt as a means of keeping disagreeable whites 'on the hook' for personal gain" (Birrell 2004). How an issue of victimization becomes an occasion for "personal gain" is beyond me; but there are those who believe that Hurricane Katrina has provided the evacuated homeless with an opportunity for gain. In a recent, widely circulated e-mail that my brother forwarded to me (knowing my disdain for such an attitude), the following exclamation is made: "I say we don't owe them anything and if anything, they OWE us, the Tax Payers that are 'WORKING PEOPLE', they owe what they have been mooching off of the Tax Payers for almost a year now. It is obvious that they don't intend to work as long as they can sponge off of the system. It is time to cut them loose and tell them the free ride is over!" (C. Arendt, personal communication, May 8, 2006). In a few short, spirited lines this e-mail reflects the following: that this tragedy is categorically being used for personal gain by the victims; that the "us" and "them" mentality typifies the splintered binary; and that the middle class resents feeling burdened by the requisite, perceived provision for others.

This bothered me immensely throughout the coverage of Katrina and that impression has never left me; I am still very disturbed. As I reflected on the nature of such attitudes, I wondered what factors might mitigate such a mindset and I began to more closely scrutinize the news coverage and a dawning realization came over me: the broadcast news media cannot be counted on to accurately depict actuality; the best we can seem to hope for is what Baudrillard called the "reality effect" (1983, p. 3). The images on the television screens and the sound bites by the victims and the reporting of the journalists were so far removed from what was actually happening, and yet it defined the attitudes and created the reality for most television viewers. It was in this media genesis of reality that stereotypes were reinforced, complicating any chance of capturing what was actually going on and furthering the gaps that already exist between whites and blacks, rich and poor, "savage" and "civil." Through its history of skewed news reporting, the media have changed the attitudes of viewers so that differences (e.g., class, race) and distance manufacture a reality that inhibits understanding, impedes altruism, and informs ignorance (as paradoxical as that might sound).

My wife and I got settled into our apartment as August turned into September and the news being reported out of New Orleans was horrific, unbelievable. But in times of national crisis, veracity takes a backseat to viewership, truth to ratings; the sensational becomes the news and the unreal becomes the real. Media Matters has cited several instances of unverified, sensationalized reporting on the part of Fox News (M., S.S. 2005). On an August 31 broadcast of *Hannity and Colmes,* correspondent David Miller reported that "a number of women have been raped" and "that there have been at least a couple of gunshot incidents taking place in the last day" (Hannity 2005). A couple of days after that broadcast, the news stories became more disturbing, more violent. On September 2, Shepard Smith described that "people have waited in line for four days in squalor, with shootings happening in there and people being raped. That's not—that's not conjecture. That's not speculation. That happened" (Neville 2005). Smith had no qualms about claiming truth, even though nothing of the sort happened; but it does not matter whether or not it happened. Once Smith makes the claim, reality is constituted. And that verbalization is integral to public perception because "the problem with voice-over direct address has often been viewed as that of self-confirmation. In this process, the accompanying images are read *both* in alignment with what is said *and* as independent verification of truth" (Corner 1999, p. 41). Once images are accompanied by utterance, "television attains meaning" (Corner 1999, p. 41) and claims are concurrently verified.

The veracity of the most sensationalized claim has since been found to be erroneous, but through her reporting at the time, Arthel Neville gave voice to the following words and provided a grotesque yet false report when she spun the following story (accompanied by the requisite sensationalist plea for children to be taken away from the room):

> One guy gets into a scuffle with a National Guardsman, takes the gun and kills the guardsman with the gun. Another guy, this is really sad, if there are any children watching take them out of the room. A man rapes and kills a 7-year old girl. About 10 guys, I don't know how many, but a group of guys turn around and beat this guy to death. This is just horrible. I cannot wrap my mind around how—the human—a human person can be reduced to such animalistic behavior. I don't understand it. (Sohnen 2005)

Never mind the fact that all of these "claims of widespread looting, gunfire directed at helicopters and rescuers, homicides, and rapes, including those of babies at the Louisiana Superdome, frequently turned out to be overblown, if not completely untrue," as later reported by National Guardsmen, operating as security in and around the Superdome during the storm (Gerhart and Gerhart 2005, p. A8). The National Guardsmen, according to Louisiana gubernatorial Press Secretary Denise Botcher, "were saying that what we were seeing on CNN was contradictory to what they were seeing. It didn't match up" (Pierre and Gerhart 2005, p. A8). Only weeks after the event were facts coming out of investigations that there were no "bands of rapists, going block to block" as CNN's Paula Zahn reported, and no discovery of "thirty to forty bodies decomposing inside a freezer in the Convention Center, including a girl whose throat was slashed" (Pierre and Gerhart 2005, p. A8). The only verified, documented shooting that occurred was that of a law enforcement individual whose leg wound was "self-inflicted," and Major Bush of the Louisiana National Guard declared that he had seen "worse fights at a Cubs game in Chicago" and that "the people never turned into these animals. They have been cheated out of being thought of as these tough people who looked out for each other. We had more babies born [in the Superdome] than we had deaths" (Pierre and Gerhart 2005, p. A8). These news reports are a small but illustrative sampling of the nature of a prevailing sensationalism that swept the nation through the media coverage of Hurricane Katrina.

In these cases it is more than merely unfortunate that national news broadcasts have an increasing influence on the viewing public because "viewers are abandoning local news in droves" (Klein and Naccarato 2003, p. 1611) and turning to the twenty-four news channels because of lifestyles that grow more and more hectic (Morris 2005). Yet, there is still another, more alluring, reason why companies like CNN and Fox command such a hold on the media market and that is directly tied to the vividness with which the reporting of trauma is produced and conveyed. CNN's success began in the early 1990s, primarily as a result of the Gulf War coverage since the "daily twists and turns of a fast-paced war were almost simultaneously transmitted back to the American public in vivid detail, and CNN did not miss a beat" (Morris 2005, p. 59). These major news broadcast companies search for "the sensational and the spectacular. Television calls for *dramatization,* in both senses of the term: it puts an event on stage, puts it in images. In doing so, it exaggerates the importance of that event, its seriousness and its dramatic, even tragic, character" (Bourdieu 2001, p. 248).

Much of the literature I encountered when researching media depictions and their impact on attitudes and the creation of reality associated with race focused on the reporting of crime. Television news has a long, and not terribly admirable, history of skewed reportage. In influential studies of television news reports on crime such as the one by Chiricos and Eschholz (2002), whites are more likely to appear as officers or role models while blacks are more likely to appear as perpetrators and criminals. The result is an association of blacks with crime that renders empathy more difficult when a tragedy like Hurricane Katrina strikes and affects primarily lower-class blacks. For it is because "the underrepresentation of Blacks as victims and overrepresentation of Blacks as perpetrators on television may have the effect of distorting viewers' perceptions of Blacks as being dangerous in our society" (Dixon and Linz 2000) and, I argue, conversely with the viewers' perceptions of blacks as victims. News report after news report depends on the simplicity of these generalizations and stereotypes when reporting the news, that they become readily identifiable motifs, or metaphors as McCarthy and others describe them:

> In the sensation-dripping evening news programs of the networks—CBS, NBC, ABC, and CNN—as they pant to keep up with the inflamed journalism of the tabloids—black and Latino youth appear metonymically in the discourse of problems.... You watch network evening news and you can predict when black and brown bodies will enter and when they will exit. The overwhelming metaphor of crime and violence saturates the dominant gaze on the inner city.... The mass media's story of inner-city black and Latino people pays short shrift to the stunning decline of opportunity and social services in the urban centers within the last fifteen years: poor public schools, chronic unemployment, isolation, the hacking to death of the public transportation system, the radical financial disinvestment in the cities, and the flight of jobs and resources to the suburbs. (236-237)

We saw this on our television throughout the hurricane coverage on New Orleans's inner-city population. The gaze on the inner city focused on and sensationalized the (alleged) criminality of the victims and paid little attention to the milieu of social decay that exacerbated the horror that these evacuees had to experience and the alienation and loss of place they are still experiencing. The news is responsible for this focus of our gaze, much like Bourdieu's glasses (2001), and we need to "[problematize] the notion of a one-way interaction between the subject and the purported object of the fantasy or gaze" as well as "[problematize] various fantasies of white (feminist or non-feminist) avowed identification (and implicit dis-identification) with 'racial' or 'subaltern others'" (Jay 1993, p. 272). The question then becomes how might we begin to break down the stock media depictions of subject and object; for Derrida and Stiegler (2002) and Esslin (1982) the answer is in education, one of the closing points I will address. But, it is this potential affect on attitudes and perceptions that I find most troubling; the depicted implausibility of blacks as victims in the media shapes attitudes through the created realities conveyed between commercial breaks.

Research has shown that this history of depiction does indeed inform the attitudes of viewers. I suspect that many of the callers I listened to in disbelief had little knowledge about Louisiana and/or limited interaction with (lowerclass) blacks and these "racially isolated whites, with no experience to fall back on, are more likely to rely heavily on media messages to make inferences about blacks" (Gilliam et al. 2002). In the study, "when exposed to negative racial stereotypes in the news, white respondents living in overwhelmingly white neighborhoods expressed more negative stereotypic evaluations of blacks, felt less close to blacks as a group" (Gilliam et al. 2002, p. 771), and it is precisely this distance that is created and upheld by media representations and result in uninformed attitudes; these whites simply "felt more distant from blacks as a group" (Gilliam et al. 2002, p. 755). Gilliam and others concluded that "in modern society the media are perhaps the most pervasive of [impersonal influences]. Most Americans are bombarded by a steady stream of mass media information, from a variety of channels.... The persistence of racial segregation means that impersonal influences such as the media are likely to play a significant role in the development of racial attitudes" (2002 p. 757) despite the fact that this "*fausse consciousness* in Sartre's sense, that television produces, ... results in attitudes toward the real world that are unrealistic, illusionary, and even harmful" (Esslin 1982, p. 72).

There is little doubt that the media influences attitudes; for "it is clear that television has exerted a wide range of influences on modern society and that its programming continues to exercise a degree of influence over viewers" (Corner 1999, p. 91). However, in situations where perceived cultural differences dominate, the news reports also have a socializing function:

> From television news, people learn for whom they should cast their ballots on election day, what products they should buy, and how to make other essential decisions in their daily lives. Mass media are a major source of expectations about various social groups in our society. For some people, particularly those who have not had direct contact with a particular group, media portrayals can provide their only socialization. It does not matter if the portrayals are misleading or distorted.... (Fuller 2005, p. 267)

The media factor predominantly in so many decisions but there is a presumption of choice in the examples Fuller chooses at the beginning of the quote. We are able to choose between candidates and among products, but the socialization element is much more troubling: how aware are we when we are manipulated socially? We're not merely being convinced to opt for one product over another; rather, we are undergoing a conditioning that affects how we view other cultures, races, and genders.

When television is the sole or primary resource on which we base our knowledge of the Other, the medium needs to be more critically examined, a plea echoed by Derrida and Stiegler (2002) and Esslin (1982) to which I'll return a bit later. The socialization aspect, meanwhile, is examined by Martin Jay as he cites Guy Debord who warned that "the spectacle is not a collection of images, but a social relation among people, mediated by images" (Jay 1993, p. 427) and these images can be misleading and the social relation adversely impacted, especially when we see the same sensationalized images (the looting, the covered body of a dead woman in a wheelchair, lines of impoverished blacks) repeated *ad infinitum, ad nauseam* on the 24-hour news channels because the news broadcasts have a tendency to "[concentrate and intensify their] action by highlighting scenes with the greatest visual and emotional impact, including scenes of violence" (Esslin 1982, p. 72). Jay continues by explaining that "it is the material objectification of alienated socioeconomic relations.... It operates by radically separating individuals, preventing dialogue, thwarting unitary class consciousness" (1993, p. 427). Again, we are returned to the need for media critique and analysis so that dialogue can be engaged and consciousness raised so that we can recognize when we are being separated.

The altruism and its impetus to which I referred earlier are explored in depth as James Rada (2000) investigates the manner in which altruism toward others operates. He begins by defining altruism as

> one person's willingness to help another in need. Empathy is the durable tendency of one person to be sensitive to another or receptive to the emotional and physical state of another—to understand feelings. The empathy-altruism, one person's willingness to help another in need, is the end result of a chain of judgments made by the potential helper. Key to the model is the focus on the motivation of the subject. (Rada 2000, p. 705)

The callers I heard on the radio and many media pundits who claimed or believed, as Jim Pinkerton did, that "the local [New Orleans] populace, which continues to get—to find itself whining all the time on TV to get more federal money" (Reina 2005) must have a low altruistic threshold and their "chain of judgments" must be heavily influenced by stereotypical media depictions. The subjection to stimuli necessarily factors into our willingness and ability to see others as victims truly in need of help; thus altruism is "influenced less by potential rewards or punishment, and more by the viewer's experience of empathy toward a potential recipient" (Rada 2000, p. 706). If the subject is not motivated toward altruism through empathy, then the result can be the ignorance or indifference to which I was exposed in the U-Haul. The group less inclined to altruism is termed *high dogmatics* (Rada 2000, p. 707), who

> are guided by inner vision rather than by the circumstances of others, and their views of legitimacy of need are dictated by their dogmatic orientations. Thus, only moderate to low dogmatics will manifest empathy to a measurable degree and can be expected to manifest empathy and altruism after exposure to media portrayals of African Americans. (Rada 2000, p. 707)

When the media portrayals are so uninformed and troubling, then viewers cannot be moved to truly altruistic ends and fall back to the stereotypes, the condition referred to earlier. But in this case, it's not the stereotypical association with blacks and crimes, for those are conditions of the criminal. I am more interested in the lower-class blacks and their condition in this instance as victims. The depictions on the news, though, rarely seemed to stir empathy; it was a spectacle. I vividly recall images of black people screaming for help, blacks "looting," blacks overcome with emotion as they cried out, but none of these images seemed to be created for the purposes of eliciting empathy. Instead, the media sought depictions that supported the long-held associations of blacks as "comical" (U.S. Commission on Civil Rights 1977) (as some laughed and danced in line before and after the hurricane), "unethical" (U.S. Commission on Civil Rights 1977) (as the alleged rapists of babies and murders), "bestial" and "brutish" (Dates 1990) (in the sensationalized stories of black-on-black violence), and "money-hungry" (Dates 1990) (as they carried out television sets and DVD players they'd taken from stores). The images of the distraught, poor blacks dominated television screens across the country for weeks and rarely did the news producers (the *production* of news is a troubling concept for me, explored in more detail later) choose sympathy over sensationalism. Through their framing, the producers and journalists were able to tell a story of their own choosing, and in doing so, created a reality for the viewers across the country who were glued to their television sets.

The notion of blacks as victims is also problematized by the association with blacks, especially those in the lower class, as social leeches in a modern-racist context as "the only users or majority users of social programs" and "either in need of or benefiting from social programs" (Fuller 2005, p. 280). This is a commonsense association according to Stuart Hall who argues that the broadcast media produces "representations and images of the social world, provide[s] and selectively construct[s] social knowledge, and order[s] a complex world by making it seem natural or by distilling complex meanings" (Hall quoted in Fuller 2005, p. 280). We have seen this distillation elsewhere in this chapter, in the assumption that poor blacks are all social leeches, manipulating white guilt to their own advantage for personal gain. We saw it in the discussion of McCarthy and others' disgust of the ubiquitous, metaphorical, metonymical association of blacks and browns with crime, with no attention being paid to a mitigating context or actuality.

Blacks, consequently, are labeled as "unfortunates" (Fuller 2005, p. 279), which brings in another element that further distances the racially isolated whites: the valorization of the white as savior. In the studies cited above, the police officers were typically white much in the same manner as the images of law enforcement in and around New Orleans after the hurricane were white. Many of the images were of whites providing supplies for the evacuees and security around the clock. I am not denying that there was such help, but the repetition of these images feed into and off of the phenomena of "redemptive fantasies" (Roman 1997), which we already see as popularized in Hollywood. I would go so far as to argue for a metonymical association of whites with heroism in mainstream media. It is in these redemption fantasies

> such as *Schindler's List, Dances with Wolves, Ghosts of Mississippi,* and *Amistad,* for example, while they seem to be "about" the histories of oppressed groups, reposition Christian-born whites as the stars of the show. In good-white narratives, the political struggles of oppressed groups serve as a dramatic backdrop to the central moral action in which the good white guy battles both the bad white guys and his own conscience. Tragic outcomes for racial minority groups, rather than undercutting the moral or political meaning of the white hero's actions, add poignancy to his moral struggles. Even if the racialized Other is doomed, at least we know that the white guy tried—and that he became a better person in the process. (Thompson 2003, p. 17)

We have to recognize our societal and cultural complicity in the perpetuation of these redemptive fantasies; we have to think neither too long nor hard to add to the list that Thompson begins. We must consider the possibility that "such fantasies display a desire for a *benevolent white redeemer*" (Roman 1997, p. 274). This "crisis of representation" between these groups "is not reducible to reified notions of racial or cultural difference—as though racist cultures could be abstracted from asymmetries of power, political enfranchisement, and material conditions. Nor is it reducible to (psychological/psychoanalytical) matters between individuals who are abstracted from racist structural practices" (Roman 1997, p. 274). Once again, we are confronted with the challenge of getting past a troublesome binary that is so pervasive, so discursively limiting and heed the call not to ignore the more complex factors in favor of the overly simplified explanations we are given through images and voice-overs. There is a discernible cultural impact of such stereotypical valorization and dependence, and these create another problem for the empathetic because it establishes a threshold for ethical exhaustion, a sense that "we've" done enough and a wonderment why "they" can't do it on "their" own and that it's time to end the reliance on government's and others' generosity or altruism to help them out of despair and difficulty (Fuller 2005).

Thus, the issue of help and the context in which it is offered needs examination and introspective reflection. There's no denying that a great number of people helped through sending money and volunteering of their time and resources in an effort to help those affected by the hurricane. Even now, the public discourse over how best to help New Orleans is still being waged by politicians and media experts, but this issue of social justice needs to be problematized within this context of the redemptive fantasy, where the normalizing, dominant discourse may not acknowledge or address the true needs of those we seek to help. Therefore, we must

> decenter whiteness from programs for social change. Among other things, this means relinquishing our cherished notions of morality: how we understand fairness, how we understand what it means to be a good person, how

> we understand what it means to be generous or sympathetic or tolerant or a good listener. When we are challenged for our whiteness, our tendency is to fall back on our goodness, fairness, intelligence, rationality, sensitivity, and democratic inclusiveness, all of which are caught up with our whiteness. (Thompson 2003, p. 17)

All of these associations and perceptions are, at least in part, due to the images depicted in the media (of both privileged and needy), particularly through the news broadcasts, whose companies produce and package just as with any other product meant for consumption. But many times the consumption takes place within a framework that has been meticulously designed and becomes similar to Baudrillard's code (1988) that we are not meant to be aware of, for

> the ultimate aim of news production [is] to erase the mechanistic construction and to make the "Real" appear as if it reveals itself. Thus, not only is the perceived and symbolic "reality" of the "world in news" sacrificed to the mechanistic artificiality of the news production process ... but that very process is then magically dissolved in the transmission of that event. (Hemmingway 2004, p. 418)

The news broadcast, then, becomes a reality, our reality. We consume the transmission passively and without question, its subtleties in stereotype also being consumed in the process. As viewers, we are at risk of being made to "wear glasses that force [us] to see the world divided up in certain ways (the young and the old, foreigners and French)" (Bourdieu 2001, p. 249). Moreover, "these divisions create groups that can be mobilized, and that mobilization makes it possible for them to convince everyone else that they exist" (Bourdieu 2001, p. 249). These are the divisions that have been at the heart of this chapter, black and white, rich and poor, valorized and demonized, deserving and nondeserving, civil and savage. During the coverage of Katrina and its aftermath, the manipulation of these divisions exacerbated the disassociation that existed between such groups, giving people justification in their feelings and claims despite any ignorance they might have with the people or places they were seeing on television.

The "glasses" to which Bourdieu refers in this instance are those that belong to the news correspondents who, most of the time, are white and likely come from at least a middle-class upbringing and privileged education. Bourdieu also points out the problem with this aspect of reporting by citing Patrick Champagne's work, which

> offers a detailed examination of how the media represent events in the "inner city." He shows how journalists are carried along by the inherent exigencies of their job, by their view of the world, by their training and orientation, and

> also by the reasoning intrinsic to the profession itself. They select very specific aspects of the inner city as a function of their particular perceptual categories, that particular way they see things. (Bourdieu 2001, 247)

In being shown the world through another's selective (knowingly or unwittingly) eyes, the scope of what we see in regard to a devastating totality is incredibly narrow, problematically limited. But that limit, despite its superficiality, which McCarthy and others have addressed, is understood as the real and becomes mythical because it "abolishes the complexity of human acts, it gives them the simplicity of essences ... it organizes a world which is without contradictions because it is without depth, a world wide open and wallowing in the evident, it establishes a blissful clarity" (Barthes 1973, p. 156). There's an absolute finality established when a reporter declares that his reporting is beyond conjecture and such an absolute statement can be made independent of reality because "television claims to report reality but largely creates its own reality" (Bourdieu 2001, p. 245) and that reality "no longer has to be rational, since it is no longer measured against some ideal or negative instance. It is nothing more than operational" (Baudrillard 1988).

This creation of reality fits into a mode of production that cannot be ignored; we must remember that there are many filters through which a news broadcast passes before being transmitted to our television sets, and each step removes it further away from the "live" event covered. Because,

> although this supposed "live" does in fact introduce a considerable structural innovation into the space we're talking about, we should never forget that this "live" is not an absolute "live," but only a live effect [*un effet de direct*], an allegation of "live." Whatever the apparent immediacy of the transmission or broadcast, it negotiates with choices, with framing, with selectivity. In a fraction of a second, CNN, for example, intervenes to select, censor, frame, filter the so-called "live" or "direct" image. To say nothing of programming decisions, whether with regard to what is "shown" or who "shows" or manipulates it. What is "transmitted" "live" on a television channel is *produced before being transmitted.* The "image" is not a faithful and integral reproduction of what it is thought to reproduce. (Derrida and Stiegler 2002, p. 40)

So "live" and "real" when it comes to news reporting become troublingly relative terms and we "should understand how this is done or made, how it is fabricated, who has the power, who chooses, what are the relations of forces, etc." (Derrida 2002, pp. 137-138), which makes media criticism an important "political task." The ambiguity in the use of the term *realism* when applied to the news results, in part, from the process of "its rendering, through a recording, of the appearances and actions of a real world" (Corner 1999, p. 27). For what we are seeing is not necessarily reality itself, as things happen or happened; this potential of reportage is merely *apparent.* Even though reporting claims to be an account of "the real," recall that reportage is "explicit in the visual claims it makes about the status of what and who we are seeing. These claims may be open to debate but this is not usually a matter of how *like* the real news appears" (Corner 1999, p. 27).

In the discussions I've had with friends, many have dismissed the racial problems resulting from Katrina by attributing it to class. I found a poignant counter, however, in an article that dealt with a similar problem in the discussion of race and crime: "It is unnecessary to speak directly of race because talking about crime *is* talking about race" (Barlow 1998, p. 151; quoted in Chiricos and Eschholz 2002, pp. 400–401). So, I believe that it is unnecessary to speak directly of class because talking about class in the context of Hurricane Katrina *is* talking about race. I don't think that there is any escaping the racial aspect of Katrina's destruction and the news coverage.

Media critics and cultural theorists (e.g., Baudrillard, Bourdieu, Derrida), internationally, have dedicated a great deal of time to the news coverage of the conflicts and wars in the Middle East dating back to the 1990's Gulf War. Domestically, images of the Twin Towers' crumbling were seen over and over again. But perhaps it is because I am closer to the events of the hurricane personally than I am to the Gulf Wars and the terrorist attacks of September 11, but I believe that the news coverage of Hurricane Katrina is a tragic yet exemplary case for the study of all the complex issues I've only managed to introduce here. The entire nation "witnessed" the decimation of one of the country's cultural centers and the resulting horrors of those who experienced it. But to believe that what we viewed was the depiction of the actual is to be naïve. How to combat that naïveté? I think our greatest potential lies in education: "The educational system in a television age must teach students how to view TV critically, with intelligence and discrimination. *Television criticism,* whether under that title or another, should become a basic subject of instruction in schools from the earliest grades" (Esslin 1982, p. 112). The context of the school, from elementary on, can equip students with the deconstructive and analytic abilities, and I will not deny that this is a political act. I also expect no denial of the fact that the school, despite the rhetoric to the contrary, is a political sphere and such means of critique, as Derrida pointed out, are likewise "juridico-political" (Derrida and Stiegler 2002, p. 33). I think it is imperative that students be able to question "who, in the end, is authorized to appear but above all authorized to show, edit, store, interpret, and exploit images.... and who owns, who is able to appropriate, who is able to select, who is able to show images, directly political or not" (33–34). I am inclined to agree with Derrida, again, that what we have here is an opportunity to teach children how to question what they see on television and what they are told via voice-overs, so that they can gain "critical access" to the images with which they are confronted every day. I believe that

> there is a chance, if it can be seized, to develop a culture of *reception.* Which might lead to another way of formulating the question of the cultural exception. The real problem here is to rethink or think otherwise what Hollywood has up to this point done in the domain of the culture industry, to which cinema and television belong. For what it has done, it has done in accordance with a *reifying schema, and by opposing production to consumption, that is to say: by putting analysis on one side (production) and synthesis on the other (consumption).* Technology is giving us the chance to modify this relation. (Derrida and Stiegler 2002, pp. 162–163)

I do not anticipate national broadcasting news corporations' altering their reporting habits to accommodate fairness when a financial bottom line and viewership are more easily increased with sensationalized and myopic reporting. After all, news media presentations are more interested in "reality effect" than reality because this effect can "make people believe in what they show. . . . The news, the incidents and accidents of everyday life, can be loaded with political or ethnic significance liable to unleash strong, often negative feelings, such as racism, chauvinism, or xenophobia" (Bourdieu 2001, pp. 248–249). It is these "negative feelings" that I heard and saw entirely too often on the part of many from the United States. True, a great deal of money was raised and the consciousness of a nation was aroused; it is not my intent in this chapter simply and summarily to discount all of the generosity of millions. But the balance of the calls favored my frustration to my encouragement. I do believe, though, that the broadcast news *apparati* did more disservice to the victims of Hurricane Katrina and their plight than it helped them. The media, generally, "transmutes reality into a kind of fictional drama" and "actually dictates the development of events in the real world" (Esslin 1982, p. 65) and in the case for Katrina specifically has already been implicated in the delay of emergency aid (Pierre and Gerhart 2005); moreover, I believe they should be implicated in the attitudes of countless others who were unable to empathize with their fellow humans. Pardon the syntactically militaristic language, but I believe that arming students with the analytical abilities can lead to generational change in the influence that television, news broadcasts specifically, has over a viewership at any time, but particularly during such times of crisis when an open dialog and awareness of the Other is so inextricably crucial.

References

Barthes, R. (1973). "Myth today." *Mythologies.* (A. Lavers, trans.). London: Paladin, pp. 117–174.

Baudrillard, J. (1983). S. Lotringer (ed.). *Simulations.* (P. Foss, P. Patton, and P. Beitchman, trans.). New York: Semiotext.

———. (1988). "Simulations and simulacra." In M. Poster (ed.), *Jean Baudrillard: Selected Writings* (pp. 166–184). Stanford: Stanford University Press.

Birrell, J. (2004). "White guilt in America." *Meridian Magazine.* Available http://www.meridianmagazine.com/ideas/040429guilt.html.

Bourdieu, P. (2001). "Television." *European Review* 9 (3), pp. 245–256.

Chiricos, T., and Eschholz, S. (2002, November). "The racial and ethnic typification of crime and the criminal typification of race and ethnicity in local television news." *Journal of Research in Crime and Delinquency* 39 (4), pp. 400–420.

Corner, J. (1999). *Critical Ideas in Television Studies.* Oxford: Clarendon Press.

Dates, J. (1990). "A war of images." In J. Dates and W. Barlow (eds.), *Split Images: African Americans in the Mass Media* (pp. 1–25). Washington, DC: Howard University Press.

Derrida, J., and Stiegler, B. (2002). *Echographies of Television* (J. Bajorek, trans.). Cambridge: Polity.

Dixon, T.L., and Linz, D. (2000, October). "Race and the misrepresentation of victimization on local television news." *Communication Research* 27 (5), pp. 547–573.

Esslin, M. (1982). *The Age of Television.* San Francisco: W.H. Freeman.

Fuller, L. (2005, March). "WLBT news in the deregulation era: Modern racism or representative picture?" *Journal of Black Studies* 35 (4), pp. 262–292.

Gilliam, F.D., Valentino, N., and Beckmann, M. (2002, December). "Where you live and what you watch: The impact of racial proximity and local television news on attitudes about race and crime." *Political Research Quarterly* 55 (4), pp. 755–780.

Hannity, S. (executive producer). (2005, August 31). *Hannity and Colmes.* New York: Fox News Broadcasting.

Hemmingway, E.L. (2004). "The silent heart of the news." *Space and Culture* 7 (4), pp. 409–426.

Jay, M. (1993). *Downcast Gaze: The Denigration of Vision in Twentieth Century French Thought.* Berkeley: University of California Press.

Klein, R.D., and Naccarato, S. (2003, August). "Broadcast news portrayal of minorities: Accuracy in reporting." *American Behavioral Scientist* 46 (12), pp. 1611–1616.

M., S.S. (2005, October 6). "*Washington Post*'s criticism of sensationalist Katrina coverage focused on CNN, ignored Fox." *Media Matters for America.* Available: http://mediamatters.org/items/200510060009.

McCarthy, C., Rodriguez, A., Meecham, S., David, S., Wilson-Brown, C., Godina, H., Supryia, K.E., and Buendia. E. (1997). "Race, suburban resentment, and the representation of the inner city in contemporary film and television." In M. Fine, L. Wies, L.C. Powell, and L. M. Wong (eds.), *Off White: Readings on Race, Power, and Society* (pp. 270–282). New York: Routledge.

Morris, J.S. (2005). "The Fox News factor." *The Harvard International Journal of Press/Politics* 10 (3), pp. 56–79.

Neville, A. (2005, September 3). *Katrina: Aftermath.* New York: Fox News Broadcasting.

Pierre, R.E., and Gerhart, A. (2005, October 5). "News of pandemonium may have slowed aid: Unsubstantiated reports of violence were confirmed by some officials, spread by news media." *Washington Post,* p. A8.

Rada, J.A. (2000). "A new piece to the puzzle: Examining effects of television portrayals of African Americans." *Journal of Broadcasting and Electronic Media* 44 (4), pp. 704–715.

Reina, C. (executive producer). (2005, September 17). *Fox News Watch.* New York: Fox News Broadcasting.

Roman, L.G. (1997). "Denying (white) racial privilege: Redemption discourses and the uses of fantasy." In M. Fine, L. Wies, L.C. Powell, and L. M. Wong (eds.), *Off White: Readings on Race, Power, and Society* (pp. 227–241). New York: Routledge.

Sohnen, A. (executive producer). (2005, September 2). *The O'Reilly Factor.* New York: Fox News Broadcasting.

Thompson, A. (2003). "Tiffany, friend of people of color: White investments in antiracism." *International Journal of Qualitative Studies in Education* 16, (1), pp. 7–29.

U.S. Commission on Civil Rights (1977). *Window Dressing on the Set: Women and Minorities in Television.* Washington, DC: Commission on Civil Rights.

CHAPTER 3

Technological Transformation, Multiple Literacies, and the Re-Visioning of Education

Douglas Kellner

The dramatic multiplication of computer, information, communication, and multimedia technologies has been changing everything from the ways people work to the ways they communicate with each other and spend their leisure time. This technological revolution is often interpreted as the beginnings of a knowledge or information society, and therefore ascribes education a central role in every aspect of life. It poses tremendous challenges to educators to rethink their basic tenets, to deploy the new technologies in creative and productive ways, and to restructure schooling to respond constructively and progressively to the technological and social changes currently underway. At the same time, important demographic and sociopolitical changes are taking place throughout the world. Emigration patterns have created the challenge of providing people from diverse races, classes, and backgrounds with the tools and competencies to enable them to succeed and participate in an ever more complex and changing world.

In this chapter, I argue that educators need to cultivate multiple literacies for contemporary technological and multicultural societies, that teachers need to develop new literacies of diverse sorts, including a more fundamental importance for print literacy, to meet the challenge of restructuring education for a hi-tech, multicultural society and global culture. In a period of dramatic technological and social change, education needs to help produce a variety of types of literacies to make current pedagogy relevant to the demands of the contemporary era. As new technologies are altering every aspect of our society and culture, we need to comprehend and make use of them both to understand and transform our worlds. In particular, by introducing multiple literacies to empower individuals and groups traditionally excluded, education could be reconstructed to make it more responsive to the challenges of a democratic and multicultural society.

Technology and the Re-Visioning of Education

To dramatize the issues at stake, we should consider the claim that we are now undergoing one of the most significant technological revolutions for education since the progression from oral to print and book-based teaching. Just as the transition to print literacy and book culture involved a dramatic transformation of education (McLuhan 1962, 1964; Ong 1988; Illich and Sanders 1988), so too does the ongoing technological transformation demand a major restructuring of education today with novel curricula, pedagogy, literacies, practices, and goals. Furthermore, the technological developments of the present era make possible the radical re-visioning and reconstruction of education and society argued for in the progressive era by Dewey and in the 1960s and 1970s by Ivan Illich, Paolo Freire, and others who sought radical educational and social reform.[1]

A re-visioning education requires a thorough examination and critique of dominant institutions of schooling, pedagogical practices, and the goals and ends of teaching. Technological change, globalization, and multicultural expansion all demand looking at things in new ways and looking back at how the world was before dramatic changes have occurred. Re-vision involves both critically seeing the past and present and imagining a different future. It implies as well reconstructing education, using informed theory to guide novel pedagogical practices and to fundamentally restructure educational institutions. Re-visioning education also involves another way of seeing and doing, grounded in historical practices of the present and looking toward a different and better future.

Put in historical perspective, it is now possible to see modern education as preparation for industrial civilization and minimal citizenship in a passive representative democracy. Modern education, in short, emphasizes submission to authority, rote memorization, and what Freire called the "banking concept" of education in which learned teachers deposit knowledge into passive students, inculcating conformity, subordination, and normalization. Today, these traits are somewhat undercut in certain sectors of the global postindustrial and networked society with its demands for new skills for the workplace, participation in emergent social and political environs, and interaction within novel forms of culture and everyday life.

A more flexible economy, based on an ever-evolving technological infrastructure and more multicultural workforce demands a more technically literate, interactive, culturally sensitive, and educated workforce, while revitalizing democracy requires the participation of informed citizens.[2] Yet, while on one hand, the demands of the expanding global economy, culture, and polity require a more informed, participatory, and active workforce and citizenship, on the other hand, a docile workforce and service industry is still the norm in many sectors of work, society, and culture. Although for a time, ideologues of the new technologies argued that information and communication technology would of themselves dramatically reorganize and democratize the workplace, schooling, the polity, and everyday life, it is by now clear that the supposed liberating effects of new technologies were greatly exaggerated. But while globalization and technological multiplication have highly ambiguous effects (Best and Kellner 2001), they provide educational reformers with the challenge of whether education will be restructured to promote democracy and human needs, or whether education will be transformed primarily to serve the needs of business and the global economy.

To some extent, constant technological transformation renders necessary the sort of thorough restructuring of education that radicals have demanded since the Enlightenment of Rousseau and Wollstonecraft through Dewey, all of whom saw the progressive reconstruction of education as the key to democracy. Today, however, intense pressures for change now come directly from technology and the economy and not ideology or educational reformist ideas, with an expanding global economy and novel technologies demanding innovative skills, competencies, literacies, and practices. It is therefore a burning question as to what sort of restructuring of education and society will take place, in whose interests, and for what ends. More than ever, we need philosophical reflection on the ends and purposes of education, on what we are doing and trying to achieve in our educational practices and institutions. In this situation, it may be instructive to return to Dewey and see the connections between education and democracy, the need for the reconstruction of education and society, and the value of experimental pedagogy to seek solutions to the problems of education in the present day. A progressive reconstruction of education will urge that it be done in the interests of democratization, ensuring access to information and communication technologies for all, helping to overcome the so-called digital divide and divisions of the haves and have nots, so that education is placed, as Dewey (1997 [1916]) and Freire (1972, 1998) propose, in the service of democracy and social justice.

Yet we should be more aware than Dewey of the obduracy of divisions of class, gender, and race, and work self-consciously for multicultural democracy and education. This task suggests that we valorize difference and cultural specificity, as well as equality and shared universal Deweyan values such as freedom, equality, individualism, and participation. Theorizing a democratic and multicultural reconstruction of education forces us to confront the digital divide, that there are divisions between information and technology have and have nots, just as there are class, gender, and race divisions in every sphere of the existing constellations of society and culture. The latest surveys of the digital divide, however, indicate that the key indicators are class and education, as well as race and gender; hence the often-circulated argument that new technologies merely reinforce the hegemony of upper-class white males must be questioned, at least for some contemporary societies.

Rob Shields has argued that the concept of the digital divide serves as a marketing device for the benefit of technology disseminators and that on the whole the development of new technologies helps increase the divide between the haves and have nots (2003). While no doubt hi-tech corporations and affiliated government institutions have promoted the challenge of a digital divide, the concept points to some serious problems and challenges. It is clear by now that providing access and computers alone without proper training and pedagogy does not advance education or social justice. Thus, more broadly conceived, the notion of a digital divide points to disparities in terms of access, training, skills, and the actual use of technologies to improve education and promote social justice.

With the proper resources, policies, pedagogies, and practices, educators can work to reduce the (unfortunately growing) gap between the haves and have nots by promoting broad training in information and computer literacy that embraces a wide range of projects from providing technical skills to engaging students in the production of media projects. Although technology alone will not suffice to democratize and adequately reconstruct education, in a technological society providing proper access and training can improve education if it is taken as a supplement.[3] That is, technology itself does not necessarily improve teaching and learning, and will certainly not of itself overcome acute socioeconomic divisions. Indeed, without proper re-visioning of education and without adequate resources, pedagogy, and educational practices, technology could be an obstacle or burden to genuine learning and will probably increase rather than overcome existing divisions of power, cultural capital, and wealth.

In the following reflections, I focus on the role of computers and information technology in contemporary education and the need for new pedagogies and an expanded concept of literacy to respond to the importance of information and communication technologies (ICTs) in every aspect of life. I propose some ways that ICTs and new literacies can serve as efficacious learning tools that will contribute to producing a more democratic and egalitarian society, and not just provide skills and tools to privileged individuals and groups that will improve their cultural capital and social power at the expense of others. How, indeed, can education be re-visioned and reconstructed to provide individuals and groups with the tools, the competencies, the literacies, and social practices to overcome the class, gender, and racial divides that bifurcate our society and at least in terms of economic indicators seem to be growing rather than diminishing?

First, however, I wish to address the technophobic argument against ICT per se. I have been developing critical theories of technology that call attention to uses or types of technology as tools of domination, and that reject the hype and pretensions of techno-utopias and techno-fixes to the problems of education and society. A critical theory of technology thus sees the limitations of pedagogy and educational proposals based primarily on technology without adequate emphasis on classroom pedagogy and on teacher and student empowerment. It insists on developing educational reform and restructuring to promote multicultural democracy, and calls for appropriate restructuring of technology to democratic education and society. Yet a critical theory also sees how technology can be used, and perhaps redesigned and restructured, for positive purposes such as enhancing education and democracy and overcoming the divide between the haves and have nots, while enabling individuals to democratically and creatively participate in a new economy, society, and culture (see Feenberg 1991, 1999; Best and Kellner 2001).

The late Ivan Illich's postindustrial model of education contains a radical critique of existing schooling and alternative notions like webs of learning, tools for conviviality, and radically reconstructing education to promote learning, democracy, and social and communal life, thus providing salient alternatives to modern systems (1971, 1973). Illich's "learning webs" (1971) and "tools for conviviality" (1973) anticipate the Internet and how it might provide resources, interactivity, and communities that could help revolutionize education. For Illich, science and technology can either serve as instruments of domination or progressive ends. Hence, whereas big systems of computers promote modern bureaucracy and industry, personalized computers made accessible to the public might be constructed to provide tools that can be used to enhance learning. Thus, Illich was aware of how technologies like computers could either enhance or distort education depending on how they were fit into a well-balanced ecology of learning.

"Tools of conviviality" for Illich are appropriate, congenial, and promote learning, sociality, and community (1973). They are tools in which ends dictate means and individuals are not overpowered or controlled by their technologies (as say, with assembly lines, nuclear power plants, or giant computer systems). Convivial tools produce a democratic and convivial society in which individuals communicate, debate, participate in social and political life, and help make decisions. Convivial tools free individuals from dependency and cultivate autonomy and sociality. They provide individuals and society with the challenge of producing convivial tools and pedagogies that will create better modes of learning and social life.

Conviviality for Illich involves "autonomous and creative intercourse among persons, and the intercourse of persons with their environment" (1973: 27). Illich proposes a normative dimension to critique existing systems and construct alternative ones using values of "survival, justice, and self-defined work" as positive norms (1973: 13). These criteria could guide a reconstruction of education to serve the needs of varied communities; to promote democracy and social justice; and to redefine learning and work to promote creativity, community, and an ecological balance between people and the Earth. Indeed, Illich was one of the few critics working within radical pedagogy in his period who took seriously ecological issues and critically appraised institutions like schooling, medicine, transportation, and other key elements of industrial society within a broad social, political, economic, and ecological framework. His goal was nothing less than a critique of industrial civilization and a project of envisaging postindustrial institutions of learning, democratization, and social justice.

Illich saw that a glaring problem with contemporary educational institutions was that they become fixed in monomodal instruction with homogenized lesson plans, curricula, and pedagogy, and neglect to address challenging political, cultural, or ecological problems. The development of tools of conviviality and radical pedagogies enables teachers and students to break with these models and to engage in Deweyan experimental education. A reconstruction of education could help create subjects better able to negotiate the complexities of emergent forms of everyday life, labor, and culture, as contemporary life becomes more multifaceted and dangerous. More supportive dialogical and interactive social relations in learning situations can promote cooperation, democracy, and positive social values, as well as fulfill needs for communication, esteem, and learning. Whereas modern mass education tended to see life in a linear fashion based on print models and developed pedagogies that broke experience into discrete moments and behavioral bits, critical pedagogies could produce skills that enable individuals to better navigate the multiple realms and challenges of contemporary life. Deweyan education focused on problem solving, goal-seeking projects, and the courage to be experimental, while Freire developed alternative pedagogies and Illich, oppositional conceptions of education and learning and critiques of schooling. It is this sort of critical spirit and vision to reconstruct education and society that can help produce new pedagogies, tools for learning, and social justice for the present age.

At a time when many were enamored of the autonomous power and emancipatory potential of the school, Illich insisted on seeing schools as part and parcel of industrial society and one of the major instruments of its social reproduction. One of Illich's enduring contributions is to see relationships between modern industrial institutions like schooling, production, medicine, transportation, and other major sectors of industrial society. In order to engage with what goes on in educational institutions, we must have far better and more critical self-understandings of what specific schools do in their institutional structure within the broader society, their hidden curriculum and how they engage in social reproduction. Understanding schooling beyond its institutional sites also requires grasping its dialectical relationships to the public pedagogies of media and the street and the networked civic and social space of the Internet, as well as how schooling relates to the oppressions and operations of workplaces, government institutions, and corporations.

Illich thus provides concrete analyses and a critique of how schooling reproduces the existing social order and is flawed and debased by the defects and horrors of the industrial system. Illich also recognizes that post-industrial society requires certain competencies and that a major challenge is to construct convivial technologies that will improve both education and social life. While he resolutely opposed neoliberal agendas and was critical of encroaching corporate domination of the Internet and information technologies, Illich's notion of "webs of learning" and "tools of conviviality" can be appropriated for projects of the radical critique and reconstruction of education and learning in the contemporary era.

It is interesting that one of the godfathers of critical pedagogy, Paulo Freire, was positive toward media and new technologies, seeing technologies as potential tools for empowering citizens as well as instruments of domination in the hands of ruling elites. Freire wrote that "technical and scientific training need not be inimical to humanistic education as long as science and technology in the revolutionary society are at the service of permanent liberation, of humanization" (1972: 157).[4] Many critical pedagogues, however, are technophobes, seeing new technologies solely as instruments of domination, and both Illich and Freire also had concerns about the Internet and globalization. In a world inexorably undergoing processes of globalization and technological transformation, one cannot, however, in good conscience advocate a policy of clean hands and purity, distancing oneself from technology and globalization, but must intervene in the processes of economic and technological revolution, attempting to deflect these forces for progressive ends and developing new pedagogies to advance the project of human liberation and well-being.

Re-visioning technology, literacy, and education should avoid both technophobia and technophilia, rejecting technological determinism, while being critical of the limitations, biases, and downsides of new technologies, but wanting to use and redesign technologies for education for democracy and for social reconstruction in the interests of social justice. This project is also, in the Deweyan spirit, pragmatic and experimental, recognizing that there is no agreed-upon way to deploy new technologies for enhancing education and democratization. Critical educators must be prepared to accept that some of the attempts to use technology for education may well fail, as have no doubt many of our own attempts to use computer-mediated technologies for education. Different parts of the world and varying groups will have different projects that computers can help them with, different needs and problems, and thus varied pedagogical projects.

A critical theory of technological literacy is aware that technologies have unforeseen consequences and that good intentions and seemingly good projects may have results that were not desired or positive. Indeed, there are ecological consequences concerning the production, use, and discarding of computer technologies; dangers of over- and misuse of computers for individual health and well-being; and costs and downsides of organizing so many activities ranging from work to communication to research around information technologies. A critical pedagogy will thus contextualize the production and use of multimedia and information technologies within social relations and contexts, criticize negative aspects and effects, and attempt to transform technologies into positive environments of education and social transformation.

Thus, the question is not whether computers and multimedia technologies are good or bad in the classroom or more broadly for education. Rather, it is a question of what multimedia and computers can do and cannot do toward helping to produce a more democratic and equalitarian society and what their limitations are for producing more active and creative human beings and a more just society. Crucially, we must ask, what sort of skills do students and teachers need to effectively deploy computers and information technology; what sort of effects might ICTs have on learning, subjectivities, and social relations; and what new literacies, forms of education, and social relations do we need to democratize and improve education today?

Media Literacy: An Unfulfilled Challenge

Literacy involves gaining the skills and knowledge to read and interpret the text of the world and to successfully navigate and negotiate its challenges, conflicts, and crises. Literacy is thus a necessary condition to equip people to participate in the local, national, and global economy, culture, and polity. As Dewey argued (1997), education is required to enable people to participate in democracy, for without an educated, informed, and literate citizenry, strong democracy is impossible. Moreover, there are crucial links between literacy, democracy, empowerment, and participation, and without developing adequate literacies, differences between the haves and have nots cannot be overcome and individuals and groups will be left out of the emerging economy, networked society, and culture.

To reading, writing, and traditional print literacies, one could argue that in an era of technological revolution, we need to develop robust forms of media literacy, computer literacy, and multimedia literacies, thus cultivating "multiple literacies" in the restructuring of education. Computer and multimedia technologies demand novel skills and competencies, and if education is to be relevant to the problems and challenges of contemporary life, it must expand the concept of literacy and develop new curricula and pedagogies.

Both traditionalists and reformists would probably agree that education and literacy are intimately connected. "Literacy" in my conception comprises gaining competencies involved in effectively using socially constructed forms of communication and representation. Learning literacies requires attaining competencies in practices in contexts that are governed by rules and conventions. Literacies are socially constructed in educational and cultural practices involving various institutional discourses and pedagogies. Literacies evolve and shift in response to social and cultural change and the interests of elites who control hegemonic institutions.

I would resist, however, extreme claims that the era of the book and print literacy is over. Although there are discontinuities and novelties in the current constellation, there are also important continuities. Indeed, in the emergent information-communication technology environment, traditional print literacy takes on increasing importance in the computer-mediated cyberworld as people need to critically scrutinize and scroll tremendous amounts of information, putting new emphasis on developing reading and writing abilities. For instance, Internet discussion groups, chat rooms, e-mail, blogs, wikis, and various Internet forums require writing skills in which a new emphasis on the importance of clarity and precision is emerging.[5] In this context of information saturation, it becomes an ethical imperative not to contribute to cultural and information overload, and to concisely communicate thoughts and feelings.

In the new multimedia environment, *media literacy* is arguably more important than ever. Cultural studies and critical pedagogy have begun to teach us to recognize the ubiquity of media culture in contemporary society, the growing trends toward multicultural education, and the need for media literacy that addresses the issue of multicultural and social difference.[6] There is expanding recognition that media representations help construct our images and understanding of the world and that education must meet the dual challenges of teaching media literacy in a multicultural society and sensitizing students and the public to the inequities and injustices of a society based on gender, race, and class inequalities and discrimination. Recent critical studies see the role of mainstream media in exacerbating or diminishing these inequalities and the ways that media education and the production of alternative media can help create a healthy multiculturalism of diversity and more robust democracy. They confront some of the most serious difficulties and problems that currently face us as educators and citizens.

Yet despite the ubiquity of media culture in contemporary society and everyday life, and the recognition that the media themselves are a form of pedagogy, and despite criticisms of the distorted values, ideals, and representations of the world in popular culture, media education in K-12 schooling has never really been established and developed. The current technological revolution, however, brings to the fore more than ever the role of media like television, popular music, film, and advertising, as the Internet rapidly absorbs these cultural forms and creates new cyberspaces and forms of culture and pedagogy. It is highly irresponsible in the face of saturation by Internet and media culture to ignore these forms of socialization and education; consequently, a critical reconstruction of education should produce pedagogies that provide media literacy and enable students, teachers, and citizens to discern the nature and effects of media culture.

Media culture is a form of pedagogy that teaches proper and improper behavior, gender roles, values, and knowledge of the world (Kellner 1995). Individuals are often not aware that they are being educated and constructed by media culture, as its pedagogy is frequently invisible and subliminal. This situation calls for critical approaches that make us aware of how media construct meanings, influence and educate audiences, and impose their messages and values. A media-literate person is skillful in analyzing media codes and conventions; able to criticize stereotypes, values, and ideologies; and competent to interpret the multiple meanings and messages generated by media texts. Media literacy helps people to use media intelligently, to discriminate and evaluate media content, to critically dissect media forms, and to investigate media effects and uses (see Kellner 1995a and 1995b).

Within educational circles, however, a debate persists over what constitutes the field of media pedagogy, with different agendas and programs. A traditionalist, "protectionist" approach would attempt to "inoculate" young people against the effects of media addiction and manipulation by cultivating a taste for book literacy, high culture, and the values of truth, beauty, and justice, and by denigrating all forms of media and computer culture (see Postman 1985, 1992). A media literacy movement, by contrast, attempts to teach students to read, analyze, and decode media texts in a fashion parallel to the advancement of print literacy. Media arts education in turn teaches students to appreciate the aesthetic qualities of media and to use various media technologies as instruments of self-expression and creation. Critical media literacy builds on these approaches, analyzing media culture as products of social production and struggle and teaching students to be critical of media representations and discourses, but also stressing the importance of learning to use the media as modes of self-expression and social activism where appropriate (Kellner 1995a).

Developing critical media literacy and pedagogy also involves perceiving how media like film or video can also be used positively to teach a wide range of topics, like multicultural understanding and education. If, for example, multicultural education is to champion genuine diversity and expand the curriculum, it is important both for groups excluded from mainstream education to learn about their own heritage and for dominant groups to explore the experiences and voices of minority and excluded groups. Thus, media literacy can promote multicultural literacy, conceived as understanding and engaging the heterogeneity of cultures and subcultures that constitute an increasingly global and multicultural world (Courts 1998; Weil 1998).

Critical media literacy not only teaches students to learn from media, to resist media manipulation, and to use media materials in constructive ways, but also develops skills that will help create good citizens and that will make them more motivated and competent participants in social life. Critical media literacy can be connected with the project of radical democracy and can be concerned with developing skills that will enhance democratization and participation. Critical media literacy takes a comprehensive approach that would teach critical skills and how to use media as instruments of social communication and change. The technologies of communication are becoming more and more accessible to young people and ordinary citizens and can be used to promote education, democratic self-expression, and social progress. Technologies that could help produce the end of participatory democracy, by transforming politics into media spectacles and the battle of images and by turning spectators into cultural zombies, could also be used to help invigorate democratic debate and participation (Kellner 1998).

Indeed, teaching critical media literacy could be a participatory, collaborative project. Watching television shows or films together could promote productive discussions between teachers and students (or parents and children), with emphasis on eliciting student views, producing a variety of interpretations of media texts, and teaching basic principles of hermeneutics and criticism. Students and youth are often more media savvy, knowledgeable, and immersed in media culture than their teachers, and can contribute to the educational process through sharing their ideas, perceptions, and insights. On the other hand, critical discussion, debate, and analysis ought to be encouraged, with teachers bringing to bear their critical perspectives on student readings of media material. Since media culture is often part and parcel of students' identity and most powerful cultural experience, teachers must be sensitive in criticizing artifacts and perceptions that students hold dear; yet an atmosphere of critical respect for difference *and* inquiry into the nature and effects of media culture should be promoted.

One of the most effective ways of teaching critical media literacy is involving students themselves in the production of media texts (see Hammer, in McLaren et al. 1995). Learning to produce different forms of media texts teaches codes, formal features, and the role of technology in constructing media artifacts. In becoming literate in semiological and ideological codes of media culture, students not only can read and critique dominant modes of cultural hegemony, but can produce oppositional forms of culture, subverting the dominant codes and ideologies and providing alternatives.

A major challenge in developing critical media literacy, however, results from the fact that it is not a pedagogy in the traditional sense with firmly established principles, a canon of texts, and tried-and-true teaching procedures.

Critical media pedagogy is in its infancy; it is just beginning to produce results, and is more open and experimental than established print-oriented pedagogy. Moreover, the material of media culture is so polymorphous, multivalent, and polysemic that it requires sensitivity to different readings, interpretations, perceptions of the complex images, scenes, narratives, meanings, and messages of media culture that in its own ways is as complex and challenging to critically decipher as book culture.

Teaching critical media literacy involves occupation of a site above the dichotomy of fandom and censor. One can teach how media culture provides significant statements or insights about the social world, empowering visions of gender, race, and class, or complex aesthetic structures and practices, thereby putting a positive spin on how it can provide significant contributions to education. Yet critical educators should indicate also how media culture can advance sexism, racism, ethnocentrism, homophobia, and other forms of prejudice, as well as misinformation, problematic ideologies, and questionable values, accordingly promoting a dialectical approach to the media that aims at critical and discriminating readers.

Computer Literacy: An Expanded Concept

To fully participate in the hi-tech and global society, teachers and students should cultivate new forms of computer literacy in ways that go beyond standard technical notions. Critical computer literacy involves learning how to use computer technologies to do research and gather information, as well as how to perceive computer culture as a terrain containing texts, spectacles, games, and interactive multimedia that call for cultivating new literacies. As technologies like computers, telephones, televisions, and new multimedia devices converge, computer-mediated culture will increasingly provide an encompassing environment in which people work, play, relate, learn, and interact. Becoming computer-literate in this broad sense thus requires expanding notions of literacy and learning how to communicate, interact, and create in novel cybercultures.

The emergent cybercultures can be seen as a discursive and political location in which students, teachers, and citizens can all intervene, engaging in discussion groups and collaborative research projects, creating Web sites, producing innovative multimedia for cultural dissemination, and engaging in novel modes of social interaction and learning. Computer culture enables individuals to actively participate in the production of culture, ranging from dialogue concerning public issues to creation of their own cultural forms. However, to take part in this culture requires not only accelerated skills of print literacy, which are often restricted to the growing elite of students who are privileged to attend adequate and superior public and private schools, but demands also multiple forms of literacy.

To respond intelligently to the dramatic technological revolution of our time, we need to begin teaching computer literacy from an early age. Computer literacy, however, itself needs to be theorized. Often the term is synonymous with the technical ability to use computers, to become proficient in the use of existing programs, and maybe to undertake some programming. I suggest expanding the conception of computer literacy from using computer programs and hardware to a broader concept of information and multimedia literacy. This necessitates promoting more sophisticated abilities in traditional reading and writing, as well as the capability to dissect and read cultural forms taught as part of critical media literacy and multimedia pedagogy.

In my expanded conception, computer literacy involves learning how to use computers, access information and educational material, use e-mail and List-servs, and construct Web sites. Computer literacy comprises the accessing and processing of diverse sorts of information proliferating in the so-called information society. It encompasses learning to find sources of information ranging from traditional sites like libraries and print media to new Internet Web sites and search engines. Computer-information literacy involves learning where information is found; how to access it; and how to organize, interpret, and evaluate the information that one seeks.

One exciting development in the current technological revolution is that library materials and information are accessible throughout the world. To some extent, the Internet is potentially the all-encompassing library, imperfectly constructed in Alexander, Egypt, that would contain the great books of the world. Yet while a mind-boggling number of the classics are found on the Internet, we still need the local library to access and collect books, journals, and print material not found on the Internet, as well as the essential texts of various disciplines and the culture as a whole. Information literacy, however, and the new tasks for librarians also involve knowing what one can and cannot find on the Internet, how to access it, and where the most reliable and useful information is at hand for specific tasks and projects.

Information literacy also requires learning how to distinguish between good and bad information, identifying what Burbules and Callister (2000) identify as misinformation, malinformation, messed-up information, and mostly useless information. In this sense, information literacy is closely connected with education itself, with learning where information is found, how to produce knowledge and understanding, and how to critically evaluate and interpret information sources and material. It also raises questions of power and knowledge, concerning who decides what privileged information is, who gets to produce and valorize various modes of information, whose ideas get circulated and discussed, and who gets marginalized.

Computer and information literacies also involve learning how to read hypertexts. This involves learning how to traverse the ever-changing fields of cyberculture, and to participate in a digital and interactive multimedia culture that encompasses work, education, politics, culture, and everyday life. Hypertext was initially seen as an innovative and exciting new mode of writing that increased the potential for writers to explore novel modes of textuality and expression (Joyce 1995; Landow 1992).[7] As multimedia hypertext developed on the Internet, it was soon theorized as a multisemiotic and multimodal form of culture. This mode is now increasingly seen as the dominant form of a new hyperlinked, interactive, and multimedia cyberculture (see Burbules and Callister 1996, 2000; Snyder 1996, 1997, 2002).

Genuine computer literacy involves not just technical knowledge and skills, but refined reading, writing, research, and communicating ability. It involves heightened capacities for critically accessing, analyzing, interpreting, processing, and storing both print-based and multimedia material. In a novel information/entertainment society, immersed in transformative multimedia technology, knowledge and information come not merely in the form of print and words, but through images, sounds, and multimedia material as well. Computer literacy thus also involves the ability to discover and access information and intensified abilities to read; to scan texts and computer databases and Web sites; and to access information and images in a variety of forms, ranging from graphics to visual images, to audio and video materials, to good old print media. The creation of new multimedia Web sites, databases, and texts requires accessing, downloading, and organizing digitized verbal, imagistic, and audio and video material that are the new building blocks of multimedia culture.

Within multimedia-computerized culture, visual literacy takes on increased importance. On the whole, computer screens are more graphic, multisensory, and interactive than conventional print fields that disconcerted many of us when first confronted with the new environments. Icons, windows, mouses, and the various clicking, linking, and interaction involved in computer-mediated hypertext dictate new competencies and a dramatic expansion of literacy. Visuality is obviously crucial, compelling users to perceptively scrutinize visual fields, perceive and interact with icons and graphics, and use technical devices like a mouse to access the desired material and field. But tactility is also important, as individuals must learn navigational skills of how to proceed from one field and screen to another, how to negotiate hypertexts and links, and how to move from one program to another if one operates, as most now do, in a window-based computer environment. And as voice and sound enter multimedia culture, refined hearing also becomes part of the aesthetics and pedagogies of an expanded computer literacy.

In my conception, computer literacy thus involves technical abilities concerning developing basic typing skills, mastering computer programs, accessing information, and using computer technologies for a variety of purposes ranging from interpersonal communication to artistic expression to political debate. There are ever more hybrid implosions between media and computer culture as audio and video material becomes part of the Internet; as CD-ROMs, DVDs, and multimedia develop; and as new technologies become part and parcel of the home, school, and workplace. Therefore, the skills of decoding images, sounds, and spectacle learned in critical media literacy training can also be valuable as part of computer literacy.

Moreover, with ever-expanding Internet subcultures and online communities, more and more people have the possibilities of participating in cultural production and expression. New Web forms of design, such as blogs and wikis,[8] have emerged as important new developments of the Net's hypertextual architecture and provide opportunities for new voices, alternative online communities, and political activism (Kahn and Kellner 2003). Participation in this new cultural and political environment accordingly requires the cultivation of multiple literacies.

Multimedia and Multiple Literacies: The New Frontier

The new multimedia environments necessitate a diversity of types of multisemiotic and multimodal interaction, involving interfacing with words and print material and often images, graphics, and audio and video material. As technological convergence develops apace, individuals need to combine the skills of critical media literacy with traditional print literacy and new forms of multiple literacies to access, navigate, and participate in the new multimedia hypertext environments. Literacy in this conception involves the abilities to engage effectively in socially constructed, emergent, and novel forms of culture and communication. Reading and interpreting print were the appropriate modes of literacy for books, while critical multiple literacies entail reading and interpreting discourse, images, spectacle, narratives, and the forms and genres of media culture. Forms of multimedia communication involve print, speech, visuality, and audio, in a hybrid field that combines these forms, all of which involve skills of interpreting and critique.

The term *multiple literacies* points to the many different kinds of always-proliferating literacies needed to access, interpret, criticize, and participate in the emergent multimedia forms of culture and society.[9] The key root here is "multiple," the proliferation of media and forms that demand a multiplicity of competencies, skills, and abilities to access, interact, and help construct a new semiotic terrain. Multiple literacies involve reading across varied and hybrid semiotic fields and being able to critically and hermeneutically process print, graphics, moving images, and sounds. Perpetually multiplying media provide the challenge for "multi-plying" uses, always recreating and reconstructing media forms and practices.

The term *hybridity* suggests the combination and interaction of diverse media and the need to synthesize the various forms in an active process of the construction of meaning. Reading a music video, for instance, involves processing images, music, spectacle, and sometimes narrative in a multisemiotic activity that simultaneously draws on diverse aesthetic forms. Interacting with a Web site, DVD, or CD-ROM often involves scanning text, graphics, moving images, and clicking on the fields that one seeks to peruse and explore, looking for appropriate material. This might lead individuals to draw upon a diversity of materials in new interactive learning or entertainment environments, whereby they must simultaneously read and interpret images, graphics, animation, and text.

While traditional literacies concern practices in contexts that are governed by rules and conventions, the conventions and rules of multiliteracies are currently evolving so that their pedagogies comprise a fresh although bustling and competitive field. Multimedia sites are not entirely new, however. Multisemiotic textuality was first evident in newspapers (consider the difference between the *New York Times* and *U.S.A. Today* in terms of image, text, color graphics, design, and content) and is now evident in textbooks that are much more visual, graphic, and multimodal than the previously linear and discursive texts of old. But CD-ROMs, DVDs, Web sites, and new multimedia are the most distinctively multimodal and multisemiotic forms. These spaces are the new frontier of learning and literacy, the great contemporary challenge to education. Critical educators need to theorize the literacies necessary to interact in these emergent multimedia environments and to gain the skills that will enable individuals to learn, work, and create in emergent cultural spaces and domains.

Cultivating multiple literacies and reconstructing education for democratization will also involve constructing traditional pedagogies and social relations. Emergent multimedia technologies enable group projects for students and more of a problem-solving pedagogy in the spirit of Dewey and Freire (1972, 1998) than traditional transmission top-down teaching models. To enable students to access information, engage in cultural communication and production, and gain the skills necessary to succeed in the global economy and culture, they need to acquire enhanced literacies, abilities to work cooperatively with others, and to navigate emergent cultural and social terrains. Such group activity may generate more egalitarian relations between teachers and students and more democratic and cooperative social relations. Of course, it also demands reconsideration of grading and testing procedures, rethinking the roles of teacher and student, and constructing projects and pedagogies appropriate to the new cultural and social environments.

Moreover, critical educators are soon going to have to rethink SATs and standard tests in relation to the new media and technologies; having the literacy and skills to successfully access material sought after, communicate, work, and create within computer and multimedia culture is quite different from reading and writing in the mode of print literacy. While traditional skills of reading and writing continue to be of utmost importance in cyberculture, they are sublated within multiliteracy, so eventually an entirely different sort of test will need to be devised in order to register individuals' multiple literacy competencies and to predict success in a new technological and educational environment. In this mutating global and technological world, it becomes increasingly irrational to focus education on producing higher test scores on exams that themselves are becoming obsolete and outdated by the changes in the economy, society, and culture.[10]

Critical pedagogies of the future must also confront the issue of online education, of how the new cultural terrain of cyberspace produces new sites of information, education, and culture, as well as novel online forms of interaction between students and teacher. In addition, possibilities of students' developing their own spaces, cultural forms, and modes of interaction and communication should be promoted. The challenge will also arise of how to balance classroom instruction with online instruction, as well as sorting out the strengths and limitations of print versus online multimedia material (see Feenberg 1999). Indeed, the emergent ICTs and cultural spaces require us to rethink education in its entirety, ranging from the role of the teacher, teacher-student relations, classroom instruction, grading and testing, the value and limitations of books, multimedia, and other teaching material, and the goals of education itself.

Online education and virtual learning also confront us with novel problems such as copyright and ownership of educational materials; collaborations between computer programmers, artists and designers, and teachers and students in the construction of teaching material and sites; and the respective role of federal and local government, the community, corporations, and private organizations in financing education and providing the skills and tools necessary for a global economy and culture. Furthermore, the technological revolution forces a rethinking of philosophical problems of knowledge, truth, identity, and reality in virtual environments. Both philosophy and philosophy of education most be reconstructed to meet the challenges of democracy and a new hi-tech economy (Kellner 2003).

Finally, adequately meeting the challenges of ever-multiplying technologies raises the question of design and reconstruction of technology itself. As Andrew Feenberg has long argued (1991, 1995, 1999), democratizing technology often requires its reconstruction and re-visioning by individuals. Within the technology world, hackers have redesigned technological systems, and much of the Internet itself is the result of individuals' contributing collective knowledge and making improvements that aid various educational, political, and cultural projects. Of course, there are corporate and technical constraints in that dominant programs impose their rules and constraints on users and the open-source movement has challenged users to participate in alternative computer programs and sites, freely providing new innovations, programs, and content of various modes. There has been an ongoing struggle within the computer world between corporations and users, with governments usually intervening on the side of major corporations.

Critical educators, however, should help teach students and themselves to become producers as well as consumers, thus helping to redesign and reconstruct the very forms and programs of computers. There are, of course, restrictions on what those without highly developed technical knowledge can do, but within limits more creative and reconstructive uses of ICTs can be devised and implemented. This leads to some final considerations on the re-vision and reconstruction of education.

Re-Visioning and Reconstructing Education in the Contemporary Era

In sum, individuals should be helped to develop the competencies to understand, critique, and transform the social and cultural conditions in which they live, gaining the ability to be creative and transformative subjects and not just objects of domination and manipulation. This requires developing abilities for critical thinking, reflection, and the capacity to engage in discourse, cultural creation, and political action and movements. Active and engaged subjects are produced in social interaction with others as well as with tools and techniques, so social skills and individual capacities for communication, creativity, and action must be part of the multiple literacies that a radical reconstruction of education seeks and cultivates.

Crucially, developing multiple literacies and alternative pedagogies must become reflective and critical, aware of the educational, social, and political assumptions involved in the restructuring of education and society currently underway. In response to the excessive hype concerning new technologies and education, it is important to maintain the critical dimension and to reflect upon the nature and effects of new technologies and the pedagogies developed as a response to their challenge. Many advocates of new technologies, however, eschew critique for a purely affirmative agenda. For instance, after an excellent discussion of new modes of literacy and the need to rethink education, Gunther Kress argues that we must move from critique to design, beyond a negative deconstruction to more positive construction (1997). But rather than following such modern logic of either/or, critical pedagogues should pursue the logic of both/and, perceiving design and critique, deconstruction and reconstruction, as complementary and supplementary rather than as antithetical choices. Certainly, we need to design alternative technologies, pedagogies, and curricula for the future, and should attempt to design more democratic and egalitarian social and pedagogical relations as well; but we need to criticize misuse, inappropriate use, overinflated claims, and exclusions and oppressions involved in the introduction of ICTs into education. The critical dimension is needed more than ever as we attempt to develop improved teaching strategies and pedagogy, and design more emancipatory and democratizing technologies and curricula. In this process, we must be constantly critical, practicing critique and self-criticism, putting in question our assumptions, discourses, and practices, as we experimentally develop novel and alternative literacies and pedagogy (see Kellner 2003).

In all educational and other experiments, critique is indeed of fundamental importance. From the Deweyan perspective, progressive education involves trial and error, design and criticism. The experimental method itself comprises critique of limitations, failures, and flawed design. In discussing new technologies and multiple literacies, we also need to constantly raise the questions: Whose interests are emergent technologies and pedagogies serving? Are they helping all social groups and individuals? Who is being excluded and why? We also need to raise the question of the extent to which multiplying technologies and literacies are preparing students and citizens for the present and future and producing conditions for a more vibrant democratic society, or simply reproducing existing inequalities and inequity.

Further, creating multiple literacies must be contextual, engaging the life-world of the students and teachers who are participating in the new adventures of education. Learning involves developing abilities to interact intelligently with the environment and other people, and calls for vibrant social and conversational environments. Education requires doing and can be gained from practice and social interaction. One can obviously spend too much time with technologies and fail to develop basic social skills and competencies. As Rousseau, Wollstonecraft, and Dewey argued, education involves developing proficiencies that enable individuals to successfully develop within their concrete environments, to learn from practice and to be able to interact, work, and create in their own societies and cultures. In the dynamically evolving and turbulent global culture, multiple literacies require multicultural literacies. Communicating and interacting with different groups and individuals demands being able to understand and work with a heterogeneity of people and spaces, acquiring literacies in a multiplicity of media and gaining the competencies to participate in a democratic culture and society (see Courts 1998; Weil 1998).

From the policy perspective, it seems clear that it is the duty of the federal, state, and local governments, as well as other interested parties, to provide the necessary equipment and tools to teachers, students, and schools in order to make it possible for education to cultivate the skills necessary for participation in the emergent global economy, networked society, and cyberculture. Second, it is important that teachers have proper training to make use of the technology in their classrooms and that there are labs with training or support people who have the proper skills and can ensure that teachers and students can effectively deploy the new media and technologies.[11] Recent studies have indicated that without proper teacher training, the technology itself will not do the teaching and may be a source of frustration, thus blocking the educational goals desired (see Rawls 2000; Zimmerman 2000). Consequently, teacher training and intelligent computer lab design and use, as well as development of more intelligent and user-friendly software, are necessary to improve education in the Information Age.

But, as I have argued in this chapter, teachers and students need to develop new pedagogies and modes of learning in the new information and multimedia environment. This could involve a democratization and restructuring of education such as was envisaged by Dewey, Freire, and Illich in which education is seen as a dialogical, democratizing, and experimental practice. New information technologies encourage the sort of experimental and collaborative projects proposed by Dewey as important for progressive education (1997 [1916]). This could also involve the more dialogical relations between student and teachers envisaged by Freire in which teachers learn from students and promote collaborative, dialogical, and nonauthoritarian teaching methods (1972, 1998), and Illich's conceptions of "webs of learning" and "tools for conviviality" (1971, 1973).

This re-visioning of education involves the recognition that teachers can learn from students and that often students are ahead of teachers in various technological literacies and technical abilities. Many of us (and this is true of myself) have learned much of what we know of computers and new media and technologies from students. We should also recognize the extent to which young people helped invent the Internet and have grown up in a cyberculture in which they may have cultivated technological skills from an early age.[12] Peer-to-peer communication among young people is highly sophisticated and developed, and democratic pedagogies should build upon and enhance these resources and practices.

One of the challenges of contemporary education is to overcome the disconnect between students' experiences, subjectivities, and interests rooted in the new multimedia cyberculture and the classroom, which is grounded in print culture and traditional learning and disciplines (see Luke and Luke, 2002). Already in the 1960s, Marshall McLuhan (1964) pointed to the disconnect between reading and listening to the radio, watching television, and participating in popular culture. Today, the disconnect is even more striking in the contrast between an interactive and multimedia cyberculture and traditional forms of authoritarian lecturing and problematic print materials, thus suggesting a generational divide as well as a digital divide.

The disconnect and divides can be overcome, however, by more actively and collaboratively bringing students into interactive classrooms or learning situations in which they are able to transmit their skills and knowledge to fellow students and teachers alike. Such a democratic and interactive reconstruction of education thus provides the resources for democratic social reconstruction, as well as cultivating the new skills and literacies needed for the global economy and cyberculture. So far, arguments for restructuring education mostly come from the high-tech and corporate sectors who are primarily interested in new media and literacies and the reconstruction of education for the workforce and economy. But restructuring can serve the interests of democratization as well as the global economy. Following Dewey, we should accordingly militate for education that is aimed at producing better democratic citizens, as well as providing skills for the workplace and social and cultural life.

Further, to cultivate new literacies for democratizing education and society in the contemporary era, we need the Deweyan experimental method of trying out and testing ideas about how computers and new information technology can aid reading, research, and teaching traditional material. This involves trial and error, attempting to discern what works and what does not in using new media to democratize and enhance education. Thus, like Dewey, we need to perceive the interconnection of science, technology, education, and democracy in the present conjuncture. To have an enlivened democracy, we must have educated and informed citizens who require training in science and technology, and acquisition of new multiple literacies. Cultivating multiple literacies involves the scientific method of trial and error, seeking collaborative solutions to problems, and working together to democratically reconstruct education and society. As Dewey noted, this experimental and collaborative method is also the ethos of democracy, which involves dialogue, cooperation, and working together, as well as designing and properly using voting machines.[13]

It appears that technology will certainly drive the reconstruction of education, but we should make sure that it works to enhance democracy and empower individuals and not just corporations and a privileged techno-elite. Producing democratic citizens and empowering the next generation for democracy should be a major goal of the reconstruction of education in the present age. Moreover, as Freire reminds us (1972, 1998), critical pedagogy comprises the skills of both reading the word and reading the world. Hence, multiple literacies include not only media and computer literacies, but a diverse range of social and cultural literacies, ranging from ecoliteracy (e.g., understanding the body and environment) to economic and financial literacy to a variety of other competencies that enable us to live well in our social worlds. Education, at its best, provides the symbolic and cultural capital that empowers people to survive and prosper in an increasingly complex and changing world and the resources to produce a more cooperative, democratic, egalitarian, and just society. Thus, with Plato, Rousseau, Wollstonecraft, Dewey, Freire, and others, I see the philosophy of education as reflecting on the good life and the good society and the ways that education can contribute to creating a better world. But as the world changes, so too must education that will be part of the problem or part of the solution as we enter and negotiate an ever-more precarious and insecure present and future.

The project of transforming education will take different forms in different contexts. In the overdeveloped countries, individuals should be empowered to work and act in a hi-tech information economy, and should learn skills of media and computer literacy to survive in the new social environment. Traditional skills of knowledge and critique should also be enhanced, so that individuals can name the system, can describe and grasp the changes occurring and the defining features of the new global order, and can learn to engage in critical and oppositional practice in the interests of democratization and progressive transformation. This process challenges us to gain a vision of how life can be, of alternatives to the present order, and of the necessity of struggle and organization to realize progressive goals. Languages of knowledge and critique must be supplemented by the discourse of hope and praxis.

In much of the world, the struggle for daily existence is paramount and meeting unmet human and social needs is a high priority. Yet everywhere education can provide the competencies and skills to improve one's life, to create a better society and a more civilized and developed world. Moreover, as the entire world becomes part of a global and networked society, gaining the multiple literacies discussed in this chapter becomes important everywhere as media and cyberculture become more ubiquitous and the world economy demands ever-more sophisticated technical skills.

This is a time of challenge and a time for experiment. It is time to put existing pedagogies, practices, and educational philosophies in question and to construct more democratic and progressive ones. It is a time for new pedagogical experiments to see what works and what doesn't work. It is a time to reflect on our goals and to discern what we want to achieve with education and how we can achieve it. Ironically, it is a time to return to a classical philosophy of education that situates reflections on education on the good life and society at the same time that we reflect on how we can transform education to become relevant to a hi-tech society and global economy and culture. It is time to return to John Dewey to rethink that intimate connection between education and democracy at the same time we address the multicultural challenges that Dewey in the midst of a still-vital melting pot ideology and liberal progressivist optimism did not address. Most saliently, it is time to take up the Deweyan attitude of pragmatic experimentation to see what it is that the new technologies can and cannot do in order to see how they can enhance education.

In the current turbulent situation of the global restructuring of capitalism and worldwide struggles for democratization, we have for the first time in decades a chance to reconstruct education and society. In this conjuncture, technology is a revolutionizing force, whereby all political parties and candidates pay lip service to education, overcoming the digital divide and expanding literacy. The time is ripe to take up the challenge and to move to reconstruct education and society so that groups and individuals excluded from the benefits of the economy, culture, and society may more fully participate and receive opportunities not possible in earlier social constellations.

Notes

1. For materials pertaining to the educational reform proposed by Dewey and Freire and the broader conceptions of relating education to creation of the good life and good society advanced by Plato, Rousseau, Wollstonecraft, and others that inform this paper, see my philosophy of education Web site, accessible from www.gseis.ucla.edu/faculty/kellner/kellner.html. See also my Education and Technology Web site, which contains materials pertinent to this study.

2. Studies reveal that women, minorities, and immigrants now constitute roughly 85 percent of the growth in the labor force, while these groups represent about 60 percent of all workers (see Duderstadt 1999–2000: 38). In the past decade, the number of Hispanics in the United States increased by 35 percent and Asians by more than 40 percent. Since 1991, California has had no single ethnic or racial minority, and almost half of the high school students in the state are African American or Latino. Meanwhile, a "tidal wave" of children of baby boomers are about to enter college (see Atkinson 1999–2000: 49–50). Obviously, I am writing this study from a U.S. perspective, but would suggest that my arguments have broader reference in an increasingly globalized society marked by a networked economy, increasing migration and multiculturalism, and a proliferating Internet-based cyberculture. There are by now a tremendous number of books and articles on the new economy, technological revolution, new cultural spaces, and the implications for every aspect of life from education to war. For example, the monumental work of Manuel Castells and the analyses of the restructuring of capital, technological revolution, and the postmodern turn in Best and Kellner (2001).

3. See the Ph.D. dissertations by two of my UCLA students, Jennifer Janofsky Rawls (2000) and Roy Zimmermann (2000). See also Bernard Warner, "Computers for youth: Spreading the Net," *The Standard,* March 27, 2000, which reports: "A study conducted recently by Denver-based Quality Education Data showed school districts across the country spent $6.7 billion on technology in the 1998–1999 school year, up almost 25 percent from the previous year. But the same study revealed that an equally crucial funding component—computer training for teachers—was startlingly low, rising just 5.2 percent over the same period." In June 2000, however, President Bill Clinton argued for increased funding for teaching training to use new technologies, so it appears that there is growing recognition of the problem.

4. Freire also stated that "it is not the media themselves which I criticize, but

the way they are used" (1972: 136). Moreover, he argued for the importance of teaching media literacy to empower individuals against manipulation and oppression, and using the most appropriate media to help teach the subject matter in question (114–116).

5. On the new forms of Internet culture and online communities, see Kahn and Kellner, 2003.

6. For an earlier and expanded discussion of media literacy, see Kellner, 1998. Carson and Friedman's (1995) work contains studies dealing with the use of media to deal with multicultural education. Examples of teaching media literacy that I draw on include Masterman (1989 [1985]); Kellner and Ryan (1988); Schwoch, White, and Reilly (1992); Fleming (1993); Giroux (1992, 1993, 1994, 1996); Giroux and McLaren (1994); Sholle and Denski (1994); McLaren, Hammer, Sholle, and Reilly (1995); Kellner (1995a, 1995b); Luke (1996, 1997a, 1997b); Giroux and Shannon (1997); and Semali and Watts Pailliotet (1999). See also the work of Barry Duncan and the Canadian Association for Media Literacy (http://www.nald.ca/province/que/litcent/media.htm) and the Los Angeles–based Center for Media Literacy (www.medialit.org). It is a scandal that there are not more efforts to promote media literacy throughout the school system from K-12 and into the university. Perhaps the ubiquity of computer and multimedia culture will awaken educators and citizens to the importance of developing media literacy to create individuals empowered to intelligently access, read, interpret, and criticize contemporary media and cyberculture.

7. Some early advocates of hypertext attacked the emergence of the World Wide Web as a debased medium that brought back into play the field of earlier media, like television, forcing the word to renegotiate its power against the image and spectacles of sight and sound, once again decentering the written word (see, for instance, Joyce 1995, and the discussion in Landow 1992; see also their more recent reflections in Snyder 2002). As the Internet becomes a multimedia hypertext, however, it is clear that contemporary education must teach reading a multimodal hypertext as a basic skill and mode of literacy.

8. On blogs and wikis, see Kahn and Kellner (2003). *Blogs* are hypertextual Weblogs that people use for new forms of journaling, self-publishing, and media/news critique, as we discuss in detail below. For examples, see our two blogs: BlogLeft: Critical Interventions, www.gseis.ucla.edu/courses/ed253a/blogger.php (accessed July 2003) and Vegan Blog: The (Eco)Logical Weblog, getvegan.com/blog/blogger.php (accessed July 2003). *Wikis* (from the Hawaiian word for "quick") are popular new forms of group databases and hypertextual archives.

9. For other recent conceptions of multimedia literacy that I draw upon here, see the discussions of literacies needed for reading hypertext in Burbules and Callister (1996 and 2000; the concept of multiliteracy Luke (1997a); the papers in Snyder (1997, 2002); Semali and Watts Pailliotet (1999); and books being published in David Barton's Routledge series *Literacies* that include Ilana Snyder's *Silicon Literacies,* as well as books on "city literacies, "situated literacies," "multiliteracies," and "global literacies and the World Wide Web."

10. On the centrality of preparation for exams in contemporary education and the role of standardized tests in the U.S. educational and social system, see Lehmann (1999). While I have not myself researched the policy literature on this issue, in the many discussions of SAT tests and their biases that I have read, I have not

encountered critiques that indicate the obsolescence of many standardized tests in a new technological environment and the need for new testing procedures based on the new cultural and social fields that we are increasingly immersed in. I would predict that proposals for devising such tests will emerge and that this issue will be hotly debated and contested in the future.

11. It was at one time encouraging that computers and new technologies were getting into the schools in the United States and elsewhere at an impressive rate. The September 25, 2000, *US News and World Report* notes that in 1994 when President Clinton vowed to connect every school to the information superhighway, only one in three schools, and just 3 percent of the classrooms, were wired to the Internet. But by 1999, according to the National Center for Education Statistics, 95 percent of schools and 63 percent of classrooms had Internet access. A survey then showed that 76 percent of the public polled believed that the U.S. government should support efforts to train teachers to use new technologies in their classrooms and said that they saw new technologies and gaining necessary literacies and skills as essential to their own professional and personal advancement. Seventy-one percent thought that the Internet could enhance their own educational level, while 86 percent thought that the Net could help their children learn more; 71 percent claimed that they had gone online for educational reasons—up from 36 percent when the same group was polled in 1999. Yet it is discouraging that the Bush administration has not continued the progressive technology and education policies of the previous administration and has reverted to conservative schooling based on training for tests and centering on traditional forms of literacy and curricula.

12. For instance, Mosaic, Netscape, and the first browsers were invented by young computer users, as were many of the first Web sites, Listservs, chat rooms, and so on. A hacker culture emerged that was initially conceptualized as a reconfiguring and improving of computer systems, related to design, system, and use, before the term *hacker* became synonymous with theft and mischief, such as setting loose worms and viruses. On youth and Internet subcultures, see Kahn and Kellner (2003).

13. I am, of course, ironically pointing to the nonfunctioning of voting technology and the system of democracy in the 2000 U.S. presidential election, suggesting a massive disconnect between the hi-tech economy and cyberculture and traditional voting machines and practices that helped the Bush machine to gain the presidency (see Best and Kellner 2001).

References

Atkinson, Richard C. (1999–2000) "The future arrives first in California," *Issues in Science and Technology* (Winter): 43–51.

Best, Steven, and Kellner, Douglas. (2001) *The Postmodern Adventure.* New York: Guilford Press.

Burbules, Nicholas C. (1997) "Rhetorics of the Web: Hyperreading and critical literacy in page to screen," in Ilana Snyder, ed., *Taking Literacy into the Electronic Era.* New South Wales: Allen and Unwin, 102–122.

Burbules, Nicholas C., and Callister, Thomas. (1996) "Knowledge at the crossroads: Some alternative futures of hypertext learning environments," *Educational Theory* 46, no. 1 (Winter): 23–50.

———. (2000) *Watch IT. The Risks and Promises of Information Technology.* Boulder, Colo.: Westview.

Carson, Diane, and Friedman, Lester D. (1995) *Shared Differences: Multicultural Media and Practical Pedagogy.* Urbana and Chicago: University of Illinois Press.

Cazden, Courtney, Cope, Bill, Fairclough, Norman, Gee, James, Kalantzis, Mary, Kress, Gunter, Luke, Allan et al. (1996) "A pedagogy of multiliteracies: Designing social futures," *Harvard Educational Review* 66: 60–92.

Courts, Patrick L. (1998) *Multicultural Literacies: Dialect, Discourses, and Diversity.* New York: Peter Lang.

Dewey, John. (1997 [1916]) *Democracy and Education.* New York: Free Press.

Dines, Gail, and Humez, Jean (eds.). (1995) *Gender, Race, and Class in Media.* Thousand Oaks, Calif., and London: Sage.

Duderstadt, James J. (1999–2000) "New roles for the 21st century university," *Issues in Science and Technology* (Winter): 37–44.

Feenberg, Andrew. (1991) *Critical Theory of Technology.* New York: Oxford University Press.

———. (1995) *Alternative Modernity.* Berkeley: University of California Press.

———. (1999) *Questioning Technology.* New York and London: Routledge.

Fleming, Dan. (1993) *Media Teaching.* Oxford: Basil Blackwell.

Freire, Paulo. (1972) *Pedagogy of the Oppressed.* New York: Herder and Herder.

———. (1998) *A Paulo Freire Reader.* New York: Herder and Herder.

Giroux, Henry. (1992) *Border Crossing.* New York: Routledge.

———. (1993) *Living Dangerously. Multiculturalism and the Politics of Difference.* New York: Peter Lang.

———. (1994) *Disturbing Pleasures.* New York: Routledge.

———. (1996) *Fugitive Cultures: Race, Violence, and Youth.* New York: Routledge.

Giroux, Henry, and McLaren, Peter (eds.). (1994) *Between Borders. Pedagogy and the Politics of Cultural Studies.* New York: Routledge.

Giroux, Henry, and Shannon, Patrick. (1997) *Education and Cultural Studies.* London and New York: Routledge.

Illich, Ivan. (1971) *Deschooling Society.* New York: Harper and Row.

———. (1973) *Tools for Conviviality.* New York: Harper and Row.

Illich, Ivan, and Sanders, Barry. (1988) *ABC: The Alphabetization of the Popular Mind.* San Francisco: North Point Press.

Joyce, Michael. (1995) *Of Two Minds: Hypertext Pedagogy and Politics.* Ann Arbor: University of Michigan Press.

Kahn, R., and Kellner, D. (2003) "Internet subcultures and oppositional politics," in D. Muggleton (ed.), *The Post-subcultures Reader.* London: Berg.

Kellner, Douglas. (1995a) *Media Culture.* London and New York: Routledge.

———. (1995b) "Cultural studies, multiculturalism, and media culture," in Dines and Humez (eds.), *Gender, Race, and Class in Media.* Thousand Oaks, Calif., and London: Sage, 5–17.

———. (1998) "Multiple literacies and critical pedagogy in a multicultural society," *Educational Theory*, 48 (1): 103–122.

———. (1999) "Multiple literacies and critical pedagogy in a multicultural society," in George Katsiaficas and Teodros Kiros (eds.), *The Promise of Multiculturalism*. New York and London: Routledge, 211–236.

———. (2000) "Globalization and new social movements: Lessons for critical theory and pedagogy," in Nicholas Burbules and Carlos Torres (eds.), *Globalization and Education*. New York: Routledge.

———. (2003) "Toward a critical theory of education," *Democracy and Nature*, 9, no. 1 (March): 51–64.

Kellner, Douglas, and Ryan, Michael. (1988) *Camera Politica: The Politics and Ideology of Contemporary Hollywood Film*. Bloomington, Ind.: Indiana University Press.

Kress, Gunther. (1997) "Visual and verbal modes of representation in electronically mediated communication: The potentials of new forms of text," in I. Snyder (ed.), *Page to* Screen. New South Wales: Allen and Unwin, 53–79.

Landow, George. (1992) *Hypertext. The Convergence of Contemporary Critical Theory and Technology*. Baltimore and London: Johns Hopkins University Press; 2nd ed.

Lehmann, Nicholas. (1999) *The Big Test: The Secret History of the American Meritocracy*. New York: Farrar Straus and Giroux.

Luke, Allan, and Luke, Carmen. (2002) "Adolescence lost/childhood regained: On early intervention and the emergence of the techno-subject," *Journal of Early Childhood Literacy*, 1 (1): 91–120.

Luke, Carmen. (1996) "Reading gender and culture in media discourses and texts," in G. Bull and M. Anstey (eds.), *The Literacy Lexicon*. New York and Sydney: Prentice-Hall.

———. (1997a) *Technological Literacy*. Melbourne: National Languages and Literacy Institute, Adult Literacy Network.

———. (1997b) "Media literacy and cultural studies," in Sandy Muspratt, Allan Luke, and Peter Freebody (eds.), *Constructing Critical Literacies*. Cresskill, N.Y.: Hampton Press, 19–50.

Masterman, Len. (1989 [1985]) *Teaching the Media*. London and New York: Routledge.

McLaren, Peter, Hammer, Rhonda, Sholle, David, and Reilly, Susan. (1995) *Rethinking Media Literacy. A Critical Pedagogy of Representation*. New York: Peter Lang.

McLuhan, Marshall. (1962) *The Gutenberg Galaxy*. New York: Signet Books.

———. (1964) *Understanding Media: The Extensions of Man*. New York: Signet Books.

Ong, Walter. (1988) *Orality and Literacy: The Technologizing of the Word*. London and New York: Routledge.

Postman, Neil. (1985) *Amusing Ourselves to Death*. New York: Viking-Penguin.

———. (1992) *Technopolis: The Surrender of Culture to Technology*. New York: Random House.

Rawls, Jennifer Janofsky. (2000) The role of micropolitics in school-site technology efforts: A case study of the relationship between teachers and the technology movement at their school. Ph.D. diss.—UCLA.

Robins, Kevin, and Webster, Frank. (1999) *Times of the Technoculture.* New York: Routledge.

Shields, Rob. (2003) *The Virtual.* London and New York: Routledge.

Semali, Ladislau, and Watts Pailliotet, Ann. (1999) *Intermediality.* Boulder, Colo.: Westview.

Schwoch, James, White, Mimi, and Reilly, Susan. (1992) *Media Knowledge.* Albany: State University of New York Press.

Sholle, David, and Denski, Stan. (1994) *Media Education and the (Re)Production of Culture.* Westport, Conn.: Bergin and Garvey.

Snyder, Ilana. (1996) *Hypertext: The Electronic Labyrinth.* Melbourne and New York: Melbourne University Press and New York University Press.

———. (ed.). (1997) *Page to Screen: Taking Literacy into the Electronic Era.* New South Wales: Allen and Unwin.

———. (ed.). (2002) *Silicon Literacies.* London and New York: Routledge.

Webster, Frank. (1995) *Theories of the Information Society.* London and New York: Routledge.

Weil, Danny K. (1998) *Toward a Critical Multicultural Literacy.* New York: Peter Lang.

Wollstonecraft, Mary. (1988) *A Vindication of the Rights of Woman.* New York: Norton.

Zimmermann, Roy. (2000) The intersection of technology and teachers: Challenges and problems. Ph.D. diss., University of California–Los Angeles.

CHAPTER 4

On Cultural Identity and Difference

Brenda Trofanenko

Introduction

One of the most powerful institutions that define identity is the museum, where "culture" is often embodied as a shared descent, or, at least, as a "people" with a historically stable and unchanging identity. What comes to be understood as culture in a museum is often a curator's authority to label and display an artifact with an interpretation projected onto an object then identified and named as culture. As a modern educational institution, broadly defined, museums have fashioned the concepts of culture and of cultural identity during the last century, in an effort to naturalize their educational imperative. Yet, this subscribed culture and cultural identity is not without question, both from within and beyond the institutional realms. What has operated as the museum's imperative of defining an unquestioned representation of culture comes up against resistance, where museums have also had to struggle to keep how they define culture and cultural identity from becoming the source of their own educational undoing.

Most recently, postcolonial scholarship has engaged the universals that define identity across a range of sites including museums, with a purpose of distinguishing shared principles and problems in the ways that culturally diverse groups are being represented, or named, today. Ethnology museums, those museums whose collections and intent focus on culture, reflect how cultural identity is defined by its imperial imperative, by the ability to define cultural identity through the circulation of certain representations. Yet, both partial and situated identities are constructed through the historically defined privileges and rights granted by the public and the museums' own professional organizations. While each museum reflects its institutional norms and values by way of its collection and display mandates, the debate concerning museums and First Nations objects and exhibitions has prompted extending and encouraging expressions of resistance.[1] Calls for self-representation and repatriation of objects from native and non-native groups both within and beyond the museum indicate that this display of identity is imbued with political and ideological questions.

This chapter is concerned with how museums define cultural identity, specifically how those holding First Nations objects are implicated in a complex, multilayered, and continually contentious relationship with First Nations.[2] It is also about how the legacy of imperialism to name and define cultural difference is to be challenged, in order to consider the conditions of possibility made available by understanding how identity is framed within difference and how employing difference serves as an educational starting point. Museums maintain a sense of knowing about the "Other" while, as many critics have made clear, continuing to question how it works against its historically defined exclusion and alienation of various cultural and ethnic groups it purports to represent.

In this chapter, I propose that the museum's defense of displayed difference be engaged by educators to understand how identity may work against its own educational promises, effecting how students have learned about culture and how educators have utilized the museum to teach about First Nations culture. I begin with a brief historical overview of the museum's educational intent. I follow with tensions that present-day museums are facing in defining *other.* I conclude with calling into question the power of museums that remain despite conflicts, contradictions, ambiguities, and tensions in defining identity.

"Desires of the Curious and the Improvement of Knowledge"[3]

Museums have long defined difference in their authority to educate. Beginning as private institutions in the sixteenth century, museums were directed by individual educational interests and purposes. These private collections were made available to a select public, an ordering of knowledge by an elite eager to show the past, in all its forms, through the possession of its remnants. While the number of private collections increased in Europe in the seventeenth and eighteenth centuries, the desire to establish institutions that defined national identity prompted the development of public, secular, and national museums where knowledge was "publicly demarcated and represented."[4] Various national acts stipulated free access to museums, having considered such advantages to the public. The British Museum Act, for example, defined the British Museum's educational imperative of "raising and vilifying the common intellect, diffusing its enjoyments, and broadening its *public* domain."[5]

From the mid-eighteenth century onward, the museum's educational undertaking situated museums, along with churches and libraries, as institutions concerned with public education. While private collections, and the spaces within which they were housed, were primarily expressions of private affluence, their transformation into public collections was an expression of the desire to shape "the moral, mental, and behaviour characteristics" of the masses.[6] This opening up of the museum was part of what Tony Bennett refers to as "the exhibitionary complex."[7] This complex consists of the "permanent [public] display of [a museum's] power/knowledge, which manifest[s] itself precisely in continually displaying its ability to command, order, and control objects and bodies, living or dead."[8] The control brought the working classes into an experience shared by the elite, for the sole purpose of informing a public audience.

During the eighteenth and nineteenth centuries, Europe was involved in Western expansion and colonization in an effort to claim, name, and inhabit.[9] The geographic expansion to unknown regions garnered objects that not only showed evidence of colonization but also provided instruction and knowledge about the new lands and the inhabitants. This expansion exposed colonialists and countries to an imagined Other, which created an interest in defining these people and justifying control of their lands, labors, and lives. Indigenous artifacts became trophies reflecting an experience of the world. The public museum became an object repository. Anne Coombes suggests that museums and their curators as "benevolent educators dispensing rational and[,] more particularly, 'scientific' knowledge" functioned to account for scientific explanations of the natural world and man as one of its elements.[10] The scholarly interest in studying difference confirmed the colonial conquests in favor of education. In defining and displaying scientific definitions for specific economic, political, and social interests, race differences were defined as determining the progress of mankind. Museums served as sites that showed the relationships between race and abilities through scientific explanation and display. Yet, the rule of race proved more than important to how the academic discipline of anthropology developed around the concepts of race and culture.

While scientific study of the Other provided countries with justification for colonial expansion, in order to tell stories of how Western society had a civilizing influence upon the rest of the world, museums affirmed anthropology as a discipline through the study of racial difference, which is the basis of anthropological knowledge, itself developed as an inquiry into the "natural history of man. Physical difference and equality between human groups, along with a scientific commitment to objectivity, produced and legitimated what were perceived to be "natural" differences. From earlier depictions of natives, for example, as savages and cannibals to the worlds' fairs and exhibitions of the nineteenth and twentieth centuries, difference was proclaimed in the public arenas through the collections, or specimens, that showed how racial difference was conceptualized and fostered. Pitt Rivers insisted, "Specimens [were to be] arranged according to their affinities, the simpler on the left and the successive improvements in line to the right of them."[11]

The idea of culturally defined differences began to disrupt the tenet of race, with anthropologist Franz Boas examining human differences as an expression of a culture. By the beginning of the twentieth century, Boas and his contemporaries' challenge of racial differences that formed the basis of Pitt Rivers' nineteenth-century exhibitions eventually gave way to anthropology's concern with describing and understanding culture in both general and specific terms. Notions of culture soon became central to "developing discourses of race, biology, and nationality."[12]

The Inability to Speak for Other

Literary critic Ania Loomba suggests that postcolonial theory engages "the contestation of colonial domination and the legacies of colonialism," in order to understand how an anticolonial resistance to imperialism and to dominant Western ways continues.[13] Postcolonial scholarship has shown how the remains of a colonial past continue in a supposedly postcolonial present. Although the era of formal colonial control is over, imperialist practices persist in the contemporary world. Gyan Prakash claims that postcolonial theory can challenge and "force a radical rethinking and re-formulation of forms of knowledge and social identities authorized by colonialism and western domination."[14] Questioning the interplay between economic, cultural, and political dominance and subordination of one group over another allows examining how power is complicit in the construction and representation of identity. The process of colonization can, as anthropologist John and Jean Comaroff proclaim, transform ethnic and cultural groups by "conceptualizing, inscribing and interacting with them on terms not of their choosing; in making them into the pliant objects and silent subjects" through assuming "the capacity to 'represent' them."[15] The museum's domination of the non-Western world is not an arbitrary phenomenon but, rather, a conscious and intentional process governed by both individual and institutional imperatives. James Clifford suggests that the public affirms the museum's traditional role of protector of cultural heritage, which then maintains its "ability to articulate identity, power, and tradition."[16] Yet the representations are never totalizing and are always unstable, suggesting that the domination of a museum over ethnic and cultural groups is active, contested, dynamic, and saturated with power.

The epistemological intent of museums that defines and displays culture faces a challenge in the recent shifts in understanding representation and identities. This shift refers to the critiques that directly challenge the ideal of museums' being solely the defining agent of identity. First Nations in Canada, along with indigenous groups in Australia and the United States, have pursued the recognition of Aboriginal rights in the legal, political, economic, territorial, and cultural spheres. Western museums have been invested with the authority to speak about and present images of First Nations, excluding First Nations from the process except as source points for artifact acquisition. As much as First Nations identity is tied up with ethnological objects located in museums, the separation of First Nations from these objects has resulted in Canadian museums' "assuming authority over aboriginal cultural interpretation."[17]

The appropriation of cultural interpretation of First Nations has a long history in Canadian museums. The conditions, contexts, and content through which the discourses of cultural identity are being produced and linked to artifacts displayed in museums are new. As art historian Anne Coombs argues, culture "does not stand apart from the socially organized forms of inequality, domination, exploitation, and power that exist in society but is implicated in and inscribed in these practices, which are maintained and contested symbolically as well as instrumentally, discursively as well as forcefully."[18] Her comments are relevant to the ways in which ethnology museums symbolically define First Nations identity through the display of objects. Through the public display of artifacts, cultural identities assume an aura of being real, while exaggerating cultural differences between First Nations and a non-native audience. In reconfiguring First Nations identity, an artifact is transformed from its symbolic or categorical use in First Nations society to an object specific to identify First Nations culture. The display and labeling of the artifact distances the object from the society, yet in this transculturation, cultural identity is attached to the object as a generalized construction of First Nations culture.

Constructing First Nations identity is often masked in a process of a museum's deciding that First Nations are incapable of representing themselves and undertaking to speak, write, and act on their behalf. In the case of the Glenbow, an artifact-based ethnology and history museum located in Calgary, Canada, the encounter between the First Nations with Euro-Canadian arrival in the late nineteenth century ignores how domination and control settled western Canada. This settlement is presented by the Glenbow as Western Heritage, which is physically separated from the displays of First Nations. The imperial legacy continues, with the Glenbow's presenting First Nations not as a group controlled by settlers to the area, but rather as a united culture separate and distinct from settlement history and Western heritage. The Glenbow symbolically defines First Nations as existing in a timeless past, where they were once colorful and vibrant cultures, ignoring First Nations as thriving cultures with contemporary problems. In addition to legitimating differences based on ideology, the Glenbow creates the nineteenth century "native," whose economic, political, social, and spiritual identities are commodified in the displays of handcrafts, garments, spiritual objects, and materials. The individual subject—native—defines a historical difference between native and non-native, which is the nexus of colonial power relations. The problematic of representation is how the Glenbow is expected to produce specific cultural identity of First Nations, the precise forms of which are policed by the museum's discourse, and where acceptable representations are encouraged by the public.

The Politics of Difference

That the Glenbow, like other museums, is not neutral territory but is a place where First Nations objects and First Nations themselves are reinvented, taking on representative qualities as special, "museum-quality" objects and individuals, invites questioning the translation of identity. In the Glenbow's salvaging of stereotypic First Nations identity, and in its constructing First Nations identity in its own image, we can begin to see the historical project of the museum while coming to appreciate its future possibilities.

At its most immediate level, the defined identities are framed by the increasingly politicized and publicized nature of debates about museums in general. Questions about the display and representation of First Nations culture have taken on prominence through vigorous and highly publicized protest over displays, the increased awareness of museum staff, and a general scholarly critique of speaking for and about others. The opportunity for First Nations to name themselves follows art historian Carol Duncan's observation that "on what terms and by whose authority [objects or peoples are named] is closely linked to the larger question [of] who constitutes the community and who defines its identity."[19] First Nations groups are requesting authority to name their own cultural phenomena within museums, which disrupts the museum's tradition of being the one who names.

An understanding of how museums define difference could well temper the fixing of culture to objects. While museums cannot completely separate themselves from their imperial legacy, they can consider how that legacy has contributed to how they once understood and now try to represent First Nations cultures. What needs to be questioned in learning about who we are, about what culture is, and about how museums circulate identity and understandings is the workings of museums so that their politics are unmasked. The changing political, economic, and social contexts facing museums in the past two decades have brought new opportunities for them to work through the tensions as part of their educational programs. It is a way of organizing the knowledge we have of First Nations, where we need to think about its history and its purposes, to ensure that institutions are capable of defining First Nations in their purpose to educate.

Yet in bringing this understanding to how museums function, I do not deny their need. They are places that bring together feelings and memories about another time. What is needed is questioning museums' purposes of defining what constitutes culture and cultural identity. As educators, we need to help our students see that museums are places where identity cannot be allowed to override the identities found beyond them. It means explaining why museums are focusing on First Nations identity as a means of realizing the tensions of naming, while worrying that how First Nations are defined is too often that of astonishment and awe. We need to explore with our students how new understandings of culture as changing and mutable may be emerging in museums. We must continue to ask how museums support a critical educational stance on the socially and historically defined identity of First Nations, and of Others defined by museums. While museums are working to make considerable gains in the critical perspective, they cannot help but remain deeply imprinted by the ongoing legacy of colonialism. In order for museums to develop a more compassionate understanding of public definitions of cultural identity, it is necessary for them to work with teachers and students in recognizing the systematic way in which museums, as the representatives of a dominant colonial culture, operate in multiple dimensions to perpetuate public attitudes that are rooted in a complex, always partial, vision of the world—one that is profoundly shaped by past and present colonial experience. How this process of identity formation secures a claim to a singular First Nations identity is affirmed by public expectations of what museums should do. As long as the attending public considers that artifacts and objects define First Nations identity, that full identity is undermined. That is, the basic premise of questioning museums' domination and control has not been realized; or, if it has, it has not been questioned publicly. How much less true is it today when journalist Stephen Hume spoke of First Nations visible presence, how "we actually prefer our native culture in museums"?[20]

In writing of how museums have been subjected to critical scrutiny, art historians Tim Barringer and Tom Flynn identify an irony within the general project of museum inquiry. They argue that museums' display of culture has been "ignored in the context of debates about colonialism."[21] The prevailing identity of First Nations that is labeled and categorized, divided and displayed, is changing in the face of calls for self-representation and repatriation. How have museums' institutional and political meanings transformed over time? The question is then one of how museums like the Glenbow can further expand the public's education about how difference is utilized, providing opportunities for greater awareness, understanding, and participation, in debating what this difference may teach. Can students understand how difference has been a way of defining identity and the privilege of being identified? Can these experiences extend into the classroom where difference is displayed more subtly through textbooks, maps, and various media? Museums will remain pedagogical in nature; what is needed are more questions about what it means to learn in and from a public institution and how these institutions reaffirm the political nature of knowing. This questioning would require, as Henry Giroux suggests in discussing public pedagogy, "subjecting the specificities of such meanings to broader interrogations and public dialogue" between museums, those they represent, and teachers and students.[22]

The politics of identity as an educational topic is significant to cultural agency and authority, and we would want to build on this significance in education. Recognizing the political character of identity in museums can become a focus for understanding the politics and agency of representation more generally for students. These practices may foster an awareness of the ideologies and mediating strategies of historical representations that shape our assumptions, and as such, our knowledge. Critical reflection on ways that representations objectify culture invites examining how students could benefit from knowing how the politics of representation facilitate particular understanding in various contexts. Can we imagine an education that begins with students' questioning how institutions define identity and control the definition of this identity? If a museum is considered, as Duncan Cameron argued many years ago, both a temple and a forum, then here is a chance to work with how cultural identity is served by an institution.[23] The modern museum has a history that we are by no means done with yet. Culture and cultural identity are not, then, to be disregarded. What is, however, ready to be questioned is how we name each other. It begins with our own Saidian challenge to our own perceptions of who or what defines culture. It means questioning our need to fix identity that cannot be fixed by cultural definitions. It means understanding how culture and identity are simplified through labeling and how these labels work within the museum and again what various groups want of the museum.

As educators, we need to ask how our work with students and with postcolonial theories can advance education in museums. We need to better understand how a museum can facilitate and structure a relationship with First Nations. The modern museum as an educational institution has worked toward improving the quality of education. We need to research and write about rethinking how museums have defined difference. If one is committed to a politics that resists identity-fixing and that resists equally the homogenizing of the stories of subjects, the claims of the political must involve a continuous recognition of persons whose ways of being are diverse. Such a politics must also involve a resistance to practices (and to the theories) that seek to contain modes of diverse presence by erasing, simplifying, or co-opting them. Such a politics will be sensitive to texts and modes of display that witness the struggle between the museum's management of diversity and the resistance to such management by those who do not fit comfortably within the range of identities supplied by a museum's imagination. Such a concern for the politics of difference is the least we can ask.

Notes

1. To identify themselves, Canadian indigenous peoples use a variety of context-dependent terms, including *Native, First Nations,* and *Aboriginal.* Throughout this chapter I use the term *First Nations* to identify Canadian Aboriginal communities, while realizing, as anthropologist Michael Ames does, that "no single term for the Aboriginal peoples of North America is universally accepted." See Michael Ames, *Cannibal Tours and Glass Boxes: The Anthropology of Museums* (Vancouver: University of British Columbia Press, 1992), 173.

2. The arguments I present in this chapter are informed by an on-going research program that examines how students engage with postcolonial theory. During 1998–99, I conducted a research study at the Glenbow, an artifact-based ethnology and history museum, art gallery, archive, and library located in Calgary, Canada. Since its establishment 35 years ago, the Glenbow has served as a mainstay in educating Calgary citizenry about "western Canadian history and culture." As a regional museum, the Glenbow is an important site for the representation of local and regional heritage, with a mandate that focuses primarily on western Canada. Influenced not only by the extensive First Nations collections that focus on members of the Treaty 7 First Nations, whose reservation areas are proximal to Calgary, the Glenbow has made First Nations a priority in both its collection practices and in its mission statements.

3. This intellectual principle that led to the founding of the British Museum in 1753 continues, with the British Museum still considering itself the epitome of museums. See Edward Edwards, *Lives of the Founders of the British Museum with Notices of Its Chief Augmentors and Other Benefactors, 1570–1870* (Amsterdam: G. Th. Van Heusden, 1870), 6.

4. Tony Bennett, *The Birth of the Museum: History, Theory, Politics* (London and New York: Routledge, 1995), 149.

5. E. Edwards, *Lives of the Founders of the British Museum,* 7 [emphasis in original].

6. Bennett, *The Birth of the Museum,* 21.

7. Bennett, *The Birth of the Museum,* 60.

8. Bennett, *The Birth of the Museum,* 66.

9. The museum did not monopolize the display of empire. The network included museums and libraries, as well as universities, governmental surveys, commercial archives, journals, and learned societies. See Thomas Richards, *The Imperial Archive: Knowledge and the Fantasy of Empire* (London: Verso, 1993).

10. Anne E. Coombes, *Reinventing Africa: Museums, Material Culture, and Popular Imagination in Late Victorian and Edwardian England* (New Haven and London: Yale University Press, 1991), 43–44.

11. Pitt Rivers, "On the principles of classification adopted in the arrangement of his anthropological collection, now exhibited in the Bethnal Green Museum," *Journal of the Royal Anthropological Institute* 6 (1874), 293–308.

12. Nicholas Dirks, *Colonialism and Culture* (Ann Arbor, MI: University of Michigan Press, 1992), 4.

13. Ania Loomba, *Colonialism/Postcolonialism* (London: Routledge, 1998), 6.

14. Gyan Prakash, *After Colonialism: Imperial Histories and Postcolonial Predicaments* (Princeton, NJ: Princeton University Press, 1995), 8.

15. John Comaroff and Jean Comaroff, *Ethnography and the Historical Imagination* (Boulder, CO: Westview, 1992), 14.

16. James Clifford, *Routes: Travel and Translation in the Late Twentieth Century* (Cambridge, MA: Harvard University Press, 1988), p. 22.

17. Loretta Todd, *Curatorship: Indigenous Perspectives in Post-Colonial Societies: Symposium Papers* (Victoria, BC: University of Victoria, 1996), 63.

18. Coombes, *Reinventing Africa,* 191.

19. Carol Duncan, *Civilizing Rituals: Inside Public Art Museums* (London and New York: Routledge, 1995), 8.

20. S. Hume, "The spirit weeps," *The Edmonton Journal* (February 14, 1988), p. B1.

21. Tim Barringer and Tom Flynn, *Colonialism and the Object: Empire, Material Culture, and the Museum* (New York: Routledge, 1998), 4.

22. Henry Giroux, "Public pedagogy as cultural politics," in P. Gilroy, L. Grossberg, and A. McRobbie (eds.), *Without Guarantees: In Honour of Stuart Hall* (London: Verso 2000), 143.

23. Duncan Cameron, "The museum, a temple or a forum," *Curator* 14, no. 1 (1990): 11.

References

Barringer, Tim and Flynn, Tom (eds.). (1998). *Colonialism and the Object: Empire, Material Culture, and the Museum.* New York, NY: Routledge, 1998.

Bennett, Tony. (1995). *The Birth of the Museum: History, Theory, Politics.* London and New York: Routledge.

Cameron, Duncan. (1971). "The museum, a temple or a forum." *Curator* 141:11-24.

Clifford, James. (1997). *Routes: Travel and Translation in the Late Twentieth Century.* Cambridge, MA: Harvard University Press.

Comaroff, John and Comaroff, Jean. (1992). *Ethnography and the Historical Imagination.* Boulder, CO: Westview.

Coombes, Anne E. (1991). *Reinventing Africa: Museums, Material Culture, and Popular Imagination in Late Victorian and Edwardian England.* New Haven and London: Yale University Press.

Dirks, Nicholas B. (1992). *Colonialism and Culture.* Ann Arbor, MI: University of Michigan Press.

Duncan, Carol. (1995). *Civilizing Rituals: Inside Public Art Museums.* London and New York: Routledge.

Edwards, Edward. (1870). *Lives of the Founders of the British Museum with Notices of Its Chief Augmentors and Other Benefactors, 1570–1870.* Amsterdam: G. Th. Van Heusden.

Giroux, Henry. (2000). "Public pedagogy as cultural politics." In P. Gilroy, L. Grossberg. and A. McRobbie (eds.), *Without Guarantees: In Honour of Stuart Hall.* London, UK: Verso, 134–137.

Hume, S. (1988, February 14). "The spirit weeps." *The Edmonton Journal,* p. B1.

Loomba, Ania. (1998). *Colonialism/Postcolonialism.* London: Routledge.

Prakash, Gyan. (1995). *After Colonialism: Imperial Histories and Postcolonial Predicaments.* Princeton, NJ: Princeton University Press.

Rivers, Pitt. (1874). "On the principles of classification adopted in the arrangement of his anthropological collection, now exhibited in the Bethnal Green Museum." *Journal of the Royal Anthropological Institute* 6: 293–308.

Todd, L. (1996). *Curatorship: Indigenous Perspectives in Post-Colonial Societies: Symposium Papers.* Victoria, BC: University of Victoria.

CHAPTER 5

The Promise of a Better Future

Four Approaches to Including Aboriginal English in Australian Classrooms

Neil Harrison

The Promise of a Better Future

There are two common discourses in Australia about Aboriginal people. The first is a discourse of enlightenment where Aboriginal people are positioned between the two poles of deficit and enlightenment. The second is a romantic discourse where the speaker marvels at the order of Aboriginal society, and this is illustrated below. An example of the first discourse comes from Linda Doherty, who refers to the poor academic performance of Aboriginal students in the NSW Basic Skills Tests (BST) as a "merry-go-round of misery" (*Sydney Morning Herald* 2003, p. 5). She positions students against an image of deficit, but she also inserts them in a competitive relation with migrant children to suggest that if Aboriginal students work hard, they too can do as well as the latter group. More recently, the *National Indigenous Times* reported on Senator Tsebin Tchen's final speech to the federal Senate where he told the chamber:

> We are lifting their [Aboriginal people] living standards and education standards and giving them hope so that they can become part of the Australian community as equals. That is true reconciliation—and I am glad to see that we are on our way. (Tsebin Tchen 2005)

Speakers of Aboriginal English (AE) are usually positioned within the discourse of enlightenment where Aboriginal students in schools, for example, are considered to speak bad English, but they are also positioned in relation to a promise that Standard Australian English (SE) will deliver them from the powerlessness of their Aboriginal lives to get a job in white society. SE is constituted with the power to provide people a better life. But better than what? A better life for Aboriginal people is often produced in discourse in relation to an Aboriginal past or a non-Aboriginal future as the following excerpts reveal:

> Student: When [the lecturer] was painting this wonderful picture about utopia in Aboriginal society about sharing and caring. I don't want to sound cynical, I'm being honest. He was painting this beautiful picture of the Aboriginal race.... It was a picture of they've got it so much together that you can't even question any aspect of Aboriginal family life. He told us that they don't fight, they share everything, they help each other. I said to [two Aboriginal students]: you know any of these blackfellas and we just all laughed. He lives in the dreamtime that muliga [man]. (Harrison 2004a, pp. 43–44)

A non-Aboriginal student at university outlines his position on Aboriginal people in research conducted at the University of New England:

> They lived in a perfect communist environment where everybody owns everything and there was no ... like you had the elders which were like the community and yes, everybody owned everything else and they lived quite happily ... if there were problems they would sit down and talk about it and they had their set rules.

Another student reflects on his thoughts about Aboriginal people:

> I admire what they have done ... they value family relationships and co-operation ... I am intrigued by them but personally I feel it would be better if they assimilated into Australian culture. I think it is a dead end for ... I am assuming that living in the bush there is very little work and there is high unemployment and they are receiving a lot of state subsidy and this is bad for everyone. (Harrison 2005)

These discourses demonstrate how Aboriginal people are positioned in relation to a "better life," a life linked in discourse to an Aboriginal past or to a non-Aboriginal future. Students in schools and universities replicate these discourses by talking about Aboriginal people as being able to make a choice between the poles of disadvantage and opportunity. Given the pervasiveness of these dichotomies and the discourses that reproduce them in Western society, it is almost impossible for students as speakers of SE to talk and think about people, including themselves, in any other way.

This has implications for teachers as models of language and behavior in the classroom because as soon as they begin to talk and teach about Aboriginal people and Aboriginal perspectives, and they are required to do so, they will situate Aboriginal people within these two discourses, and therefore between the poles of disadvantage and advantage, "misery" and progress. Furthermore, they will reveal their own thoughts and values about Aboriginal people to their students as much as they will teach about Aboriginal Australia. Teachers cannot avoid making judgments about others, and passing "their" values about Aboriginal people on to their students simply because they are required to teach about Aboriginal Australia. Their values and attitudes will be transmitted through these discourses and students will leave the classroom with "pictures" of Aboriginal people situated unconsciously in their own ways of talking and thinking. Students learn syllabus content, and while they are doing this, they also learn to replicate the discourses of the classroom; along with these discourses they imitate particular ways of thinking about others. This chapter searches for a position outside these two discourses, and outside that which has historically positioned Aboriginal students and non-Aboriginal teachers in an unequal power relation in the classroom.

The chapter focuses on those classrooms with students whose home dialect is AE. I suggest that attempts to teach Aboriginal perspectives, or even to use *culturally appropriate methods* in these classrooms without linking them to AE will function to objectify and distance these perspectives in the eyes of both Aboriginal and non-Aboriginal students. In particular, speaking about AE and its *relation to* culture could help teachers to traverse some of the most common pitfalls outlined above, and to teach about Aboriginal people outside the discourses of enlightenment and romanticism.

I will first address the relationship between language and culture in the context of analyzing how Aboriginal perspectives are currently taught as an end in themselves. The curriculum requirements for including AE in classrooms throughout New South Wales will then be described. I will review the literature on how nonstandard varieties of English have been incorporated in Australian education and elsewhere to highlight the benefits of including AE in the school curriculum. AE has remained largely an academic exploration, and in the final section I will outline four approaches that teachers could use to *include* AE in their program.

The Relationship Between Knowledge and Language

Most research over the last 30 years has suggested that recognition of the culture is "fundamental to achieving Aboriginal student engagement" (New South Wales Department of Education and Training and New South Wales Aboriginal Education Consultative Group 2004, p. 89). The Quality Teaching Framework in New South Wales (New South Wales Department of Education and Training 2003, p. 15) expects that teachers have a "cultural knowledge" of their students, and that they are also capable of incorporating this knowledge in their teaching assessment tasks. These expectations are also reflected in the New South Wales Aboriginal Education Policy (1996b) and in the primary English syllabus requirements (New South Wales Board of Studies 2001, pp. 10–11, 23). A *culturally relevant pedagogy* focuses on academic achievement and explicitly recognizes and affirms the student's cultural identity (Mellor and Corrigan 2004, p. 34).

However, most teachers readily admit that they know very little about Aboriginal people and Aboriginal cultures (New South Wales Department of Education and Training and New South Wales Aboriginal Education Consultative Group 2004; Malcolm 1994b, p. 161). They have little to do with Aboriginal people and have few perspectives on what it is like to be Aboriginal, and furthermore, what they do know comes from stories *about* Aboriginal people rather than from the people themselves (Langton 1993). I suggested above that these stories about Aboriginal people are transmitted through two discourses, and it is these discourses that are positioning Aboriginal people in relation to a pathology. Students are learning to reproduce cultural knowledge and perspectives that already position Aboriginal people within a deficit relation.

As a consequence of teachers' perceived lack of knowledge, most universities have now included a unit for preservice teachers on how to include Aboriginal perspectives in their classrooms (Craven et al. 2005; Harrison 2005). Students are learning about the art of Tracey Moffat, Clifford Possum Tjapaljari, and David Page; about Aboriginal science and sports stars; and the importance of relationships in Aboriginal families. They are also reading emotionally charged stories about the stolen generations. But for some students at university and in schools, these lessons will constitute objectified knowledge divorced from who they are and what they want, and more particularly, separated from the context in which the knowledge is produced. The cultural context is perceived to be a nebulous reality lying outside the school yard, waiting to be presented by an Aboriginal speaker or reproduced by teachers and students through reading and writing. And language continues to be viewed as a tool for teaching this cultural knowledge, as if it is knowledge that is already there and we use language to communicate it to students.

The relation between cultural knowledge and language has been clearly demonstrated in linguistics (for example, Sharifian 2005; Malcolm 1994a; Salzmann 1993), and yet in Aboriginal education throughout Australia it is often assumed that we can somehow learn and talk and even teach about the cultures without knowing anything about the language or dialect or home talk of the student. Sharifian (2005, p. 77) highlights this relation when he observes that the "language maps out a particular terrain that allows the speaker to talk and write in pre-ordered ways." How the child in any classroom structures knowledge and makes sense of it is constituted through how he or she talks and writes, and yet some teachers assume through their planning that knowledge exists before the class begins.

Sharifian (2005) observes how the language carries the culture, and I will suggest that teachers could be demonstrating and explaining some of these links for students. For example, the significance of situated knowledge, silence, information-seeking techniques, conceptions of time, gender, and agreement for many Aboriginal speakers takes on meaning in the context of how AE is used in its cultural and social context (Sharifian 2002; Eades 1992). Malcolm (1994a) shows how some verb tenses and conjugations in AE are linked to how knowledge is produced by and for some Aboriginal students. Both AE and the knowledge it produces need to be read together, but taken on their own they can look inappropriate and boring to students.

Curriculum Requirements for Including Aboriginal English

The New South Wales Department of Education and Training's Aboriginal Education Policy (1996b) stipulates that AE must be incorporated in the classroom (for requirements in other states, see Harrison 2004c). The New South Wales Board of Studies (1998, p. 10) English K-6 Modules require teachers to *accept* AE, and to "collect and develop resources that use AE." These modules state (1998, p. 9):

> Appreciation of Aboriginal English is fundamental to understanding the cultural differences of Aboriginal students and to enhancing their education ... research also indicates that giving Aboriginal students opportunities to engage with curriculum content in their home language positively supports their cognitive development.

The English K-6 Modules (1998, p. 23) emphasize that "encouraging home language use in the classroom is an important means of showing acceptance of the student's home background language, culture and ethnicity." While some linguistic studies of the structure and usage of AE have been conducted by Eades (1992, 1995, 2004), Malcolm (1992, 1994a, 1994b, 2001), Malcolm et al. (1999), Sharifian (2002, 2005), Sharifian et al. (2004), Konigsberg and Collard (2000, 2002), and Harkins (1994), extensive research at the local level remains to be done. Research in local communities is crucial because it would reveal how AE could be applied and taught within the school, which is the focus of this chapter (see, for example, Hitchen's 1992 study on Moree in New South Wales).

While AE has been accepted by many teachers as a legitimate dialect of their Aboriginal students, there are no guidelines provided to show how it could be incorporated in the classroom. The important findings on the structures and usage of AE by linguists such as Eades and Malcolm (see previous paragraph) are only now beginning to reach teachers, with some useful ideas coming from Western Australia including projects like *Deadly Ways to Learn: A Collection of Two-Way Bidialectal Teaching Strategies* (Konigsberg and Collard 2000); *Ways of Being: Ways of Talk* (Konigsberg and Collard 2002); *Solid English* (Cahill 1999); and *Making the Jump* (Berry and Hudson 1997). Malcolm (2003) has developed alternative approaches to incorporating AE in the classroom. The New South Wales Department of School Education (1996a) produced a video on working with Aboriginal English with visual demonstrations of how the dialect is incorporated in four primary schools in New South Wales. The New South Wales Department of Education and Training (2004a, 2004b, 2005) has also published a range of materials to help teachers link the statewide English Literacy and Language Assessment (ELLA) in high schools and Basic Skills Tests in primary schools to AE, although these provide only implicit support for AE while privileging the teaching of SE. A bidialectal pilot project was tested in central New South Wales in 2004 and a draft report and recommendations are now being finalized (New South Wales Department of Education and Training and New South Wales Aboriginal Education Consultative Group 2004, p. 71). There have been some articles from educators supporting the inclusion of AE in schools and classrooms (for example, Daly 2004; Harrison 2004c; Simpson, Munns, and Clancey 1999; Farrell 1997; Enemburu 1989).

This chapter attempts to apply some of the linguistic findings on AE to the classroom, and to present a range of approaches that teachers could use to incorporate AE in the school curriculum. These approaches are proposed in the current political climate of economic rationalism where there is considerable pressure on teachers to increase the scores for Aboriginal students in statewide testing (see Siegel 2005, who meticulously debunks the popular arguments used against incorporating the home dialect of students in the classroom, namely that AE would detract from the students' ability and time to learn SE, or that AE would interfere with the students' learning of the target dialect). I propose several alternatives, each of which requires varying degrees of time, expertise, and money. Teachers and schools could therefore choose from these alternatives to develop a particular approach to including AE in their teaching. A description of these approaches will also clarify what it means to *accept* and *incorporate* AE in the curriculum.

Benefits of Including Aboriginal English in the Curriculum

Unequal power relations. One of the strongest positions put in regard to the incorporation of AE in classrooms is that Aboriginal students should be allowed to speak their home language at school, but the dominance of SE effectively denies them a place to produce an identity that reflects a continuity with their life outside the school. At present, many Aboriginal students are permitted only to express themselves through the dominant dialect of SE, and consequently stories abound from Aboriginal people over the generations (for example, Harrison 2004a) who have never been able to see themselves in the discourses of the classroom, particularly those dominant discourses outlined at the beginning of this chapter. In the American context, Delpit (2002, p. 47) draws on the experiences of her own daughter at school to demonstrate that to reject a person's language can feel as if we are only rejecting him or her.

Aboriginal students are often expected to perform in schools as if they are white (Malcolm 2003), and this has been the case for the last 200 years:

> Willy: Being educated from school onwards, we've been suppressed with white culture. We've had to learn the white culture even from school onwards. What the white people did, how do they think, how do they speak, we've had to learn all that, how to read and write their way. (Harrison 2004a, p. 85)

Of course, we all perform and act out in particular roles, but historically Aboriginal students have been expected to *act white* all day, and to speak like white people at school with little opportunity to see and perform themselves through the dominant discourses of SE. Some Aboriginal children are taking their work home, and parents are saying, "My kid doesn't speak like that." There continues to be an enormous gap between Aboriginal homes and the school, a gap that is perpetuated not only through the absence of the student's home language in the school, but also through unequal power relations that are reproduced through the dominance of SE. This gap is a question of power as much as it is one of cultural discontinuity (cf. Nakata 2004, p. 26). Teachers cannot be expected to know about the home background and culture of every student, or to teach these perspectives, but they can be expected to recognize how the student's home language is used in the classroom, and how this impacts on his or her learning.

I have highlighted an assumption pervading the discourses of Aboriginal education that Aboriginal students must acquire mastery over SE in the hope of a "better life" (see Siegel forthcoming; Pennycook 2001). Malcolm (1992, p. 16) points out that a condition for success in learning SE is that "non-standard dialect speakers identify with the speakers of the standard variety, and, often that precondition is not met." One of the reasons for this is because there has always been an unequal power relation between Aboriginal and non-Aboriginal people, and one that has been perpetuated through the privileging of SE as the key producer of identity in the classroom. The incorporation of AE in the school curriculum could redress this unequal power relation and act as the foundation on which to build literacy skills in SE.

Improved Results in Literacy Skills

Those involved in bilingual education highlight that "in order to gain maximum academic benefit from schooling, language minority students must develop high levels of language proficiency in both English and their first language" (McMahon and Murray 2000, p. 39). Siegel (forthcoming, p. 2) observes that while the educational practice of moving from the known to the unknown is commonly accepted, schools have thus far ignored the home dialect of most Aboriginal students and expected them to move from the unknown to the known. Aboriginal students are expected to learn, in the first instance through a second dialect, yet studies demonstrate that the use of the student's own dialect or language "in long-term educational programs (but not always short-term experiments) leads to higher scores in tests measuring reading and writing skills in standard English and to increases in overall academic achievement" (Siegel 2005, p. 12). Improved results here are explained in terms of five factors: easier acquisition of literacy, children's being able to speak and *see* themselves in their own dialect or language without the fear of correction, teachers' improved understanding of language and power, increased motivation and self-esteem, and ability to separate codes and contrast differences (Siegel 2005, pp. 12–14). A key lesson here for teachers is that a focus on the student's first dialect does not detract from the time devoted to learning SE; to the contrary, research suggests that using AE as a bridge to learning SE actually enhances the student's grasp of SE. Siegel (2005, p. 12) shows that learning in the first dialect has a positive effect on D2 attainment. It is well known that students find it easier to acquire literacy in their first language or dialect and then apply these skills to the standard (Cummins 2000), but there are also dangers and limitations.

The potential for improved results in literacy skills is limited by the recognition that people who can switch effortlessly from their first dialect into the standard are usually those who had access to it starting from a very young age (Siegel forthcoming; Lippi-Green 1997). Siegel (forthcoming, p. 6) explains that there is sensitive period for the acquisition of a second dialect while Chambers (1992, p. 689) demonstrates in relation to the acquisition of phonology that "a person seven or under will almost certainly acquire a new dialect perfectly, and a person 14 or over almost certainly will not" (acquire these phonological features). These are important revelations about dialect acquisition in the context that attendance for Aboriginal students in New South Wales begins to decline around year 5 (10–11 years old) onward, along with literacy and reading levels, while the average gap between Aboriginal and non-Aboriginal students' outcomes in writing almost triples between 10 and 13 years of age or between years 5-7 (New South Wales Department of Education and Training and New South Wales Aboriginal Education Consultative Group 2004, pp. 21–23). Furthermore, by the age of 14 or 15, when, according to this research, the capacity for learning a second dialect is declining, most Aboriginal students have left school or are no longer attending (New South Wales Department of Education and Training and New South Wales Aboriginal Education Consultative Group 2004, pp. 19–29).

Contrastive analysis. Research (see Siegel 2005) suggests that when students are able to learn two dialects together, they are then in a position to examine the patterns of speech, rules of grammar, vocabulary, sounds, tonal features, and so on of their own dialect and observe how they differ from those of other students. A discussion of these differences would allow students to separate the two dialects rather than confuse them because they are perceived to be similar (see examples from Konigsberg and Collard 2000; Baker 2002). Their home dialect would provide them with a metalanguage, a way of talking about and analyzing SE, and this in turn would help students to reduce the interference, rather than increase it as is sometimes feared (see Siegel 2005). Contrastive analysis would not only assist both Aboriginal and non-Aboriginal students in recognizing dialect differences, but could also encourage them to critically analyze the historical power relation that has traditionally existed between AE and SE, and therefore between the speakers.

Climate of acceptance of AE and its speakers. In the context of African American English, Lisa Delpit (2002, p. 47) proposes that "the negative responses to the children's home language on the part of adults around them insures that they will reject the school's language and everything else the school has to offer." Judith Baker (2002, p. 50), a high school English teacher in the United States, discovered from her students that "when formal English no longer threatens to demean them, they are more than willing to master it." Cummins (1986) notes that raising the status of the minority language speakers and their language or dialect is determined by the attitudes held by members of the dominant society (also Malcolm 1992, 2003; DEET n.d.). Delpit (2002, pp. 41–42) adds that if teachers view a dialect as deficient, "then no amount of instructional modification would make much difference." Teachers' attitudes do make a difference (Malcolm 2003, p. 23); the teacher will position the two dialects in either a symmetrical or asymmetrical power relation through his or her *own* ways of speaking, and these will govern the students' relation to each dialect, and more particularly to their speakers. The status of the minority dialect and its speakers in the school could be renegotiated through how the teacher talks, and subsequently through the *relations* that are produced through these classroom conversations.

Defining the role of Aboriginal education assistants in schools. The Aboriginal education assistant (AEA) has an important role to play in the classroom and in teaching (about the) dialect. Raising the status of AE could provide AEAs with a clearly defined role where they are seen by all students and staff to have a strong position in the school *and* the classroom. In 2003, there were 320 AEAs employed in schools across New South Wales with more than 33,600 full-time enrollments, an average of 105 students per AEA (New

South Wales Department of Education and Training and New South Wales Aboriginal Education Consultative Group 2004, pp. 18–19; 40). Although the main responsibility of AEAs is to improve educational outcomes for Aboriginal students (New South Wales Department of Education and Training and New South Wales Aboriginal Education Consultative Group 2004, p. 40), is such an outcome best achieved through work inside or outside the classroom?

Applying the Theoretical Findings on Aboriginal English to the Classroom?

This chapter is directed at applying linguistic findings on AE to the classroom and outlining four alternative approaches to teaching the dialect. Ian Malcolm (2003) outlines a number of similar approaches to teaching AE in the classroom in his presentation to the Association for Teaching English to Speakers of Other Languages (ATESOL) conference in Sydney. There are two ways of going about this, given that it is already departmental policy in New South Wales. One way is for teachers to implement the policy on an individual basis, according to the desires of the community and how it uses AE, the number of Aboriginal students in the classroom, and the teacher's understanding of language. Of course, the decision to include AE in the school needs to come from the local indigenous community. Shnukal (1992) highlights the fact that this can be a highly complex and controversial issue in places like the Torres Strait where parents may decide against the incorporation of the home language in the school curriculum (also see Delpit 2002 for a U.S. context). Consideration would need to be given to the best ways of equipping teachers with a knowledge of AE structures and usage as well as how they differ from SE. Teacher education institutions could already be doing some of this teacher preparation. The second approach could be to incorporate AE on a whole-school basis, which would require extra time on behalf of teachers, strong school management, and especially the prioritizing of Aboriginal education within the school. Long-term planning would be required to devise and pilot a program, decide how AE can be included in the curriculum, as well as train teachers and gradually improve the status of AE in the eyes of all students in the school. Siegel (2005, p. 12) demonstrates that improvements in literacy and numeracy outcomes will result, but they will be long term rather than immediate.

Approach 1: Focus is on Standard English. Individual teacher provides implicit recognition of Aboriginal English.

Description. The teacher recognizes and supports the speech of Aboriginal students as per Aboriginal Education Policy (NSW Department of School

Education 1996b) and Department of Education and Training curriculum requirements. Teacher and student focus is on teaching SE, with the Aboriginal students' home language being supported orally and implicitly recognized in the classroom. Explicit teaching and learning occurs in SE, with support for AE in oral contexts only.

Advantage. AE is included orally and is not corrected. Implicit support for the home language of Aboriginal students is provided. Aboriginal students have an opportunity to hear themselves in classroom discourse.

Limitation. AE continues to be compared against SE. Aboriginal students continue to operate within the teacher's discourse structure (see Malcolm 1994b, pp. 160–161) and so the model does not challenge historical relations (Baker 2001; Cummins 2000). It is likely that AE will continue to be regarded as an inferior version of SE, and the Aboriginal learners will be positioned within a deficit theory of education. No explicit teaching of AE occurs, and there is no guarantee that students will pick up the differences between the dialects (Malcolm 2003, p. 13). Students learn SE through repetition and modeling; comparisons are made only in relation to the dominant dialect rather than between dialects. Code-switching continues as students do not learn conscious control of the two dialects (see Berry and Hudson 1997, pp. 38–41 for some useful activities to control code-switching). Aboriginal students are still expected to learn through an assimilation to the position of the non-Aboriginal teacher. Baker (2001, p. 110) observes that the dominance of the second language, in this case SE, and the repression of the home language, in this case AE, "often [aim] at rapidly integrating minority language groups into mainstream society." Language continues to be the primary medium of social control (Fairclough 1989).

Research, preparation, and implementation. This approach complies with current curriculum expectations and could be implemented in both primary and secondary schools. Teachers would need to learn some local AE structures, how the dialect is used in their classroom, and how it differs from SE. Teacher education institutions could draw upon some of the linguist findings outlined above to train preservice teachers in some of the general grammatical features of both AE and SE so that they could begin to recognize how these might be applied in the local setting during their practicums. This would also constitute a useful action research project for preservice teachers.

Approach 2: Focus is on both Aboriginal English and Standard English in specific texts. Implemented by individual teacher.

Description. The teacher recognizes speaking, reading, and writing in AE in the specific texts of recount, narrative, and information reports. AE is recognized across all key learning areas. SE is used in texts of explanation and exposition. Teacher models SE, and Aboriginal students make the implicit comparisons between the two dialects. No explicit teaching and learning is done in AE, and students are left to establish unconscious comparisons in grammar and usage.

Advantage. Students learn to speak and write competently according to identified text structures. AE is recognized in speech and writing. Teacher does not need to know a lot about AE.

Limitation. AE is unconsciously compared against the higher-order genres or text types. Unequal status of dialects (and students) is maintained. Aboriginal students continue to be compared against a white standard (see earlier discussion on historical power relations).

Research, preparation, and implementation. This approach could be implemented in both primary and secondary schools. Background research and teacher preparation similar to Approach 1 would be required.

Approach 3: Whole school recognizes Aboriginal English in all contexts for Aboriginal students. The first dialect is used as a bridge to teaching Standard English to Aboriginal students.

Description. The whole school recognizes speaking, reading, and writing in AE for all texts (not only recount, narrative, and information reports). The first dialect is used as a bridge to teaching SE to Aboriginal students. The teacher highlights and models the grammatical differences between the two dialects for Aboriginal students in speaking, reading, and writing. Aboriginal students are involved with community members in developing and producing readers in AE (and these people would therefore need to be paid).

Advantage. Aboriginal students learn conscious control of two dialects and therefore two social contexts. They are able to observe the differences between the home talk and the school talk (SE), although these differences are not taught explicitly. These comparisons (or contrastive analyses, previously discussed) can allow students to recognize when they are code-switching and reduce the likelihood of interference from AE in the acquisition of SE. Aboriginal students learn that they are code-switching rather than assuming that they are making mistakes in SE or that their language skills are deficient. The fear of correction can be great, especially when the student is positioned, or positions him- or herself against a deficiency (Delpit 2002; Baker 2002). Foucault (1979) demonstrated the extent to which people internalize external disciplinary powers to control their own ways of thinking and talking.

Limitation. How can the teacher work with two (or more) different groups of students, and dialects?

Research, preparation, and implementation. In high school this could be included as part of the Aboriginal Studies years 7–10 elective, or Aboriginal Studies in year 12. Generally, this alternative would be best suited to K–6. Schools in New South Wales now receive funding of about $700 per teacher for professional development purposes. They can also apply for regional funding to prepare a grammatical description of AE in their area, and to develop and produce readers in AE.

Approach 4: Whole school is seen to be a strong advocate of Aboriginal English in all contexts for all students. Grammatical differences between the two dialects are taught explicitly.

Description. The whole school recognizes speaking, reading, and writing in AE in all texts and contexts and uses the first dialect of Aboriginal students as a bridge to teaching SE. Teachers highlight and model the grammatical differences between the two dialects for all students and link these differences to cultural knowledge. AE is attributed equal status in the classroom and non-Aboriginal students are expected to be familiar with its grammar and usage. It is widely recognized that "acceptance of AE is one of the most important steps in establishing a positive environment for language and literacy learning" (DEET n.d., p. 28).

Advantage. Differences are compared against AE as well as against SE. Unequal historical power relations are addressed. Teachers and schools can now be seen by all students and the community as strong advocates of the minority dialect (Cummins 1986). AE is given a strong position across the school curriculum, and Aboriginal identity is given a voice (see DEET n.d., p. 28). Both student and teacher negotiate their relationship to speech (and being heard) in the classroom. Knowledge and language are linked. A second dialect will not only help students to talk about the other dialect, it will also allow them to make comparisons that will ultimately assist them to talk about language and to interpret their differences. They learn through comparison as well as through the repetition of a model of SE. Such explicit comparisons on behalf of student and teacher will allow students to separate the two dialects and to reduce the likelihood of AE's interfering with acquisition of SE. Furthermore, explicit recognition of the patterns of speech, rules of grammar, vocabulary, sounds, and tonal features are more likely to give students control over code-switching (Konigsberg and Collard 2000, p. 17).

Research, preparation, and implementation. This approach requires the involvement of Aboriginal people in the classroom as speakers and models of AE. While they may not be able to explicitly describe the features of AE and how these function, it would provide Aboriginal people with a clearly delineated teaching role in the school. This approach would be restricted to primary schools, and could be piloted in one class at the outset to prepare materials and to test and evaluate methodologies (see Approach 3 regarding funding options). Teachers would need to learn some of the features of AE and SE and be able to compare how they are used.

Talking and Teaching about Indigenous Australia Outside the Discourses of Enlightenment and Romanticism

In conclusion, I want to return to the question I first raised at the beginning of this chapter. I have suggested that another way in which we can think about this question is in terms of historical power relations, namely, the unequal relation between AE and SE in Australian classrooms. In the past, AE has usually been positioned as bad English and consequently its speakers have been constituted within a deficit relation to learning the King's English, as a lecturer once described it to me (Harrison 1991, p. 31). Aboriginal students not only have the King's English to contend with, they are rarely able to recognize themselves in the discourses of the classroom when their home language is excluded. This is a recipe for an unsafe and alienating classroom climate. These students are further disempowered when SE is constituted as capable of delivering them from a life of poverty and misery unto a better life (see the introduction). I have suggested that nonindigenous teachers need to take great care in how they represent indigenous perspectives to their students because of these colonizing effects of discourse. Rather than trying harder to increase the cultural awareness of teachers, I have taken the position that language needs to be foregrounded in the teaching of indigenous perspectives, and this requires a whole-school approach if the historical relation between indigenous students and nonindigenous teachers is to change.

Acknowledgments

I would like to thank Diana Eades, Hilary Webster, and David Baxter for their insightful comments.

References

Baker, C. (2001). *Foundations of Bilingual Education and Bilingualism* (3rd ed.). Buffalo, NY: Multilingual Matters.

Baker, J. (2002). Trilingualism. In L. Delpit and J. K. Dowdy (eds.), *The Skin That We Speak: Thoughts on Language and Culture in the Classroom*. New York: New York Press.

Berry, R., and Hudson, J. (1997). *Making the Jump: A Resource Book for Teachers of Aboriginal Students.* Broome: Catholic Education Office.

Cahill, R. (1999). *Solid English.* Perth: Education Department of Western Australia.

Chambers, J. K. (1992). Dialect acquisition. *Language* 68 (4), pp. 673-705.

Craven, R. G., Halse, C., Marsh, H. W., Mooney, J., and Wilson-Miller, J. (2005). Teaching the teachers mandatory Aboriginal studies: Elucidating recent successful strategies and overcoming enduring barriers. Vol 1. DEST. Canberra: Commonwealth of Australia. Retrieved October 7, 2005, from: http://www.dest.gov.au/sectors/higher_education/publications_resources/profiles/teaching_teachers_volume_1.htm.

Cummins, J. (1986). Empowering minority students: A framework for intervention. *Harvard Educational Review* 56 (1), pp. 18-36.

———. (2000). *Language, Power and Pedagogy: Bilingual Children in the Crossfire.* Buffalo, NY: Multilingual Matters.

Daly, A. (2004). *Investigating literacy achievement for students who speak AE.* Paper presented at the "Get real and all that spiel: Real texts, real lives, real learning, real pleasure" Conference, Sydney.

Delpit, L. (2002). No kinda sense. In L. Delpit and J. K. Dowdy (eds.), *The Skin That We Speak: Thoughts on Language and Culture in the Classroom.* New York: New York Press.

Department of Employment, Education and Training (DEET) (n.d.) *Langwij Comes to School: Promoting Literacy among Speakers of AE and Australian Creoles.* Canberra: Department of Employment, Education and Training.

Doherty, L. (2003, November 15-16). System has failed Indigenous Students, *Sydney Morning Herald,* p. 5.

Eades, D. (1992). *Aboriginal English and the Law: Communicating with Aboriginal English Speaking Clients: A Handbook for Legal Practitioners.* Brisbane: Continuing Legal Education Department of the Queensland Law Society Inc.

———. (1995). *Aboriginal English.* Sydney: New South Wales Board of Studies.

———. (2004). Understanding Aboriginal English in the legal system: A critical sociolinguistics approach, *Applied Linguistics* 25 (4), pp. 491-512.

Enemburu, I. G. (1989). *Koori English.* Melbourne, Victoria: State Board of Education.

Fairclough, N. (1989). *Language and Power.* London: Longman.

Farrell, K. (1997). Bidialectalism and the potential educational status of Aboriginal English. In S. Harris and M. Malin (eds.), *Indigenous Education: Historical, Moral and Practical Tales* (pp. 59-70). Darwin: Northern Territory University Press.

Foucault, M. (1979). *Discipline and Punish: The Birth of a Prison.* New York: Vintage Books.

Harkins, J. (1994). *Bridging Two Worlds: Aboriginal English and Crosscultural Understanding.* St Lucia, QLD: University of Queensland Press.

Harris, S. (1990). *Two Way Aboriginal Schooling: Education and Cultural Survival.* Canberra: Aboriginal Studies Press.

Harrison, N. (1991). It's a world of constant tensions: Lecturer's views on language choice and language use by Aboriginal students of the Northern Territory University. Unpublished manuscript. Darwin, Northern Territory, Australia.

———. (2004a). *Indigenous Education and the Adventure of Insight: Learning and Teaching in Indigenous Classrooms.* Flaxton, QLD: Post Pressed.

———. (2004b). The reproduction of historical relations in the crosscultural classroom at university, *Australian Journal of Education* 48 (3), pp. 282–294.

———. (2004c). Self-recognition and well-being: Speaking AE in healthy classrooms. *Australian Journal of Indigenous Education* 33, pp. 7–13.

———. (2005). The romantics: Preservice teacher fantasies of Indigenous people. Refereed paper presented to Multiliteracies & English Teaching K–12 in the Age of Information & Communication Technologies Conference (November 25–27, 2004), Armidale, Australia.

Hitchen, M. M. (1992). Talkin Up: Aboriginal English in Moree. Master of Letters in Linguistics, University of New England.

Konigsberg, P., and Collard, G. (2000). *Deadly Ways to Learn: A Collection of Two-Way Bidialectal Teaching Strategies.* Perth: Education Department of Western Australia.

———. (2002). *Ways of Being, Ways of Talk.* Perth: Education Department of Western Australia.

Langton, M. (1993). "Well, I heard it on the radio and I saw it on the television … " An essay for the Australian Film Commission on the politics and aesthetics of filmmaking by and about Aboriginal people and things. North Sydney: Australian Film Commission.

Lippi-Green, R. (1997). *English with an Accent: Language, Ideology and Discrimination in the United States.* London: Routledge.

Malcolm, I. (1992). English in the education of speakers of Aboriginal English. In J. Siegel (ed.), *Pidgins, Creoles and Nonstandard Dialects in Education: Occasional Paper 12.* Armidale, NSW: Applied Linguistics Association of Australia.

———. (1994a). Discourse and discourse strategies in Australian Aboriginal English, *World Englishes* 13 (3), pp. 289–306.

———. (1994b). Aboriginal English inside and outside the classroom, *Australian Review of Applied Linguistics* 17 (2), pp. 147–180.

———. (2001). Aboriginal English: Adopted code of a surviving culture. In D. Blair and P. Collins (eds.), *English in Australia.* Amsterdam/Philadelphia: John Benjamins.

———. (2003). English language and literacy development and home language support: Connections and directions in working with Indigenous students. Paper presented to the 13th ATESOL NSW Biennial Summer School and ACTA National Conference (20–22 January), Furama Hotel Central, Surry Hills.

Malcolm, I., Haig, Y., Konigsberg, P., Rochecouste, J., Collard, G., Hill, A. and Cahill, R. (1999). *Two-Way English: Towards More User-Friendly Education for Speakers of Aboriginal English.* Perth: Education Department of Western Australia.

McMahon, K., and Murray, F. (2000). Bilingual education: Looking for the big picture, *TESOL in Context* 10 (2), pp. 37–44.

Mellor, S., and Corrigan, M. (2004). *The Case for Change: A Review of Contemporary Research on Indigenous Education Outcomes.* Camberwell, Victoria: Australian Council for Educational Research.

Nakata, M. (2004). Indigenous knowledge and the cultural interface: Underlying issues at the intersection of knowledge and information systems. In A. Hickling-Hudson,

J. Matthews, and A. Woods (eds.), *Disrupting Preconceptions: Postcolonialism and Education.* Flaxton, QLD: Post Pressed.

New South Wales Board of Studies. (1998). *English K-6 Modules.* Sydney: NSW Board of Studies.

———. (2001). Aboriginal Studies Stages 4 and 5, Years 7–10 Syllabus. Retrieved August 30, 2004, from: http://www.boardofstudies.nsw.edu.au/syllabus_sc/pdf_doc/aboriginal_710_syl.pdf.

New South Wales Department of Education and Training (2003). Quality teaching in NSW public schools. Discussion paper. Sydney: Department of Education and Training.

———. (2004a). *Speakers of Aboriginal English and the Year 5 Basic Skills Tests: Teaching Strategies.* Sydney: Department of Education and Training.

———. (2004b). *Speakers of Aboriginal English and the Year 3 Basic Skills Tests: Teaching Strategies.* Sydney: Department of Education and Training.

———. (2005). *Literacy 2005: Linking ELLA to Aboriginal English.* Sydney: Department of Education and Training.

New South Wales Department of Education and Training and New South Wales Aboriginal Education Consultative Group Inc. (2004). *The Report of the Review of Aboriginal Education/ Yanigurra Muya: Ganggurrinyma Yaarri Guurulaw Yirringin.gurray Freeing the Spirit: Dreaming an Equal Future.* Darlinghurst, NSW: New South Wales Department of Education and Training.

New South Wales Department of School Education (1996a). *A Place of Belonging: Working with Aboriginal English.* Sydney: Department of School Education.

———. (1996b). *Aboriginal Education Policy.* Sydney: Aboriginal Education Unit, NSW Department of School Education.

Pennycook, A. (2001). *Critical Applied Linguistics: A Critical Introduction.* Mahwah, NJ: Lawrence Erlbaum.

Salzmann, Z. (1993). *Language, Culture, & Society: An Introduction to Linguistic Anthropology.* Boulder, CO: Westview.

Sharifian, F. (2002). Chaos in Aboriginal English discourse. In A. Kirkpatrick (ed.), *Englishes in Asia: Communication, Identity, Power and Education* (pp. 125–141). Melbourne: Language Australia.

———. (2005). Cultural conceptualisations in English words: A study of Aboriginal children in Perth, *Language and Education* 19 (1), pp. 74–88.

Sharifian, F., Rochecouste, J., and Malcolm, I. (2004). "But it was all a bit confusing . . . ": Comprehending Aboriginal English texts, *Language, Culture and Curriculum* 17 (3), pp. 203–228.

Shnukal, A. (1992). The case against a transfer bilingual program of Torres Strait Creole to English in Torres Strait schools. In Siegel, J. (ed.), *Pidgins, Creoles and Nonstandard Dialects in Education: Occasional Paper 12.* Armidale, NSW: Applied Linguistics Association of Australia.

Siegel, J. (forthcoming). Language ideologies and the education of speakers of marginalised language varieties: Towards a critical awareness approach.

———. (2005). Keeping creoles and dialects out of the classroom: Is it justified?

In N. Shondel (ed.), *Dialects, Englishes, Creoles and Education*. Mahwah, NJ: Lawrence Erlbaum.

Simpson, L., Munns, G., and Clancey, S. (1999). Language tracks: Aboriginal English and the classroom, *Pen* 120, pp. 1-6.

Tsebin Tchen. (2005). Final speech to the federal Senate, in *National Indigenous Times*. Retrieved June 24, 2005, from: http://www.nit.com.au/breakingNews/story.aspx?id=5193.

CHAPTER 6

Transcreation, Transformance, and the Fertility of Difference

Reading Language Difference Through the Lens of Translation

Lisa Taylor

> I hated the seeming arbitrary blindness of the two languages. Each left me out while stumbling all over the other invisible entity that occupied the same territory—me. Finally, I thought that if the two languages could only "see" each other within me, I would stop feeling haunted and cheated. *(Michelut, 1994)*

> A boundary is not that at which something stops but, as the Greeks recognized, the boundary is that from which something begins its presencing. *(Heidegger, cited in Bhabha, 1994)*

It has been argued that any understanding of the contemporary context of globalization, with its exponential rate of expansion since the end of World War II and particularly the end of the Cold War, needs to be contextualized within an analysis of earlier colonial processes of global circulation, specifically universalist modernity's incorporation/configuration and deployment of difference (Liu, 1999). In his article, "The Local and the Global: Globalization and Ethnicity," Stuart Hall (1997) describes the current era in which (at least) two forms or configurations of globalization coexist. The first is organized by imperial grand narratives and raced, ethnicized, gendered, and classed discourses of national identity that depend upon the absolute separation and binary opposition of difference. This "older, embattled, more corporate, more unitary, more homogenous" system of globalization is challenged by a newer "global postmodern" form that, catering to and promoting an Americanized, anglophone mass culture, presents itself as an embrace and celebration of difference and the endless pleasure of its proliferation; in the consumption and commodification of diversity and "exotica," this system capitalizes upon cultural, gendered, and classed difference in order to enhance global marketing and exploit divisions of labor (Hall, 1997: 182).

What visions of difference are being naturalized in these two coexisting forms of globalization? In the first, violently re-entrenched since September 11th, 2001, and exemplified by Huntington (1996) and his post-9/11 celebrants, difference is absolute, insuperable, incommensurable and a source of inevitable violence, remystified as some religio-cultural essence.[1] But Empire's global reach is also fueled by a voracious appetite for diversity (contrasted with difference by Bhabha) as Benetton pluralism promises a garden of consumption, reducing difference to benign and depoliticized variation (Hardt and Negri, 2000).

In both forms of globalization, which we are living today, the figure of difference is pivotal to social, cultural, political, and economic relations of power, value, and access to resources, opportunity, and security. Consequently, it remains crucial to the many long traditions of education for social justice addressed in this anthology, as the political and conceptual terrain of our transformative work. As Trifonas argues in his introduction, difference is also highly contested ground, upon which the different critical pedagogical traditions stake their claims to theoretical and methodological validity in the project of nurturing communities of learners able to deconstruct and challenge discrimination.

Both concepts of difference outlined above prove highly dangerous as they inform educational projects: The first has fueled assimilationist pedagogies (such as English-only approaches to the education of ESL students) and essentialist identity-based politics within critical education. The second can be associated with reductive forms of multicultural education that celebrate a show-and-tell ethnotourism approach to difference and are silent on issues of discrimination. The question remains: Which imaginings of difference might ground an integrative, radically equitable project for social change?

In this chapter, I explore this question with reference to feminist and postcolonial translation theory. I ground my discussion in ethnographic material excerpted from a qualitative case study of the experiences of discrimination shared and collectively explored by 30 English as a Second Language (ESL) high school students within the context of a Freirean-style, integrative antiracism (Dei, 1996) leadership program in Toronto, Canada (Taylor, 2003a). In order to understand the ways their experiences of difference were discursively framed and reframed as strategic, relational epistemic and locutory standpoint, I reframe these as translational negotiations of identity, meaning, and value that strive to articulate what Bhabha (2001) has described as "an intercultural ethic of contiguity." Finally, I return to the urgent questions facing us as educators for social change, sketching an initial proposal for a pedagogy of critical cultural translation.

Theoretical Framework

This question of difference, posed in the present anthology, is raised by Bhabha in relation to what he calls the "linguistic turn" in contemporary theory. He observes that within the project of cultural studies to integrate and "institutionalize a range of transgressive discourses" whose distinct histories, forms of subjectivity, and strategies of resistance often set them at odds; "contemporary critics resort to the peculiar temporality of the linguistic metaphor ... [t]o provide a social imaginary that is based on the articulation of differential, even disjunctive, moments of history and culture" (1994: 176). That is, in the struggle between competing differences and interventionist projects, the linguistic metaphor makes possible certain radical concepts: of difference as the enunciative articulation, in the present, of incommensurable, contiguous but not continuous temporalities of expression; and of translation as the productive friction of this heterochronous contiguity located in the performative crucible of cultural meaning and subjectivity. Here, *contiguity* references the way that in any intercultural moment of contact and translation, different histories and memories, different geographically and culturally particular standpoints and ways of being are articulated[2] through a particular linkage that is contingent upon specific conditions and formations (Hall, 1996: 141–142).

In this chapter I propose bringing to questions of social difference, and specifically relations of language difference, this conceptual framework within which translation and difference are reconfigured as the complex grounds of learning, transformation, ethical engagement, and community.

Specifically, in bringing this framework to an analysis of the social relationships and maneuvers ESL students engage in every day as they pass through "media of varying [discursive] density" (Benjamin cited in Bhabha, 1994), I'm advocating that those of us who work in the field of language in education engage in a theoretical retranslation. My sense of urgency arises from my observation, made from the location of my teaching and research at the intersection of social justice and second language education, that while strong critical traditions have developed that ground their activist pedagogy in an analysis of gendered, racialized, ethnicized, classed, and sexualized difference, linguistic difference has tended to be treated, even by progressive educators, as a *cognitive* more than *social* phenomenon. Alternatively, language difference is treated as a subset of racialized or ethnicized differentiation, governed by the same discursive mechanisms, except that it is assumed to dissipate once English is mastered (and one's accent "reduced").

At the same time, the social sciences have been profoundly enriched through the use of the metaphor of language to understand social relations of power, meaning/representation, and position/identity. I'm thinking of sociological and educational research that grounds its analysis in the work of such theorists as Foucault (1972, 1982), Derrida (1976, 1978), Bakhtin (1981), and Bhabha (1990, 1994). The field of second language education has only recently begun to explore the possibilities of importing the fruits of this innovation back to questions of educating and empowering immigrant language learners (see, e.g., Canagarajah, 1993; Ibrahim, 1998, 1999; Luke and Lin, 2006; Pennycook, 1999; Norton, 2000; Toohey, 2000; Walsh, 1991).

What is to be gained in such a venture? To begin, I am making the case that *language difference must be treated as social difference:* as a unique form that, though inextricably conditioned by other forms, cannot be considered simply interchangeable with or incorporable into the others. Clearly, we need to recognize that immigrant ESL students are socially, institutionally (including education), and materially marginalized as racialized, ethnicized, and classed others on the borders of society and discourses of national identity. Furthermore, neocolonial structures of racialized, gendered, and classed divisions of labor adjudicate global access to migration[3] and to the material and symbolic capital (education, professional qualifications, savings, etc.) required of immigrant applicants (Mohanty, 1997; Shohat, 1998; Grewal and Caplan, 1994).

At the same time I want to stress the particularity of language difference as a grounds of struggle. Why? While "ESL" does constitute a social category in the world of work and particularly in schools, languages are more than social markers; they are expressive idiolects, epistemological and hermeneutic universes of intersecting heterogenous valencies and trajectories of meaning in continual process of reconfiguration. They are also aesthetic and ideological technologies of identity, relation, and comprehension, "touchstone[s], loc[i] of difference, the site[s] of political and poetic imagination" (de Zavalia, 2000: 199). Thus, in mechanisms of linguistic marginalization, (de)legitimation, and resistance, there is a struggle over meaning and authority, not only in relation to a certain shared though contested vocabulary, but also to entire lexicons of alternative worldviews and configurations of power/knowledge, memory, and identity.

This particularity raises the question of which analytical framework(s) might most fruitfully be brought to pedagogical research of language difference as social difference. I am proposing turning to scholarly traditions built upon the study of the politics of language, language difference, and exchange to enrich our sociological frameworks. I'm referring to recent developments in translation studies that have seen this narrow, Eurocentric and male-dominated literary tradition transformed through the influence of cultural studies, which insists on critically grounding analyses of intertextual dynamics, semantic negotiation, and exchange within historical contexts of racialized, sexualized, and classed colonizing global relations of power (Apter, 2001). Sherry Simon writes: "[We now] are attentive to the fact that cultural traffic does not circulate freely about the globe, that its flow is regulated by the existence and condition of trade routes, the availability of willing vehicles and the needs and pleasures which cultural commerce caters to.... [We] know that the circulation of translations is not to be equated with the logic of the gift but with the rules of commodity exchange" (Simon and St.-Pierre, 2000: 13). This shift has brought translation studies as a field closer in relevance to sociological and pedagogical concerns with the conditions, constraints, and possibilities within which intercultural contact and relations of social difference and disparity take place today.

In this chapter I hope to identify and promote a similar shift within second language education through a cultural studies' attention to the politics of meaning in contests of cultural authority in order to open up a space for a more richly informed, rigorous sociological engagement of the lived politics of language difference and possibilities for pedagogical intervention.

Specifically, I will argue that bringing certain concepts from translation theory to an analysis of language difference as social difference makes available a model of difference as neither absolute nor transparent, but as a space of becoming, of the multiplication and rearticulation of meaning, positionalities, and relations. Reframing social difference as a multivalent, "interstitial space brings out to the full the tensions which inform [all] cultural identities ... [tracing] the negotiations between mother tongue and other tongue" (Simon, 1996: 162–168). Just as the language learner must bend her/his tongue to words she/he never invented even while bending them to her/his tongue, this transformative tension of surrender and appropriation, addressivity and assertion (Derrida, 1998) can be seen to play out in other forms of social difference our students negotiate every day. This conceptual framework makes it possible to trace the power-saturated movements and dissonant temporalities of emergent cultural meaning and stuttering subjectivities that are "multi-accentual" and palimpsestal, authorized by incommensurable yet conjugated histories and worldviews (Bhabha, 1994). I am not proposing the power-blind proliferation of "pluralist anarchy" (Bhabha, 1994: 6), rather, a critical engagement of difference as nonsynchronous (Bhabha, 1994) and a promise (Derrida, 1998).

I will also argue that the concept of translation reorients discussions of the *deconstructive* in-between—the space of the differential—toward a critical *creativity* and *expanded field of possibility*. This is a vital response to the question launching this anthology: despite the antagonistic positioning of divergent political projects and definitions of social difference, "each position is always a process of translation and transference of meaning. Each objective is constructed on the trace of that perspective that it puts under erasure; each political object is determined in relation to the other and displaced in that critical act" (Bhabha, 1994: 26). Understanding any political enterprise as a translation—a process of differential elaboration—and difference as a space of "transcreation" (de Campos, 1981) radicalizes the project of integrative critical pedagogies by asserting that we are always already speaking to each other, that we develop our theoretical groundwork, methodologies, and critical reflexivity in this very space of the differential. It suggests that this boundary dividing our transformative labor might instead act as the place from which other understandings and trajectories might begin their presencing. It also inspires an insistently hopeful, integrative pedagogy by focusing our work on what Bhabha (2001) calls an "ethic of intercultural contiguity."

The critical concepts I draw from translation studies are elaborated by postmodern feminist and postcolonial authors whose work on *textual* translation within the context of unequal sociopolitical relations elaborates an analysis of the dynamics and terms of the *social and discursive* negotiation of these colonizing relations.

Within Canada, for example, a movement in Francophone-Anglophone feminist translation, literature-in-translation, and literature about translation provocatively traces the play of language difference and the vectors of desire and authority within, as well as between, the formation of gendered subjects in relation to literary and also broader social texts. Making the comparison between gender relations and translation, Banting asserts: "Women's language is a simultaneous translation between language and the body, between the spoken and the unspeakable.... Furthermore, this (m)other tongue ... [n]o one's mother tongue ... is a language which emerges in a complex and multivalent act of translation and can only be comprehended in two or more languages at once ... [like] an interlanguage"[4] (1994: 175). Authors/translators/theorists in this tradition reconfigure translation as a process of differentiation within gendered subjects living at the intersection of dominant and silenced discourses, a transgressive practice which inf(l)ects the monologism of dominant discourse through their divergent performance: "Positing the existence of two language worlds, [Gagnon] advocates that women use the language of the dominant to persuade and to transform it.... This doubled language, male discourse re-marked by the multiplicity of women's speech, will transform scientific discourse and its poetics of transparence" (Godard, 1990: 87–89). Most striking are the fertile metaphors engendered by this link to performative collaboration and political resistance: renovating a field "dominated by tired clichés of betrayal and failure ... [and] an economy of loss ... [c]hallenging the traditional master-slave view of translation vis-à-vis writing," this movement rearticulates translation as creative rather than derivative (Simon, 1996: 158–160).

In the emerging tradition of postcolonial translation, the latter is taken as a paradigm for understanding sociopolitical relations of difference in a postcolonial world. As Liu (1999) writes, "We can no longer talk about translation as if it were a purely linguistic or literary matter" since it describes practices through which the universalizing tendencies of Euro-imperial modernity configure, incorporate, and deploy difference within global circulations of meaning as value. That is, within colonial and postcolonial economies of transcultural exchange, translation hosts ongoing contests for epistemic and cultural authority. In this sense, it becomes "an overarching metaphor for the unequal power relationship which defines the condition of the colonized [Niranjana, 1992]. The colonial subject fixed to his native site as well as the unsited migrant post-colonial are thus equally translated persons" (Bassnett and Trivedi, 1999: 12–13).

As a powerful lens through which to examine not only individual experiences of geographical and social rupture, but also global struggles for social and political priority fought in the arena of cultural representation, translation maps the "intricate processes of cultural contact, intrusion, fusion and disjunction" (Young, in Simon and St.-Pierre, 2000: 11). In this way, translation radicalizes our understanding of culture as "an uneven, incomplete production of meaning and value, often composed of incommensurable demands and practices, produced in the act of social survival" (Bhabha, 1994: 172). It is in this reconception of cultural signification within histories of displacement that the space of difference is reconfigured as not simply *geographical* but *temporal*. Bhabha, for example, pushes us to comprehend the terms of intercultural engagement from a minoritized, resistant positionality as a claim to the "right to signify,"[5] in which recognition and authority as a speaking subject are resourced through the contingent and contradictory reinscription and deployment of alternative cultural traditions. "The recognition that tradition bestows is a partial form of identification. In restaging the past it introduces other, incommensurable cultural temporalities [into the present conjuncture]" (Bhabha, 1994: 2). These differential modalities of meaning, "striving to exclude each other," render translation an agonistic "state of contestation and flux" in which the simultaneity of communicative engagement is riven by the palimpsestal temporalities of cultural traditions whose citation authorizes resistant speech (1994: 227). Thus, Bhabha helps us reconceptualize translation as the *performative* staging, in the "nervous temporality of the transitional, ... the emergent provisionality of the present," of the resistant foreignness of other-timely cultural difference (1994: 216–227). He explains: "The sign of translation tells, or 'tolls' the different times and spaces between cultural authority and its performative practices. The 'time' of translation consists in that *movement* of meaning" (1994: 227–228). Within this movement, difference as dissonant contiguity becomes a search for new forms of affiliation, for an ethic of survival together (Bhabha, 2001).

It is this concept of cultural difference and translation as an enunciative space of intervention and invention, as "the place from which *something begins its presencing*" (Bhabha, 1994: 5) that I am bringing to understand ESL students' negotiations of language difference.

Context of Research

This chapter draws from a qualitative practitioner study of the pedagogical possibilities of antidiscrimination education for new Canadian adolescent language learners (Taylor, 2003; in press). Examining a unique equity leadership program, the case study pursued questions central to the paradigm of difference raised by multicultural and antiracism education: How is difference experienced by racialized immigrant and refugee language learners? How are these youth able to reconfigure difference from the assimilatory and reductive terms set by dominant Eurocentric narratives of Canadian settler/immigrant identity, into a critical relation of transformation? How might a social justice program, developed in the specific cosmopolitan context of Toronto, open itself to the challenges of cultural difference by its own addressees?[6]

Part of a multipronged approach developed over the past 20 years of increasing demographic diversity and commitment to equity-promoting[7] learning environments, the Toronto School Board (and the amalgamated Toronto District School Board [TDSB] after 1997) has run *Equity Leadership Retreats* to students from more than 16 secondary schools in this urban area. Among the specialized camps were the ESL camps.

Explicitly designed as a pedagogical model for individual, social, and institutional change (McCaskell, 2005), the camps combine elements of popular education, critical and feminist pedagogy, and integrative antiracism education. Drawing from the first three pedagogical approaches, the camp program centers students' personal embodied experience as the basis of discussion, shared insight, analysis, holistic knowledge-construction, and positive identity-building (Luke and Gore, 1992; Arnold et al., 1985), as well as leadership development. Understanding leadership as the capacity to analyze and collectively act upon the architectures of power shaping the social and material conditions of learners' immediate worlds, activities are designed to elaborate and extrapolate personal understandings and individual interests to a process of building collective commitment and effective alliances around shared values and visions. Grounded in *integrative* antiracism education (Dei, 1996), this approach takes racism as an analytical starting point, but in implementation insists on the urgency of *all* forms of discrimination. Facilitators consistently encourage participants to "see" how xenophobia, ethnocentrism (and not only Eurocentrism), linguicism, sexism, classism, and heterosexism play out in different societies and communities, how they intersect in everyday interactions (Essed, 1991; Razack, 1998). This has proven crucial to underlining crosscutting shared values and interest in social change, and to ensure that, for example, male students do not dominate action plans to challenge racism in home schools, or that female students of prominent ethnic or class backgrounds do not dominate antisexism projects.

As an extracurricular program, running from 9:00 a.m. until 3:30 p.m. for four consecutive days in the late spring of 2000 in one of the recreational buildings of the University of Toronto, the activities were focused solely on values education, without the pressure to cover grade-level subject content. This creates an ambience of support for the often uncomfortable exploration of students' personal experience.

The participants in the Year 2000 ESL Equity Leadership Camp came from two downtown high schools, were aged 16 to 19, and hailed from 15 countries of origin. Data collection included participant observation in the camp and schools and one-hour postprogram, individual, semistructured interviews with 30 participants, carried out within ten months of the program's completion. These data were supplemented by one-hour individual interviews with four adult graduates of past camps (from 1990–1999), which allowed the refinement of interview questions and unique insights available through a mature retrospective vision. The scope of this chapter, however, encompasses quotes from only eight participants (seven from the Camp 2000 and one adult graduate of an earlier camp) and focuses particularly on two detailed portraits of camp participants, Khatra and Luiza.[8]

The Fertile Turbulence of Heterochronous Multilingualism

What does translation as an "anachronistic moment of transition" (Bhabha, 2001) look like in this pedagogical project? This can be seen in relation to one of the central goals of the program: the collective analysis by ESL students of their past experiences of discrimination and the construction of an alternative *community of difference* (my term, explained in the following paragraph) upon values that challenge discrimination. To this end, activities and discussions encourage students to translate their memories, concepts/definitions, and values from their immigration experiences in Canada—and also *from their home culture and previous country*—into camp discussions of their lives now in their schools. For most students this is an unprecedented invitation; according to interviews, they have found no space that offered a place for the values, cultural worldview, meanings, or language they brought with them within their new context, except perhaps in their families or friendship groups who share the same language. For many, the severing of these lines of connection feels like a "loss," which inspires varying degrees of melancholy (the words "loss" and "lost" arise repeatedly in students' descriptions of early immigration/settlement experiences) and their memories from before immigration can be somewhat nostalgically idealized. To a certain degree this disposition seems to shape their descriptions of community, which many recall from childhood as free from discrimination, animated by the values of egalitarianism, humanity, mutual support, generosity, and trust. When probed regarding this absence of discrimination or disparity, their responses attest to a naturalized vision of a community that coheres based on commonality and sameness. "No, there was no racism or discrimination; we're all just same people! Always, like we live there since Adam and Eve! Not like here, we're all different countries' people" (George, male, 18, Ghana). These students' notions of ideal community seem to be haunted by echoes of archaic temporalities that refuse translation into this present moment of engagement and authorize a profound sense of identity and commitment.

Without attacking these loyalties, the camp program is designed to encourage the construction of what I term a *community of difference*: that is, as a community, what ESL students have in common—experiences of dislocation, marginalization, and discrimination based on their positionality as non-native English speakers, immigrants, and members of non-Anglo Saxon ethnicities—also marks the differences between them (the group does not share mother tongue, first culture, ethnoracial affiliation, or country of origin). The participants are therefore challenged to import and perform the values learned from their childhood contexts in the deliberate collective construction of a community, sharing no histories save those of the present and future: a community engaged in the present with an eye to the future but host to heterogenous, incommensurable pasts. While this translation is attempted within the physical space of the camp—a space defined by the dominant culture of the program's social justice pedagogy in which the "texts" of these values and memories are valued—it is with the consciousness that the community's test will be its survival back in the space of the school, in which it is very much a minority culture. Thus, while there is less of a demand that the students "bring the text to the audience"—that is, to explain, justify, and translate the values and meanings of community that they bring from their "home country"[9] into popular discourses and images already familiar to this nascent community—the community as a new whole will have to work very hard to communicate and promote these values, understandings, and goals to the larger school community.

This paradigm for negotiating difference should be distinguished from what Banting characterizes as univocal, unquestioning celebrations of dialogue across the accepted fact of difference (Banting, 1994: 176–178), or what Bhabha (2001) terms the "sublatory dialectic," which rushes to resolve a binary opposition through transcendence within a teleological unity or universalism. This critique is eloquently expressed in Davor Marjanovic's explanation of his complex film *My Father's Angel* about war-traumatized Bosnian Muslims and Serbians trying to live together in multicultural Canada. "Canada tells immigrants, 'Don't bring your ancient feuds here with you' but what if your feuds brought you? I can't evacuate my memory, leave my soul at [the ministry of] Immigration. This is cultural amnesia, not cultural pluralism" (Marjanovic, 1999). He seems to be underlining the danger of a monologic reductionism unable to recognize translation as anything more than assembling "an accurate collection of synonyms" (Spivak, cited in Simon, 1996: 142), as calculating a fair rate of exchange. Similarly, Banting warns that flattening and containing difference within a sole mode of tolerant, liberal variation unilaterally smothers the transfigurative labor of "the vagaries, errors, slippages, transferred syntax, slips of the tongue and (in)felicities" of interlanguaging.

The experience of language difference illustrates graphically that the very vocabulary for any "dialogue" needs to be sought, struggled for, and created in the process: like a sort of interlanguage, it is not a given, nor may it preexist the encounter (Banting, 1994: 178). In the camp discussions, it is not enough for each participant to simply "transpose" her/his experiences, concepts, and values of community into this context, She/he also needs to discover what is happening to this "text" in its transference and reception by this audience: what some of the intertexts are that accompany its decipherment by the others, what elements resist translation, how it is signifying both more and less to the listeners than she/he intends, how she/he might supplement this meaning. For example, Mohammed (male, 16), an Ethiopian student, recalling an absence of discrimination between ethnolinguistic groups in his "home community," held the eyes of Fatma (female, 16), a female Eritrean coparticipant, while speaking with a rising consultative tone at the end of his sentence. Fatma responded in both a shared language (Amharic) and in English, suggesting that this apparent harmony may have changed since the war for Eritrean independence, and that relationships may feel different when one ventures outside one's ethnolinguistic community now. The English word that resisted translation in this discussion, which they inserted into Amharic speech, was "prejudice"; other terms remained in Amharic. After two to three minutes, an English summary was related by both to the rest of the group. In the ensuing group discussion in English, each recognized that neither held the other responsible for the larger conflict; the pedagogical agenda and affective barrenness of English words created partial closure and emotional distance. Later, in his individual interview, the Ethiopian student commented that while he didn't remember forms of discrimination similar to those discussed at the camp in his "home" town, he did remember groups of older men and sometimes women sitting in conversation and "judging" passing girls in terms of the modesty of their dress. Asked why he chose this word, he replied, "Well, it's like this word in Amharic we use . . . maybe it's like prejudice, maybe they are prejudice to the girls."[10] In this example it seems that terms and concepts of *both* languages are imported back and forth, forming a nascent interlanguage as they re-inscribe and are re-inscribed by at least three heterochronous, conjugated yet non-equivalent contexts of cultural meaning and identity (Ethiopia/Eritrea in the past and now, the school in Toronto and the camp community).

As I bring this theoretical framework to analyze ESL students' exploratory process of multivalent difference, I find myself in the position of translating concepts such as "text" and "context," "author" and "reader" into social and discursive interactions. In interpreting my data, I have found it most revealing to regard any element of culture as a text: values, practices, collective narratives, discursive tropes, images, beliefs and notions of identity, belonging, legitimacy, worth, relationality, truth, and normalcy. That is, I am including anything in the social imaginary or cultural realm that can be apprehended and interpreted by a social subject and may influence their relation or interaction with others. This is because, in order to analyze the mechanisms and negotiations of power and positioning within the multiply articulated sociocultural worlds in which ESL students live, I consider that anything that is brought from one context to another that communicates a message regarding relationships, social positionalities, and meaning in either world is acting as a text (whether it is actively performed, verbally or bodily, or simply serves to inform understandings). The context, then, is the sociocultural world of relationships and meaning where these students dwell, shaping it and being shaped as subjects.[11]

In a second example, there emerged in a discussion during the camp among a group of ESL students a common sentiment that there currently exists no space for them at their particular school, that the ESL program is being ghettoized in student life and hidden from public events or view. One "action plan" developed to address this consisted of starting a multicultural dance troupe. I understand this as a process of the students' reading the culturally and linguistically exclusionary "text" of the school's extracurricular cultural events, and claiming the right to inflect it with (initially) the language of Angolan dance and music.[12] When the troupe asked the vice-principal for the chance to perform at school events, and it was invited to the first upcoming event, the November 11 Remembrance Day assembly,[13] a new relation to the new text needed to be hammered out: wasn't the group supposed to be just about dancing? Why should it be about war? But wasn't the idea also to show the rest of the school about ***their lives, their stories***? Hadn't the Angolan students talked about the war in Angola, how it had infused society with such violence that their families had come to Canada to simply live in peace and security? Had the group not also learned about the history of colonialism in the camp, and discussed the historical reasons for poverty and war in Africa that don't stereotype Africans as "lazy" or "savage"? Could this dance show some of the historical roots of war and poverty and corruption, to teach "Canadians" that Africans aren't violent by nature? What about showing peace in Africa in the future (a time when one of the female students plans to return to Angola and run for president in order to end corruption)? Within this conversation, then, the troupe shifted its intention to performing the text of the commemoration of violence, introducing the histories of pre- and postcolonial African societies and cultures, European colonization, slavery, and emigration/exile. The initial choice of Angolan music was narrowed down to the music of Bongo, a political dissident, once political prisoner and exile of 20 years, making connections between war and migration. The supervising teacher was somewhat surprised at the revised theme; she checked with the vice-principal, a meeting was held with an invited "equity facilitator," and the student decision was approved. During these weeks following September 11, 2001, however, doubts were raised by the school administration, the troupe members, and their families, particularly in regard to safety and public response. The presentation went ahead in the end; the troupe's organizer and eldest member felt strongly that, in the current context of war, Afghani women and children should be receiving not bombs but food, medical care, and access to education. However, this specific antiwar message was not stated in the program notes; only the title of the autobiographical pacifist song of exile from Bongo is being translated from Kimbundu[14]: "Mona Ki Ngi Xica" [My Child I Have to Leave You].

This example illustrates the dynamics of power and status in the translation of cultural "texts" between "dominant" and minoritized cultures.[15] The ESL students are both claiming the right to bodily perform dominant texts of cultural expression and war memorial, and asserting the need to read the ethnocentric, selectively commemorative, dominant Canadian narratives of war and peace in performative counterpoint with minoritized texts from European colonialism's "intertwined histories" (Said, 1993) or "tethered twin[s]" (Bhabha, 2001). These texts from across the imperial divide (Said) consist of dance, music, historical memories and analyses from an African perspective as expressed by these participants in their Toronto context. Furthermore, the patriarchal nationalist time-space and androcentric commemoration of fallen soldiers are populated by the young women's embodied testimonies of the gendered impact and casualties of war, the social fabric and cultural wealth that are also lost. Thus, the students can be seen as "transtextualizing" the institutional space of official ritual, in de Campos's sense (incorporating Bakhtinian dialogism and Kristevan intertextuality) of translation as "a 'parallel canto', a dialogue not only with the original's voices but with other textual voices" (de Campos, 1981: 191). In the students' contrapuntal canto, the discourses of cultural authority lose their univocal claim to finalize meaning, close down eccentric references, and totalize a "prior moment of being or meaning—an essence" (Bhabha, 1990: 210).

Two points drawn from postcolonial translation studies are relevant here. First of all, it has been noted that when translation moves from less powerful cultures into the context of more powerful ones, the minoritized text tends to have to be "brought to the audience" rather than vice versa. That is, the burden of translation tends to fall more heavily upon the translator of the minority text—to "bend and twist" the foreignness of the text into the service of the dominant culture's repertoire of intelligibilities, interests, and homogenizing conventions, to smooth the dissonant edges, traces, and accents into a fluent reading—than it does upon the dominant audience to adapt its ear, disposition, and background knowledge to the minority language (Venuti, 1996; Simon and St.-Pierre, 2000: 23). This trend is resisted by some postcolonial theorists, who see the translator's task as "not to turn Hindi, Greek, English into German [but] instead to turn German into Hindi, Greek, English" (Pannwitz, cited in Bhabha, 1994: 228); that is, "to 'translate' the foreign reader into a native one" (Ramanujan, cited in Bassnett and Trivedi, 1999: 16). In this specific case of cultural translation, a meeting was required in order to explain to school administrators the intention of the dance performance, the meaning of the dance, music, lyrics, song title, and singer's biography, as well as the history and personal stories being retold. Furthermore, it was necessary to justify the legitimacy of this minority text's being performed within a dominant temporal and spatial context (one teacher thought that the performance should be postponed until February's Black History Month activities when it would be "more appropriate" than within the national November 11th event).

In terms of the second point, it is worth revisiting the differential role of translation in colonial settings. In their introduction to postcolonial translation, Bassnett and Trivedi remind us of the Filipino experience:

> For the Spaniards, translation was always a matter of reducing the native language and culture to accessible objects for and subjects of divine and imperial intervention. For the Tagalogs, translation was a process less of internalizing colonial-Christian conventions than of evading their totalizing grip by repeatedly marking the differences between their language and interests and those of the Spaniards. (Rafael, in Bassnett and Trivedi, 1999: 3)

In this case, the dance troupe's performance of the dominant theme of war and commemoration consciously marks the particularity of the students' subaltern perspective through the enunciative citationality of their bodies, movements, images, memories, music, and identifications. Their translation of these minoritized historical and aesthetic texts into their performance in a space of nationalist ritual and pedagogical narration (Bhabha, 1994) takes pains to resist reductive assimilation into settled archaic time, and to keep the nervous, transitional temporality of semantic contestation in flux and open in the present. Their turbulent enunciation thus opens up a "discontinuous intertextual temporality ... the 'inter'—the cutting-edge of translation, negotiation, the in-between space—that carries the burden of meaning of culture" (Bhabha, 1994: 38) from which complex, intercultural understandings might begin their presencing.

In this sense, while these ESL students seek inclusion within dominant collective Canadian identities, their attempts to translate elements from other cultural formations or to inflect dominant artifacts/texts with an ethnicized, gendered performance may be best understood in terms of their desire to claim the signifying authority of cultural difference as a "grounds for intervention" (Simon and St.-Pierre, 2000), to triangulate social and power relations within their school/peer contexts with rival value systems. This is similar to how Rampton and Ibrahim theorize subversive linguistic performance within the frame of "crossing" and the practice of ritual (Rampton, 1995: 81, cited in Ibrahim, 1998: 106–107) as the invocation, activation, and recognition of alternative symbolic marketplaces (following Bourdieu, 1991).

The above example attests to the weight and texture of institutional interventions into the spheres of contested authority within which ESL students need to stake out enunciative positions; that is, it illustrates the power of educational institutions and actors to stage and police the terms and spaces of intercultural traffic.

The next example explores the dynamics of cultural translation within an institutionally less powerful but perhaps affectively more influential symbolic marketplace: the sphere of peer culture with its competing and exclusionary narratives of collective identity and belonging. This example also highlights the embodied *performativity* of cultural translation when it is understood as inherent to all social interactions (in distinction from conceptualizing translation in relation to written literary texts). As an enunciative temporality of signification and subjectivity, the performativity of cultural translation can open a space of resistance and possibility in the very heart of social relations. The distinct dynamics of this embodied negotiation of difference are best captured by Godard's (1990) concept of "transformance": in the performative act of cultural translation, in the process of physically constructing cultural meaning in which one's body is both a text to be read and an enunciative dialogic intervention into the discursive context of available narrative codes, there is a transformative interstitial moment that holds open the possibility for rearticulating meaning and relations.

One of the camp participants, a young Somali woman, recounts what she considers a personal experience of discrimination:

> It was after the March break, this girl just pushed me in the hall, and I was with my Ethiopian friends: "What you looking at fat girl?" It was a Jamaican girl. Then my friends called the principal. (Khatra, female, 16, Somalia)

The most powerful culture among many groups in this school is anglophone Afro-Caribbean (based on student and teacher interviews) even though this is an extremely marginalized ethnic group in Canadian society (in fact, many teachers consciously and actively work to empower Afro-Caribbean students and support their cultural expression and identifications). In this local context, however, Khatra may not represent particular dominant images of feminine beauty, either in relation to normalized white femininity or to marginal Afrocentric images of female beauty that have developed within historical contexts of racism, cultural colonization, and the de-/hyper-sexualization of black women (hooks, 2002). In addition to contesting exclusionary gendered aesthetics, however, her body is also read as performing an identity which unsettles dominant notions of blackness and Africanness in this social context of her peers:

> They say, "You're not African, you're not Somali. You got, like big eyes and your hair is straighter." I say, "Excuse me, I'm telling you I'm Somali. My people don't look the same, they're all different! ... Like my grandmother from my mom, she doesn't look like Somali people: she looks Arabic or Italian. And other Somali people, they have really light light skin, like white, really white. Some people have red hair, some people look different, we're not all look the same! Somali people, they know that. Like my older sister people think she's Indian; she says, like 'Give me a break! I am Somali so don't call me that other thing!' (Ethiopian friend interrupts in Dutch, both laugh) ... my friend says we were like the oldest kings and queens in the world!"[16]

At stake are definitions of blackness and Africanness that, in this interaction within this social context, seem to depend upon hair and skin shade, and to be buttressed by not only black/white but apparently also Indian/African distinctions.[17] Khatra's performance of "authentic" African identity inflects it with abject markers—imperfect English, nonidealized femininity, hair and skin that look "Indian"—even as it minoritizes the anglophone West Indian culture of blackness in the school. Here I am referencing the Deleuzian sense of how Khatra minoritizes a dominant discourse of blackness/Africanness through the multiplication of its "radical heterogeneity by submitting [it] ... to constant variation, forcing it to become minor, delegitimizing, deterritorializing, alienating it," speaking it as a foreigner, speaking where it is foreign to itself (Venuti, 1996: 92).

In several incidents Khatra's "Indian" features are repeatedly pointed out as visual evidence that disqualify her from credible African identity—as if the two ethnicities were constitutively mutually exclusive. In this particular encounter, one of the strongest reactions is drawn by Khatra's performance of an "authentic" Africanness that stages markers of another ethnicity at its hybrid heart. Finding herself a "translated person" expected to perform in mysterious fluctuating languages of pigmentation, hair consistency, sometimes shape and height, Khatra asserts the alien outside of each discourse as a heterotropic inside, as a "denied knowledge" whose introduction into the essentialist black African identity being imposed "estrange[s] the basis of its [univocal] authority" (Bhabha, 1994: 114). Located within a transitional space of dissonance, "translat[ing] between body and language, between the spoken and the unspeakable" (Banting, 1994: 175), she performs the text of

Africanness not as an absolute, timeless object but as a "process of translation and transference of meaning." (1994: 26).

As Bhabha (2001) warns, "Ambivalence and antagonism accompany any cultural translation because it unsettles settled meaning." Khatra's translation introduces the deconstructive (and generative) friction of disjunctive yet contiguous iterative temporalities (Bhabha, 1994: 182) at the palimpsestal heart of cultural meaning: her references to slavery, ancient Nubian kingdoms, Arabic and Italian colonialism/migration/miscegenation invoke and reinscribe dissonant historical narratives and traditions for her strategic purposes in the present engagement (Bhabha, 1994: 2). In this deconstructive performance she translates a minority "text"—the ways she understands ethnicity and social difference to be measured in "Africa"—into the Caribbean-dominant context, minoritizing and triangulating this context with the authority of incommensurable difference:

> It's like back home: we never do that kind of stuff. We have white people come to live there in Somalia, but we never did those kinds of stuff. It's like, we saw, like, Somali people, especially men married Italian women, so they live in Somalia and the guy works so the neighbors help the woman, how to dress, how to make her husband something to eat. It's like we never, usually look, the people don't even like what, she has different color, we have different color, so what! Not there, we never did that kinds of stuff . . . It's like, I was sitting in the library, and this girl came to and she touch my hair and say, "It's so smooth? How come?" And I say, "What do you mean, how come?" And she said, "This is your hair?" And I said, "Yes," and she said, "What did you put?" I said, "W-what did I put? I didn't, I never put anything, it's just my natural hair! Since when I came out of my mother, this is the hair I was born!' . . . And she said, "I put everything, you see? My hair still looks ugly!! But yours looks fine!" And I said, "So we are different! That's what I'm telling you! We're not the same!"

Khatra also deploys the discourses of the civil rights movement—already circulating in the school with teacher sponsorship[18] and made explicitly available through the camp curriculum and discussions—in a translation that presents this text, not as a symbol of her oppression by European imperialist power, but by the local black-centered culture that delegitimates her enunciative status as a speaker and renders her body a sign of miscegenation or of an imposter. Framing this within Haroldo de Campos's theory of cannibalistic translation, I would suggest she is drawing linguistic nourishment and strategic support from popular culture's performance of an American-centered discourse of civil rights and slavery commemoration, while refusing a stance of imitation or adulation (Vieira, 1994: 67–70; 1999: 103). In fact, her response, "What're you tryin' to do, slave me?" suggests that, in articulating a stuttering, nascent metalanguage or interlanguage of defense, she is ingesting and incorporating the language of U.S. civil rights discourses as part of an alternative global history. Of course, Khatra's resistant history shouldn't be romanticized; in contesting the young Jamaican woman's practices of intragender relations and raced identity, she elides what she may well not know: the histories of racialized stratification and gendered competition institutionalized in slave-based economies such as those in the Caribbean.

Invoking alternative histories of antagonisms, betrayals, and losses, Khatra asserts her own synchronic and diachronic pluri-accentual reading of both women's bodies as multiply translated, transculturated, and transvalorized (Vieira, 1994; 1999) through colonization and slavery. It is possible that this transtextual performative reading is intended to shock; she recognizes that her own amazement at the other woman's attack was not only at its black-on-black nature, but its "girl-on-girl" violence. Earlier in the interview she had related her experience watching Spielberg's *Amistad* with a white female friend:

> I remember seeing the film *Amistad*. It was like, sometimes, like, you don't feel like watching, sometimes you get mad and you say, "Why this happen, how they treated the people?" (You're mad because this person and this person are the same: this person is a human being, and has real pain!) ... I was like, my eyes were red, and she said, "Why? It's just a film? I know white people are not that good" ... And I say, "No, no no no no! It's like, you're white, you have a ... you're a person, you're a human being same as me, like, I'm concerned about those kind of women because they are poor people who shouldn't have to do that kind of stuff!" It's the same, like, when you touch your skin and do something that's gonna cause you pain, if I do the same thing I feel the same! And I say, "I'm just concerned about the way they're treated, not their color" ... You see a lot of women naked, they're hitting, they're like doing that kind of stuff, raping ... it like gives you a lot of mad, but not for the color. Because you will see a lot of the white people—like, you see the history and you will see a lot of white women getting killed or raped by a white man, so you feel mad, because you're a woman, you're feeling that—how can he do that? He's stronger than her? How is she gonna protect herself? Why is he doing that? ... But I don't like anyone to hit a woman! I don't like it! I hate a person hitting women! I hate it, it's like, it's like I can't stand it! I say, "It's just a poor woman! Why!" ... Oh yeah, I hate it! Like, when I was back home in Somalia, I had a brother, he died too in the war (not just my sister), during the war, he was killed: he was protecting my mother. That's why he was killed, because those kind of guys came and there were three girls and my brother and my mother, and my mother said, "Please don't hurt my daughters because they are still young and they have to have a future!" Because I was the youngest of 10 children and I was almost 9! Almost a woman! And she said, "Please don't hurt her!" And the guy was hitting my mother, he just pushed her. And this guy, like, my brother said, "Don't kill my mother! I swear to God I'm gonna kill you!" And they said, "What do you want?" And he said, "What do I want? Don't kill her!" And so they just shoot him. And my mother just started crying and he just said, "Stupid woman." Because of that, I always hated—my sister too, we always hated a man or a boy hurting a woman.

Tracing her repulsion at violence against women back to the violence she witnessed against her own female family members during the war in Somalia, Khatra asks listeners to travel back and forth with her, as she weaves these disparate moments in a trans-Atlantic history of gendered violence into her position of passionate opposition to its perpetuation. Considering the affective impact the images in *Amistad* had on her, it is possible that this visual text of violence against women under colonialism and slavery, and the more personal traumatic text of gendered violence during war, are both powerful intertexts in her response to the young Jamaican woman. I would suggest that there are two unspoken values or wishes behind Khatra's response: first, a gendered solidarity that can "see" (in Michelut's sense) histories of *both* racialized and gendered violence; and secondly, the hopes of some kind of peaceful coexistence that have brought Khatra and her family to this contemporary Toronto context. Spanning both contexts, haunting her passage from one to another, asserting an ethical relation between the two, these heterochronous values make their presence felt as a demand and a promise in present engagements.

The Transcreative Back-and-Forth of Double Translation

The examples above risk portraying the process of agonistic friction in cultural translation as unidirectional. This raises the phenomenon that first jumped out of the data at me, and I'm indebted to Walter Mignolo (2000a, 2000b) for how his theory of double translation helped me name what I was seeing. Exploring this phenomenon in the following examples, I also want to refocus my analysis on the mediating role of the camp's social justice pedagogical agenda and curriculum in relation to the commerce in hermeneutic authority within cultural translation.

As explained above, the pedagogy of the camps is designed along Freirean lines to be experiential: to encourage ESL students to draw from their experiences of marginalization as part of the process of collectivizing and analyzing this experience with the goal of defining actions to challenge these relations in their lives. While the analytical vocabulary (the terms *stereotype, prejudice,* and *discrimination*) of the camp's antiracist critical pedagogy is introduced by camp facilitators and defined within a discourse of collective action, the explicit pedagogical intent of activities associated with this introduction is that students negotiate the meaning of these words according to their different experiences, such that the working definitions collectively arrived at reflect the reality of their lives and their perceptions of it.

Perhaps less prominent in relation to the initial intents of the program's design was the fact that ESL students draw from experiences, not only from the Toronto context, but also from the sociodiscursive and linguistic contexts of their "home countries" that until now have been given virtually no place in their current institutional and even social spheres. This reflects the dynamic spirit of ongoing innovation in this program; developed as an integrative antiracism (Dei, 1996) experience for general public school populations, then specialized into ESL-only camps (among others) to maximize ESL students' opportunities to speak and be heard, it became possible within the camp to focus on the particular forms of marginalization and silencing experienced by immigrant/refugee language learners.

The specificity and complexity of students' experiences that became the curriculum of the program gave rise to a certain phenomenon in my data. While I heard students in camp discussions and in subsequent individual interviews negotiating different possible meanings of the three new analytical terms (*stereotype, prejudice,* and *discrimination*), it was clear that there was a particular "movement of meaning" emerging: there was a back-and-forth motion happening, a lateral traversing of definitions between different contexts such that the traversals transmuted each new insight into the possible meaning of the term in question, as well as altering the student's view of and self-positioning toward the sociodiscursive relations in each context. All of this took place very much within, and not escaping, local and global colonial power relations. This is the "movement of meaning" Mignolo's work helps explain.

Mignolo describes the process undergone by Subcommandante Marcos, an urban Marxist intellectual of European descent, in discussion with indigenous Chiapan Mayan elders, in which certain words (for example, the figure of Emiliano Zapata) came, through attentive conversation, to act as portals; they figured in both cosmologies, though they were related through entirely different logics to the other elements of the two incommensurable yet conjugated systems of meaning. Mignolo calls these certain words or figures "points of connection."[19] I believe Bhabha (2001) would describe them as "new forms of affiliation in the project of ethical intercultural survival" that allow for contemporaneous relations of contiguity, contact, interdependence, contrapuntal entwinement and engagement between disjunctural temporalities, memories, narrations, and cosmologies.

Mignolo calls this attentive conversation "double translation"; in relation to my research, I understand this to describe a process that transforms not only the term (or text) under consideration, but the semantic configurations and logic, the silences and exuberances, internal to each "language" or culture, while also transmuting the mode, terms, and expectations of engagement between these languages. I also understand double translation as a process that profoundly inhabits and lives the effects of unequal epistemological and ontological status and power relations between two semantic and sociocultural systems. In relation to postcolonial translation studies, this concept further elaborates and highlights the way that translation transforms both target and source language to the point of displacing the hierarchical temporalities and authority embedded in the binary of "source/target."[20] In terms of the model of cultural translation I have been developing in this chapter, I'd like to incorporate the sense in which double translation as a concept foregrounds the bidirectionality of translation and its spiraling multivector transformative processes, while resisting the assumption of symmetricality or the sublatory logic of dialectics.

In this case, ESL students can be understood to be translating concepts of discrimination and its opposite, the conditions and characteristics of ethical community, between at least three contexts/spheres: their "home country" (and language and culture), their social sphere of peers at school, and the alternative "community of difference" being proposed and attempted at the camp.

Luiza, for example, (female, 16, Albania) spirals around several constantly shifting intertextual definitions of discrimination, freedom, and community in her enunciative movement between the three spheres. Describing her grandfather's experience of political repression and her father's experience of an inherited infamy in Albania, she says she hadn't thought of them as a form of discrimination before, but now does: "It wasn't race-discrimination, it was social. [In terms of your political reputation?] And beliefs." She also recognizes discrimination in Canada:

> Personally, I haven't experienced difference towards me ... but I think, there was still a kind of racism, but towards more the races, mostly, the country. Because we are white people, so maybe we don't feel it as much as black or Chinese people do, because I have friends from all over the world, so, I know like when they tell me that "this happened to me" and it's like some kind of discrimination but they're not white and they're black or Chinese. So I think there's a kind of discrimination but not from the countries between countries, I think it's between the *race*.

Other forms of discrimination she points out in Canada include "sexism," "ageism," and "social—about the job that the people have, like, the place in society, the status. They don't want to mix with, like, they think someone is lower."

In the interview, she recognizes these forms of discrimination in Albanian society, yet makes the qualification:

> But I think communism helped, 'cause before Albania was like, the male was always on front on the table and he was always the one who made decision and everything. And the council of the men, I don't know they had like this stuff. But after like when the communism came, it gave the women the same rights: to work, to do everything. Yeah, it made it equal. That's a good thing they did. 'Cause I'm saying they [communism] had all this bad stuff: but like

> they had the discipline, like there has never been so much crime in Albania as now, 'cause everybody knew if they did something they would go to jail. Maybe it was because the people were afraid, but at least it kept, like under, like they didn't commit crimes, or they didn't have so many divorces. Because the men knew, like if he cheated on his [wife], if he drank, if he beat her, the people, of the—it was like the council in the neighbor—they would take him in front of the neighborhood and, like, make him admit his errors and try to change him and everything. So, yes, so no man would do that, 'cause the one who did that ... So communism was teaching people, 'cause the society, like, my mom tells me, like the society: at that time they didn't know better than that. And if there was the son of somebody in their class, they wouldn't talk to him: they would make him feel isolated, because if they talked to him, the other people would be like "who're you talking to? Are you crazy? He's the son of this, and he did all this stuff."

In this process of viewing each context through an imported concept, what begins in Luiza's interview as a ping-pong movement of comparing forms and degrees of freedom and discrimination in each society seems to trace a spiraling passage through continua of transformation as the image of each cultural formation erupts into its own disunity, its unspeakable contradictions unraveling toward a tentative yet radicalizing standpoint:

> But people say to me, "That's terrible, you had no freedom under communism!" But I remember the Democrats came in power in 1991, so I was 6 years old, and it was like the Mafia came in: the borders opened, but the people didn't know any better. So the Italian and Russian Mafia came in, they were getting girls into prostitution ... So I never enjoyed my life there, because before, even though [before] it was like Communism and everything, it was more freedom: nobody would touch you, nobody would say anything bad to you because they knew that something bad would happen to them: prison or something else. But now there was nothing, so I stayed mostly at home, *it wasn't free: it was supposed to be like freedom but it wasn't safe.* And after the war in 1987 we would like sleep on the ground because everyone was armed, so ... And there were like the local mafia, not like the big Mafia, and they would fight with each and it would be like you could go on the street and get killed for nothing because there were like guns everywhere and it wasn't safe ...
>
> So my family came to Canada for freedom. Like, you have the freedom of speech, you have the freedom to do whatever you want, to go wherever you want ... Your right to do whatever you want but not step on somebody's right. But then there is something bad with freedom too: well there's too much drugs and, the teens, I don't know, there's too much violence, too much sex, people are growing up so much faster, and they're not having their childhood, 'cause they're going immediately to drugs, to violence, to sex, all that stuff. I see it at this school a lot. Like, it seems exciting, it seems like everybody else is doing it. *So it's kind of not free and kind of too free!* Because there are people that know it, but don't really care, but I don't think they really know: they think

> they know it and they say, "I don't care, I think I'm safe" or whatever. But I don't think they really know it: *if they knew it, they would care* . . . So that's why, I remember in the camp we said discrimination is something it's gonna, like make people have less freedom if they are some group like Chinese or black. *But if you are in danger that's gonna take away your freedom too!* And teenagers can get into danger from too much drugs, or maybe they just get pregnant. (pause) But the mafia can shoot you too! Or like when the Kosovo mothers and children came to Albania because the husbands were in the war.

Clearly, Luiza is traversing back and forth between the three contexts (Albania, her school, and the camp), each with their own incommensurable demands and practices, their own understandings of freedom and discrimination—concepts and practices that, from the "inside," could not be imagined otherwise—yet with her own keen, liminal awareness that each culture does not share equal status and "truth" value in relation to the others. Conscious that values developed under communism are delegitimized texts within North American society—including the camp—she makes an extra effort to qualify and justify this translation, to resist a reductive reading of these ideas and values. Sketching the emergent provisionality of the present as her grounds for intervention, she articulates heterochronous mobile positions as processes of differential elaboration built upon the trace of other perspectives they put under erasure (Bhabha, 1994). This minoritizes the univocal pretensions of dominant definitions (of "freedom," for example) in this society *as well as in the program's social justice pedagogical agenda.*

She does this in order to develop her meditation on how to balance the attractions of freedom with its loss at the hands of discriminatory systems such as uneducated peer pressure, social custom, and ignorance. These are discriminatory impulses that she describes, based on a translation of her Albanian experience *and* her analysis of her Canadian experience, as innate to human beings and societies without the intervention of education. Hers are clearly gendered insights that clarify the differentially greater threats to women's freedom posed by North American society's apparent sexual freedom (in terms of such consequences as pregnancy and moral judgment) and Albania's lower civil security (in terms of women's heightened vulnerability to physical and sexual violence). Thus, it is her interlingual understanding that the freedom of some may end up sacrificed to the freedom of the more powerful, and that the un-freedom of all, effected through social regulation, can safeguard certain freedoms invisible to those who base their evaluation of a society on their own personal (or family) experience alone. This heterochronous, plurilingual intertext (Godard, 1993) that she speaks to the gaps in North American individualist visions of unhampered freedom resists monolingual readings, demanding that her listeners open themselves to a translational double consciousness (Wolf, 2000: 141) of the complex and contingent conditions, effects, and dimensions of freedom.

Luiza's traversals can be read together with Dôre Michelut's description of the moment when two languages, each with its distinctive "undertow" of felt meaning and sensibility, its "inner ear" that "occupied the same territory—me," are finally able to "see each other within me." Her heterotropic spiraling translations of these culturally particular concepts allows each cultural perspective to see what happens to the other in the process of translation; to reflect each other's impressions of sense, presence, and absence, each other's silence, un/thinkability and un/speakability. In Luiza's reflection on the relation between freedom, ignorance, education, and community, there is a moment when "the outside of each language takes a place in relation to the inside and vice versa," when each cultural worldview bends and speaks in relation to the other's sensibilities, possibilities, and incapacities, opening to her new ranges of possible imaginable relationships, dispositions, potentialities, and becomings (Michelut, 1994: 168–170). The "something" that begins its presencing on this activated boundary holds the promise of *an ethic of heterolingual and heterologic affiliation,* a working notion of a community of difference engaged in "differential consciousness" (Sandoval, 2000).

Communities Engaged In-Between

In fact, the productive agonistic friction of translation is clearest in the vectors of meaning traced by students as they develop new values and conceptions of community and collective identity during the course of the program.

Many ESL students initially perceive the community of difference proposed in the camp as a microcosm of the official narratives of Canadian identity: a collectivity supposedly united in its respectful nondifferentiating appreciation of difference, not the abjection and suppression of difference. However, dissonant experiences of ESL students of color or anecdotes of individual Canadians' racialized xenophobia tell another story: they attest to the exclusionary "European settler" discourse underlying dominant narrations of Canadian identity. What Walcott has called the "heritage model of ethnicity" (Walcott, 1995; 1997) is a pedagogical narration of the nation (Bhabha, 1994) that recuperates unfolding cultures of people on this land into the "backward-looking authenticity" and archaic temporality of "Two Founding Nations" (British and French; officially expanded to include First Nations only in 1986). This elides all experiences of immigration, asylum-seeking, and ethnicity within the universalized paradigm of European settlers' arriving in an empty land to work their way from the bottom of society to the top, while denying the experiences of First Nations peoples (Sleeter, 1993).

Performing a *clôtural* reading of this narrative (Derrida, 1976), letting the exuberances and incapacities, the stumbling contradictions, eccentric echoes, and silences of the concept of "settler/settling" open up to release the violence of the colonial difference (Mignolo, 2000a, 2000b) erased in this history, students at the camp assert the contiguity of this hoary narrative with their own immigration stories, repositioning themselves and opening both contexts up to radical reinscription. Below, one student responds to a newspaper article on a xenophobic right-wing parliamentary candidate who had campaigned to reduce Canada's refugee acceptance rates (on the claim that refugees are often criminals or "not the best clientele"):

> I don't know if these people ever studied history. Because I think their grandparents and ancestors were immigrants too. So I don't think just because she was born here so she calls herself a Canadian. But she's not a Canadian, because she or her grandfather, they came from some place else. So now, the time changed, but there are still people who are looking for a better future. Because her ancestors came here to give her the place that she has now. So why shouldn't other people have the right to do the same thing too? ... And when she says, "They are not the best clientele": they want, like, educated people to come to Canada and do slave work? Because that's what they're trying to do. But there are people who work, like, not slave work (maybe that was a bad definition) but, you know, people who were advocates, lawyers, doctors and come here and work in anything. Like there are people who did that work at home and here they're doing it again. And she's like, "It's [they're] lower." Why? If she's doing the same thing they do? It's not like they're criminals: they're poorer people who are coming here for a better future. But if she thinks that, other people in other countries even in Europe, like even if they have university they are stupider than her, then she is the stupid one. Because they're [Canadian Immigration] not taking smart people—I'm not saying smart people, but people that have the chance to go to school and get a career—they're not taking them to places where they can work in same where they belong: they're taking them for stupid work with no thinking. (Nadia, female, 16, Russia)

In this reading, students minoritize the dominant discourse of Canadian identity, speaking it as a foreigner, speaking where it is foreign to itself (Venuti, 1996). This can be seen as exteriorizing *différence*: staging the heterophemy of the monolingual dominant culture's intended self-narration (as an immigrant meritocracy, as a land of equal opportunity); triangulating it with its constitutive outside (the ongoing exclusion of First Nations Peoples and exploitation of new Canadians' dreams), with an "otherwhere" and an "otherwise" (Taylor, in press). As a double movement this process can be seen as both *deconstructive*—undermining the binary concepts of self/other, inside/outside, and citizen/alien that anchor dominant discourses of identity—and *creative,* as students develop new models of community and identity based on elected affiliation (Derrida, 1998); opening up "a fund of syncretisms, recombinations and mechanisms of acculturation ... [that]

resist categorization and renaturalization" (Bhabha in Simon and St.-Pierre, 2000: 21).

In response to the same article, other students volunteer the missing pieces of information—the silences and absences, the careful ignorance, and closing down of meaning—needed to maintain this Eurocentric national narrative: "Anyone who says refugees are criminals, they've never met a refugee! Just tell that *politico* to come, let her live five minutes normal person's life in my country in Africa, even one minute! Let her meet a refugee, see how is her life: I'm sure she'll never more say a refugee is a criminal. I'm sure!" (Rosina, female, 19, Angola). This "difficult knowledge" (Britzman, 1998), which must remain outside conscious knowing for most Canadians in order to maintain the face of a benign liberal national identity, is translated from the other-time, other-where of students' experiences into the collective space of this interrogative community. Here, it erupts, "mak[ing] something happen to this language ... [like an] ineffaceable archive ... a tattoo, a splendid form, concealed under the garments in which blood mixes with ink to reveal all its colours to the sight" (Derrida, 1998: 51–52). This translation against the grain of dominant monolingual amnesia may not be heard outside this audience without the institutional creation and sanctioning of a pedagogical space of listening (with teacher or principal support). Yet this speech act is powerfully transformative for these students, and is remembered by them in subsequent interviews when other details have faded. It acts as a portal or point of connection to other values of humanity and interdependence that students insert and assert in this emerging community, sundering "culturally collusive" (Bhabha, 1994: 9) narratives of this land of opportunity with the undeniable authority of these values' untranslatability, their semantic obstinacy:

> This is absolutely wrong. This is what I think. If I would be them, kind of, well, first I would be a guy, Canadian, speaking English, I would care about other people, because they're human too, they have the same feelings as you! If someone reacted to them or called them stupid or dumb, maybe some day it can happen to you too. Like maybe you go to other country: you try, but you won't learn all languages of a country. It's not like—you won't feel—just think about it, like, they are, like, same, kind of person as you are, right? (Nelofer, female, 15, Afghanistan)
>
> Listen, as far as I can see, it makes no sense. I mean, if I see someone all blood dying on the ground, I'm not gonna ask, "Are they my color?" I'm just gonna help! So it makes no sense. You never know what's gonna happen. She says she don't want no "boat people," coming, but maybe one of them is a doctor gonna save her life some day. You never know what's gonna happen, that's what I say. (George, male, 18, Ghana)
>
> What does discrimination mean? War. It makes for everybody war. (Vladimir, male, 15, Kazakhstan)

Toward a Decolonizing Pedagogy of Language Difference

As an educator, participant observer, and researcher in relation to these students and their learning, my most urgent conclusion relates to the role of teachers and cultural workers in fostering spaces of translation such as those I have described. As powerful designers of the infrastructure of classroom pedagogy and interpersonal culture, as well as active, institutionally sanctioned actors in this space, educators can work to create and encourage a classroom culture with certain (clearly not all) elements of the alternative community of difference attempted within the ESL equity camps. These elements might include: a knowledge base of the histories of colonialism and resistance from subaltern and not only dominant perspectives; a critical analysis of and proactive disposition toward social relations of marginalization, discrimination, and colonization; high value or symbolic capital associated with multilingualism, and awareness of the existence of gaps in meaning between languages and cultural systems; a comfort with complex relations of difference; awareness of the range of meanings in any term, image, or idea, and of the responsibility of any speaker to pay attention to its reception by the listeners; a taught and fostered culture of listening that involves attempting to bring oneself as a listener to the text of a speaker's message, to expand one's interpretive resources rather than demanding easily accessible messages in familiar dominant packaging/language; positive experiences of creativity and expanded understanding resulting from teacher-supported (and taught) processes of negotiating differential meaning between divergent perspectives; an expanded repertoire of "normal" (in terms of attracting identification) or at least accepted, identificatory sites; collectively discussed and debated visions of community, freedom, and diverse collective identities. My research attests that the way difference is understood and welcomed (or regulated) in relation to community is crucial: students cannot engage in a transformative double translation of their worlds if spaces of listening, hospitality (Derrida, 1998), and the critical interruption of agendas are not actively promoted by the teacher and maintained by all. Even social justice pedagogies need to confront their conceptual and cultural monolingualism.

Clearly, these educational aims go against the grain of the dominant cultural contexts we inhabit every day; this means that seeding and cultivating them within any classroom community will require an accretionary, multifaceted and multipronged approach, incorporating a complex range of interventions and pedagogical conditions. In this project, protecting the kinds of relations of difference and translation I've tried here to describe is crucial, a task that returns us to the fertile promise of our own differential traversals: the various traditions of feminist, antiracist, post/anticolonial, queer, and critical pedagogy have all elaborated highly sophisticated frameworks, methods, strategies, and activities for creating various elements (already described) in classroom communities, even while focusing on historically particular discriminatory tropes. In view of the multiply intersectional nature of our students' lived experience as heterogenously positioned subjects of shifting discourses of difference in a range of social spheres, there is an immediate need for us as transformative educators to engage our own boundaries, in a pedagogical translation across competitively opposed stakes that might enrich the cultural spaces of our practice as we collaborate in "the much larger task of creating a just intercultural world" (Bhabha, 2001).

Notes

1. Echoed by countless editorials and political speeches in the aftermath of 9/11, Huntington's theory of the "clash of civilizations" fully affirms this vision of difference: "It is my hypothesis that the fundamental source of conflict in this new world will not be primarily ideological or primarily economic. The great divisions among humankind and the dominating source of conflict will be cultural. Nation states will remain the most powerful actors in world affairs, but the principal conflicts of global politics will occur between nations and groups of different civilizations. The clash of civilizations will dominate global politics. The fault lines between civilizations will be the battle lines of the future" (Huntington, cited in Said, Oct. 11, 2001).

2. I'm referencing Hall's sense of "articulation": how things "can, but need not necessarily, be connected ... in different ways because they have no necessary ... transhistorical 'belongingness'" (1996: 141–142).

3. Almost 30 percent of the ESL students in my research were sponsored by a single parent who came first as a laborer; two thirds of these parents came as nannies.

4. Banting applies to feminist activism the translation concept of an interlanguage: a language that emerges during the learning or translation from a source to a second language, existing as an intermediate system between the two (1994: 175).

5. See Bhabha's discussion of Walcott's poem, "Sainte Lucie" (1994: 234).

6. Space does not allow me to address these questions in this chapter (see Taylor, 2003, in press).

7. *Equity* is defined as an approach to education that does not presume equality between students in terms of their current positions of social status and access to opportunity and resources, but actively works to achieve this through curriculum and policy (McCaskell, 2000).

8. All personal and school names are pseudonyms. Citations from interviews are followed in parentheses with the indication of participants' names, gender, age at the time of the interview, and country of origin.

9. This is the term that the students use to refer to either the country of their birth or that of the majority of their childhood; I use it in order to keep in circulation the many affective and discursive vectors of the term *home* (Bhabha, 1997; Mohanty and Martin, 1986).

10. Asked if he had heard of the words discrimination, stereotype, or prejudice

before learning to use them in the camp, he recalled learning one from two close friends (Ethiopian and Afghani) whose English is better than his; he'd often heard them discuss how "prejudiced" certain TV shows were and looked it up.

11. My conceptualization of translation in sociodiscursive interactions draws from Foucault's (1982, 1972) use of language metaphors to theorize power/knowledge discourses, such that discursive tropes, images, truths, narratives/histories, or identities might be performatively translated texts. In this interpretation I am also profoundly influenced by Bakhtinian concepts of the dialogic and social heteroglossia, in which a subject appropriates language, adapting to her/his own "semantic and expressive intention" words (or texts) that are already "saturated, shot through ... [and] populated with the intentions and accents of others"; my caveat is that, as translators, subjects are never in a prior, pure, or whole state, but already complexly, multiply shaped by competing logics and modalities of affect, meaning, and truth, just as cultural "texts" informing intercultural exchanges were never pure (Bakhtin, 1981: 288–295).

12. The troupe was originally five to six young Angolan women and one Brazilian; they were later joined by friends from Pakistan and Russia.

13. In Canada, this day officially commemorates the fallen Canadian soldiers of World Wars I and II.

14. The choice to translate only the title of this song arose in part from the fact that the students speak Portuguese but almost no Kimbundu, the latter being the language of rural areas outside the capital where they are from, spoken by peasants with far slimmer chances of ever immigrating to Canada. While the students all knew the idea behind this song, the title's translation had to be taken from the notes of a "world music" CD liner, bought here in Canada. The ironies of the differential life and traffic of languages in "the new world border" (Gómez-Peña, 1996) highlight the coexisting forms of globalization described by Hall (1997).

15. My qualification of "dominant cultures" is intended to signal that the dominant culture(s) or discourse(s) at play in specific social spheres and spaces vary widely according to a number of factors, especially in diverse public schools. Particularly in relation to language use, Rampton's study illustrates that there exist a range of symbolic marketplaces (following Bourdieu, 1991) within the larger context of a school: in a certain social space African American hip-hop culture may dominate or define the symbolic value of different languages; in another, this dominance or marketplace may be challenged by established, middle-class "white" culture; in more policed spaces a very narrow official culture of "culture-blind" Anglocentric citizenship may be enforced (Rampton, 1995).

16. While these young women do not share their mother tongue, they speak Dutch together as both have spent a period of time in Holland as refugees.

17. I am not comparing black/white ethnic relations with Indo/Afro-Caribbean relations, but do wish to signal how the complexity of interethnic relations and collective identity negotiation in one society may be further complicated and intensified under the pressures of migration and integration into Canadian society with its marginalizing and culturally reifying structures and inter-/intradiasporic relations among multiethnic populations (Hall, 1997; Baumann, 1996; Whitten and Torres, 1998).

18. The school has a reputation as a black-focused school, and there are posters

of Martin Luther King, Jr., on classroom walls; school trips have included viewings of *Amistad* (Spielberg, 1997), *The Hurricane* (Jewison, 1999), and *Remember the Titans* (Yakin, 2000).

19. Bakhtin also proposes that a single term can exist in more than one language allowing double-voiced/accented/styled speech to ironically unmask the other ideological semantic system. As Wolf points out, however, Bhabha's theory of cultural translation radically politicizes this double-voicedness as an "active moment of challenge and resistance to the dominant cultural power" (Wolf, 2000: 133–134). I believe Mignolo's concept further explores possible modalities of connection across colonizing inequity and cosmological incommensurability that would neither ignore difference/disparity nor declare it absolute.

20. In relation to hierarchy of the source/target language binary in translation studies, Simon writes: "Translation, like ethnography, is faced with issues of asymmetrical authority and legitimacy in the production of cultural knowledge. Wolf uses Homi Bhabha's definition of the hybrid as an 'active moment of challenge and resistance to the dominant cultural power' which transforms the cultural from the source of conflict to an element of production, opening onto a 'Third Space' which accommodates a whole fund of syncretisms, recombinations and mechanisms of acculturation. The Third Space is a space of cultural creation, where translation is a 'grounds for intervention,' creating texts that resist categorization and renaturalization" (Simon and St.-Pierre, 2000: 21).

References

Apter, Elizabeth (ed.). Translation in a Global Market. Special Issue of *Public Culture* 13, no. 1 (Winter, 2001).

Arnold, R., Barndt, D., and Burke, B. *A New Weave: Popular Education in Canada and Central America.* Toronto: OISE Press, 1985.

Bakhtin, M. M. *The Dialogic Imagination: Four Essays.* M. Holquist (ed.), C. Emerson and M. Holquist (trans.). Austin: University of Texas Press, 1981.

Banting, Pamela. "S(m)other Tongue? Feminism, Academic Discourse, Translation." In *Collaboration in the Feminine: Writings on Women and Culture from Tessera,* Barbara Godard (ed.). Toronto: Second Story Press, 1994.

Bassnett, Susan, and Trivedi, Harish (eds.). *Post-colonial Translation: Theory and Practice.* London; New York: Routledge, 1999.

Baumann, Gerd. *Contesting Culture: Discourses of Identity in Multi-ethnic London.* Cambridge; New York: Cambridge University Press, 1996.

Bhabha, Homi K. (ed.). *Nation and Narration.* London; New York: Routledge, 1990.

———. *The Location of Culture.* London; New York: Routledge, 1994.

———. "The World and the Home." In *Dangerous Liaisons: Gender, Nation, and Postcolonial Perspectives,* A. McClintock, A. Mufti, and Ella Shohat (eds.). Minneapolis: University of Minnesota Press, 1997.

———. Keynote Address. Symposium on Globalization and Postcolonialism: Definitions of Visual Culture V. Musée d'Art Contemporain de Montréal. Montréal, Canada: October 5, 2001.

Bongo. "Mona Ki Ngi Xica." In *Telling Stories to the Sea: Adventures in Afropea (3), Afro-Portugal* (CD). New York: Luaka Bop, 1995.

Bourdieu, Pierre. *Language and Symbolic Power,* John B. Thompson (ed.). Gino Raymond and Matthew Adamson (trans.). Oxford: Polity Press, 1991.

Britzman, Deborah P. *Lost Subjects, Contested Objects: Toward a Psychoanalytic Inquiry of Learning.* Albany: State University of New York Press, 1998.

Canagarajah, Suresh. "Critical Ethnography of a Sri Lankan Classroom: Ambiguities in Student Opposition to Reproduction Through ESOL." *TESOL Quarterly* 27, no. 4 (Winter 1993): 601–626.

Cummins, J. *Negotiating Identities: Education for Empowerment in a Diverse Society.* Ontario, CA: California Association for Bilingual Education. 1996.

De Campos, H. *Deus e o Diablo no Fausto de Goethe.* Sao Paolo: Perspectiva, 1981.

Dei, George J. S. *Anti-racism Education: Theory and Practice.* Halifax, NS: Fernwood, 1996.

Derrida, Jacques. *Of Grammatology,* Gayatri Chakravorty Spivak (trans.). Baltimore: Johns Hopkins University Press, 1976.

———. *Writing and Difference* Alan Bass (trans.). Chicago: University of Chicago Press, 1978.

———. *Monolingualism of the Other, or, the Prosthesis of Origin,* P. Mensah (trans.). Stanford, CA.: Stanford University Press, 1998.

de Zavalia, J. "The Impact of Spanish-American Literature in Translation on U.S. Latino Culture." In *Changing the Terms: Translating in the Postcolonial Era,* Sherry Simon and Paul St.-Pierre (eds.). Ottawa: University of Ottawa Press, 2000, 187–206.

Equity Studies Office. "ESL Leadership Camp Facilitator's Handbook." Toronto: Toronto District School Board, 2000.

Essed, P. *Understanding Everyday Racism: An Interdisciplinary Theory.* Newbury Park, CA: Sage, 1991.

Foucault, Michel. *The Archaeology of Knowledge,* A. M. Sheridan Smith (trans.). London: Tavistock, 1972.

———. *The History of Sexuality,* Robert Hurley (trans.). New York: Vintage Books, 1982.

Godard, Barbara (ed.). "Theorizing Feminist Discourse/Translation." In *Translation, History, and Culture,* Susan Bassnett and André Lefevere (eds.). London; New York: Pinter Publishers, 1990.

———. Intertextuality." In *Encyclopedia of Contemporary Literary Theory: Approaches, Scholars, Terms,* Irena R. Makaryk (ed.). Toronto: University of Toronto Press, 1993, 568–572.

———. *Collaboration in the Feminine: Writings on Women and Culture from Tessera.* Toronto: Second Story Press, 1994.

Godard, Barbara, et al. "In Conversation." In *Collaboration in the Feminine: Writings on Women and Culture from Tessera,* B. Godard (ed.). Toronto: Second Story Press, 1994.

Gómez-Peña, Guillermo. *The New World Border: Prophecies, Poems, and Loqueras for the End of the Century.* San Francisco: City Lights, 1996.

Grewal, Inderpal, and Kaplan, Caren (eds.). *Scattered Hegemonies: Postmodernity and Transnational Feminist Practices.* Minneapolis; London: University of Minnesota Press, 1994.

Hall, Stuart. *Stuart Hall: Critical Dialogues in Cultural Studies,* D. Morley and K. H. Chen, (eds.). London; New York: Routledge, 1996.

———. "The Local and the Global: Globalization and Ethnicity." In *Dangerous Liaisons: Gender, Nation, and Postcolonial Perspectives,* A. McClintock, A. Mufti, and Ella Shohat (eds.). Minneapolis: University of Minnesota Press, 1997.

hooks, bell. *Communion: The Female Search for Love.* New York: Morrow, 2002.

Huntington, Samuel P. *The Clash of Civilizations and the Remaking of World Order.* New York: Simon and Schuster, 1996.

Ibrahim, Awad el Karim M. "'Hey, Whassup Homeboy?' Becoming Black: Race, Language, Culture, and the Politics of Identity." Unpublished doctoral diss. Toronto: Ontario Institute for Studies in Education, University of Toronto, 1998.

———. "Becoming Black: Rap and Hip-Hop, Race, Gender, Identity, and the Politics of ESL Learning." *TESOL Quarterly* 33, no. 3 (1999): 349–369.

James, Winston, and Harris, Clive (eds.) *Inside Babylon: The Caribbean Diaspora in Britain.* London; New York: Verso, 1993.

Jewison, Norman (director). *The Hurricane.* Burbank, CA: Azoff Entertainment, 1999.

Lin, A. "Doing-English-Lessons in the Reproduction or Transformation of Social Worlds?" *TESOL Quarterly* 33, no. 3 (1999): 393–412.

Liu, Lydia. "Introduction." In *Tokens of Exchange: The Problem of Translation in Global Circulations,* Lydia Liu (ed.). Durham; London: Duke University Press, 1999.

Luke, C., and Gore, J. (eds.). *Feminisms and Critical Pedagogy.* New York: Routledge. 1992.

Marjanovic, Davor. Question and Answer Session after Première of *My Father's Angel.* Toronto: Toronto International Film Festival, September 1999.

——— (director). *My Father's Angel.* Vancouver: Ranfilm Productions, 1999.

McCaskell, T. *Race to Equity: The Struggle for Change in Our Schools.* Toronto: Between the Lines, 2005.

McClintock, Anne, Mufti, A., and Shohat, Ella (eds.). *Dangerous Liaisons: Gender, Nation, and Postcolonial Perspectives.* Minneapolis: University of Minnesota Press, 1997b.

Michelut, Dôre. "Coming to Terms with the Mother Tongue." In *Collaboration in the Feminine: Writings on Women and Culture from Tessera,* B. Godard (ed.). Toronto: Second Story Press, 1994.

Mignolo, Walter D. "The Many Faces of Cosmopolis: Border Thinking and Critical Cosmopolitanism." *Public Culture* 12, no. 3 (2000a): 721–748.

———. *Local Histories/Global Designs: Coloniality, Subaltern Knowledges, and Border Thinking.* Princeton: Princeton University Press, 2000b.

Mohanty, Chandra T., and Alexander, M. J. *Feminist Genealogies, Colonial Legacies, Democratic Futures.* New York: Routledge, 1997.

Mohanty, Chandra, and Martin, Biddy. "Feminist Politics: What's Home Got to Do with It?" In *Feminist Studies/Critical Studies,* Teresa de Lauretis (ed.). Bloomington: Indiana University Press, 1986.

Norton, B. *Identity and Language Learning: Gender, Ethnicity and Educational Change.* New York: Longman, 2000.

Ortiz, Fernando. *Cuban Counterpoint: Tobacco and Sugar.* Durham, NC: Duke University Press, [1940] 1995.

Pennycook, A. "Introduction: Critical Approaches to TESOL." *TESOL Quarterly* 33, no. 3 (1999): 329–348.

Pratt, Mary Louise. *Imperial Eyes: Travel Writing and Transculturation.* London; New York: Routledge, 1992.

Rampton, Ben. *Crossing: Language and Ethnicity among Adolescents.* London; New York: Longman, 1995.

Razack, S. *Looking White People in the Eye: Gender, Race, and Culture in Courtrooms and Classrooms.* Toronto: University of Toronto Press. 1998.

Said, Edward. *Culture and Imperialism.* New York: Knopf, 1993.

———. "The Clash of Ignorance." *ZNet.* Retrieved October 11, 2001, from: http://www.zmag.org.

Sandoval, Chela. *Methodology of the Oppressed.* Minneapolis: University of Minnesota Press, 2000.

Shohat, Ella. "Introduction." In *Talking Visions: Multicultural Feminism in a Transnational Age,* E. Shohat (ed.). Cambridge; London: MIT Press, 1998.

Simon, Roger I., Rosenberg, Sharon, and Eppert, Claudia (eds.). *Between Hope and Despair: Pedagogy and the Remembrance of Historical Trauma.* Lanham, MD: Rowman and Littlefield, 2000.

Simon, Sherry. *Gender in Translation: Cultural Identity and the Politics of Transmission.* London; New York: Routledge, 1996.

Simon, Sherry, and St.-Pierre, Paul (eds.). *Changing the Terms: Translating in the Postcolonial Era.* Ottawa: University of Ottawa Press, 2000.

Sleeter, Christine. "How White Teachers Construct Race." In *Race, Identity and Representation in Education,* C. McCarthy and W. Crichlow (eds.). New York; London: Routledge, 1993.

Spielberg, Steven (director). *Amistad.* Glendale, CA: Dreamworks, 1997.

Taylor, Lisa K. (in press). "Creating a Community of Difference: Understanding Gender and Race in a High School ESL Anti-Discrimination Camp." In *Gender and TESOL,* B. Norton and A. Pavlenko (eds.). TESOL Publications.

———. "Longing to Become, Coming to Belong: ESL Students' Engagement of Social Justice Leadership Education." Unpublished doctoral diss. Toronto: Ontario Institute for Studies in Education, University of Toronto, 2003.

Toohey, K. *Learning English at School: Identity, Social Relations, Classroom Practice.* Toronto: Multilingual Matters, 2000.

Trifonas, Peter. "Introduction." In *Pedagogies of Difference: Rethinking Education for Social Justice.* New York: Routledge, 2002.

Venuti, Lawrence. "Translation, Heterogeneity, Linguistics." *TTR Traductio, Terminologie, Rédaction: Études sur le Texte et Ses Transformations* IX, no. 1 (1996): 91–116.

Vieira, Else Ribeiro P. "A Postmodern Translation Aesthetics in Brazil." In *Translation Studies: An Interdiscipline,* Mary Snell-Hornby, Franz Pöochhacker, Klaus Kaindl (eds.). Amsterdam; Philadelphia: J. Benjamins, 1994.

———. "Liberating Calibans: Readings of *Antropofagia* and Haroldo de Campos'

Poetics of Transcreation." In *Post-colonial Translation: Theory and Practice,* Susan Bassnett and Harish Trivedi (eds.). London; New York: Routledge, 1999.

Walcott, Rinaldo. "Performing the Postmodern: Black Atlantic Rap and Identity in North America." Unpublished doctoral diss. Toronto: Ontario Institute for Studies in Education, University of Toronto, 1995.

———. *Black Like Who?* Toronto: Insomniac Press, 1997.

Walsh, C. E. *Pedagogy and the Struggle for Voice: Issues of Language, Power, and Schooling for Puerto Ricans.* Toronto: OISE Press, 1991.

Whitten, Norman E., Jr., and Torres, Arlene (eds.). *Blackness in Latin America and the Caribbean: Social Dynamics and Cultural Transformations.* Bloomington: Indiana University Press, 1998.

Wolf, M. "The Third Space in Postcolonial Representation." In *Changing the Terms: Translating in the Postcolonial Era,* Sherry Simon and Paul St.-Pierre (eds.). Ottawa: University of Ottawa Press, 2000, 127–146.

Yakin, Boaz (director). *Remember the Titans.* 2000.

CHAPTER 7

Contesting the New "Young Hegelians"

Interrogating Capitalism in a World of "Difference"

Valerie Scatamburlo-D'Annibale and Peter McLaren

Introduction

> None of the New Social Movements ... can confront capitalism on its own terms ... they have all foundered on the barrier reef of class ... In fact, many of those swept up in the politics of identity have made their peace with capital and have prospered accordingly ... For many of these "cultural radicals" textual analysis is raised in their imagination to the same system-shaking level as revolutionary action ... Safely sequestered in the universities but still playing at resistance, their "discourse radicalism" has led them into a dead end dalliance that fetishizes language. When not promoting the "politics of complaint," these masters of theory-in-and-for-itself engage in the hollow puffery of introspection, creating occupationally safe crusades, and demanding bad faith reforms that deftly side-step the enduring conundrums of class struggle ... Against a sobering background of cheapened discourse and opportunistic politics, the New Social Movements have been stripped of their self-advertised radicalism. A decade ago they contested socialism's privileging of the producing classes and promoted their own alternative theories of liberatory politics. Now they are reduced to the role of supplicants in the most degraded form of pluralist politics imaginable ... the class war rages unabated as liberals and radials alike seem either unwilling or unable to focus on the

> unprecedented economic carnage occurring around the globe . . . What is needed at this juncture is a cadre of engaged intellectuals who can speak the . . . voice of . . . socialism. (Harvey, 1998: 29–31)

We begin with David Harvey's scorching criticism of contemporary post-Marxist, postsocialist "Left" theory and practice since it provides an apt entry point into the main argument of our chapter, namely, the importance of resuscitating the concepts of class, class analysis, and class struggle in this age of globalized capitalism. As Harvey suggests, quite rightly in our opinion, the "discourse radicalism" of contemporary Left poseurs in the academy has led to a fashionable apostasy that has severed the critical links between theory and revolutionary praxis. Harvey's remarks are also reminiscent of those made by Marx (1978: 149) in his criticism of the Young Hegelians who were, "in spite of their allegedly 'world-shattering' statements, the staunchest conservatives." Marx further suggested that the Young Hegelians were simply fighting "phrases" and yet they forgot that to those phrases they themselves were only opposing other phrases, and in no way "combating the real existing world." Taking a cue from Marx and substituting "phrases" with "discourses," we contend, following Harvey, that much of what falls under the rubric of "post-al" theory and politics is rather superficial and esoteric; little more than an academic exercise of nominalism and excessive discursivism. The fetishization of language has led us willy-nilly down a path where politics takes a back seat to aesthetics, where form takes precedence over substance, and where pseudoradicalism replaces genuine political engagement with inequitable social and economic arrangements.

Well over 40 years ago, the renegade sociologist C. Wright Mills (1959) complained about the retreat of the intellectual and the failure of scholars to ask the "big" questions. Of course, Mills was then lamenting the methodological inhibition and fact fetishism of positivistic social science that provided intellectuals with "busy work" by counting more and more about less and less. Yet, the point of his polemic rings true today, albeit in a somewhat different form. Today, equal amounts of busy work are carried out by many "Left" intellectuals in the form of a flighty theoreticism that bears little connection to the realities of our contemporary world. They no longer ask or explore the "big" questions because they've painted themselves into a corner of particularisms, fetishized conceptions of "difference," tropicity, and the rhetoricity of discourse. More starkly, they have also expunged questions of class and the interrogation of capitalism from the theoretical and political canvas. What then, must be done, both theoretically and politically? To these questions there are no easy answers or prescriptions, and we do not purport to offer simple solutions or to exhaust all political possibilities. But if social change is the aim for the "Left"—as it has traditionally been—it must resuscitate a sustained and unrelenting interrogation of capitalism and it must overcome the corrosive skepticism of those narratives that have rendered visions of social transformation as hopelessly obsolete. Indeed, transcending the debilitating political pessimism that characterizes whatever remains of the Left is the most important issue anyone seriously interested in social change must confront (Panitch and Gindin, 2000). The criticisms launched in the following pages are, as we hope to make abundantly clear, not an indictment of theory itself. In short, we are not advocating an antitheory stance. Rather, we are concerned with the kinds of theoretical discourses that have become so common in leftist circles—those that have become sufficiently trapped in the prison house of discursivity and textuality that they have contributed little to understanding the actual complexion of contemporary capitalism; those that revel in theorizing endlessly about gender, race, ethnicity, and class but that tend to say very little about the latter and that have even less to say about the material conditions of actual people. To this end, we must seriously examine the enduring relevance of Marx and the tradition of historical materialism.

The Ghosts of Marx

For years, Marxian theory has been maligned by the prevailing centers of intellectual power as "totalizing," "reductionist," and even "repressive." In the heady, halcyon days of postmodernism's apogee when the ideals of revolution, emancipation, and social transformation were swept away in a swirl of incommensurable language games, the heartbeat of Marxism was flatlined into a stasis that signified coma or death. To overcome the presumed inadequacies of Marxism, an entire idational/discursive apparatus, sometimes called post-Marxism arose to fill the void. Serving as academic pallbearers at the funeral of the old bearded devil, post-Marxists (who often go by other names including postmodernists, poststructuralists, postcolonialists, radical multiculturalists, etc.) have tried to entomb Marx's legacy while simultaneously benefiting from it. Yet, despite the desperate attempts to devise the definitive requiem for Marxism, they have never quite managed to drive that irrevocably terminal nail into that legacy's coffin. The crypt designed for Marx, while reverential in its grand austerity, has never been quite able to contain his impact on history. For someone presumably dead, Mr. Marx has a way of escaping from his final resting place and reappearing with an uncanny regularity in the world of ideas. His ghost, as Greider (1998: 39) notes, "hovers over the global landscape" as he continues to shape our understandings of the current crises of capitalism that haunt the living present.

Irrespective of Marx's enduring relevance and even though much of post-Marxism is actually an outlandish "caricature" of Marx and the entire Marxist tradition, it has eaten through the "left like a cancer" and has "established itself as the new common sense" (Johnson, 2002: 129). Nowhere has this been more evident than in the North American academy where the works of post-Marxists are generally animated by a widespread reluctance to engage seriously Marx's *oeuvre*. This is most often accomplished by invoking academic buzzwords (i.e., universalizing, totalizing, essentializing, etc.), which have gained such currency and become so pervasive that it is no longer necessary to explain what these terms imply. What is particularly paradoxical here is that while many post-Marxists rhetorically celebrate difference, particularity, historicity, and the like, they do not bring these positions to bear when they critique Marxism—that is, they do not put into practice, methodologically, that which they champion in theory. Rather they construct Marxism as a unified phenomenon informed by a variety of erroneous and naïve assumptions and reject it *in toto*. Beyond the baleful farrago of assertions that Marx and his heirs have sunk into a "solidarity of defeat" in the wake of advanced capitalist society, Marxism is considered to be theoretically bankrupt and intellectually passé. In many instances, Marxism has been dismissed as a form of ideological Neanderthalism, an antediluvian memory invoked by those trapped in the mental furniture of a bygone era.

Yet, as conditions for the many continue to deteriorate, as human misery escalates under the rule of globalized capitalism, it is increasingly difficult to ignore Marx. Indeed, when Marx and Engels penned their agitational pamphlet—the *Communist Manifesto*—capitalism as we know it was still confined to a few countries. Today the reign of capital is more absolute than ever and Marxism remains the best implement for analyzing its rule, its nature, and its inner contradictions (Singer, 1999). Marx's description of capitalism as the sorcerer's dark power that has become uncontrollable is even more apt today than it was in Marx's time, despite the fact that Marxism has been relegated by post-al theorists to the Icarian status of failed aspiration. No other individual has been able to analyze the Frankensteinian dimensions of capital accumulation with the same intensity and foresight as Marx. His "ghost" can no longer be ignored at a time when present-day social conditions are reverting back "to those of the 19th century" (Petras and Veltmeyer, 2001: 45). Indeed, key passages of the *Communist Manifesto* ring truer today than they did in 1848 as "key features of nineteenth-century capitalism are clearly recognizable, and even more strongly developed, in the early twenty-first century" (Saad-Filho, 2003: 1).

Ours is a world internationally connected but dominated by the whims of the capitalist class and corporate globalization;[1] a world where the profit motive reigns supreme and where it subordinates every area of society and every corner of culture; a world where the many are oppressed for the benefit of the few. It is a world where free trade has become nothing more than coerced compliance, where local control over economies has been superseded by the most powerful global interests and a world in which "half of the world's one hundred largest economies are corporations" (Starr, 2000: 18). It is a world where "consumer choice" has trumped the notion of citizenship as the preeminent right and where democracy has become nothing more than a buzzword, a "brand" that is marketed along with neoliberal global capitalism as a panacea for all that ails the world. It is a world where imperial ambitions are making a comeback in the form of a belligerent, war-mongering U.S. administration that is doing the bidding for the transnational capitalist class, a world where resources such as oil are determining the future of global relations between nations and affecting the lives of scores of innocent people killed in imperialist wars, a place where cowboy capitalism enflames an unprincipled frenzy of economic deregulation causing financial impoverishment and insecurity for the vast majority of the world's poor. Indeed, we have recently witnessed a rise in abject poverty, unemployment, inequality, and environmental degradation in *every* country of the world (Wallach and Sforza, 1999; World Health Organization, as cited in Canadian Centre for Policy Alternatives, 2002). Today, roughly 2.8 billion people—almost half the world's population—struggle to sustain themselves on less than U.S. $2 a day (McQuaig, 2001: 27). These are the concrete realities that currently exist in our world—tales of desperation, destitution, and despair. Given this sobering context, it seems somewhat perplexing that many "radicals" and "leftists" have championed (in theory) "the decentering of capitalism," the "emphasis on language" and its priority over "social forces," and the "abandonment of revolutionary politics" (Wray, 1998) at precisely a time when a critical and unrelenting interrogation of capitalism seems more necessary than ever. As we shall argue, the harsh objective realities of global capitalism and class exploitation cannot be grasped by theoretical narratives that confine themselves to the discursive realm, that banish class analysis to the dustbin of history, and that, beneath their radical-sounding patinas, merely reinscribe the banality of liberal pluralism and reproduce precisely those forms of idealism chastised by Marx. Rather, these are realities that can be grasped only by attending to matters of capitalist social relations. This implies the necessity of moving beyond what Bannerji (2000) has called the "culturalization" of theory and politics—a theme to which we now turn.

Hyper-Culturalism and Its Discontents

> It is perhaps best to let this "exhorbitation of language" run its course. It seems New Age criticism has chosen of its own invention to enter the prison house of language. If so, it should be allowed to go in and remain there. (Harvey, 1998: 32)

Adam Katz (2000: 57) notes that much of the contemporary critique of Marxism has "become a series of unthinking reflexes and slogans that are mobilized to dismiss historical materialist critique as quickly as possible." Among those slogans, the charge of "economic determinism" has become one of the most common and, by now, hackneyed criticisms of Marx. While there is abundant evidence of determinist versions of Marxism, the charge that Marxism is *inherently* determinist and that Marx himself was an economic determinist are demonstrably dubious (Amin, 1998; Meyerson, 2000). Nonetheless, much of contemporary "radical" social theory can be conceptualized as a revolt against the presumed economism of Marxian formulations. In their rush to avoid the "capital" sin of economism, however, post-Marxists have fallen prey to an ahistorical and generally apolitical form of culturalism that holds, among other things, that cultural struggles external to class organizing provide the cutting edge of emancipatory politics (Ebert, in press; Ebert and Zavarzadeh, 2008). It is necessary to acknowledge that there exists a marked distinction between underscoring the importance of culture and the atavistic rhetoric of culturalism, which not only reduces everything to questions of culture but also has a reductionist conception of culture. This reductionism honors "all manifestations of cultural difference as political" and in doing so not only encourages an excessive particularism but also a "narcissistic dissolution of politics"—one that "has dissolved the very possibility of politics" and the "possibility of culture itself as a field of struggle" (Mulhern, 1997: 48). Despite assertions to the contrary, the cultural cannot wholly encompass the political. In his critique of contemporary cultural politics, Eagleton (2000) argues that theorists working in this vein fail to make the distinction between culture and politics. Not all political problems stem from cultural antagonisms, nor can all cultural differences be classified as political. When culture subsumes everything, politics loses meaning and when everything is political, "nothing is—or nothing is more political than anything else" (Jacoby, 1999: 40). Yet this seems to escape the collective consciousness of those who valorize the "cultural" to excessive extremes.

Even those who invoke Gramsci to accentuate the relevance of the cultural domain denude his thought of its fundamental concern with class struggle and the economic constitution of given social formations, largely because they adopt Laclau and Mouffe's (1985) poststructuralist—not to mention, partial—rendering of Gramsci's thought derived from *Hegemony and Socialist Strategy,* arguably the manifesto of post-Marxism.[2] Indeed, Laclau and Mouffe repeatedly, and mistakenly, took Gramsci's critiques of economism to mean that analyses of economic and class relations were epiphenomenal or subordinate to cultural considerations.[3] While Laclau and Mouffe (1985) did not employ the term *culture* in any strict sense, their theory of discourse as constitutive of meaningful social relations and identities is generally understood as an argument in favor of viewing culture as universally constitutive (Nash, 2001). Taking their cue from Laclau and Mouffe, many contemporary narratives treat the "cultural" as a separate and autonomous sphere severed from its embeddedness within sociopolitical and economic arrangements (Ebert, in press). Such culturalist assertions about the "autonomy" of culture represent the most contorted perversions of Gramsci's thought.[4] His critiques of economism were not intended to downplay the central importance of the economic foundations; nor were they intended to obscure the dialectical interplay of the base and superstructure. What Gramsci was assailing was a specific version of Marxism that tended to reduce everything to the economic level, thereby simplifying the structure of social formations and their complexities by flattening the *mediations* between different levels. As several critics have argued, post-Marxist (not to mention idealist) readings of Gramsci have committed the errors of overemphasizing the status of culture and ideology while deemphasizing the power and function of capital and abstracting class struggle out of existence.[5] As McNally (1997: 38) aptly notes, Gramsci is insistent that the building of

> mass counter-hegemonic movement does not take place on a strictly cultural plane or as some rarefied intellectual process of ideological dissent. Counter-hegemonies, he argues, are created through political struggle, movements in which economic resistance and ideological combat go hand in hand.

In this regard, it is imperative to emphasize that Gramsci developed his ideas to serve not an abstract academic purpose but rather the aim of political praxis. The current deployment of Gramscian terms without acknowledging their origins in political practice and class analysis is, at best, a liberal dilution of his radical formulations and, at worst, a dissolution of his political aspirations into an abysmal, postmodern cul-de-sac. As Verdicchio (1995: 172) argues, if "Gramscian thought may be regarded as post-Marxist, it is due only to its decontextualization."

In addition, Gramsci's appropriation by post-Marxists has too often accentuated the priority of language and discourse. In fact, Laclau and Mouffe tend to portray Gramsci as a "forerunner of a poststructural perspective in which politics becomes entirely contingent, entirely detached from class position" (Epstein, 1996: 134).[6] On the idealist, linguistic or discursive turn in social theory, McNally is again worth quoting:

> We are witnessing today a new idealism, infecting large sections of the intellectual left, which has turned language not merely into an independent realm, but into an all-pervasive realm, a sphere so omnipresent, so dominant, as virtually to extinguish human agency. Everything is discourse, you see; and discourse is everything. Because human beings are linguistic creatures, because the world in which we act is a world we know and describe through language, it allegedly follows that there is nothing outside language. Our language, or "discourse" or "text"—the jargon varies but not the message—defines and limits what we

> know, what we can imagine, what we can do.... This new idealism corresponds to a profound collapse of political horizons. It is the pseudoradicalism of a period of retreat for the left, a verbal radicalism of the word without deed, or, rather, of the word *as* deed. In response to actual structures and practices of oppression and exploitation, it offers the rhetorical gesture, the ironic turn of phrase ... The new idealism and the politics it entails are not simply harmless curiosities; they are an abdication of political responsibility, especially at a time of ferocious capitalist restructuring, of widening gaps between rich and poor, of ruling class offensives against social programs. They are also an obstacle to the rebuilding of mass movements of protest and resistance. (1997: 26–27)

We have quoted McNally at considerable length to emphasize three points. First, the effect of inflating the concept of discourse to the extent that post-Marxists have not only elides the crucial distinction between material reality and thought; it also undermines the critique of ideology (Ebert, in press; Ebert and Zavarzadeh, 2008). Of course, the notion of ideology has been deemed obsolete by several post-Marxist discourse theorists and it is therefore necessary, in this context, to clarify how we are using the term since it has been subjected to a variety of definitions and interpretations. The formulation of ideology that we are invoking is not used to refer to political beliefs—that is, ideology as an "ism" although certain political beliefs would be one instance of ideology. Nor is ideology being used here to draw boundaries or dichotomies between some mythical notion of impartiality and disinterestedness as opposed to ideology. Rather, following Kellner (1978) and Smith (1987), ideology is understood here as those concepts, categories, and ideas that give experience its social form, ideas and concepts that originate within a specific historical formation. Ideology, defined in this way, necessitates contextual understanding for we are required to direct our attention to who is producing these ideas for whom, for what purpose, under what material conditions, etc. Such a formulation directs us to examine where our social forms of consciousness are derived from. In addition, it accords attention to the "actual," practical production and organization of ideas, thereby accentuating the ontological dimensions of "the social." In other words, it seeks to illuminate the material conditions undergirding the production of particular knowledges and to reveal the contradictions that enable the articulation of certain ideas to the exclusion of others. However, in post-Marxist narratives that valorize discourse such questions are marginalized. That is, if "ideas and material reality are given indissolubly together" (as discourse theorists contend), "there can be no question of asking where social ideas actually hail from" (Eagleton, 1991: 219). Contrary to the dominant trend of marginalizing the concept of ideology, we agree with Katz (2000: 85) that a rigorous concept of ideology is more necessary now than ever.

Secondly, it is imperative to note that our critique of an exaggerated discursivism does not suggest a cavalier dismissal of the concept of discourse.[7]

Historical materialism does not seek to undermine the importance of discourse and the cultural and it has no difficulty in accommodating an appreciation of the materiality of texts and the significance of cultural apparatuses in maintaining aspects of hegemony. However, to treat culture as a mere theatre of significations and to detach cultural production from its basis in economic and political processes (as post-al theories are prone to do) *dis-embeds* culture from its constitutive *embeddedness* in the materiality of social life and can emasculate the very practice of radical critique. As Katz (2000: 104) argues,

> the move away from an understanding of culture in terms of . . . the economic makes a radical cultural critique impossible. This is because the autonomy of culture removes any external standpoint from which one could theorize cultural products in relation to systemic contradictions. It follows, then, that one can only critique culture from within, which, I argue, reduces cultural critique to the function of pointing out the uselessness of outmoded cultural forms. This provides an important service for the ruling class, by updating dominant institutions and developing more subtle and sophisticated modes of domination.

There is more than enough room in historical materialist narratives for the concepts of discourse and culture but only when they are used as valuable supplements to Marxism's historical materialist premises and not when they are proffered as ontological alternatives. Nonetheless, what we have witnessed over the last two decades or so is the absolutization of language and discourse divorced from considerations of capitalism. This has been symptomatic across the entire spectrum of what has come to constitute the reservoir of "Left" theory. At the heart of the post-alization and culturalization of politics is the displacement of material reality (the nondiscursive) by the discursive and the abandonment of transformative politics in favor of semiotic play (Ebert, in press; Ebert and Zavarzadeh, 2008). The post-al emphasis on micropolitics and localized struggles transforms what are essentially social struggles into discursive struggles. In doing so, they overvalue economies of desire and discourse at the expense of political economy. In many post-Marxist narratives, exploitation is often reduced to a linguistic process (in a purely semantic universe) that can presumably be struggled against by producing counterdiscourses, alternative representations/interpretations and "ever-alterable articulations" that are as "fluid and malleable as words on a page" (Dyer-Witheford, 1999: 188). It is as though interpreting the world is more important than changing it—as though changing the interpretation is all that can be done to change the world. As Sivanandan acerbically noted, "Marxists interpret the world in order to change it, postmodernists change the interpretation" (cited in Bourne, 2002: 204).

Finally, while it is not our intention to rehash the arguments and counterarguments between Marxist critics and Laclau and Mouffe's post-Marxist sycophants, we would argue that they provide their readers with a choice that is untenable and misleading—a choice between a reductionist version of Marxism in which class position determines politics and a poststructuralist position that seems to suggest that there is no relationship between class interest and politics at all. They suggest:

> Here, the alternative is clear: either one has a theory of history according to which ... an absolutely united working class will become transparent to itself at the moment of proletarian chiliasm—in which case its "objective interests" can be determined from the very beginning; or else, one abandons that theory and, with it, any basis for privileging certain subject positions over others in the determination of the "objective" interests of the agent as a whole—in which case this latter notion becomes meaningless. (Laclau and Mouffe, 1985: 84)

In essence (no pun intended), Laclau and Mouffe succeeded in constructing an entire theoretical narrative around the concept of automization. Social relations, in that context, are not viewed as part of a unitary economic and political system but rather "in a field criss-crossed with antagonisms" (Laclau and Mouffe, 1985: 153). In this schemata, class struggle is but one of many presumed "articulations" of antagonism. Having dispensed with a materialist explanation for history based on a frontal assault on a caricature of Marx and Engel's ideas, Laclau and Mouffe proceed to explain history as a series of contingencies and always shifting antagonisms. In their formulations, antagonisms are not only viewed as autonomous from each other, but there is no way to locate and name a primary course of oppression. Rather, oppression is something that becomes self-articulated and self-defined and presumably has no basis in the larger society. By virtue of their argument, it appears that anyone could assume the identity of the "oppressed" through mere articulation—oppression becomes completely subjective.

If their argument were simply that workers are not automatically, by virtue simply of being workers, socialists, one could hardly find that assertion objectionable.[8] However, Laclau and Mouffe (1985) take an extreme position that seems to dissolve any relationship between class location and politics for they contend that there are no class interests prior to their articulation in discourse. To suggest otherwise would be tantamount to suggesting that these interests exist prior to the discourse in which they are formulated and articulated and, hence, would constitute a form of dreaded essentialism. The problem with this is that oftentimes oppressed and exploited classes do take part in resistance movements but not because they have necessarily articulated their resistance in political terms (in discourse); rather, such resistance often occurs as a result of material impact—the concrete material conditions that they endure may compel them to act. While Laclau and Mouffe are certainly correct in arguing that objective class position does not, in and of itself, transparently constitute a revolutionary subjectivity or subject position, a point that Gramsci made quite forcefully, their rejection of any "interest" that might exist prior to its articulation has the effect of textualizing people's location in actually existing social relations. Indeed, it would appear that a subject position is only "real" to the extent that it expresses itself discursively, and yet history has demonstrated that at times basic economic struggles are precisely those that lend themselves to a deepening of class consciousness as Cohen and Moody (1998: 112–113) aptly note.[9] Laclau and Mouffe, however, tend to downplay such notions and, in doing so, undermine Gramsci's original formulation in which there remained a profound, albeit not transparent, connection between class and politics. Furthermore, *Hegemony and Socialist Strategy* has arguably done more than any other single text to shift the terms of intellectual debate to a discussion of radical democracy and "new social movements" and away from socialism and an examination of capitalist social relations—a point that we will subsequently explore in greater detail.

The Difference of Class

The hyperculturalism that permeates the post-Marxist "new times" exegesis has generally chastised Marxist theory for privileging "class" over other "differences" (i.e., gender, race, etc.).[10] Marxism has been taken to task for its perceived lack of attention to issues of difference and while some post-al theorists fancifully adorned in avant-garde guises have suggested a wholesale dismissal of Marxism, others have tried to reconstitute Marxism as a form of radical pluralist theory in which all social axes (gender, race, class, etc.) are equally important. In such formulations class relations "are no longer 'privileged' but rather seen as only one among a diversity of semiotically constructed identities" (Dyer-Witheford, 1999: 9). The resistance to historical materialism is generally premised on the assertion that foregrounding capitalist social relations necessarily undermine the importance of "difference" or trivialize struggles against racism, sexism, etc., in favor of an abstractly defined class-based politics. It is argued that a politics of difference could work to further the interests of those subordinated by dominant social relations. Yet many advocates of difference politics have not adequately addressed the constitution of class nor have they explored the machinations of capitalist social organization. Rather, they have overemphasized the priority of language and discourse in the hegemonic processes of identity formation to the detriment of acknowledging how the constructions of "difference" (be they based on race, gender, etc.) are structurally imbricated in the antinomic configurations of capitalism and implicated in the international division of labor. As Ahmad (1998: 22) contends:

> Marxism is today often accused of neglecting all kinds of "difference," of gender, race, ethnicity, nationality, culture, and so on. But it is not Marxism that recognizes no gender differences. These differences are at once abolished by capitalism, by turning women as much as men into instruments of production. These differences are also maintained through cross-class sexual exploitation, not to speak of the differential wage, in which women are paid less than men for the same work, or the direct appropriation of women's labour in the domestic economy.

Post-Marxist theorists of difference tend to ignore that capitalism is a "ruthless totalizing process which shapes our lives in every conceivable aspect" and that capitalism also subjects all "social life to the abstract requirements of the market, through the commodification of life in all its aspects," thereby making a "mockery out" of all aspirations to "autonomy, freedom of choice and democratic self-government" (Wood, 1995: 262–263).

Part of the problem, as we perceive it, is the manner in which "difference" has been taken up in post-al narratives. For the most part, the dominant modes of conceptualizing difference have been developed within culturalist frameworks that have, in effect, marginalized and, in some cases, completely ignored the economic and material dimensions of "difference." This posturing is nowhere more evident than in the current constellation of post-al theories of "discourse" and the realm of "ludic" cultural studies that have tended to valorize an account of difference in exclusively "superstructuralist" terms. The pitfalls of this approach are two-fold. First, the reification of "superstructural" differences into "almost intractable social and political disjunctions" has rendered "dialogue and communication among groups impossible" (San Juan, 2002: 337). Any discussion of commonalities, particularly in terms of material and class interests, has essentially been undermined. Secondly, as a result of the inflated culturalism of much contemporary social theory, political struggles have been limited to those over signs, signification, and the textual—something which Teresa Ebert (1996) attributes to the "theory as play" motif epitomized in what she calls "ludic" theory. For Ebert, ludic theory has served to undermine progressive political agendas, and the politics advocated by such intellectual "movements" has generally remained limited to the cultural and the discursive while cutting these off from the material relations underlying the cultural and the discursive.[11] As a result, culturalist narratives have produced autonomist and reified conceptualizations of difference that "far from enabling those subjects most marginalized by" categories of difference have in effect reduced "difference to a question of knowledge/power relations" that can presumably be "dealt with (negotiated) on a discursive level without a fundamental change in the relations of production" (Sahay, 1998: 10). By privileging cultural forms of oppression and circumventing the material dimensions of difference, they have tended to sever questions of difference from analyses of class formation and capitalist social relations—a position which we argue is flawed. We contend that such positions are deeply problematic in terms of their penchant for de-emphasizing the totalizing (yes totalizing!) power and function of capital and for their attempts to employ culture as a construct that would diminish the centrality of class analysis. In a proper historical materialist account, "culture" is not the "other" of class but rather constitutes part of a more comprehensive theorization of class relations in different contexts (Ebert, in press). Furthermore, we agree with E. San Juan (2002: 161), who argues that it is "imperative" to "attend to the political economy of differences" in this era of globalized capital.

How then can we (re)conceptualize difference in relation to class formation and capitalist social relations? The first step, we would argue, is to ground our understanding of difference by drawing upon Marx's materialist and historical formulations that enable us to apprehend "difference" in relation to social and economic organization rather than seeing "difference" as something that is merely cultural or discursive. Because systems of difference almost always involve relations of domination and oppression, we must concern ourselves with the economies of relations of difference that exist in historically specific formations. Drawing on the Marxist concept of mediation enables us to unsettle the categorical, and often rigid, approaches to both class and difference for it was Marx himself who warned against creating false dichotomies in the situation of our politics—that it was perilous to choose between consciousness and the world, subjectivity and social organization, etc. In a similar vein, it is equally perilous to view "difference as a historical form of consciousness unconnected to class formation, development of capital and class politics" (Bannerji, 1995: 30). Bannerji points to the need to historicize difference in relation to the history and social organization of capital and class (inclusive of imperialist and colonialist legacies) and to acknowledge the changing configurations of difference and "otherness." Unlike the "refined particularism and individualism of the politics of difference," which "avoids naming and mapping out the general organization of social relations" (Bannerji, 1991: 84), apprehending the meaning and function of difference in this manner necessarily highlights the importance of exploring (a) the institutional and structural aspects of difference; (b) the meanings and connotations that are attached to categories of difference; (c) how differences are produced out of, and lived within, specific historical, social, and political formations; (d) the production of difference in relation to the complexities, contradictions, and exploitative relations of capitalism.

Moreover, it presents a challenge to those theorizations that work to consolidate an "identitarian" understanding of difference that apprehends difference exclusively as a question of cultural and/or racial hegemony. In such approaches difference is rendered opaque in that it is often unhinged from its historical embeddedness in colonial/imperialist relations and relations of production and valuation. Indeed, in culturalist narratives, the answer to oppression often amounts to creating greater discursive/textual space for the formerly excluded to have their voices heard (represented). Much of what is called difference politics, in this regard, is little more than a demand for inclusion into the club of representation—something that reinscribes a neoliberal pluralist stance rooted in the ideology of free-market capitalism. In short, the political sphere is modeled on the marketplace and freedom amounts to the liberty of all vendors to display their different "cultural" goods. A paradigmatic expression of this position is encapsulated in the following passage that champions a form of difference politics whose presumed aim

> is to make social groups appear. Minority and immigrant ethnic groups have laid claim to the street as a legitimate forum for the promotion and exhibition of traditional dress, food, and culture ... [This] is a politics of visibility and invisibility. Because it must deal with a tradition of representation that insists on subsuming varied social practices to a standard norm, its struggle is as much on the page, screen ... as it is at the barricade and in the parliament, traditional forums of political intervention before the postmodern. (Fuery and Mansfield, 2000: 150)

This passage would be comical, if the political implications of it were not so tragic, for it appears as though struggle has been redefined in the image of a liberal multiculturalism that shouts: "Look, marvel at our inimitable crafts, performances, apparel, idioms—we contribute to making America a colorful salad bowl of differences" (San Juan, 2002: 136). What is offered here as a presumably "radical" postmodern challenge to cultural homogeneity is a "peaceful management of difference" where the celebration of "difference" acts as a "cover for foundational inequality" (San Juan, 2002: 152). As Steinberg (1981) convincingly argued, no amount of glorifying ethnic myths and other cultural symbols of identity can hide or downplay the inequality of wealth, power, and privilege in our society. Multicultural add-ons or changes in the discursive/cultural realm, in this sense, do not adequately address the historical and material conditions of colonialism, racism, etc., in any substantive way. If anything, the passage cited reinforces the discourse of liberal pluralism at its very core. Amin (1997: 137) argues that postmodernism's "penchant for the uncritical adulation of difference" makes it an approach that is "quite compatible with conventional, economistic management practices designed to perpetuate capitalist practices" and that as a result it is an "ideology compatible with the interests of the privileged."

Furthermore, such positions foster a fetishized understanding of difference in terms of primordial and seemingly autonomous cultural identities and treat such "differences" as inherent, as ontological or cultural traits of the individuals of particular cultural communities. Rather than exploring the construction of difference within specific contexts mediated by power differentials, we are instead presented with a plethora of ontological cultural particularities that serve as markers of ethnicity, race, group boundaries, and so forth. In this instance, the discourse of difference operates ideologically—cultural recognition derived from the rhetoric of tolerance and acceptance of difference averts our gaze from power relations and presents a strategy for attending to difference as solely an ethnic, racial, or cultural issue.

What uncritical champions of difference fail to acknowledge is that the forces of diversity are allowed to flourish provided that they remain within the prevailing forms of capitalist social arrangements. Indeed, "difference" has been extensively commodified and sold to consumers seeking a bit of the "other." As Jonathan Rutherford (1990: 11) has noted, from "World Music to exotic holidays in Third-World locations, ethnic TV dinners to Peruvian knitted hats, cultural difference *sells*. This is the 'difference' of commodity relations . . ." In this context, difference is offered to us as one of the many colors of Benetton, a piece of pottery from afar at Pier One Imports, an instant whiff of the exotic from the Body Shop. Furthermore, the neopluralism of difference politics cannot adequately pose a substantive challenge to the productive system of capitalism that is able to accommodate a vast pluralism of ideas and cultural practices. In fact, the post-al themes of identity, difference, diversity, and the like mesh quite nicely with contemporary corporate interests precisely because they revere lifestyle—the quest for, and the cultivation of, the self—and often encourage the fetishization of identities and differences in the marketplace as they compete for "visibility" (Boggs, 2000; Field, 1997). Milner (1994: 150) contends that the cultures of difference are sustained, "not so much by the existence of effectively organized political counter-cultures, as by an effective monetary demand for commodifiable" difference. Finally, the mere toleration of difference/diversity is as Lorde (1984: 111) suggests "the grossest reformism" and also has the potential to undermine emancipatory political projects. Bannerji (2000: 7–8) argues:

> In the case of Western elites and their governments, for example in Canada, Germany or the United States, it would no doubt be far easier for the states to tolerate or recognize cultural nationalism or religious fundamentalism than class based social movements among the immigrants and "foreigners." It is a safe bet to say that if the U.S. government had to choose between a revival of the left wing Black Panther Party and a growing power of the Nation of Islam as the burden of its tolerance, it would undoubtedly choose the latter and offer cultural sensitivity as an excuse. It is the culturalization of antiracist and other oppositional politics in the last decade or so that has largely made it possible for the government of the U.S. or of Canada to maintain the appearance of a democracy.

The uncritical and celebratory tone of various forms of difference politics can also lead to some disturbing paradoxes. For example, if we take to their logical conclusion the statements that "postmodern political activism fiercely contests the reduction of the other to the same," and that post-al narratives believe that "difference needs to be recognized and respected at all levels" (Fuery and Mansfield, 2000: 148), their political folly becomes clear. Commenting contemptuously, Eagleton (1996: 126–127) foregrounds the implications:

> ... Almost all postmodern theorists would seem to imagine that difference, variability and heterogeneity are "absolute" goods, and it is a position I have long held myself. It has always struck me as unduly impoverishing of British social life that we can muster a mere two or three fascist parties ... The opinion that plurality is a good in itself is emptily formalistic and alarmingly unhistorical.

The liberal pluralism manifest in discourses of difference often means a plurality without conflict, contestation, or contradiction. In the realm of politics, this posturing easily lends itself to a form of cultural and ethical relativism that not only renders the very practice of critique impossible but buttresses the status quo. As Norris (1996: 182) states, post-Marxism and postmodernism does "great service to the interests of state and corporate power in diffusing the idea that there is *really no difference* between things as they seem, things as they are, and things as they might be ... it is only by maintaining a sense of these distinctions ... that theory can lay any claim to possessing a transformative or ethico-political force." Moreover, the inherent limitations of the "all difference is good" formulation are also evident if we turn our attention to issues of class. Expanding on Eagleton's observations and adopting the logic that informs the unqualified celebration of difference, one would be compelled to champion class differences as well. Presumably, the differences between the 475 billionaires whose combined wealth now equals the combined yearly incomes of more than 50 percent of the world's population are to be celebrated—a posturing that inevitably lends itself to a triumphant endorsement of capitalism and inequitable conditions. One is inclined to ask how the celebration of such differences could be heralded as "democratic." San Juan (1995) has noted that the cardinal flaw in current instantiations of culturalism lies in their decapitation of discourses of intelligibility from the politics of antagonistic relations. He frames the question quite pointedly (pp. 232–233): "In a society stratified by uneven property relations, by asymmetrical allocation of resources and of power, can there be equality of cultures and genuine toleration of differences?" More recently, San Juan (2002: 152) asks whether the vogue of difference politics has "ever questioned private property or the surplus value created by unpaid labor." Undoubtedly, the answer to that question is a resounding no.

A historical materialist approach adopts the imperative that categories of difference are social/political constructs that are often encoded in dominant ideological formations and that they often play a role in "moral" and "legal" state-mediated forms of ruling. It also acknowledges the "material" force of ideologies—particularly racist ideologies—that assign separate cultural and/or biological essences to different segments of the population that, in turn, serve to reinforce and rationalize existing relations of power. But more than this, a historical materialist understanding foregrounds the manner in which difference is central to the exploitative production/reproduction dialectic of capital, its labor organization and processes, and the way labor is valued and remunerated. The real problem is the internal or dialectical relation that exists between capital and labor within the capitalist production process itself—a social relation in which capitalism is intransigently rooted.[12] This social relation—essential or fundamental to the production of abstract labor—deals with how already existing value is preserved and surplus value is created. Saad-Filho (2003: 35–36) explains that exploitation "through the extraction of surplus value is a systemic feature of capitalism" and suggests that "this system of production operates like a pump for the extraction of surplus value ... exploitation is the fuel that moves capitalist production and exchange. Without surplus value there would be no wage employment, no capitalist production and the system would grind to a halt."

We can take Saad-Filho's observations one step further: if, for example, the process of actual exploitation and the accumulation of surplus value are to be seen as a state of constant manipulation and as a realization process of concrete labor in actual labor time—within a given cost-production system and a labor market—we cannot underestimate the ways in which difference—racial, ethnic, and gender difference—is encapsulated in the production/reproduction dialectic of capital. It is this relationship that is mainly responsible for the gross inequalities and an unjust distribution of resources. A deepened understanding of this phenomenon is essential for understanding the emergence of an acutely polarized labor market and the fact that disproportionately high percentages of "people of color" are trapped in the lower rungs of domestic and global labor markets. "Difference" in the era of global capitalism is crucial to the workings, movements, and profit levels of multinational corporations, but those types of complex relations cannot be mapped out without attending to capitalist class formations. To sever issues of difference from class analysis therefore conveniently draws attention away from the crucially important ways in which "people of color" (and more specifically "women of color") provide capital with its superexploited labor pools—a phenomenon that is on the rise all over the world. The "K-Marting of the labor force" has yielded unprecedented record profitability for transnational corporations, especially in "third-world" countries where a combination of cheap labor markets and violent suppression of union activism has created extremely ripe conditions for the economic exploitation of what Moody (1997) calls the transnational working class. Contrary to conventional political wisdom and the post-al declarations that we live in an age without classes, the transnational working class is in fact growing—there are growing numbers of people who "now depend—directly or indirectly—on the sale of their labor power for their own daily reproduction" (Panitch et al., 2000: ix). Although it is certainly apparent that there have been major changes in the class structure, they have not been "in the direction that post-Marxists point to." In fact, the major changes have reinforced class differences and capitalist exploitation. Petras notes that there are now more "temporary wage workers than in the past" and that there are many more workers toiling in "unregulated labour markets (the so-called informal sector today) than in the past." He adds that the issue of "unregulated exploitation does not describe a system that 'transcends' past capitalism"; rather, it represents a "return to nineteenth century forms of labour exploitation" (1998: 5).

Although post-Marxists encourage us to think of the "extraction of surplus value" as merely one "within a range of dominations and oppressions"—none of which "can be accorded any priority over the other"—they "have seriously mistaken the target of their attack" for the major "source of practical, brutally effective reductionism and totalization at work on the planet is not Marxism, but the world market" (Dyer-Witheford, 1999: 9). Drawing on the work of Dunayevskaya and others, we would contend that because the logic of capitalist work has insinuated itself across the vast expanse of the globe and invaded all forms of human sociability, society can be conceptualized as a totality of different types of labor. Dyer-Witheford seems to encapsulate this quite well when he argues that capitalism

> is a system based on the imposition of universal commodification, including, centrally, the buying and selling of human life-time. Its tendency is to subordinate all activity to the law of value—the socially imposed law of exchange. It relates a monological master-narrative in which only money talks. Such a system operates by process of massive reduction—Marx called it "abstraction"—that perceives and processes the world solely as an array of economic factors. Under this classificatory grid—this "classing" of the world—human subjects figure only as so much labor power and consumption capacity, and their natural surroundings as so much raw material. This reductionism—the reductionism of capital—has today a totalizing grip on the planet. Other dominations, too, are reductive—sexism reduces women to objects for men, racism negates the humanity of people of color. But neither patriarchy or racism has succeeded in knitting the planet together into an integrated, coordinated system of interdependencies. This is what capital is doing today ... In doing so, it is subsuming every other form of oppression to its logic. Contrary to the post-Marxist belief that different kinds of domination politely arrange themselves in a nonhierarchical, pluralistic way the better not to offend anyone's political sensibilities, capitalism is a domination that really dominates ... Indeed, it is possible now to see much better than Marx in his day could how the capitalist international division of labor often incorporates, and largely depends on discrimination by gender or ethnicity to establish its hierarchies of control. (1999: 9–10)

Dyer-Witheford's assertions suggest that it is necessary to acknowledge that most social relations constitutive of difference—including those of race, ethnicity, gender, etc.—are considerably shaped by the relations of production and that there is undoubtedly a racialized and gendered division of labor whose severity and function vary depending on where one is situated in the capitalist global economy. That racism and sexism are necessary social relations for the organization of contemporary capitalism and new forms of emerging neocolonialism seems to escape the collective imaginations of those who theorize difference in a truncated and exclusively culturalist manner. Indeed, it is remarkable, in our opinion, that so much of contemporary social theory including strands of postcolonial theory (ostensibly concerned with marginalized peoples, i.e., the subaltern)—have been so seduced by French intellectual fashion, that they have largely abandoned the problems of class, labor exploitation, and socialist struggle at a time when colonialism is making a comeback in the form of global trade rules and structural adjustment programs. The so-called third world is being reconquered—not with gunboats—but with the protocols articulated by organizations like the WTO and the IMF. Yet hardly a whisper from those presumably most concerned with the "subaltern." Postcolonial preoccupation with indeterminancy, ambivalence, otherness, and the like has "not translated into a serious engagement with the geopolitics of the global assembly line" or the "internationalization of migrant labor comprised primarily of women of color" (San Juan, 2002: 236). Then again this should not come as a big surprise since the majority of intellectual work often collected under the rubric of postcolonialism tends to treat colonialism and imperialism as mere discursive and/or epistemological practices.[13] In short, most contemporary postcolonial theory tends to exhibit far greater concern for the texts of colonialism than the actual relations of neocolonialism manifesting themselves across the globe.

Callinicos (1995: 106) notes that again and again the interest of "various struggles against colonial domination turns out to be the way in which they instantiate 'aporia, ambivalence, indeterminancy' and all the other items of the poststructuralist repertoire" where resistance to Western imperialism is "reduced to yet another variation on the well-worn theme of the endless flow of signification." While we would not discount the problems of representation and the forms of epistemological violence perpetrated by Western theories of knowledge, to reduce the concerns of postcoloniality solely to the regime of discursive relations ignores the reality of capitalism and that what is often called "Western domination is actually a capitalist universalization" (Ahmad, 1997: 58). With sincerest apologies to those post-al theorists who may find this observation too crude for their academic taste, we contend that hegemonic postcolonial theories that tend to view postcoloniality as simply a problem of cultural politics (as Foucauldian-inspired geneaology problems) are woefully remiss and conceptually incapable of engaging material relations of post- and neocolonialism and the configuration of the global proletariat. Postcolonial theory's hostility toward historical materialism and its concomitant metaphysical idealism have revealed "the paralysis and inconsequentiality" of this discourse in "the face of globalized capitalism" (San Juan, 2002: 255). Echoing San Juan, Aguilar (2000: 7) argues that only a class analysis is capable of comprehending the "glaring inequalities that characterise international relations." She continues:

> To begin to know how transnationals operate in conjunction with governments and international lending agencies demands an overarching perspective, a grand narrative that is anathema to postmodernists. As a consequence of this rejection, academic discussions on transnationalism and transculture (trendy topics that elide the economic globalization processes from which they arise) tend to omit, in my experience, any reference to the operations of predatory capitalism embodied by transnational corporations. Academics can indulge in this omission because they consciously chose to talk about "transculture" in purely aesthetic terms safely removed from the international political economy. (Aguilar, 2000: 7)

Like other culturalist discourses of difference, postcolonialism has had the effect of "deflecting critical attention" from an increasingly "racialized" political economy (Bannerji, 2000: 8–9) and has, in some instances, actually served to normalize and naturalize the assumptions of neoliberalism (Ahmad, 1997; San Juan, 2002). If theorists of the various "posts" want to "confront colonization and the production of otherness, it must confront capital" and if they wish "to deconstruct universal categories," they might do well to begin with those categories of "political economy" as Marx did for those that "are the most universal categories in which power resides" (Bologh and Mell, 1994: 86). It follows that in order to counteract the debilitating political tendencies of such narratives, we must critically examine from a Marxist perspective the dynamic mechanisms that enable capitalist social relations of oppression to persist. To this end, Bannerji advocates a broad, class-based approach:

> Having a concept of class helps us to see the network of social relations constituting an overall social organization which both implicates and cuts through racialization/ethnicization and gender ... [A] radical political economy [class] perspective emphasizing exploitation, dispossession and survival takes the issues of ... diversity [and difference] beyond questions of conscious identity such as culture and ideology, or of a paradigm of homogeneity and heterogeneity ... or of ethical imperatives with respect to the "other." (2000: 7, 19)

Bannerji's plea for resuscitating the concept of class comes at a time when class analysis is largely out of intellectual fashion among the gatekeepers of the bourgeois intelligentsia. Class, as we are reminded incessantly, is not everything. Yet we would remind our readers that neither is class "nothing." We agree with Panitch (2000: 368) who suggests that the "costs of the marginalization of class in the intellectual and political arena are becoming increasingly severe, especially in the context of 'globalization'—which is another word for the reach of American imperialism."

Despite the fact that anti-imperialism has generally "disappeared from the political lexicon" of post-Marxists (Petras et al., 1999: 73) and contrary to Hardt and Negri's (2000) giddy proclamations about the death of imperialism, *these are the days of empire.* The court-appointed jester who serves as the president of the United States can barely contain his exuberance for military aggression and might as was recently evidenced when King George swaggered onto the world stage after landing on the *USS Abraham Lincoln* to declare "victory" in the war on Iraq. Without discounting or denying the tyranny of Saddam Hussein and his dictatorial regime, engineering regime change in Iraq was merely a stepping stone in the larger imperialist project.[14] The real prize, according to Pilger, is "nothing less than the world: all the riches above and below the earth and seas" (cited in Street, 2003: 2). The drive toward "American empire" may not constitute a classical imperial mission for control of another territory. It may not be about establishing a set of colonies around the globe. But it does reflect the use of political and military power on behalf of an ideology—a radical, procorporate, antigovernment, free-market fundamentalism—one we are tempted to call the terrorism of global capitalism. The assertion that today's imperialism, represented above all by the corporate elite of the United States, is somehow lessened by the fact that there is little direct political rule of other territories fundamentally misses the central issues confronting us. What is at stake today is the "extreme violent rule of the whole world by one hegemonic imperialist country" (Meszaros, 2001: 73) dedicated to serving the interests of the capitalist class.

Long before the body bags started piling up in Iraq, however, the carnage wrought by free-market policies presumably intended to "help" the world's oppressed populations was already in plain view. Global capitalism has paved the way for the growing concentration of wealth in fewer and fewer hands and a world that is increasingly divided between those who enjoy opulent affluence and those who live in dehumanizing servitude and economic misery. Indeed, we are in the midst of returning to the "most fundamental form of class struggle" in light of current global conditions (Jameson, 1998: 136). Today's climate suggests that class struggle is "not yet a thing of the past" and that those who seek to undermine its centrality are not only "morally callous" and "seriously out of touch with reality" but also largely blind to the "needs of the large mass of people who are barely surviving capital's newly-honed mechanisms of globalized greed" (Harvey, 1998: 7–9). In our view, a more comprehensive and politically useful understanding of the contemporary historical juncture necessitates foregrounding class analysis and the primacy of the working class as the fundamental agent of change.[15]

Our concern about the forfeiting of class analysis is largely directed at the danger of the governing tropes of difference politics that are displacing the issues of capitalist class relations. We believe this is a legitimate concern given the evidence that has amassed. While we have argued elsewhere (Scatamburlo-D'Annibale and McLaren, 2003) that it is virtually impossible to conceptualize class without attending to the forms and contents of difference—i.e., race, ethnicity, gender, etc.—that does not imply that class analysis and struggle are now outdated by the politics of difference. Nor does it imply that we rely on the conceptually anemic race/class/gender triptych that has gained currency in recent years. While this "triplet" can sound both radical and vaguely Marxian, it is not. Although race, class, and gender may invariably intersect in particular contexts, they are not coprimary. On the surface, the trio may sound convincing as a way to articulate the multiple forms of oppression that exist in our world. That is, some people are oppressed because of their race, some as a result of their gender, and others because of their class. This formulation, however, is misleading and often leads to conceptual confusion or what philosophers might call a "category mistake." For it is not that "some individuals manifest certain characteristics known as 'class' which then results in their oppression; on the contrary, to be a member of a social class just *is* to be oppressed," and in this sense, class is a "wholly social category" (Eagleton, 1998: 289).

Furthermore, class is not simply another ideology that serves to legitimate oppression; rather class denotes "exploitative relations between people mediated by their relations to the means of production" (Gimenez, 2001: 24). Such an understanding of class has largely been marginalized by those who invoke the aforementioned triptych. In such formulations, class is usually gutted of its practical, social dimension or treated solely as a cultural phenomenon or category—as just another form of difference. In these instances, class is transformed from an economic and, indeed, social category to an exclusively cultural/discursive one or one in which class merely signifies a "subject position." The category of class is presumed to acquire "its subjective weight as a meaningful identity from cultural elements" and in relation to other (i.e., ethnic, racial, gender, etc.) identities (Buechler, 2000: 126). In such theoretical trickery, class is effectively cut off from the political economy of capitalism and class power is severed from exploitation and a power structure in which those who control and benefit from collectively produced resources only do so because of the value generated by those who do not. To conceptualize class in this manner not only replaces a historical materialist understanding of class with a cultural analysis of class, it also conflates individuals' objective locations in the intersection of structures of inequality with individuals' subjective understandings of how they are situated based on their "experiences."[16] That is, merely because one may not articulate one's sense of self (or identity) in terms of class does not negate the fact of one's objective location within larger class formations. Classes, in other words, "do not come into being by subjective fiat"; rather "they are organized by the capitalist class to appropriate value" (Petras et al., 1999: 63). Therefore, the notion that class is merely a subjective concept presumably dependent on perception, time, place, and in relation to other identities as implied above, confuses class and class-consciousness. Class has an objective status; class consciousness, on the other hand, is undoubtedly shaped and conditioned by social and cultural factors. Class, of course, cannot and has not ever disappeared. However, in being "*identified* as simply one of many plural subjectivities, class has actually been obscured from analytic and political view by poststructuralism's analytic edifice, erected at just the moment that the Left is in dire need of the clarity and direction that class, as a category and an agency, a structure and a politics, can provide" (Palmer, 1997: 72). In addition, as a result of post-Marxist tendencies to treat class as merely another form of difference, the very concept of class has been stripped of that element that, for Marx, made it radical—namely, its status as a universal form of exploitation whose abolition required (and was central to) the abolition of all manifestations of oppression (Marx, 1978: 60).

Post-Marxists regularly invite us to mourn the passing of socialism, class analysis, and class struggle in favor of a post-al future filled with the proliferation of more and more forms of valorized difference, but the narcissism of little differences will never be able to overturn "capitalist universality" (Ahmad, 1998: 22). Instead, such gestures often result in a pragmatic fetishization of particularity and difference that precludes systemic critique, a serious analysis of capitalism and coherent political action. The refined particularism and individualism of difference politics often operate in a fashion that thwarts revolutionary politics and that confuses the epistemological with the ontological. As Harvey (1998: 7–9) argues, "Class struggle, rooted as it is in the objective structures of capital itself, is *ontologically distinct* from those forms of oppression" that drive the agendas of those practicing and advocating the politics of difference. The "expressive content of movements seeking relief from cultural oppressions vary widely across generations" and given their shifting, transitory nature, "clarity demands" we treat them and their incarnations in the "various New Social Movements as being conditioned by the ever-present realities of class struggle." Concomitantly, the "objectivity of capitalist exploitation" cannot be relativized by "treating it as a mere reflex of hermeneutic self-understanding," as a mere discursively articulated subject-position. The struggles involving the politics of difference must be "situated within the overarching context of class struggle." This is especially the case today in light of the increasing polarization of wealth that is "reinstating class privileges for the few, while creating barbarous uncertainty for the many."

Harvey's comments suggest that we cannot abandon class analysis given contemporary realities. Rather, class analysis needs to be deepened in order to explain its connections with configurations of difference. Multiple forms of oppression do exist, but these are best understood within the overarching system of class domination and the variably discriminatory mechanisms central to capitalism as a system. This does not entail engaging in a reductionist exercise of collapsing forms of oppression into class relations. However, social oppression and economic exploitation are much more than tangentially linked to class background and the social relations of production. In treating class as a mere abstraction (when discussing it at all) by removing it from all determinate historical content and the terrain of wider social relations, post-Marxists conveniently forget that the "vast majority of the working class consists of women and people of color" (Foster, 2002: 45). The ways in which the contradiction between capital and labor is lived at the level of everyday life are almost certainly racialized and gendered, but it is important to seriously examine the specific ways in which capitalist social relations shape and configure various forms of oppression. As Meyerson (2000: 1) argues:

> Marxism properly interpreted emphasizes the primacy of class in a number of senses. One of course is the primacy of the working class as a revolutionary social agent—a primacy which does not render women and people of color "secondary." This view assumes that "working class" means white—this division between a white working class and all the others, whose identity (along with a corresponding social theory to explain that identity) is thereby viewed as either primarily one of gender and race or hybrid ... the primacy of class means ... that building a multiracial, multi-gendered international working-class organization or organizations should be the goal of any revolutionary movement so that the primacy of class puts the fight against racism and sexism at the center. The intelligibility of this position is rooted in the explanatory primacy of class analysis for understanding the structural determinants of race, gender, and class oppression. Oppression is multiple and intersecting but its causes are not.

Among other things, Meyerson explodes the image of the "working class" that many people, including many on the left, have about the category—that is, as an exclusively white male phenomenon.[17] To suggest this today is patently absurd since the global working class today is very diverse and in this regard the fact that labor is changing in terms of its racial and gender composition makes the working class a much more inclusive social agent (Panitch, 2000: 369). Meyerson's remarks also remind us of the necessity of a cohesive approach that is able to apprehend the manner in which forms of exploitation and oppression are related internally to the extent that they are located in the same totality—one that is currently defined by capitalist class rule. Capitalism is an overarching totality that is, unfortunately, becoming increasingly invisible in post-Marxist narratives that valorize difference as a primary explanatory construct.

From a historical materialist perspective, the dynamic process of "social reality cannot be grasped without comprehending the manifold internal relations and linkages that constitute the totality of its objective determinations. Several levels of abstraction have to be clarified" (San Juan, 2002: 267). The importance of attending to totality in this manner is based on the ontological insight that phenomena must ultimately be understood contextually and relationally—that one would "always have to specify and historicize the determinations which constitute any given field" (Ahmad, 1992: 21). Rejecting all notions of totality (which post-al theorists tend to do) summarily runs the risk of trapping oneself in particularistic theories that obscure the real connections and relationships that constitute forms of social organization. The valorization of difference, fragmentation, and indeterminancy characteristic of post-al narratives is not sufficient to grasp the current formations of global capitalism that are becoming more and more totalizing—through such a framework we cannot see the overall social relations that organize the concrete experiences of oppression.[18] Palmer (1997: 72) suggests that those "thinkers who have failed to see the transitory nature" of post-al thought, many of "them academic fair-weather friends of Marxism" may well be "among the last to acknowledge the blunt revival of class in the face of contemporary capitalism's totalizing materiality."

At this juncture, some may object to our general orientation and the argument about the primacy of class analysis and the necessity of foregrounding capitalist social relations. However, we agree with Ahmad (1997: 104) who bluntly contends that the reality of oppressive class relations must be forcefully and unabashedly brought to light:

> One may speak of any number of disorientations and even oppressions, but one cultivates all kinds of politeness and indirection about the structure of capitalist social relations in which those oppressions are embedded. To speak of any of that directly and simply is to be "vulgar." In this climate of Aesopian language it is absolutely essential to reiterate that most things *are* a matter of class. That kind of statement is ... surprising only in a culture like that of the North American university ... But it is precisely in that kind of culture that people need to hear such obvious truths.

We believe that the retreat from class (in theory) by "leftists" represents an abdication of ethical and political responsibility especially at a time when the conditions of immiseration are growing the world over. Theory aside, there is a pragmatic justification that is sufficient for organizing around "class." As Reed (2000: xxvii) argues, the goal of building a mass movement "requires proceeding from that which unites as much of the society as possible around a vision and program that most directly challenges the current power relations." For the vast majority of all people—"of all racial classifications or identities, all genders and sexual orientations—the common frame of reference ... the concerns and aspirations that are most widely shared are those that are rooted in the common experience of everyday life shaped and constrained by political economy." Reed's position echoes and incorporates Marx's notion of "unity of difference" in which people share widely common class and material interests. Such an understanding extends far beyond the realm of theory for the manner in which we choose to interpret and explore the social world, and the concepts and frameworks we use to express our sociopolitical understandings represent more than just abstract cogitations. They imply intentions, organizational practices, and political agendas. Identifying class analysis as the basis for our understandings and class struggle as the basis for political transformation implies something quite different from constructing a sense of political agency around issues of race, ethnicity, gender, etc. Contrary to "Shakespeare's assertion that a rose by any other name would smell as sweet," it should be clear that this is not the case in political matters. Rather, in politics "the essence of the flower lies in the name by which it is called" (Bannerji, 2000: 41).

Contesting TINA, or Socialism Without Apologies

> This is definitely not a postcapitalist world, nor is it a post-Marxist one (Foster, 2002: 43).
>
> It is not Marxism but its revisions that are becoming outdated in the era of free market capitalism and globalization. (Kagarlitsky, 1999: vii)
>
> Cutting ourselves off from Marx is to cut off our investigative noses to satisfy the superficial face of contemporary intellectual fashion. (Harvey, 2000: 12)

One of the major critiques of Marxism offered by post- and ex-Marxists suggests that the "avalanche of historical mutations" (Laclau and Mouffe, 1985: 1) has rendered Marxist theory both irrelevant and invalid. The proliferation of struggles, typically grouped under the rubric of "new social movements," presumably indicates ahistorical mutation in the forms of political organization. Whereas "old social movements" were generally organized around class and oriented toward economic issues and social inequality, "new social movements" are allegedly more concerned with "recognition" and cultural change (Fraser, 1996). Hence, it is argued that there has been a shift in social activism from the materialist to the postmaterialist class to identity (difference) and the like. New social movement theory has generally been suspicious, if not hostile, toward class and to Marxist class analysis (Philion, 1998). It is generally held that the rise of new social movements dealt a "crippling blow" to Marxism since advocates and practitioners of the politics of difference and so on were unable to "find a theoretical home in Marxism."

s a result, some have suggested that "the rise of these movements and their apparent incompatibility with Marxism has revealed an important lacuna in Marxist theory" (Hekman, 1999: 2).[19] Rather than socialism, proponents of new social movements championed radical plural democracy that they held would unleash a new, more powerful kind of radicalism, resulting in a democratic revolution that would represent a step forward from the Marxist and socialist traditions. Additionally, many theorists of radical democracy argued that only postmodernism enabled us to understand the complexity and heterogeneity of contemporary social movements and the multiplicity of subject positions (Mouffe, 1988: 34).[20] The cardinal principle for Mouffe is the concept of difference; radical democracy, she argues, "demands that we acknowledge difference—the particular, the multiple, the heterogeneous" (Mouffe, 1988: 36). We have already pointed out the folly of such uncritical appeals to respecting/tolerating difference, yet we believe it is important to reiterate that the neoliberalism of "radical democracy" is completely compatible with capitalist social relations. Capitalism is not necessarily endangered by the ethnic, racial, sexual, gender, etc., "differences" of the social groups that it seeks to exploit; nor is it endangered by single-issue struggles around issues of racism, sexism, etc. Capitalism has already demonstrated that it can survive the challenges of activism based on the precepts of difference politics, for the system as a whole is rooted, above all, in economic exploitation and the abstraction of surplus value. As we have attempted to demonstrate, the failure to recognize capitalism as a fundamental determinant of social oppression and the tendency to delink struggles against racism, sexism, and the like from the international division of labor result in a facile culturalism and a toothless liberal pluralism.[21]

The abandonment of socialism, however, has given way to a concomitant post-al pessimism that has revealed itself as a paralyzing influence on transformative political thought and action. In the years that difference politics has taken hold of large sections of the "Left," global disparities in wealth have increased and more and more people have entered into the exploitative realm of capitalism's productive apparatus. The voguish academic brigandism of those that have given primacy to incommensurability as the touchstone of analysis has had the effect of diverting critical attention from the global sweep of advanced capitalism and imperialist exploitation. In their deconstructive dalliances, theorists of the "post" have abandoned metanarratives (particularly those of Marxism and socialism) while ignoring the most "meta of all metanarratives"—namely, "the creeping annexation of the globe for the dominance of capital over laboring humanity" (Ahmad, 1997: 364). It seems that the only "ism" that hasn't garnered the interest of these self-proclaimed radicals is that of capitalism and to speak of socialism is to invite the self-righteous snickers of those who know that "There Is No Alternative." The best that can be hoped for is a seat at the table of radical democracy, a mere "rearrangement of the existing distribution of power" and some kind of "vague hope for egalitarianism" (Bologh and Mell, 1994: 86). Rather than challenging the core of capital and seeking change in the direction of socialist democracy, post-Marxists have altered the very meaning of change to fit what capital and liberalism are capable of accommodating.

While "radical democracy" has assumed a set of positive connotations given its association with various social movements of the 1970s and 1980s including feminism, environmentalism, gay and lesbian rights, etc., we nonetheless agree with Epstein, who claims that it is a problematic and limited political project for the Left. She argues that

> the term radical democracy is anchored in the "new social movements," a category that did not entirely fit the map of social change activism even at the moment when it was most useful—roughly the mid-seventies to the mid-eighties—and which is considerably less relevant to social movements of the mid-nineties than it was a decade or so ago. The "new social movements" are a thin basis for a left perspective for the nineties. If one regards radical democracy as rooted in the particular kinds of movements described by new social movement theory but associated simply with the range of existing movements, then this is an even thinner basis for a radical perspective. If the left has nothing more to contribute than to refer to the current map of social activism, it has little reason to exist. Furthermore, current activism includes as much on the right as on the left: in fact, the term "radical" is easily appropriated by the right. The turn toward radical democracy involves a turn away from class as a key category of left politics ... The shift away from class ... is a big mistake, especially at a moment when class polarization is proceeding rapidly both in the United States and internationally, and when economic globalization is raising the question of who will hold power and what those who hold it will do with it. (1996: 128–129)

We have quoted from Epstein extensively to make a series of major points. First is the issue of class politics that has been threaded throughout this chapter. Writing in 1996, Epstein could not have anticipated the events of 1999 (the infamous Battle of Seattle) and beyond, but she was prescient enough to argue that the paradigm of new social movements and aspirations toward radical democracy constituted a thin basis for a Left political project in the 1990s. They hold even less conceptual and political rigor as we find ourselves in the new millennium since such formulations are clearly insufficient in analyzing the rapidly changing political landscape that has recently emerged. For example, Joel Harden (2002: 8) has argued that contemporary activism—particularly around anticorporate globalization—has "provoked a shift away from the single-issue campaigning and parochialism" that marked the difference politics pervasive in the 1970s, 1980s, and early 1990s. Today's activists are explicitly naming "capitalism as the source of their problems" and in the course of their resistance, a new generation of protesters is daring to name the *totalizing* system of capitalism that until recently had no name (Gindin, 2002). In her study of the anticorporate globalization movement (ACGM), Amory Starr (2000: 1-3) situates the movement among the "relevant intellectual discussions that pre-date it" and argues that the fact that contemporary activists are "naming the enemy" (that of capitalism) presupposes an ability to coherently and systematically recognize it in a manner that flies in the face of many post-al assertions. The attention accorded to a plethora of different sites of oppression in various post-al accounts wreaks havoc with the attempt to get organized about political economy (and against capitalism), which as she claims represents the heart of the anticorporate globalization movement.

Theorists of social movements and advocates of radical democracy have focused on questions of difference and identity; however, the "empirical realities of corporate hegemony suggest promising possibilities for a shift beyond the difficulties" of politics based on difference and identity. Starr argues that

> the empirical work of critical globalization scholars shows how corporations are using all possible opportunities to exploit women, people of colour, workers, poor communities ... the experience of multiple oppressions no longer requires multiple theories of oppression because corporations multiply oppress ... anti-corporate movements do not deny the idea of multiple oppressions, but centre it in their analysis of the enemy and in their visions of rebuilding the worlds ... They have redefined enemies in ways that do not depend on ... a subtle and fragile "politics of difference"... What is at stake is political economic. (2000: 166-167)

Starr further notes that her study suggests that difference may "no longer be the most important organizing principle for social movements" for they do not "propose that there are multiple truths about the world"; rather "they speak with clarity about the enemy" (Starr, 2000: 167).

These observations would seem to emasculate the theoretical agendas of "academic radicals" who have been busily decentering the analysis of capitalism, deconstructing the category of class and championing multiplicity and difference. The chants of "Another World Is Possible" that echoed in the streets of Seattle, Genoa, Quebec, and elsewhere seem to belie the chorus refrain "There Is No Alternative" (TINA) sung by liberals and conservatives and buttressed by post-Marxists. All over the globe there are large anticapitalist movements afoot and their explicit rallying cries challenge the oppressive system of capitalism in its current "global" and imperial forms. Banners declaring "One World, One Humanity" reveal shades of the kinds of universalism and humanism disparaged by post-Marxists. It seems that those struggling in the streets haven't read about the end of grand narratives, the triumph of

TINA, the death of universalism, and other such vainglorious decrees emanating from seminar rooms. Moreover, recent developments intimate that those who have been crowing about the death of class politics and socialist struggle since 1989 may have been too premature in their announcements, too quick in championing the "new social movements" as the beacons of emancipatory change (Singer, 1999). Perhaps it is time for theorists and advocates of new social movements to acknowledge that which millions of protesters presumably have: that "sooner or later" we have to "confront the inescapable fact that" it is capitalism that "cripple[s] our capacities, stunt[s] our dreams and incorporate[s] our politics" (Panitch and Gindin, 2000: 5). The struggle must therefore be against those debilitating aspects of life under capitalism.

Noted historian Howard Zinn (2000: 20) recently pointed out that after years of single-issue organizing (i.e., the politics of difference and new social movements), the WTO and other anticapitalist protests signaled a turning point in the "history of movements of recent decades," for it was the issue of "class" that more than anything "bound people together." Class, as both a category of potential and becoming, seems to have reasserted itself as more and more of humanity face the destruction and havoc of capitalism's totalizing impulses. There is no doubt that die-hard post-Marxists will still find some variant of "difference" to cling to, the better to avoid the necessarily difficult work of engaging with the nature of capitalism's metanarrative of exploitation, but they do so at their own peril and at the risk of irrelevancy. The changes in political activism we are witnessing today do not indicate that socialism will inevitably come about; nor are we implying that the ACGM (as it is currently configured) is Marxist in terms of its underlying ideological predilections (although large sections of it certainly are, and others clearly employ a Marxist-influenced critique of capitalism). Rather, we are merely arguing that given the present historical juncture, Marxist class analysis has assumed even greater import and that the line of thought derived from Marx is far from obsolete since its enduring legacy lies in its indictment of capitalism. Parenti (1997: 122) contends that

> Marx's major work was capital, a study not of "existing socialism" which actually did not exist in his day, but of capitalism—a subject that remains terribly relevant to our lives. It would make more sense to declare Marxism obsolete if and when capitalism is abolished, rather than socialism. I wish to argue not merely that Marx is still relevant but that he is more relevant today than he was in the nineteenth century, that the forces of capitalist motion and development are operating with greater scope than when he first studied them.

That is not to say that everything Marx said or anticipated has come true for that is certainly not the case; however, Marx did provide us with *fundamental* insights into class society that have held true to this day despite the many and varied changes which capitalism has undergone. As long as capitalism isn't dead, neither is the heart of Marxism; and a return from the "ill-defined and ambiguous post-Marxist theorizing to the tough, simple truths" that lie at the core of Marx's analyses is "an essential condition of effective political practice" (Kagarlitsky, 1999: 74).

Rather than jettisoning Marx and discrediting socialist struggle, there is a need to vigorously challenge the questionable assumptions that have come to constitute the core of "radical" theory, pedagogy, and politics. Endemic class exploitation, racism, poverty, and other forms of human degradation will not disappear if leftists limit themselves to turning texts on their heads. Nor will they disappear if the very system that produces and perpetuates them is decentered or treated as little more than a signifying system. In lending their voices to the symphony of TINA, post-Marxists have served as ideological ventriloquists of the capitalist class and have revealed the utter superciliousness of their radical posturing couched as it is in the netherworld of discourse. Much like the Young Hegelians, they have forgotten that fighting the existing phrases, representations, etc., of the world does not a revolution make. Indeed, such discursive politics do not constitute an adequate, let alone substantively radical, challenge to the bleak material conditions under capitalist rule. Forms of contemporary social theory that have sought to "displace an activist culture with a textual culture" and that have tended to reformulate "in a postmodernist direction" questions that had previously been associated with a "broadly Marxist politics" (Ahmad, 1992: 1) must be vigorously challenged.

Contrary to TINA, the legacy of Marx and historical materialism reminds us that there are always alternatives. As a form of emancipatory critical knowledge that offers a systematic way of making sense of contemporary social life, historical materialism simultaneously serves as an agent for changing it. Historical materialist critique, then, is not merely oriented toward what was, or what is, but also toward what *could be*. In this regard, historical materialism remains the "necessary intellectual ground for all those who seek, not to revel in the 'carnival' of capitalist productive and market relations, but to transcend them" (Foster, 1997: 193). The challenge before us lies, partially, in the recognition that alternatives to capitalism do exist—that they are not merely idealistic, utopian pipe dreams in the face of the capitalist behemoth. Amin (1998) states the challenge explicitly: humanity may let itself be led by capitalism's logic to a fate of collective suicide or it may pave the way for an alternative humanist project of global socialism. Of course, one of the greatest challenges is convincing people that forms of social ugliness wrought by the reality of the new corporate feudalism sweeping the globe can be fought—that this thing called "globalization" is not something historically ordained, the inevitable result of new technologies, the collapse of "communism," etc. In reality, the seemingly inexorable corporatization of the world is the result of specific policies that made it happen—conscious choices of a self-interested minority who, "over the past half-century, have designed, shaped and now control the institutions that dominate global economic activity" (Korten, 1998: 15).

We live at a time when capitalism has become an unrepentant universal system. As such we must base our resistance to it in an equally universalist narrative—that of socialism. On this topic Ahmad is worth quoting at length:

> Contrary to prevailing fashions, I am a shameless advocate of the idea of universality. This is so despite the fact that colonialism has been intrinsic to the kind of universality that we have had so far and that the only universal civilization that exists today is the capitalist civilization. I think that human beings are perfectly capable of waking up to the barbarities of this civilization and making a far better universality—for which my word continues to be "socialism," but you are welcome to use some other word so long as you mean the same thing ... No struggle against ... any kind of collective oppression is possible without some conception of universality." (Ahmad, 1997: 57)

What Ahmad advocates here is a form of radical universalism that animated the work of Marx. While Marx clearly interrogated (and oftentimes mocked) the liberal bourgeois conceptualizations of universalism, it was he who "created the master narrative of radical universalism, its most brilliant version" (Heller and Feher, 1991: 1). Radical universalism is, of course, not a term used by Marx but it sums up the major features of his materialist conception of history and his critique of political economy from the vantage point of his eleventh thesis of Feuerbach. Hobsbawn provides historical succor with respect to the importance of radical universalism in progressive leftist politics:

> The mass social and political movements of the Left, that is, those inspired by the American and French revolutions and socialism were ... held together not by aims that were specific to the group, but by great, universal causes through which each group believed its particular aims could be realized ... The political project of the Left is universalist: it is for *all* human beings. (1996: 42–43)

While we agree that critique of the uncritical, false universalism of bourgeois thought is, undoubtedly, warranted, it is nonetheless essential to preserve the validity of socialism (as a form of concrete, radical universalism) as a political referent for it enables us to forge a third space—one that traverses the rigid boundaries fostered by binary oppositions of universalism/particularism, etc. To this end, radical universalism, or socialism, as Ahmad calls it, remains a crucial weapon in our theoretical and political arsenal. Kagarlitsky (1999: ix) goes as far as suggesting that the global conditions of stark inequality clearly demonstrate the "vital need for a universalist left as the *only real alternative* to diverse forms of barbarism." One is a socialist precisely because universality ***doesn't*** exist at present in any positive, as opposed to merely descriptive or ideological, sense. As Eagleton has argued, "Not everyone, as yet, enjoys freedom, happiness and justice." This is due in large part to the false universalism that animates the rhetoric of "liberal democracy." Socialism, however, "is a critique of this false universalism, not in the name of cultural particularism" but rather in the "name of the right of everyone to negotiate their own differences in terms of everyone else's." The "political goal of socialism" is then not a "resting in difference, which is then just the flipside of a spurious universalism, but the emancipation of difference at the level of human mutuality and reciprocity." This is a development that would be "indispensable for the discovery or creation of our real differences, which can only in the end be explored in reciprocal ways, and which may then well turn out to be different from what we currently consider them to be" (Eagleton, 1996: 118-120).

The historical task for committed leftists today is to seize this moment and develop a transformative socialist political agenda that is grounded in historical realities and possibilities (utopistics rather than utopias as Wallerstein [1998] suggests) and that is able to cultivate a common project committed to overcoming exploitative conditions. In terms of effecting change what is needed now is a collective vision—not one based on discrete differences for such visions have not worked in eradicating oppressive social relations. Socialism remains a theory of social and economic justice rooted in a critique of capitalism and exploitation. Whatever the misunderstandings or confusion surrounding the notion of socialism—largely bound up with a mistaken identification of Marxism with its opposite, Stalinism—the ***democratic*** and ***internationalist*** principles of socialism need to be reinvigorated among those serious about resisting the domination of capital and social relations that create inequality. We agree with Harvey (1998) who contends that while the fragmentation engendered by difference politics and the transformation of capitalism pose significant challenges to conventional ways of imagining socialist democracy, it need not sound the death knell of socialist struggle. It is time, however, to move from the proverbial prison house of language to the slaughterhouse of history, time to move beyond the text to gritty reality. We can no longer afford to remain indifferent to the horror and savagery committed by capitalism's barbaric machinations. We need to recognize that capitalist democracy is unrescuably contradictory in its own self-constitution. Capitalism and democracy cannot be translated into one another without profound efforts at manufacturing empty idealism. Capitalism fails to realize its own truth in practice. But capitalism cannot realize its own truth in practice because it cannot do so and continue to survive as capitalism. It is a constitutive impossibility for capitalism to create equal access to education, to feed and shelter the homeless, and to bring dignity and freedom to the lives of aggrieved communities. Denys Turner notes that "capitalism has to live its own morality ideologically, that is to say, it can sustain its moral convictions only as a way of recognizing the fact that it installs the very conditions under which those conditions are unrealizable. It cannot abandon the moral language it cannot live" (1983, p. 151). Progressive leftists must illuminate the little shops of horror that lurk beneath the shiny façade of "globalization"; they must challenge the true "evils" that are manifest in the tentacles of global capitalism's reach. And more than this, socialists need to search for the cracks in the edifice of "globalized" capitalism and shine light on those fissures that give birth to alternatives. To this end, the corpse of Marx must be exhumed from the necropolis of post-Marxism and the spirit of socialism nascent in the present must be resurrected by those seeking to change the world. Rosa Luxembourg's famous challenge—socialism or barbarism—has never been more apposite as the world has clearly moved closer to the latter.

Notes

1. While we employ the term *globalization* in our work, we believe that the term *globalization* is most often used as a smoke screen to disguise the real nature of the capitalist system. Indeed, the term that best characterizes contemporary capitalism is *imperialism*.

2. Laclau and Mouffe's *Hegemony and Socialist Strategy* has had a major influence in displacing socialism as a point of reference for leftist politics and setting the terms for the discussion of cultural politics and "radical democracy." As is well known, Laclau and Mouffe consign something they call Marxism to the foul Enlightenment brew of foundationalism, essentialism, and universalism. Marx is in effect collapsed back into Hegelianism and historical materialism into idealism. This is accomplished through a variety of fundamentally dogmatic maneuvers that systematically misread Marx and the Marxist tradition.

3. For early critiques of Laclau and Mouffe's "interpretation" of Gramsci, see, for example, the works of Norman Geras, Hennessy (1993), and Wood (1986).

4. While Gramsci's theory of hegemony clearly demonstrated the importance of culture in winning consent to rule, he never discounted the importance of the "economic." Rather, it was Laclau and Mouffe (1985) who dispensed with what they perceived to be a form of residual economism in Gramsci.

5. John Holst (2001) has recently addressed these selective and often problematic culturalist renditions of Gramsci's work in the context of his discussion of contemporary adult educators (see also Allman, 1999, 2001). Holst addresses these shortcomings not only in the contemporary culturalist appropriations of Gramsci's work, but also in relation to the writings of Marx and Freire. In particular, Holst sets out to differentiate between the work of classical Marxist critique as espoused and advocated by socialist adult educational scholars and that produced by what he labels as radical pluralists and post-Marxists. In doing so, Holst returns to the actual writings of Gramsci, Freire, and Marx to reveal the ways in which he believes that radical pluralists, identity politicians, and post-Marxists have vulgarized and domesticated the writings of these revolutionary thinkers—through selective and/or misconstrued

"readings" of their writings—in a manner that is conducive to their various "reformist" educational and political agendas. He contrasts their interpretations of Freire, Gramsci, and Marx with those adult education scholars working from a socialist/Marxist perspective. One of Holst's major premises is that where adult educators locate themselves on the radical-pluralism/radical-socialist divide largely determines their position on the question of political alliances. The radical pluralists, according to Holst, largely champion the cause of the new progressive social movements and organizations dealing with feminism, antiracism, sexuality, and environmental issues because they view this as a necessary defense of the lifeworld and a courageous deepening of democracy through their engagements with civil society. While some socialist adult educationalists seek to forge alliances between the old (community-labor organizations/trade unions) and new social movements, others reject the new social movements outright. For the most part, they reject them on the basis that they cleave away from the basic tenets of classical Marxism, especially when read directly against the work of Marx and Gramsci. Many socialist adult educators, such as Allman and Wallis, believe that while the issues addressed by the new social movements are urgent and important, they nevertheless constitute what Gramsci would call "secondary questions." Holst himself, unapologetically, takes such a position and is deeply skeptical of the new social movements dedicated to "democratizing" civil society while leaving state apparatuses largely untouched. In short, he has little interest in strategies that seek to democratize civil society if that means (and it usually does) that the system of capitalism (and the state's role in facilitating class rule) itself remains relatively unscathed. Contrary to the opinion of mainstream social and political theorists, the power and influence of the state in regulating the capitalist economy have not been vanquished. Indeed, the state continues to play a number of fundamental functions in maintaining capitalist social relations of exploitation—including its complicity in various trade agreements that have buttressed the power of corporations in unprecedented ways (McQuaig, 2001). In addition, the state still serves as a vehicle for viciously repressing social movements through such state apparatuses as the police, the military, and the judicial system. As such, the state remains an important terrain of radical struggle as Holst demonstrates by referring to actual concrete social actions that have been undertaken in France, South Korea, Italy, Belgium, Canada, Argentina, Bolivia, and elsewhere.

6. Epstein (1996: 134) goes on to argue that what "Laclau and Mouffe leave out is that for Gramsci there remained a profound connection between class and politics" and that according to Gramsci, "socialism remained the most authentic expression of the interests of the working class."

7. Harvey (2000: 12) argues that Marx himself was "deeply concerned with language (discourse) and was acutely aware of how discursive shifts (of the sort he examined in depth in *The Eighteenth Brumaire*) carried their own distinctive political freight."

8. Indeed, one of Gramsci's (1971) fundamental concerns was to explore why Italian workers had been drawn to fascism rather than socialism.

9. Contrary to Laclau and Mouffe, who reduce exploitation to a discursive process, the oppressed know differently. For them,

> exploitation takes place in a concrete fashion, in the bowels of everyday contradictions that expel relations of equality. Workers might not be able to

> theorize this, or link it up to a working definition of resistance, but they live such contradictions in their bones ... we do not believe that resistance has to be conscious on the part of workers in order to stipulate that exploitation has occurred. (McLaren and Farahmanpur, 2002: 49)

10. Some sections included under the subheading "The Difference of Class" first appeared in Scatamburlo-D'Annibale and McLaren, 2003.

11. To suggest that culture is generally conditioned/shaped by material forces does not reinscribe the simplistic and presumably deterministic base/superstructure metaphor that has plagued some strands of Marxist theory. Rather, such a formulation draws on Marx's own writings from both the *Grundrisse* (Marx, 1858/1973) and *Capital* (Marx, 1867/1967) in which he contended that there is a consolidating logic in the relations of production that permeates society in the complex variety of its "empirical" reality. This emphasizes Marx's understanding of capitalism and capital as a "social" relation—one that stresses the interpenetration of these categories and one that offers a unified and dialectical analysis of history, ideology, culture, politics, economics, and society.

12. Marx never argued that the contradiction between labor and capital was the only contradiction in society, but he and Engels did argue (quite rightly in our view) that the contradiction was crucial and without transforming it, "other problems and contradictions could not be resolved" (Kagarlitsky, 1999: 77).

13. Of course, there are important exceptions—Ahmad, Amin, and Dirlik—all of whom have assailed the type of postcolonial theory produced in the Western academy.

14. Should anyone doubt the intentions of Bush and his minions, one need only peruse the unsettling canon of the Project for the New American Century (www.newamericancentury.org). There, in plain sight, one will find Bush's blueprint for the establishment of Pax Americana.

15. It is imperative to note that arguing that the working class is the fundamental agent of change is not the same as suggesting that it is the only agent of change.

16. We do not intend to renounce the concept of experience. As we have argued elsewhere (Scatamburlo-D'Annibale and McLaren, 2003: 158–159), we believe that it is imperative to retain the category of lived experience as a reference point. We do not, however, advocate the uncritical fetishization of experience that animates some versions of identity politics. Rather we advance a framework that seeks to make connections between seemingly isolated situations and/or particular experiences by exploring how they are constituted in, and circumscribed by, broader historical and social conditions. Experiential understandings, in and of themselves, are initially suspect because dialectically they constitute a unity of opposites—they are at once unique, specific, and personal but also thoroughly partial and the products of historical forces about which individuals may know little or nothing.

17. As we have argued elsewhere (Scatamburlo-D'Annibale and McLaren, 2003) foregrounding class struggle and the primacy of class analysis does not render people of color as secondary as is often suggested in the culturalist narratives of post-Marxists. Indeed, such formulations often rest on a bizarre but generally unspoken logic that assumes that racial "minorities" are only conjuncturally related to the working class. This stance is patently absurd since the concept of the "working class" increasingly includes blacks, women, and often black women workers as well as other women of color. A good

deal of post-al critique of Marxism is subtly racist (not to mention essentialist) in this regard insofar as it suggests that people of color could not possibly be concerned with issues beyond those concerning their racial identities. This posits "people of color" as single-minded, one-dimensional caricatures and undermines the rich complexity of their lives. Presumably, their working lives are less crucial to their self-understanding than is the case with their "white male" counterparts.

18. We also agree with Eagleton (1996: 12) who argues that discarding the idea of totality has become a convenient excuse for post-Marxists because "not looking for totality is just a code for not looking at capitalism."

19. This, of course, is a questionable and certainly debatable assertion. See, for example, McLaren and Farahmanpur, 2002: 51.

20. Despite the raft of theoretical commentaries that have linked new social movements and a postmodern sensibility, empirical studies have demonstrated that the purported link is quite thin. See, for example, Carroll and Ratner, 1996.

21. Noam Chomsky illustrates this point well while arguing that class transcends both race and gender:

> The United States *could* become a color-free society. It's possible. I don't think it's going to happen, but it's perfectly possible that it would happen, and it would hardly change the political economy at all. Just as women could pass through the "glass ceiling" and that wouldn't change the political economy at all. That's one of the reasons why you commonly find the business sector reasonably willing to support efforts to overcome racism and sexism. It doesn't matter that much for them. You lose a little white-male privilege in the executive suite, but that's not all that important as long as the basic institutions of power and domination survive intact. (1994: 70–71)

Chomsky here suggests that the demands for greater inclusion (i.e., more diversity) are easily co-optable by the institutional structures of power. Indeed, one need look no further than the current administration of George W. Bush, which is often commended for being diverse in its racial and ethnic makeup, for having "people of color" like Condoleezza Rice and Colin Powell in high-ranking positions. Yet, the political ideologies and policies being pushed by these exemplars of diversity and difference are clearly not in the interests of people of color at home or abroad. When the "politics of difference" can be exemplified and embodied in an administration that is very far to the right of the political spectrum, it should encourage honest, progressive people to pause and rethink their chosen political strategies.

References

Aguilar, D. (2000). Questionable Claims: Colonialism Redux, Feminist Style. *Race and Class* 41(3): 1–13.

Ahmad, A. (1992). *In Theory*. London and New York: Verso.

———. (1997). Culture, Nationalism, and the Role of Intellectuals. In E. Meiksins-Wood and J. B. Foster (eds.), *In Defense of History: Marxism and the Postmodern Agenda* (pp. 51–64). New York: Monthly Review Press.

———. (1998). The Communist Manifesto and the Problem of Universality. *Monthly Review* 50(2): 12–23.

Allman, Paula. (1999). *Revolutionary Social Transformation: Democratic Hopes, Political Possibilities, and Critical Education*. Westport, CT: Bergin & Garvey.

———. (2001). *Critical Education Against Global Capitalism: Karl Marx and Revolutionary Critical Education*. Westport, CT: Bergin & Garvey.

Amin, S. (1997). *Capitalism in the Age of Globalization*. London and New York: Zed.

———. (1998). *Spectres of Capitalism: A Critique of Current Intellectual Fashion*. New York: Monthly Review Press.

Bannerji, H. (ed.). (1991). But Who Speaks For Us? Experience and Agency in Conventional Feminist Paradigms. *Unsettling Relations* (pp. 67–108). Toronto: Women's Press.

———. (1995). *Thinking Through: Essays on Feminism, Marxism and Anti-Racism*. Toronto: Women's Press.

———. (2000). *The Dark Side of the Nation: Essays on Multiculturalism, Nationalism and Gender*. Toronto: Canadian Scholars' Press.

Boggs, C. (2000). *The End of Politics*. New York: Guilford Press.

Bologh, R., and Mell, L. (1994). Modernism, Postmodernism, and the New World (Dis)order: A Dialectical Analysis and Alternative. *Critical Sociology* 20(2): 81–120.

Bourne, J. (2002). Racism, Postmodernism and the Flight from Class. In D. Hill, P. McLaren, M. Cole, and G. Rikowski (eds.), *Marxism Against Postmodernism in* Buechler, Steven. (2000). *Social Movements in Advanced Capitalism: The Political Economy and Cultural Construction of Social Activism*. New York: Oxford University Press.

Buechler, Steven. (2000). *Social Movements in Advanced Capitalism: The Political Economy and Cultural Construction of Social Activism*. New York: Oxford University Press.

Callinicos, A. (1995). Wonders Taken for Signs: Homi Bhabba's Postcolonialism. In M. Zavarzadeh, T. Ebert, and D. Morton (eds.), *Post-ality: Marxism and Postmodernism* (pp. 98–112). Washington, DC: Maisonneuve.

Canadian Centre for Policy Alternatives. (2002). *The CCPA Monitor* 8(7).

Carroll, W., and Ratner, R. (1996). Master Frames and Counter-Hegemony: Political Sensibilities in Contemporary Social Movements. *Canadian Review of Sociology and Anthropology* 33(4): 407–436.

Chomsky, Noam. (1994). *The Prosperous Few and the Restless Many*. Berkeley, CA: Odion Press.

Cohen, S., and Moody, K. (1998). Unions, Strikes and Class Consciousness Today. In L. Panitch and C. Leys (eds.), *The Communist Manifesto Now* (pp. 102–123). London: Merlin.

Dyer-Witheford, N. (1999). *Cyber-Marx: Cycles and Circuits of Struggle in High-Technology Capitalism*. Urbana and Chicago: University of Illinois Press.

Eagleton, T. (1991). *Ideology: An Introduction*. London and New York: Verso Press.

———. (1996). *The Illusions of Postmodernism*. Cambridge, MA: Blackwell.
———. (1998). Defending the Free World. In S. Regan (ed.), *The Eagleton Reader* (pp. 285-293). Malden, MA: Blackwell.
———. (2000). *The Idea of Culture*. Oxford: Blackwell.
Ebert, T. (1996). *Ludic Feminism and After*. Ann Arbor: University of Michigan Press.
———. (in press). *Cultural Critique (with an Attitude)*. Champaign: University of Illinois Press.
Ebert, T., and Zavarzadeh, Mas'ud. (2008). *Class in Culture*. Boulder, CO: Paraadigm.
Epstein, B. (1996). Radical Democracy and Cultural Politics: What about Class? What about Political Power? In D. Trend (ed.), *Radical Democracy: Identity, Citizenship and the State* (pp. 127-139). New York and London: Routledge.
———. (1998). Interpreting the World (Without Necessarily Changing It). *New Politics*, vol. 6, no. 4. Retrieved June 14, 2000, from: http://www.wpunj.edu/~newpol/issue 24/epstei24.htm.
Field, N. (1997). Identity and the Lifestyle Market. In R. Hennessy and C. Ingraham (eds.), *Materialist Feminism: A Reader in Class, Difference, and Women's Lives* (pp. 259-271). New York: Routledge.
Foster, J. B. (2002). It Is Not a Postcapitalist World, Nor Is it a Post-Marxist One. *Monthly Review* 54(5): 42-47.
Fraser, Nancy (1996). *Justice Interruptus: Critical Reflections on the Postsocialist Condition*. New York: Routledge.
Fuery, P., and Mansfield, N. (2000). *Cultural Studies and Critical Theory*. Melbourne, Australia: Oxford University Press.
Gimenez, M. (2001). Marxism and Class, Gender and Race: Rethinking the Trilogy. *Race, Gender and Class* 8(2): 23-33.
Gindin, Sam. (2002). Social Justice and Globalization. *Monthly Review*, vol. 54, no. 2: 1-11.
Gramsci, A. (1971). *Selections from the Prison Notebooks*. Quintin Hoare and Geoffrey Nowell Smith (trans. and eds.). New York: International Publishers.
Greider, W. (1998). *One World, Ready or Not: The Manic Logic of Global Capitalism*. New York: Touchstone.
Hardt, M., and Negri, A. (2000). *Empire*. Cambridge, MA: Harvard University Press.
Harvey, D. (1998). The Practical Contradictions of Marxism. *Critical Sociology* 24(1/2): 1-36.
———. (2000). *Spaces of Hope*. Berkeley: University of California Press.
Hekman, S. (1999). Radical Plural Democracy: A New Theory for the Left? *HRC* 4. Retrieved June 14, 2000, from: http://pages.globetrotter.net/charro/HERMES$/hekman.htm.
Heller, A., and Feher, F. (1991). *The Grandeur and Twilight of Radical Universalism*. New Brunswick, NJ: Transaction.
Hennessy, R. (1993). *Materialist Feminism and the Politics of Discourse*. New York & London: Routledge.
Hobsbawn, E. (1996). The Cult of Identity Politics. *New Left Review*, no. 217: 38-47.
Holst, John. (2001). *Social Movements, Civil Society, and Radical Adult Education*. Westport, CT: Bergin & Garvey.

Horkheimer, Max. (1947). *Eclipse of Reason.* New York: Oxford University Press.

Jacoby, Russell. (1999). *The End of Utopia: Politics and Culture in an Age of Apathy.* New York: Basic.

Jameson, F. (1998). *The Cultural Turn.* London: Verso.

Johnson, A. (2002). The Legacy of Rosa Luxemburg: A Critical Reply to Stephen E. Bronner. *New Politics,* 8(4): 128–140.

Kagarlitsky, B. (1999). *New Realism, New Barbarism: Socialist Theory in the Era of Globalization.* London: Pluto Press.

———. (2000). *The Return of Radicalism: Reshaping the Left Institutions.* London: Pluto Press.

Katz, Adam. (2000). *Postmodernism and the Politics of "Culture."* Boulder, CO: Westview.

Kellner, D. (1978). Ideology, Marxism, and Advanced Capitalism. *Socialist Review* 8 (6): 37–65.

Korten, David. (1998). *Globalizing Civil Society.* New York: Seven Stories Press.

Laclau, E., and Mouffe, C. (1985). *Hegemony and Socialist Strategy.* London: Verso.

Lorde, Audre. (1984). *Sister Outsider.* Berkeley, CA: Crossing Press.

Marx, K. (1967). *Capital: A Critical Analysis of Capitalist Production—Volume 1.* New York: International. (Original work published in 1867).

———. (1973). *Grundrisse: Foundations of the Critique of Political Economy* (M. Nicolaus, trans.). Harmondsworth, UK: Penguin. (Original work published 1858).

———. (1978). *The Marx-Engels Reader* (2nd ed., R. Tucker, ed.). New York: Norton.

McLaren, Peter, and Farahmandpur (2002).

McNally, David. (1997). Language, History, and Class Struggle. In E. Meiksins Wood and J. Bellamy Foster (eds.), *In Defense of History: Marxism and the Postmodern Agenda* (pp. 26–42). New York: Monthly Review Press.

McQuaig, L. (2001). *All You Can Eat: Greed, Lust and the New Capitalism.* Toronto: Penguin.

Meszaros, Istvan. (2001). *Socialism or Barbarism: From the "American Century" to the Crossroads.* New York: Monthly Review Press.

Meyerson, G. (2000). Rethinking Black Marxism: Reflections on Cedric Robinson and Others. *Cultural Logic,* 3(1/2). Retrieved December 3, 2002, from: http://eserver.org/clogic/3-1%262/meyerson.html.

Milner, A. (1994). *Contemporary Cultural Theory.* London: UCL Press.

Mills, C. Wright. (1959). *Sociological Imagination.* New York: Oxford University Press.

Moody, Kim. (1997). *Workers in a Lean World: Unions in the International Economy.* London: Verso.

Mouffe, C. (1988). Radical Democracy: Modern or Postmodern? In Andrew Ross (ed.), *Universal Abandon* (pp. 46–62). Minneapolis: University of Minnesota Press.

Mulhern, F. (1997). The Politics of Cultural Studies. In E. Meiksins Wood and J. Bellamy Foster (eds.), *In Defense of History: Marxism and the Postmodern Agenda* (pp. 43–50). New York: Monthly Review Press.

Nash, K. (2001). The "Cultural Turn" in Social Theory: Towards a Theory of Cultural Politics. *Sociology* 32(1): 77–95.

Norris, C. (1996). *Reclaiming the Truth: Contribution to a Critique of Cultural Relativism*. Durham, NC: Duke University Press.

Palmer, B. (1997). Old Positions/New Necessities: History, Class, and Marxist Metanarrative. In E. Meiksins Wood and J. Bellamy Foster (eds.), *In Defense of History: Marxism and the Postmodern Agenda* (pp. 65-73). New York: Monthly Review Press.

Panitch, L. (2000). Reflections on Strategy for Labour. In L. Panitch and C. Leys (eds.), *Working Classes, Global Realities* (pp. 367-392). New York: Monthly Review Press.

Panitch, Leo, and Gindin, Sam. (2000). Transcending Pessimism: Rekindling Socialist Imagination. *Necessary and Unnecessary Utopias, Socialist Register 2000* (pp. 1-29). New York: Monthly Review Press.

Panitch, L., et al. (2000). Preface. In L. Panitch and C. Leys (eds.), *Working Classes, Global Realities* (pp. viii-xi). New York: Monthly Review Press.

Parenti, M. (1997). The Increasing Relevance of Marxism. Retrieved April 4, 2000, from: http://www.job.cyberius.net~/luzah/essays/parenti.html.

Petras, J. (1998). A Marxist Critique of Post-Marxists. *Links* 9. Retrieved December 3, 2002, from: http://www.hartford-hwp.com/archives/26/154.html.

Petras, J., and Veltmeyer. H. (2001). *Globalization Unmasked: Imperialism in the 21st Century*. New York: Zed.

Petras, J., et al. (1999). *The Left Strikes Back: Class Conflict in Latin America in the Age of Neoliberalism*. Boulder, CO: Westview.

Philion, S. (1998). Bridging the Gap Between New Social Movement Theory and Class. *Rethinking Marxism* 10(4): 79-104.

Reed, A. (2000). *Class Notes*. New York: New Press.

Rutherford, J. (ed.). (1990). *Identity: Community, Culture, Difference*. London: Lawrence and Wishart.

Saad-Filho, A. (ed.). (2003). Introduction. *Anti-Capitalism: A Marxist Introduction*. London: Pluto Press.

Sahay, A. (1998). Transforming Race Matters: Towards a Critique-al Cultural Studies. *Cultural Logic* 1(2). Retrieved May 7, 2000, from: http://eserver.org/clogic/1-2/sahay.html.

San Juan, E., Jr. (1995). *Hegemony and Strategies of Transgression: Essays in Cultural Studies and Comparative Literature*. Albany, NY: State University of New York.

———. (2002). *Racism and Cultural Studies: Critiques of Multiculturalist Ideology and the Politics of Difference*. Durham, NC: Duke University Press.

Scatamburlo-D'Annibale, V., and McLaren, P. (2003). The Strategic Centrality of Class in the Politics of "Race" and "Difference." *Cultural Studies/Critical Methodologies* 3(2): 148-175.

Singer, D. (1999). *Whose Millennium? Theirs or Ours?* New York: Monthly Review Press.

Smith, D. (1987). *The Everyday World as Problematic*. Toronto: University of Toronto Press.

Steinberg, Stephen. (1981). *The Ethnic Myth*. Boston: Beacon Press.

Starr, A. (2000). *Naming the Enemy: Anti-corporate Movements Confront Globalization*. London: Zed.

Street, Paul. (2003). "Anti-Empire." *ZNet.* Retrieved February 19, 2003, from: http://www.zmag.org.

Turner, Denys. (1983). *Marxism and Christianity.* Oxford: B. Blackwell.

Verdicchio, P. (1995). Reclaiming Gramsci: A Brief Survey of Current and Potential Uses of the Work of Antonio Gramsci. *Symposium* 49(2): 169–177.

Wallach, L., and Sforza, M. (1999). *The WTO: Five Years of Reasons to Resist Corporate Globalization.* New York: Seven Stories Press.

Wallerstein, Immanuel. (1998). *Utopistics: Or Historical Choices of the Twenty-First Century.* New York: New Press.

Wood, E. (1995). *Democracy Against Capitalism: Renewing Historical Materialism.* New York: Cambridge University Press.

Wood, Ellen Meiksins. (1986). *The Retreat from Class.* London: Verso.

Wray, M. (1998). Left Conservatism: A Conference Report. *Bad Subjects.* Retrieved October 22, 2000, from: http://english-www.hss.cmu.edu/bs/37/wray.html.

Zinn, H. (2000). A Flash of the Possible. *The Progressive* 64(1): 20.

CHAPTER 8

Learning the Real, Theorizing the Virtual II

From Technology to Worlds of Difference

Peter Pericles Trifonas and Paulo Ghiraldelli, Jr.

Experience, Reason, and Education

How do we characterize the phenomena of virtual learning and its environments when we look at its theoretical presuppositions, its pragmatics, and technologies through a contemporary philosophical perspective on experience and education?

Early on in the twentieth century, John Dewey told us that the most important philosophical notion for education was "experience." According to the pragmatic focus of his doctrine, experience was deemed to be not just a relation between consciousness and "the real world," but a living learning environment—a contextualization of educational phenomena generated from the relation between elements of the universe that included the interaction between subjects and objects. Experience, for Dewey, was the central point in his real and virtual cosmology of education and constituted the nature of learning environments. This empirical epistemology posited that knowledge was possible because we *were* our experiences, and education—as the pragmatic ability to solve problems—was a simple job of discovering the dimensions of reality and making meaning from it for ourselves. Dewey was firm in the belief that we should "reload" our experience with diversity, thus enabling us to give life and living new meaning, leading from one experience to another experience at breakneck speed via the epistemological curiosity of the subject. And so, to new kinds of new experience. The regeneration of experience from experience itself constitutes a never-ending cycle of learning and an infinite resource for education. Sometimes Dewey's philosophy shows an odd equation: experience = life = education. Education as a concept and process is grounded in "the real" world of nature, not "the virtual" world of cyberspace. The institutional context of learning in virtual spaces would constitute schooling as an artificial educational environment. Dewey's "philosophy of experience" was undergirded by a theory of social reconstructionism and ethics that focused the pragmatics of education as discovery learning for a moral purpose. He viewed education and schooling as a way to the self-actualization of the subject as a critical citizen with the ability to change society for the better and uphold democracy for morality and justice. Consequently, John Dewey has been called "the philosopher of the Democracy." Education and democracy presuppose a condition for the creation of a "special environment" for public discussion. Not a "virtual" discourse removed from experience through any techno-logical means, but grounded in experience and in the intersubjective possibilities of experience, therefore, meaningful in the subjective formations of reality as a meaningful context for learning within community formations. The authenticity of the real experiences was thought to generate socially conscious subjects able to interpret and evaluate natural and social phenomena for the purpose of informed discussion in the public sphere. Dewey showed us how the sustained exchange of the diversity of perspectives upon experience, with luck, can create the dissemination of new ideas to generate a better world.

After Dewey and the high period of American Pragmatism, two schools of philosophy questioned the belief that we could take the truth of our experiences at face value. Modernity ushered in the age of technological development and industrialization that created learning environments rooted in the economic division of classes by the systems of production and labor. The Frankfurt School tried to persuade us that in the Modern Period objective reflection on experience was impossible. Empirical reality linked reason to the senses. Thus, the effects of nature on the subject could be measured only in relation to experimental procedures that gauged the cause-and-effect relations between phenomena as percieved by a self-conscious ego. Using the Marxist notion of reproduction theory, social interest, and false consciousness, the Frankfurt School drew a picture of Modernity that showed the relation between the subject and real-world phenomena as inevitably ideological and based in the means of production and the class struggles that structured the institutions and social foundations of all capitalist societies. Karl Marx talked about the power of commodification and economic self-interest to influence the formation of subjectivity, but the Frankfurtian philosophers used reproduction theory to further critique the closed nature of the learning process prominent in capitalist and socialist societies. Reproduction Theory was governed by a notion of reason as instrumental—or a calculus for limiting meaning to finite interpretations. Reason defined in this way does not permit a questioning of the ground of subjectivity and the interpretative structure of educational environments. The transparent relationship posited between words or signs and natural phenomena renders the truth an object indisputable. The relationship between words and objects provides the philosophical cover of reason and its claims to truth. The Frankfurt School exploded the idea of reason as "disinterested" and therefore questioned its validity as a basis for pedagogical action, consequently highlighting the need for the creation of effective learning environments that involved thinking rather than the reproduction of acceptable ideas. They critiqued Dewey's notion that all experience was a pragmatic experiment, on the part of the subject, involving interaction, relation, and movement in nature and cultural history. The Frankfurt philosophers defined a special kind of experience. In German, the words *Erlebniz* describes psychological experience and *Erfahrung* refers to historical and social experience. For the Frankfurt School, Dewey's notion of "pragmatic experimentalism" would not adequately conceptualize the idea of "experience." In the *Eclipse of Reason* (1947), Max Horkheimer charged that Dewey seemed to be reducing thinking to instrumental method. Horkheimer objected to the fixed notion of reality and the universal picture of the world that Dewey advocated via a process of reification with problematic trajectories for securing social justice, if the world were to emerge for the epistemic subject through an "instrumental rationality." According to the Frankfurtian philosophers, "instrumental reason" was an objective rendering of reason arriving *after* a social transformation made by Modernity and its technological mastery of nature by human ingenuity. Theodore Adorno and Herbert Marcuse argued that subjects should strive for social and intellectual emancipation from the circumstance of political and economic domination enshrined by the powers that be. This core Marxian tenet applied to the concept of reason promoted by the status quo of the state and its ideology. The Frankfurtian philosophers sought to maximize the subject's capacity for a revolutionary move to a state of freedom and the possibility of self-actualization without external cohersion or force. That meant analyzing the ideological conditions for exploitation and how reason exuded the potential for an interpretative plurality within hegemonic discourses and called for an illumination of the structural conditions of oppression, power, and its working through the educational institution and its apparatus. A negative critique of reason was aimed at derailing the effects of false consciousness on the rendering of the subjective world of experience and learning. This estrangement of the incorporate shell of subjective identity was thought to be a fundamental step to the individual's emancipation from the hegemony of ideology's infusing the site of unabashed exploitation. A counterhegemonic practice well versed in the nuances of negative critique is the intellectual instrument for a sustained resistance to the imposition of meaning from ideologically overdetermined sources outside the self. To liberate subjectivity, in this sense, does not mean to deny self-identity, but to assert independence and control over the homeostatic effects of ideology that enslave the subject to a living-through of the interests and desires of the system.

So, for the Frankfurt School, Dewey's philosophy was a mirror of Modernity and not a reflection of the *rational life* per se. Dewey's conception of experience, it was argued, constructed an empty relation between the subject and reality using a positivist perspective on science to forge artificial links between the consciousness and the external environment in relation to class structures and the economic power base of the status quo. The objection to Dewey that comes from the Frankfurt School forms the basis for an insurrection against the potential tyranny of learning environments constructed through a blind obedience to technological rationalism. The Frankfurt School was influenced by the meditations of Martin Heidegger on technology, thinking, and the principle of reason.

Heidegger argued that in the principle of reason there is an element of accountability (*Rechenschaft*) for the "truth-value" of representation (*Vorstellung*). That is, the judgments made about an object placed and positioned *before* a subject—an ego who is sure of itself, thinks "I" (*sum*) am. The justification (*Rechtfertigen*) of the certainty of such a self-grounding of knowledge yielded of the *cogitation* rests on the security of demonstrating the proof of the "evident correctness" of an explanation. The logic of perception, Heidegger explained, is set back on the source of the response (e.g., the subjective consciousness) as mental instructions directed by language. Reason is sufficiently rendered, "given back," and *it has to be* for the determinacy of the *ens rationis* (intellect) to piece together an *idea of reality.* If and when a "representation that judges" reality can display the "truth" of its propositional outcomes by redirecting the ground of the "connection" between subject and predicate—the "what" of "is"— back to a cogitating "I." This structure of repetition orders the chain of consequence and organizes the syntagm of language in the coming-back of its returning of presence to the "double effigy" of the sign/picture for concept (*Begriff*). It has the function of "holding" or "keeping" the world of beings firmly-fixed (*fest-gestellt*) in the bright light of "objectivity" (*Gegenständlichkeit*), over and against the underlying filter of the projecting self-consciousness of the "knowing self" as *subjectum* or *hypokeimenon,* "that-which-lies-before" (*qua* prior).[1] Heidegger showed how the firmament of the truth of experience depicted as such bears an anthropocentric foundation and the unmistakable mark of a *metaphysical humanism.* To expand in a slightly different way: On the one hand, the productive reflexivity of the ego sustains the "purity" of the ground of its reasoning. Simply put, its "power-of-bringing-back-to-presence" the self-presence of itself ensures the *truth of representation* from within the abiding swells of an inwardly spectating imago of the mind. But this is not enough. On the other, a collective form of the responsibility to *give an account of reason (logon didonai)* is coaffirmed outright by the *auto-poietic* reflexivity—a self-consciousness of self and self-*hood.* It disengages itself from empirical reality to set apart the Sub-ject from Ob-ject, the Self from Other. It subordinates nature to itself and mortgages its fore-closure in a nature that is always ready-to-hand (*das Zuhanden*). Taking these together: the sense of *ratio* understood in the affirmative form of the principle of reason, *Omnes ens habet rationem* (Every being has a reason), is interpretable as a reckoning to account *for* the calculability (*Berechenbarkeit*) of entities (*Seinden*). The subject thus precedes the object in and ensuing the Cartesian age of modernity. Thus, the ground for the predictable equationing of reason convenes the primacy of calculation as the fate of Western thought and rationality.

The *techne* of this amenability of a reductive reason that we have outlined is the characterizing feature of the historical evolution of "philosophy" to "science" that after the epistemological trailblazing of the early Greeks (not the pre-Socratics) stimulates the onto-genesis of modern "techno-science." The method of "Reason" as the "closure" of representation is not, nor could it ever be, outside the *scope of technology and learning environments,* but rather is a precursor of, and, moreover, integral to, *the necessity for a critical questioning of the grounding of the foundation of the institutional frameworking of knowledge.* Mainly because the metaphysical (logocentric) assumptions behind the objective setting of the value of truth are reductive, autarchical, and protective, of the *practical ends of the task of thinking. Reason and the technologies of Reason are not without interest, not without ground or a grounded grounding that withdraws, refracts, is concealed.*

The issue of the "properness" of response becomes more radical after the Frankfurt School and Heidegger in conjunction with what has become a *post*modern "crisis of representation," a suspiciousness of reference and referentiality formed as a question of the *Question of Reason* and its "must" in the space of a virtual signifier.

Knowledge and Techno-Epistemology: The Rise of the Virtual Teaching Machines

A question we must always ask in education and research is: Can truth be reduced to an archive? Is it possible? Knowledge is nothing if it is not grounded upon the possibility of a permanent record of physical data that can then be used to establish "laws of science" as the demonstrable evidence of the self-certainty of the truth of research. Culture depends upon the feasibility of referring to relative archives of meaning to endow expressions of understanding with the evidence of empirical value and predictive power. The failings of conscious memory require the continuing, demonstrable proof of a past and a future to secure the possibility of a genealogical rendering of human experience.[2]

Language intervenes nevertheless to question the validity of laws as denotative statements based on the power of the archive to stabilize the ground of meaning-making. The signs of knowledge thus exteriorized are transformed into the more general category of "information"—its "use-value" not withstanding the effects of representation that mediate for the limitations of human understanding by giving way to the instrumentality of technological reason. Lyotard states that "scientific knowledge is a kind of discourse" (*PC* 3)[3]—a postmodern proclamation. Knowledge is not a technology in itself. The a posteriori of practice is lacking. Knowledge as discourse need not be instrumental. Commands can be disobeyed and disavowed, consciously or unconsciously. We must consider the significance of Lyotard's statement regarding scientific knowledge with respect to language and technology—the two sides of a postmodern techno-epistemological understanding of real-world phenomena through information and communications media (e.g., the computer).

Postmodern epistemological doubt settles in between the apparatus used for the technical manipulation of information and its archival containment of data as virtual signs of understanding. The need for a techno-epistemology—or a view of virtual knowledge that takes into account the influences of technological mediation upon the sources of its production and perception—arises out of the lack of faith in the truth of science. Representation deforms, denatures, and supplements the originary eidetic structures of conceptual formations. Technology redeems a postmodern epistemological doubt by quelling it in the practice of facilitating pragmatic ends through the supplementation of human weakness. Despite ineptitude. Lyotard isolates the origins of technology in prosthetics, or devices that are "aids for the human organs or as physiological systems whose function it is to receive data or condition the context." (*PC* 44) Such a post-Darwinian supplementation of nature readily follows the "principle of optimal performance," (*PC* 44) whereby God-given deficiencies are minimized and one purposeful action "expends less energy than another." (*PC* 44) Technology presupposes the need for the proof of the efficacy of research "as the pragmatics of scientific knowledge replaces traditional knowledge or knowledge based on revelation." (*PC* 44) The concreteness of its manifest structures and operations objectify the union of thought and action. Instrumental reason is born when the root of technology becomes competence rather than invention or *poiesis,* utility rather than creativity or art. Lyotard refers to the fact that after the sixteenth and seventeenth centuries, but especially during the industrial revolution, the quest for "technical apparatus require[d] an investment" (*PC* 45) of capital and energy predicated on the promise of optimizing efficiency for greater productivity, which in turn gave it a "surplus-value derived from this improved performance." (*PC* 45)

The economizing of reason as "instrumental," of course, has commercial implications for the production of knowledge by promoting the logic of end-oriented research. The point is to add to the cultural archive of information for social profit. A lack of ecological and intellectual altruism directs the reason of technology toward capital incentives rather than educational imperatives. Technology is put to use for the benefit of private interests that guide the progress of science and the production of knowledge regardless of the public good. We do not need to give examples; we live them and know them.

The dubious talent of *homo faber* as researcher is revealed in how the raw materiality of the human world can be used as "standing-reserve" (*Bestand*) for material production. That is, a resource always present-at-hand (*Vorhandenheit*) and ready to be used for the artificiality of a ready-made "techno-ecology," whereby nature is brought to a standstill by the enframing (*Gestell*) of a prefabricated world picture (*Weltbild*). Like Heidegger, for Lyotard, techno-science contributes to a postmodern spirit of pessimism caused by feelings of alienation and homelessness (*Unheimlichkeit*).[4]

Technology and capital can coexist; and they do, one supporting the other and vice versa through collaborations and partnerships. However, the epistemological legitimacy of knowledge suffers when the ethics of research are compromised for "learning circulating along the same lines as money." (*PC* 6) And research becomes tied to funding and science to capital for specific outcomes related to application. The economic terms of the exchange then result in what Lyotard calls "payment knowledge" and "investment knowledge," (*PC* 6) whose first priority is not ideological or "communicational transparency." (*PC* 6) The philosophical and ethical disinterestedness of "higher learning" that Kant champions becomes redundant relative to the economic viability of sustaining publicly supported educational institutions.[5] A new academic responsibility toward the production of applied knowledge is thus consecrated in the context of the total subjugation of educational institutions to the technologies of informatization or data creation. A cross-contamination occurs between the "instrumental" and the "*poietic*" aims of research, where and when the specificity of the goals or purposes of knowledge is blurred by economic interests. Education cannot but become the site of modern TECHNO-SCIENCE, Lyotard tells us, although not without a cost to basic research within the university. The amenability of reason to technology is the characterizing feature of the institutional evolution of knowledge from "philosophy" to "science," from theory to practice, and the necessity for the empirical justification of knowledge. The application of reason as the structure and end of research is not, nor could it ever be, outside the scope of a critical questioning of the grounding of the foundation of the institutional frameworking of knowledge. For Lyotard, the metaphysical assumptions behind the attempts made at an objective setting of the values of truth are reductive, autarchical, and protective of the practical modality of a teleological thinking. Reason and the use of technologies of reason in the process of research and teaching cannot be legitimated without interest—without the power of a subjective ground of logic—an ideologically grounded grounding that withdraws, refracts, is concealed by the self-sustaining logic of a closed system exemplified by the epistemological hierarchy of disciplines. In this articulation is reflected the arbitrary structure of social interests actualized via the institutional hierarchy of the disciplines as the practice of knowledge generation gets worked out through the "crossing-over" of science from theoria to praxis. Normative criteria come to govern the optimal performance of "ideas in action" for the purpose of subordinating the quality of information to the augmenting effects of technological performativity. Lyotard calls this accretion of the power of truth—its principle of reinforcing reality through a supplementation of the deficiencies of reality—"the best possible input/output equation." (*PC* 46) This techno-epistemological cultivation of efficient representations of phenomena both prefigures and supports the existence of metanarratives of academic responsibility that appeal to narrowly defined ethical standards of research for the purpose of authenticating and legitimating the means used for the production of practical knowledge. Technology propels the work of science toward the facilitation of an instrumental rationality outside the scope and interests of intellectual inquiry *in* and *of* itself. According to Lyotard, the "rising complexity" of proof becomes the goal for the axiomatic demonstration of truth. Techno-epistemological claims to knowledge require the mysticism of an "other" language of science reconcilable only to the binary logic of its own expression of decidability. The limits of truth are programmatic and incommensurable to the presence of otherness within the interpretative frameworking of a system that constructs meaning according to the "principle of a universal metalanguage." (*PC* 43) Techno-epistemology facilitates the proof of science by modeling the laws of reality as a simulation of real phenomena. It produces a simulacrum of experience faithful to the conceptual structures of experience. Reality is heightened by the virtual expression of empirical knowledge. Technology, it can be said, is more than just the principle of verification required for the legitimacy of research. Scientific proof has power through the performativity of "good verdicts" (*PC* 47) that concretely represent the meaning of experience. Technology "reinforces" science, Lyotard maintains, because "one's chances of being just and right [about a knowledge of reality] increase accordingly" (*PC* 47) through efficient research applications. There is another side to it nevertheless.

Technology cannot bridge the difference between reality and experience because it is predicated on principles of practice governing the consistent production of instrumental reason that mimics verisimilitude. And yet, technology also functions as a difference engine, creating "a plurality of formal and axiomatic systems capable of arguing the truth of denotative statements," (*PC* 43) but is unable to show how empirical proofs support the logic of conclusions. Techno-epistemology illustrates the postmodern paradox of science as applied research when the status of reality is questioned and academic responsibility is at stake. For Lyotard, "proof is problematical since proof needs to be proven." (*PC* 44) Technology does not compute (for) interpretative alterity, and so, unwittingly augments the unlikely probability of its commensurability or the conceptual reduction of difference via a paradigmatic rendering of the full presence of the other within the possibility of a mechanized reproduction of the same. Ironically, the result of techno-epistemology is a crisis of legitimation in the postmodern age of science. The rapid proliferation of paradoxical theorems and conflicting findings undermines the power of the grand master narratives to persuade research worlds to reach a consensus of meaning. The principles of techno-epistemology create a performativity of simulations that offer a substitute for empirical proof. For the purposes of legitimation, the outcomes of applied research practices come to determine the effectivity of scientific inquiry. Technology, however, exacerbates the postmodern condition of incommensurability between the metanarratives of science because it "cannot fail to influence the truth criterion." (*PC* 46) The paradoxes of techno-epistemology are produced by the proliferation of competing interpretations that threaten the credibility and legitimacy of claims to knowledge. Science surrenders to paralogy: the game of language played from within the axiological framework of a system of meaning-making to undermine the self-certain truth of research.

Legitimation Crisis and Language Games

It is not difficult to ascertain why Lyotard cautions against adopting the principles of techno-epistemology without reservation. He believes that the instrumental aims of corporate and government funding of research for the purpose of orienting the efficiency of scientific performativity "subordinate the institutions of higher learning to the existing powers." (*PC* 50) The pursuit of a techno-epistemological justification of knowledge is not necessarily a "bad" thing. That is, if it is just one more available method of testing, among others, to query the validity of scientific protocol. The desire to implement a system of research based on the logic of performativity is, however, misguided. An "imperative of performance" placed upon the "task of science" to generate usable information supports the "'organic' connection between technology and profit." (*PC* 45) This is true. Although to be fair, the application of knowledge can be ethical whether it is originally directed or not. Free will is involved. And Lyotard does leave room for the power of the imagination and aesthetic inspiration to shape scientific discovery as an intangible influence upon the limitations of instrumental reason. But, if the point of research is to improve the performance of the social system through a techno-epistemological rendering of science, then what can learning be tied to other than the creation of "skills that are indispensable to that system"? (*PC* 48)

Here again in Lyotard's postmodern futurology are echoes of our contemporary dilemma, especially in the higher echelons of the education machine. Now, more than ever, the surplus-value of knowledge is molded though the use-value of technology because global competition requires the citizen to be capable of supporting the economic mission of the nation-state on an international scale. On the one hand, Lyotard predicts that there will therefore be a "growth in demand for experts and high and middle management executives" (*PC* 48) in "any discipline with applicability to training in 'telematics' (computer scientists, cyberneticists, linguists, mathematicians, logicians...)" (*PC* 48) We most certainly have seen this to be the case with the explosion of the World Wide Web and the Internet and the rapid rise of a new global economy of virtual proportions. The architecture of technology itself is not the obstacle to intellectual and economic self-actualization now as much accessibility to it is. On the other hand, Lyotard sees the delegitimization of liberal education and a discrediting of its "emancipation narrative" (*PC* 48) that has informed the disciplinary construction of knowledge within institutions of higher learning since the beginnings of the modern university in Prussia under the guidance of Wilhelm von Humboldt. The need to create citizen subjects "with the skills [to fulfill] society's own needs" (*PC* 48) diminishes the necessity for dabbling in philosophical ideals, so there are only

> so many doctors, so many teachers in a given discipline, so many engineers, so many administrators, etc. The transmission of knowledge is no longer designed to train an elite capable of guiding the nation toward its emancipation, but to supply the system with players capable of acceptably fufilling their roles at the pragmatic posts required by its institutions. (*PC* 48)

Learning in the postindustrial age promotes the development of skills, for competence and productivity, not the value of speculation, for invention and discovery. No interest is taken in science for its own sake. The principles of "liberal humanism" no longer ground the model of an emancipatory education through which autonomous self-actualization is attainable. Occupational horizons and careerism do. Consequently, the professionalization of work is informed by the ethical imperative of gathering the situational knowledge needed to perform and excel at a job skill as opposed to engaging in the speculative production of knowledge for general inquiry. Functionalism overtakes learning. But this could not happen without the delegitimation of philosophy and science in light of the distinction between theory and practice that collapses under the weight of an interdisciplinary questioning of the universal premises of truth. Postmodernism can be held accountable here, if it is as Lyotard states, "an incredulity toward metanarratives" (*PC* xxiv) or legitimating stories that seek to explain the meaning of experience. To quell epistemological doubt and control the transmission of established knowledges, didactics takes over learning after the ground of certainty has disappeared under it.[6] Method supersedes for the reproduction of a cultural archive and its paradigmatic and self-conscious teachings. The result after postmodernism is that philosophy and science are no more capable of extrapolating truth than any other disciplines, since the decline of the grand narrative, "whether it is a speculative narrative or a narrative of emancipation," (*PC* 37) reduces knowledge to a method of language games.

It is crucial to recognize the semantic elision that Lyotard makes—but does not specifically state—between the archiving of knowledge and the constitutive means and methods of doing so, that delegitimize grand narratives and create a crisis of meaning. The paradigmatic shift from discourse to technology changes the social and epistemological definitions of research and truth. Not to mention the cognitive and affective preconditions of teaching and learning. The speculative dimension of reason comes into question after the instrumental push of technology to recode human experience according to its own nature is made. And yet, teaching and learning require creativity and imagination. It is moved forward by epistemological curiosity—the quest for infinite human progress—and not the inculcation of procedural outcomes that render subjectivity as the products of coded instructions performed via electronic commands. Lyotard is enamored neither by the prospects of a "cyborg subjectivity"—and the potential it foresees for a new information society of techno-automatons—nor by the vision of a learning culture that prioritizes the ethical value of the digital enterprising of knowledge. He details how research in such a techno-epistemological milieu will begin to be legitimated according to the power of information as a commodity to be used by nation-states "in the world wide competition for power." (*PC* 5) Lyotard's predictions about the future of knowledge in an economic globalization here are uncanny—"the breakdown of the hegemony of American capitalism, the decline of the socialist alternative, a probable opening of the Chinese market." (*PC* 6) Furthermore, he envisions the influence of the digital age on higher education. He anticipates the miniaturization of technology and the increase in computing power through which "learning is translated into quantities of information." (*PC* 4) These "bytes of knowledge"—channeled by finite systems of translation with discreet programmable languages—will produce highly directed areas of inquiry. Consequently, the legitimacy of research is determined in accordance with its potential viability to serve "industrial and commercial strategies on the one hand, and the political and military strategies on the other." (*PC* 5) The field of scientific inquiry narrows drastically when it is tied to the circulation of capital. Basic or fundamental research becomes shaped in relation to the interests of multinational corporations and nation-states vying for control of information.

In a postindustrial, postmodern age, where knowledge is reinterpreted as information—and its value is determined by the capacity to incite profitable exchanges between social actors—Lyotard explains how learning is also commodified in the public sphere. Education no longer becomes the sole "purview of the State," (*PC* 5) but is determined through the socioeconomic and ideologico-political forces that structure and mercantilize knowledge. An information society and its "new economy" is predicated to grow through the open exchange of information on a global scale. Lyotard was perhaps the first modern philosopher after Martin Heidegger to predict the future impact of technology on knowledge without referring to more recent inventions such as the World Wide Web and the Internet. The need for the flow of information supersedes and overrides the necessity to censor the quality of the information made available. *All information is created equal.* That is the motto of the new information age and its pseudointellectual economy. Lyotard outlines the implications of what this contemporary perspective proselytizes. The hidden significance of information is posed as a future problem of equitable access to data: "Who will know?" (*PC* 6). Ideology is now joined to the question of the status of knowledge. Another more personal question arises: "Why should I know?" Quite simply, because the telematic system of communication and its open exchanging of messages that techno-epistemology has effectualized now oblige a citizenry to be responsible for the dissemination and growth of information. And, of course, the obligation extends to the direction of the language games of science that are played in the public sphere. Ignorance of technology no longer contitutes an excuse when the stakes for a way of life and living are high.

Language is the foundation of technology and of science. Narrative constitutes the source of subjectivity. Postmodern doubt complicates the self-certainty of identity from which the empirical value of science as a discourse of truthful knowledge is constructed vis-à-vis the Greek *logos.* Lyotard appropriates the Wittgensteinian concept of "language games"—the rules of expression governing the constative and performative instances of utterance within the field of communication—to articulate the paradoxical essence of knowledge under the influence of a postindustrial techno-epistemology. Narration is antagonistic to "hard science" because it exposes data to an interpretative modality of analysis that in effect cannot be controlled. For Lyotard, narrative creates an *agonistics,* whereby a community of truth is transformed into a community of dissensus through *paralogy,* or the proliferation of paradoxical discourses that contradict meaning though the games played with the rules of science via language. At least, this is Lyotard's hypothesis. The problem with language games—and all "games theory" in general—is the supposition that each "move" both incites and merits a "counter-move" to offset the structure of the system, to keep it in balance. The binary modality of the logic is totalizing as well as simplistic: if there are no rules, there is no game; if there is a move, it requires a response. This is not necessarily the case. Sometimes a game has only one player who knows the game is being played. Technology renders the use-value of knowledge incalculable as new information is produced, publicly archived, and made accessible at a faster rate than ever before in history. Interpretability is open. Information can be recoded into existing systems of knowledge and can be used to build new structures and frameworks of understanding. Language enables the constant changing of rules that characterize the validity of a denotative or prescriptive statement referring to a state of knowledge or knowing. So, it is essential for those in the private and public domains who may well benefit from it the most to attempt to stimulate the circulation of messages that are "rich in information and easy to decode." (*PC* 5)

From Technology to Worlds of Difference

Now, more than ever, there is an obligation to recognize the presence of infinite possibilities and multiple horizons of alterity that destabilize the grounding of knowledge and subjectivity in worlds of difference. This responsibility highlights the problem of exposing or creating locations within communitarian-based cultures that still occupy the colonized space of traditional knowledge archives and are at the same time alterior to the logic of the status quo.[7] If so, how and where are gestures toward the spaces of these new locations enacted as worlds of difference by which we define the difference of ourselves as another?

The inside and outside borders of any cultural spaces we define according to the age-old concept of community open up the material locations within which theory and praxis are renewed through the syncretic nature of subjectivity as a condition of impossibility fueled by a global vision of a shared community's running rampant today around the technology. The idea of global citizenship nurtures the idea of a communal proclivity of the autotelic Subject and produces the call for a leveling of difference in what Jacques Derrida has called the cosmopolitical point of view. In relation to culture, language, and technology, the alterity of subjectivity and systems of representation in worlds of difference are conjoined and yet render them unique in the difference of themselves by the forces of globalization. Otherness is present, yes, but with a debt and duty to the historicity of what has gone before. The cosmopolitical defines worlds of difference through the necessity of marking the interior and exterior limits of culture through language and the rise of other technologies of representation. The logic of the cosmopolitical within the notion of worlds of difference broaches the question of human rights and education. It asks us to rethink the certainty of knowledge as a philosophical project of genealogical excavation in relation to social justice and educational equity. The ethical problem of who can, should be, or is capable of determining the propriety of the formal location of inquiry—the space and place of the cultural-institutional indexicality marking the public paths of difference, its entrances and exits—is a flash point of conflict. Pedagogy is always already implicated in the perennial question of democracy and discipline, of knowledge, difference, otherness, social justice, and the right to education for each and every subject and citizen.

The moment of questioning the nature or community directly addresses the academic responsibility of educational institutions and by extension those who teach, work, and live *in* and, perhaps, *for* them, as the teaching body (*le corps enseignant*),[8] to value difference. What does this mean exactly? To say that a pedagogical institution and those who are a part of it, are it, possess total and unabiding and hence *irresponsible and unaccountable* control of the intellectual domain they survey is to surmise a legacy of exclusion. There is no space left to welcome another. It is a question of affinity and openness toward embracing the difference of the Other without giving way to hesitance or reservation, empirical qualification and moral judgment, let alone indignation.

The question of a "proper domain" of the question of rights, of institutions, of community and difference—of propriety and domination, appropriation, expropriation, of property, participation, ownership and fairness, and therefore of law, ethics, and ultimately, of social justice—brings us back to the connections between culture and knowledge. It extends the problem of democracy and *democraticity,* governance and governmentality, of the responsibilities and principles relating to the formation and formativity of a system of public education on an international scale. It is a matter of locating the axiomatic difference of these terms, the difference of their axiomaticity, and their interrelatability, within a hospitable space and place that only an open concept of community can entreat them to because there is difference. Concept excavation as a genealogy of difference eventually leads to a productive recognition of alterity. That is, an ethical expansion of thought and thinking without limitations or borders.

The heterogeneous scope of this impossible territory wherein the struggle over difference and human rights occurs, after Immanuel Kant and his "risky" envisioning of the cosmopolitical condition: a hypothetical situation of geoglobal interconnectivity or "mondialization" having an "inter-national or inter-state dimension"[9] and related to the question of the *emanation* and diaspora of the *polis* and *politeia as a way of life.* The idea of the cosmopolitical solidifies the problem of a universal history or "the link among the cities, the *poleis* of the world, as nations, as people, or as States."[10] However, we cannot in good conscience subscribe to the constellations of a panoptic vision of an "abstract universalism"[11] that strangles difference in the name of a general culture of homogeneous worlds. Kant postulated the cosmopolitical as an organic global synthesis of cultures and subjects upon which a template for writing the blueprint of any and all institutions *to come* can be. In many ways, the vision still guides us and the pedagogical imperatives of today's educational and social institutions. Interrogating the modality of this desire for sameness demands a rethinking of the future of thinking and works toward illuminating and transforming rather than dismissing or deriding the historicity of "philosophical acts and archives."[12] Questioning the ground of institutions and the reason of their institutionality with respect to the formation of subjectivity engages the real-world effects produced by the performative force of epistemological discourses and their responsibility as instances of founding and therefore of foundation. The notion of worlds of difference arise from an antiutopian thrust, contrary to the ideal of a natural universalism of thought and action uniting thinking and subjectivity in the image of the global citizen. It enables us to link the problem of human rights and difference with the Kantian conception of a cosmopolitical point of view and community in a positive rather than a negative way. We must remember that knowledge and knowing are articulated by the continual reaggregation of the logic of the letter, the terms of its reading as production and reproduction, and the domain of its archive. The problem of how to go about securing both private and public "access to this language and culture, first and foremost by means of education,"[13] involves, more or less, the working out of the problems of community and difference central to answering the question of academic privilege (who has the right to knowledge?) and the power of location (how? and why?).

The pedagogical onus on an affable (simple, crude, vulgar) modality of cultural production and reproduction without the complexity of resistance or complications of difference fixes the parameters of an institutional ethic of response and responsibility. But this reduction of the frame of reference to categorical imperatives that willfully ignore the limitations and boundaries of a project of repeating the historicity of Western education occurs only if and when the cosmopolitical nature of difference as a source for community is not taken into account. It would be wrong to ignore the diversity within the composition of difference and to cull a universal difference without diversity. The emanation of the cosmopolitical view is a gathering of multiplicity in worlds of difference that articulate the ethical terms of a responsibility to acknowledge the profundity of difference, the unimaginable manifestation of many of its parts and partners, nations, states, and peoples whose materiality comprises and cannot but exceed the conceptual totality of its essence. These aspects are not unrelated insofar as such ethico-qualitative judgments require an identification of who would have the privilege and opportunity of participation regarding curricular decisions about the future of the right to education, and why. The global diaspora of subjectivity is the open ground of a *democracy-to-come,* with a *pedagogy-to-come,* and the potentially diverging paths of its filiations, friendships, what is held close, in affinity, to the spirit and the heart, not the mind.

Kant's ethical universalism, and its Eurocentric bias, can be used in a novel way by turning it toward the question of human rights, community, and difference to mobilize the cosmopolitical as a viewpoint *not only* for reconceptualizing the "eternal becoming"[14] of being-in-the-world, *but as a new approach to realizing the impossible futures of a "progressive institutionality" to come and the unforeseeability of its educational methods and apparatus.* This does not simply mean a securing of the opportunity for freedom in thinking and teaching via technological archives of knowledge; neither does it defer pedagogically, nor ethically, to the teaching of thinking without reference to the tradition of Western episteme, however it may be defined in curricular terms. The notion of the cosmopolitical reawakens and resituates the Eurocentrism of the concept and its implications for reinscribing the "horizon of a new community"[15] of the question around the virtual and the impossibility of worlds of knowledge that teach the Other to question the sources of the Self and the Other through meditations on difference. We have to accept the reality of the forces of globality and cosmopolitanism articulated via technology and yet safeguard the right to difference for everyone.

The Virtual Future?

Expanding the question of the status of knowledge to include a generalized overview of postindustrial, postmodern virtual learning environments brings to light how the location and the nature of learning are being integrated with the practices of everyday life. Lyotard does not address the consequences of the intellectual engagement of virtual archives as a cultural practice. He prefers to concentrate on the use-value of knowledge in relation to its performative commodification through technology. The "computerization of society" (*PC* 7) instantiates a "legitimation crisis" according to Lyotard. Although not in the Habermasian sense of a community's reacting to iconoclastic attitudes that question the validity of scientific truths. A digitally driven information society inheres the relation of knowledge to power and the ideological underpinnings of claims to reason. The focus of a "post-theory" of discourse instantiates, after Dewey, a critique of the principle of reason that governs the philosophical genealogy of the Western epistemological tradition and its privileging of a naïve concept of representation.[16] What distinguishes a postmodern vision of a computerized information society is the recognition of the ethico-political dimension of knowledge that an instrumental rendering of science and research technologies diminishes. Years ago, we heard people talking about the Internet as a kind of mass media and telecommunications system. They assimilated its reliance on language and images conceptually into the familiar real-time landscapes of the media—newspaper, TV, radio, phone, magazines, and so on. It was thought that the Internet could not be a teaching and learning machine of virtual information. But the Internet is not a communication channel. It is a complex environment. And it is not just any environment; it is *a virtual* environment. The virtual environment has its proper time, space, coordinates—and semantics! It is *almost* a kind of new dimension without boundaries. It has the cache of being a universe of infinite possibility and yet it could also be a fictional construction of space. But if we invoke it as a fiction, we can say it is a special kind of fabrication, since it produces fiction and reality without boundary. This is its power. It is a postmodern feature highlighting the virtual education that Lyotard's perspective took in almost 30 years ago when he wrote *The Postmodern Condition.* In questioning modern philosophy and its closed epistemology we are breaking down blind hierarchies between fields of knowledge and their metadiscursive rationality. Mathematics is not more true than Literature, or Music is not less scientific compared to Physics. The Internet is an educational situation that breaks down hierarchies within a virtual learning environment inasmuch as it upholds them. So, the old discussion about who is against the possibility of "experience" or who defends the notion of experience is rather pointless. What happens between a computer user and the virtual Web is not what Dewey called "experience" or what Horkheimer and Heidegger denied could be "real." *Between* virtual Web and learner we have a unique relation—a virtual one. We do not have an interaction. We have just a unique fiction of symbiotic union between human beings and machines that covers the reason of both. The computer user is a virtual learner and the computer a piece of technology, but we cannot think of the two parts separately when the virtual environment starts to work. When we realize what the specificity of the environment entails we cannot imagine an "inside" and an "outside." That fiction creates the *ether* or the *web* of connectivity and virtual space—the Web is not "inside" or "outside." The Web is a new way station to knowledge and meaning creation—it is knowledge in process but it is not an "experience of reality" or the discovery of new meaning from experience. The Deweyan cosmological model does not work here. We do not see subject or object because the Web is not constructed by *one,* and it is not *there* like an object fixed by a subject. It keeps itself growing and improving like an autogenerative plasma, but a plasma without an arterial system. It is not possible to know what is in *the* learner's brain. The cognitive apparatus does not stay *on* the Web and govern its manifestations. "Online" is an English word, but in the rest of the Planet it is metaphor, maybe a bad metaphor. The cognitive apparatus does not stay *in* the Web. We can spell "*In*ter-net" looking for a meaning, but you would not find a satisfactory meaning covering the multiplicity of conceptions associated with the words. Virtual learning and teaching do not happen in the virtual camp, but it *is* the virtual camp, that is, the Web, the virtual environment working fast and suggesting that we are living in a special dimension. It does not stop. It does not have a break when someone turns off a computer. And maybe what we call "the real world" breaks down if the Web stops for even just one second.

And yet, the archiving of information is not benign, but subject to the governance of the means of representation by external forces, mechanical and ideological, though ultimately grounded in the logic of cultural practices. The translatability of messages and other sensory data (visual, auditory, haptic) permeating the virtual public sphere remains greatly under the power of controlling forces who shape their form according to the reason of exposition. But given that the field of interpretation may be open to aberrant codings and responses, the power of information is undecidable. Intentionality is factored into representation, but cannot control it. Signs are not autogenic, therefore virtual. Responsibility is involved in representation. The desire for technological determinism characterizes the reason of "the most highly developed societies." (*PC* 7) Cybernetics becomes the terrain for the struggle over knowledge that manifests itself according to the Occidental passion for decidability and appropriation. Justice is not an issue when nature is fixed as experience. A community of learning grows from a commensurability of perspectives wherein truth is qualified by the adherence to traditions of inquiry. Certain discourses are accepted, while others are not. Censorship comes by way of a paradigmatic modality of knowledge. The master narratives that are generated to support the ideology of the system of representation are in need of excavating to explore the truth of reason in the virtual realm of learning environments, that is, if we are to question the ethics of techno-epistemology and the democratic status of knowledge in the information age after postmodernism.

Notes

1. See Martin Heidegger, *The Question Concerning Technology and Other Essays,* trans. William Lovitt (New York: Harper and Row, 1977), for the discussion of technology as a mode of *aletheuein* revealing—the essence of technology being nothing "technological" but *poietic.* Also see Martin Heidegger, *The Principle of Reason,* trans. Reginald Lilly (Bloomington: Indiana University Press, 1991). We can follow the trail that leads from the transformation of the pre-Socratic notion of Being as *physis* and *aletheia* into the conception of Being as *eidos* and *idea* from Plato to Being as humanity's idea to technology.

2. Jean-François Lyotard, *The Postmodern Condition: A Report on Knowledge.* Originally published in France in 1979. All further references to this work in the

text are to the English trans. Geoff Bennington and Brian Massumi (Minneapolis: University of Minnesota Press, 1984).

3. J-F. Lyotard, *The Postmodern Condition.* Henceforth cited as: (*PC* followed by page number).

4. See Heidegger, *The Question Concerning Technology and Other Essays,* for the discussion of technology as a mode of *aletheuein* revealing—the essence of technology being nothing "technological" but *poietic.* Also see Heidegger, *The Principle of Reason.* We can follow the trail that leads from the transformation of the pre-Socratic notion of Being as *physis* and *aletheia* into the conception of Being as *eidos* and *idea* from Plato to Being as humanity's idea to technology.

5. See Immanuel Kant, *Critique of Practical Reason,* trans. Lewis White Beck (New York: Macmillan, 1956), and Immanuel Kant, *The Conflict of the Faculties/Der Streit der Fakultäten,* trans. Mary J. Gregor (New York: Abaris Books, 1979). See also Jacques Derrida, "Mochlos; or, The Conflict of the Faculties," trans. Richard Rand and Amy Wygant, in *Logomachia: The Conflict of the Faculties,* ed. Richard Rand (Lincoln: University of Nebraska Press, 1992).

6. See Jacques Derrida, "On a Newly Arisen Apocalytic Tone in Philosophy," trans. John P. Leavey, Jr., in *Raising the Tone of Philosophy: Late Essays by Immanuel Kant, Transformative Critique by Jacques Derrida,* ed. Peter Fenves (Baltimore: Johns Hopkins University Press, 1993), 117–171.

7. "Jacques Derrida's 'Des humanités et de la discipline philosophiques'/'Of the Humanities and Philosophical Disciplines,'" in *Surfaces* VI.108 (v.1.0A-16/08/1996). The page references are from the Web-site version of the text (http://www.pum.umontreal.ca/revues/surfaces/vol6/derrida.html).

8. See Jacques Derrida, "Où commence et comment finit un corps enseignant," in *Du droit à la philosophie* (Paris: Galilée, 1990), 111–153.

9. Derrida, "Of the Humanities and the Philosophical Disciplines," 2.

10. Ibid.

11. Ibid.

12. Ibid.

13. Ibid.

14. The "Roundtable Discussion" on "Jacques Derrida's 'Des humanités et de la discipline philosophiques'/'Of the Humanities and Philosophical Disciplines,'" pp. 5–40, involved Hazard Adams, Ernst Behler, Hendrick Birus, Jacques Derrida, Wolfgang Iser, Ludwig Pfeiffer, Bill Readings, Ching-hsien Wang, and Pauline Yu. All further quotations from this text are comments made by Derrida. The page references are from the Web-site version of the text at http://www.pum.umontreal.ca/revues/surfaces/vol6/derrida.html. This endnote refers to a quotation from page 3.

15. Derrida, "Of the Humanities and the Philosophical Disciplines," 3.

16. Gianni Vattimo, *The End of Modernity: Nihilism and Hermeneutics in Postmodern Culture,* trans. Jon R. Snyder (Baltimore: Johns Hopkins University Press, 1988), gives an excellent rendering of the crisis of meaning after the questioning of representation.

CHAPTER 9

Youth and the Politics of Education in Dark Times

Henry A. Giroux

Introduction

We live at a time in which the loss of American standing in the world is related directly to the United States' ill-fated war in Iraq, its reckless free-market triumphalism deciding the fate of most nations of the world, its disregard for human rights at home and abroad, and its increasing support at the highest levels of government for radical Christian religious groups. What is often ignored by many critics with their singular fixation on the war abroad is the war that is also being waged on the home front.[1] This war can be seen not only in the crushing assault on unions and civil liberties, but also in the restructuring of the tax system to benefit the rich and drain resources from the poor and the middle class. The war at home has been exacerbated by the ascendancy of neoliberal corporate culture into every aspect of American life. Neoliberalism consolidates economic power in the hands of the few, aggressively attempts to destroy the welfare state, subordinates the needs of society to the dictates of corporate power, views misfortune as a weakness, and deems public services and goods an unconscionable luxury.[2] With few exceptions, the project of democratizing public goods, redistributing resources, and addressing important social problems has fallen into disrepute in the popular imagination as the logic of the market undermines the most basic social solidarities. The consequences include not only a weakened social state, but a growing sense of insecurity, cynicism, and political retreat on the part of the general public. The incessant calls for self-reliance that now dominate public discourse betray an eviscerated and refigured state that neither provides adequate safety nets for its populace, especially those who are young, poor, or racially marginalized, nor gives any indication that it will serve the interests of its citizens in spite of constitutional guarantees.

In fact, rather than disappearing as some theorists have argued, the state is being reconfigured; that is, it is increasingly becoming a punitive state more concerned with punishing and policing than with nurturing and investing in the public good. Stanley Aronowitz elaborates on this issue by arguing that the core functions of the state have shifted, not disappeared:

> Contrary to some recent arguments, the nation-state has not disappeared; instead its core functions have shifted from the legitimating institutions such as those of social welfare to, on the one hand, providing the monetary and fiscal conditions for the internal, but spurious expansion of (fictitious) capital, among whose elements is a reverse redistributive program, and on the other, to supplying a vastly expanded regime of coercion, that is, the growth of the police powers of government at home and abroad directed against the insurgencies that object to the growing phenomenon of an authoritarian form of democracy.[3]

Democracy increasingly appears damaged, if not fatally wounded, as those who are young, poor, immigrants, or people of color are excluded from the operations of power, the realm of politics, and crucial social provisions. For over a century, Americans have embraced as a defining feature of politics the idea that all levels of government would assume a large measure of responsibility for providing the resources, social provisions, security, and modes of education that enable young people to be prepared for the present while offering them a better future as the meaning and depth of an inclusive democracy are simultaneously expanded. But just as education has been separated from any viable notion of politics, youth have been separated from the discourse of either the social contract or any ethical notion of what it might mean for society to provide young people with the prospects of a decent and democratic future. Youth increasingly have come to be seen as a problem rather than as a resource for investing in the future. Framed largely as a generation of suspects, they are now treated as either a disposable population, fodder for a barbaric war in Iraq, or the source of most of society's problems. Youth now constitute a crisis that has less to do with improving the future than with denying it. Punishment and fear have replaced compassion and social investment as the most important modalities mediating the relationship of youth to the larger social order.

No longer "viewed as a privileged sign and embodiment of the future,"[4] youth are now demonized by the popular media and derided by politicians looking for quick-fix solutions to crime. Bestselling authors such as Lt. Col. Dave Grossman and Gloria DeGaentano argue in their *Stop Teaching Our Kids to Kill* that young people are more violent than ever before because of what they learn in popular culture and, by default, the authors suggest that young people need to be subjected to more extended disciplinary measures.[5] Hollywood movies consistently represent youth as either dangerous, utterly brainless, or simply without merit. The marketplace only imagines students either as consumers or as branded billboards as it offers for sale sexuality, beauty, and athleticism embodied in music, clothes, accessories, and a host of other consumer products. Market relation executives are now gloating over their discovery that eight- to fourteen-year-olds constitute a new market for "sexy" fashions such as La Senza Girl bra, heavy makeup, and magazines like *Twist*, *J-14*, *Teen Vogue*, and *M* that read like adult fashion magazines. At the same time, in a society deeply troubled by their presence, youth prompt in the public imagination a rhetoric of fear, control, and surveillance as well as laws and policies that threaten to fine youth for wearing baggy pants, subject youth to antigang laws that punish kids for violating certain dress codes, and offer them schools that are modeled after prisons. In the case of the latter, federal laws now provide financial incentives to schools that implement zero-tolerance policies, in spite of their proven racial and class biases; drug-sniffing dogs and cameras have become a common feature in schools; and administrators willingly comply with federal laws that give military recruiters the right to access the names, addresses, and telephone numbers of students in both public schools and higher education. Trust and respect now give way to fear, disdain, and suspicion. Children have fewer rights than almost any other group and fewer institutions protecting these rights. For instance, while young children need a parent's permission to get a tattoo or abortion in many states, they can be convicted of a serious crime and put to death long before their eighteenth birthday. The United States is one of the few countries in the world that sentences minors to death while spending more on each incarcerated inmate than on each public school pupil. As Marian Wright Edelman, founder and president of the Children's Defense Fund, points out,

> Fifty years after *Brown v. Board of Education* and 40 years after President Johnson declared a War on Poverty, many minority and lower income children still lack a fair chance to live, learn, thrive and contribute in America. The great unfinished business of our nation in this first decade of the 21st century is to open wide the doors of equal education and economic opportunity to every child in America. It's time to build a powerful 21st century movement to emancipate our children from racial injustice and poverty. We must summon the moral, political, and financial courage to make sure that we truly leave no child behind.[6]

Yet the Bush administration seems intent on pursuing a "war [in Iraq] whose central feature is the government's consistent, disastrous denial of reality,"[7] just as it drains the public treasury of billions of dollars through tax cuts for the rich and appropriations for a bloated military budget. The idea, not to mention the reality, of justice seems dead on arrival, as the Bush regime consistently and aggressively attempts to generate retrograde policies that are intent on increasing corporate power, expanding the reach of its influence, and wasting billions of dollars on a rapacious empire-building agenda. Justice seems to take a backseat in Bush's 2006 budget proposal. For instance, the Bush administration proposes to cut back funding for Upward Bound and Talent Search, two programs that benefit disadvantaged students, while at the same time it has allocated $127 billion to the Pentagon to build a robot army.[8] According to a representative from the U.S. Joint Forces Research Center, the virtue of the robot army is that there "are no prohibitions against robots making life-or-death decisions."[9] All of this may be good news for those die-hard members of the Christian Right, free-market fundamentalists, and power-hungry neoconservatives who are doing everything they can, not only to render democracy irrelevant, but also to disempower an entire generation of children whose future is being mortgaged off to the vagaries of corporate power and religious fanaticism. Instead of providing a decent critical education to poor young people, President Bush and his cohorts serve them more standardized tests,[10] enforce abstinence programs instead of sex education, hand out Bibles, inculcate right-wing Christian values, and advocate creationism at the expense of reason and freedom.[11] Youth who are poor fare even worse and often find themselves in classes that are overcrowded, lack basic resources, and are subject to policies largely designed to warehouse young people rather than educate them with even minimal basic literacy skills. Instead of providing young people with vibrant public spheres, the Bush government offers them a commercialized culture in which consumerism is the only condition of citizenship.

Rather than being viewed as at risk, children in George Bush's America are now seen as the risk and are treated as either disposable or a drain on the national treasury. Equal education, economic opportunity, decent healthcare, and the most basic social provisions are now out of reach for millions of children who are poor, deprived of health insurance, abused, and sadly undereducated. The Bush administration's answer to the plight of children in America can be seen in his proposed $2.5 trillion budget for 2006. Laura Flanders defines Bush's budget as a hit list targeting teens and kids because it "calls for cuts in emergency medical services for children, cuts in K–12 education funding, cuts in vocational education and cuts in programs like Head Start. There are food-stamp cuts and a five-year freeze on child care. A $41 million college loan program is eliminated. The whole National Youth Sports Program which has provided athletics for low income kids is cut, as in cut out."[12] The hypocrisy underlying these cuts becomes more obvious when cuts in education are examined, especially since Bush's "compassionate conservativism" defines itself largely through educational reforms. In fact, of the 150 programs designed to be radically cut back, "one out of every three of the targeted programs concerns education ... [including] $2.2 billion for high school programs, ... $440 million in Safe and Drug-Free School grants,

$500 million in education technology state grants, $225 million for the Even Start literacy program, [and] $280 million for Upward Bound programs for inner-city youths."[13] Paul Krugman calls Bush's latest budget projections a form of class warfare since he "takes food from the mouths of babes and gives the proceeds to his millionaire friends."[14] In his 2006 budget proposals, Bush calls for terminating aid for over 300,000 people receiving food stamps and denies childcare assistance to over 300,000 children from working-class families, while at the same time phasing out a limit on tax exemptions for high-income families that would give taxpayers with incomes over $1 million an average tax cut of more than $19,000.[15] In this case, savage cuts in education, nutritional assistance for impoverished mothers, veterans' medical care, and basic scientific research would help fund tax cuts for the inordinately rich.

How might youth fare in the midst of such a crisis, particularly around their need for decent schools, qualified teachers, and a critically informed education? Rather than invest in young people, the Bush administration either punishes them through retrograde policies or simply ignores their needs. One example of how the Bush administration views the education of young people is in a recent incident in which the newly appointed Secretary of Education Margaret Spellings, on the second day of her job, launched a public attack against the children's television show *Postcards from Buster.*[16] The show is about a rabbit who travels all over America visiting families of various and diverse backgrounds. Unfortunately, according to Spellings, the show was no longer fit to be aired because in one of the episodes a family consisted of a lesbian couple with children. This does not simply suggest an inept public official who would like to teach children that tolerance rather than bigotry is the enemy of democracy. It also reveals a powerful representative of the Bush administration whose disregard for children is evident in her undemocratic embrace of censorship and her politically inspired tirades and threats to decrease funding for PBS, another apparently left-wing public service that poses a threat to free-market fundamentalism. Ms. Spellings' actions inspired Frank Rich, a writer for the *New York Times,* to claim that "Ms. Spellings' threats against PBS are only the latest chapter in a continuing saga at an education department that increasingly resembles an authoritarian government's ministry of information"[17] and that clearly has little regard for young people.

Youth have become one of the most visible symbols onto which class and racial anxieties are projected. The very troubled state of young people confronts us with the broken promises of capitalism in the age of outsourcing, contract work, deindustrialization, and deregulation. It also represents a collective fear of the consequences wrought by systemic class inequalities, racism, and a culture of downsizing and deficits that have created a generation of unskilled and displaced youth who have been expelled from shrinking markets, blue-collar jobs, and any viable hope in the future. Indeed, more than five million youth between the ages of eighteen and twenty-four are out of school, work, and hope. In the inner cities, youth hopelessness is increasingly matched with a mix of violence, drug trafficking, and an exaggerated "tough-guy" masculinity. But as Earl Ofari Hutchinson points out,

> It's not just drugs and hopelessness that drive young men, especially young Black men, to kill and dodge bullets. The huge state and federal cutbacks in job training and skills programs, the brutal competition for low and semi skilled service and retail jobs from immigrants [along with] the high number of miserably failing inner-city public schools ... have turned thousands of Blacks into education cripples. These students are desperately unequipped to handle the rapidly evolving and demanding technical and professional skills in the public sector and the business world of the 21st century.[18]

In the degraded economic, political, and cultural geography of neoliberal capitalism, youth occupy a "dead zone" in which the spectacle of commodification exists side by side with the imposing threat of the prison-industrial complex and the elimination of basic civil liberties. As market fundamentalism frees itself from political power, it has disassociated economics from its social costs, and "the political state has become the corporate state."[19] Under such circumstances, the state does not disappear but, as Pierre Bourdieu has brilliantly reminded us,[20] is refigured as its role in providing social provisions, intervening on behalf of public welfare, and regulating corporate plunder is weakened. The neoliberal state no longer invests in solving social problems; it now punishes those who are caught in the downward spiral of its economic policies. Punishment, incarceration, control, and surveillance represent the face of the new, expanded state. One consequence is that the implied contract between the state and its citizens is broken, and social guarantees for youth as well as civic obligations to the future vanish from the agenda of public concern. Similarly, as market values supplant civic values, it becomes increasingly difficult "to translate private worries into public issues and, conversely, to discern public issues in private troubles."[21] Alcoholism, homelessness, poverty, and illiteracy, among other issues, are seen not as social but as individual problems—matters of character, individual fortitude, and personal responsibility. Ardent consumers and disengaged citizens provide fodder for a growing cynicism and depoliticization of public life at a time when there is an increasing awareness not just of corporate corruption, financial mismanagement, and systemic greed, but also of the recognition that a democracy of critical citizens is being replaced quickly by a democracy of consumers. The desire to protect market freedoms and wage a war against terrorism has, ironically, not only ushered in a culture of fear, but also dealt a lethal blow to civil freedoms. At the heart of this contradiction are both the fate of democracy and the civic health and future of a generation of children and young people.

For many young people and adults today, the private sphere has become the only space in which to imagine any sense of hope, pleasure, or possibility. Culture, as an activity in which young people actually produce the conditions of their own agency through dialogue, community participation, public stories, and political struggle, is being eroded. In its place we are increasingly surrounded by a "climate of cultural and linguistic privatization"[22] in which culture becomes something that is consumed, and the only kind of speech that is acceptable is that of the fast-paced shopper. The war against youth can be understood, in part, through those central values and practices that characterize a market fundamentalism that emphasizes market forces and profit margins while narrowing the legitimacy of the public sphere by redefining it around the related issues of privatization, deregulation, consumption, and safety. In spite of neoconservative and neoliberal claims that economic growth will cure social ills, the market has no way of dealing with poverty, social inequality, or civil rights issues. It has no vocabulary for addressing respect, compassion, decency, and ethics, or, for that matter, what it means to recognize antidemocratic forms of power. These are political issues, not merely economic concerns. In contrast, a political system based on democratic principles of inclusiveness and nonrepression can and does provide citizens with the critical tools necessary for them to participate in investing public life with vibrancy while expanding the foundations of freedom and justice.

The current state of youth bears heavily on both public and higher education. Childhood as a core referent for a vibrant democracy and for an embrace of social justice appears to be disappearing in a society that not only rejects the promise of youth, but the future itself "as an affective investment."[23] The crisis of youth signals a dangerous state of affairs for the future; it also portends a crisis in the very idea of the political and ethical constitution of the social and in the possibility of articulating the relevance of democracy itself. In what follows, I want to argue that youth as a referent refers not only to young children, but also to those youth who inhabit the institutions of higher learning and who are poised to become adults by virtue of the knowledge, capacities, and skills they learn as critical citizens, workers, and intellectuals.

Higher Education and the Crisis of the Social

Within the last two decades a widespread pessimism about public life and politics has developed in the United States. Individual rights now outweigh collective concerns as market ideals have taken precedence over democratic values. In the vocabulary of neoliberalism, the public collapses into the personal, the personal becomes "the only politics there is, the only politics with a tangible referent or emotional valence,"[24] and it is within such an utterly personal discourse that human actions are shaped and agency is privatized. Under neoliberalism, hope becomes dystopian as the public sphere disappears and, as Peter Beilharz argues, "politics becomes banal, for there is not only an absence of citizenship but a striking absence of agency."[25]

As economic and financial power is increasingly separated from the specificity of traditional politics and public obligations, corporations are less subject to the control of the state, and "there is a strong impulse to displace political sovereignty with the sovereignty of the market, as if the latter has a mind and morality of its own."[26] Under the auspices of neoliberalism, the language of the social is either devalued or ignored, as public life is reduced to a form of pathology, and all dreams of the future are now modeled around the narcissistic, privatized, and self-indulgent needs of consumer culture and the dictates of the alleged "free" market. Samuel Weber has suggested that what seems to be involved in such a transformation is "a fundamental and political redefinition of the social value of public services in general, and of universities and education in particular."[27]

Within this impoverished sense of politics and public life, the university is increasingly being transformed into a training ground for the corporate workforce, with the loss of any notion of a future that views higher education as a crucial public sphere in which critical citizens and democratic agents are formed. In the age of money and profit, academic subjects gain stature almost exclusively through their exchange value on the market. This is all the more so as the Bush administration attempts to privatize higher education, cut student aid, plunder public services, and push states to the brink of financial disaster. As higher education increasingly becomes a privilege rather than a right, many working-class students either find it impossible financially to enter college or, because of increased costs, have to drop out. Those students who have the resources to stay in school are feeling the tight pressures of the job market and rush to take courses and receive professional credentials in business and the biosciences as the humanities lose majors and downsize. Not surprisingly, students are now referred to as "customers," while faculty are rewarded less for their scholarship than their ability to secure funds and generate grants from foundations, corporations, and other external sources. Rather than being rewarded for critically inventive teaching and rigorous research, faculty are now valued as multinational operatives, even as the majority of their colleagues are increasingly reduced to contract employees.

Under the reign of neoliberalism and corporate culture, the boundaries between commercial culture and public culture become blurred as universities rush to embrace the logic of industrial management while simultaneously forfeiting those broader values central to a democracy and capable of limiting the excesses of corporate power. As higher education is corporatized, young people find themselves on campuses that look more like malls, and they are increasingly taught by professors who are hired on a contractual basis, have obscene workloads, and can barely make enough money to pay the loans for their cars. Tenured faculty are now called upon to generate grants, establish close partnerships with corporations, and teach courses that have practical value in the marketplace. There is little in this vision of the university that imagines young people as anything other than fodder for the corporation.

Educated Hope in Dark Times

In opposition to the corporatization of higher education and the devaluing of the capacities of young people, there is a prominent educational tradition in the United States extending from Thomas Jefferson to John Dewey in which the future of the university is premised on the recognition that in order for freedom to flourish in the worldly space of the public realm, citizens have to be formed, educated, and socialized. John Dewey, for example, argued that higher education should provide the conditions for people to involve themselves in the deepest problems of society, to acquire the knowledge, skills, and ethical responsibility necessary for "reasoned participation in democratically organized publics."[28] C. Wright Mills challenged schooling as a form of corporate training and called for fashioning higher education within a public philosophy committed to a radical conception of citizenship, civic engagement, and public wisdom.[29] Education in these contexts was linked to public life through democratic values such as equality, liberty, and freedom, rather than as an adjunct of the corporation whose knowledge and values were defined largely through the prism of commercial interests. Education was crucial to a notion of individual agency and public citizenship, integral to defending the relationship between an autonomous society—rooted in an ever-expanding process of self-examination, critique, and reform—and autonomous individuals, for whom critical inquiry is propelled by the need to engage in an ongoing pursuit of ethics and justice as a matter of public good. In many ways, higher education has been faithful, at least in theory, to a project of modern politics, in which its purpose was to create citizens capable of defining and implementing universal goals such as freedom, equality, and justice as part of a broader attempt to deepen the relationship between an expanded notion of the social and the enabling ground of a vibrant democracy.

If the rise of the corporate university is to be challenged and education is to become a meaningful site for educating youth for a democratic future, educators and others need to reclaim the meaning and purpose of higher education as an ethical and political response to the demise of democratic public life. At stake here is the need to insist on the role of the university as a public sphere committed to deepening and expanding the possibilities of democratic identities, values, and relations. This approach suggests new models of leadership based on the understanding that the real purpose of higher education means encouraging people to think beyond the task of simply getting a lucrative job. Beyond this ever-narrowing instrumental justification there are the more relevant goals of opening up higher education to all groups, creating a critical citizenry, providing specialized work skills for jobs that really require them, democratizing relations of governance among administrators, faculty, and students, and taking seriously the imperative to disseminate an intellectual and artistic culture. Higher education may be one of the few sites left in which students can learn how to mediate critically between democratic values and the demands of corporate power, between identities founded on democratic principles and identities engulfed by forms of unbridled individualism that promote competitiveness, self-interest, profit-making, and greed. This view suggests, once again, that higher education needs to be defended through intellectual work that self-consciously recalls the tension between the democratic imperatives and possibilities of public institutions and their everyday realization within a society dominated by a market fundamentalism. Higher education should be defended as a space of critical education where teachers and students have the chance to resist those modes of pedagogy, time, and rationality that refuse to include questions of judgment and issues of responsibility. Understood as such, higher education should be viewed exclusively as neither a consumer-driven product nor a form of training and career preparation, but as a mode of learning that renders all individuals fit "to participate in power. . . . to the greatest extent possible, to participate in a common government,"[30] and to be capable, as Aristotle reminds us, of both governing and being governed. Addressing education as a democratic endeavor begins with the recognition that higher education is more than an investment opportunity; citizenship is about more than consuming; learning is about more than preparing for a job; and democracy is about more than making choices at the local mall.

Reclaiming higher education as a public sphere begins with the crucial project of challenging corporate ideology and its preference of market time over public time. Market time fosters a narrow sense of leadership, agency, and public values and is largely indifferent to those noncommercial concerns that are critical to a just society. The values of hierarchy, materialism, competition, and excessive individualism are enshrined under market time and play a defining role in how it allocates space, manages the production of particular forms of knowledge, guides research, and regulates pedagogical relations. Market time accentuates privatized and competitive modes of intellectual activity, largely removed from public obligations and social responsibilities. Public time, on the other hand, rejects the fever-pitch appeals of "just-in-time" or "speed-time," demands often made within the context of "ever faster technological transformation and exchange"[31] and buttressed by corporate capital's golden rule: "Time is money." Public time slows time down, not as a simple refusal of technological change nor as a rejection of all calls for efficiency, but as an attempt to create the institutional and ideological conditions that promote long-term analyses, historical reflection, and deliberations over what our collective actions might mean for shaping the future. Rejecting an instrumentality that evacuates questions of history, ethics, and justice, public time fosters dialogue, thoughtfulness, and critical exchange. Public time offers room for knowledge that contributes to society's self-understanding, enables it to question itself, and seeks to legitimate intellectual practices that are not only collective and noninstrumental, but that also deepen democratic values while encouraging pedagogical relations that question the future in terms that are political, ethical, and social. At stake here is the important task of redefining higher education as a democratic public sphere not only to assert the importance of public time, but also to reconfigure it so that "economic interests cease to be the dominant factor in shaping attitudes"[32] about the social as a realm devoid of politics and democratic possibilities. Higher education is a hard-won democratic achievement, and it is time that parents, faculty, students, college alumni, and concerned citizens reclaim it as a fundamental public good rather than a mere training ground for corporate interests, values, and profits. Education is not only about issues of work and economics, but also about questions of justice, social freedom, and the capacity for democratic agency, action, and change as well as the related issues of power, exclusion, and citizenship. These are educational and political issues and should be addressed as part of a broader concern for renewing the struggle for social justice and democracy.

Academics Making Public Connections

Institutions of higher education must be seen as deeply moral and political spaces in which intellectuals assert themselves not merely as professional academics, but as citizens whose knowledge and actions presuppose specific visions of public life, community, and moral accountability. This view suggests that higher education be defended, not as an adjunct of the corporation, but as a vital public sphere in its own right, one that has deeply moral and educative dimensions that directly impact on civic life. This defense must be maintained by academics' redefining their roles as public intellectuals who can move between academic institutions and other public spheres in which knowledge, values, and social identities are produced.

If the university is to remain a site of critical thinking, collective work, and public service, educators will have to redefine the knowledge, skills, research, and intellectual practices currently being favored in the university. Central to such a challenge is the necessity to define intellectual practice "as part of an intricate web of morality, rigor and responsibility"[33] that enables academics to speak with conviction, enter the public sphere in order to address important social problems, and demonstrate alternative models for what it means to bridge the gap between higher education and the broader society. Under such conditions, it is crucial to construct intellectual practices that are collegial rather than competitive, that refuse the instrumentality and privileged isolation of the academy, that link critical thought to a profound impatience with the status quo, and that connect human agency to the idea of social responsibility.

Increasingly as universities are shaped by a culture of fear in which dissent is equated with treason, the call to be objective and impartial can easily echo what George Orwell referred to as the official truth or the establishment point of view, however unconscious or unintentioned. Lacking a self-conscious democratic political project, the role of the university intellectual is often reduced to that of a technician or functionary engaged in formalistic rituals and unconcerned with the disturbing and urgent problems that confront the larger society. In opposition to this view, I argue that public intellectuals—and perhaps especially those concerned with research into aspects of childhood and youth—should combine the mutually interdependent roles of critical educator and active citizen. This suggests finding ways to connect the practice of classroom teaching to the operation of power in the larger society. I think Edward Said is on target when he argues that the public intellectual must function within institutions, in part, as an exile, as someone whose "place it is publicly to raise embarrassing questions, to confront orthodoxy and dogma, to be someone who cannot easily be co-opted by governments or corporations."[34] In this perspective, the educator as public intellectual becomes responsible for linking the diverse experiences that produce knowledge, identities, and social values in the university to the quality of moral and political life in the wider society. Vaclav Havel captures this sentiment in arguing that intellectuals have a responsibility to engage in practical politics, to see "things in more global terms.... build people-to-people solidarity.... foster tolerance, struggle against evil and violence, promote human rights, and argue for their indivisibility."[35]

I think that these concerns about the responsibility of academics as public intellectuals are especially important with respect to how young people in education programs are taught to educate and nurture people younger than themselves. One of the ways in which university teachers in education programs can reach out to influence the future is to make it clear to their own students that they bear a responsibility to educate critically the students they will be interacting with once they graduate from college. The importance of such an educational challenge and project can be seen in a recent survey conducted by the John S. and James L. Knight Foundation, which found that 36 percent of U.S. high school students believed that "newspapers should get government approval of stories before publishing."[36] Clearly, it is precisely the lack of education about student rights, First Amendment freedoms, and the meaning of a substantive democracy that provides the conditions for such views that are much closer to fascism than to what it means to be a critical citizen in a democracy. Moreover, this type of political illiteracy and historical amnesia poses as much of a threat to Canadian children as it does to American youth.[37] Critical education cannot be decoupled from political democracy and should take place at all levels of schooling; but it must gain its momentum in those colleges and universities among students who will go back to the schools, churches, synagogues, and business world in order to produce new ideas, concepts, and democratic ways of understanding the world in which young people live.

Intellectuals who feel an increased sense of responsibility for humanity may not be able to, and do not necessarily have to, explain the problems of the world in terms that purport to be absolute or all-encompassing. Nor should they limit their responsibility to the sphere of the university or the media. On the contrary, public intellectuals need to approach social issues with humility, mindful of the multiple connections and issues that tie humanity together; but they need to do so as border intellectuals moving within and across diverse sites of learning as part of an engaged and practical politics that recognizes the importance of "asking questions, making distinctions, restoring to memory all those things that tend to be overlooked or walked past in the rush to collective judgment and action."[38] Within this discourse, the experiences that constitute the production of knowledge, identities, and social values in the university are inextricably linked to the quality of moral and political life of the wider society.

If educators are to function as public intellectuals, then they need to provide the opportunities for students to learn that the relationship between knowledge and power can be emancipatory, that their histories and experiences matter, and that what they say and do count in their struggle to unlearn dominating privileges, productively reconstruct their relations with others, and transform, when necessary, the world around them. More specifically, such educators need to argue for forms of pedagogy that close the gap between the university and everyday life. Their curriculum needs to be organized around knowledge of communities, cultures, and traditions that give students a sense of history, identity, and place. Edward Said is again helpful. Said urges academics and students to accept the demands of "worldliness," which implies "lifting complex ideas into the public space," recognizing human injury outside the academy, and using theory as a form of criticism to change things.[39] Worldliness requires not being afraid of controversy, making connections that are otherwise hidden, deflating the claims of triumphalism, and bridging intellectual work and the operation of politics. It means combining rigor and clarity, on the one hand, and civic courage and political commitment, on the other. Following Said, I am calling for the transgressing of the often rigid division between academic culture and popular culture as well as between disciplines, and for expanding pedagogical practice as a form of cultural politics by making all knowledge subject to serious analysis and interrogation, and, in so doing, making visible the operations of power that connect such knowledge to specific views of authority, cultural practice, and the larger world.

Educators need to construct pedagogical approaches that do more than make learning context-specific; in effect, they need to challenge the content of established canons and, similarly, to expand the range of cultural texts that count as "really useful knowledge." As public intellectuals, university teachers must begin to use those electronically mediated knowledge forms that constitute the terrain of mass and popular culture. I am referring here to the world of media texts—videos, films, music, and other mechanisms of popular culture that operate through a combination of visual and print culture. What I am suggesting here is that educators challenge the traditional definition and site of pedagogy by widening the application of pedagogy to a variety of cultural locations and, in doing so, alert students to how public pedagogy operates through the educational force of the culture at large.

The content of the curriculum should affirm and critically enrich the meaning, language, and knowledge forms that students actually use to negotiate and inform their lives. Academics can in part exercise their role as public intellectuals via such curricula by giving students the opportunity to understand how power is organized through the enormous number of "popular" cultural spheres that range from libraries, movie theaters, and schools, to high-tech media conglomerates that circulate signs and meanings through newspapers, magazines, advertisements, new information technologies, machines, films, and television programs. University intellectuals must draw a lesson from cultural studies in extending the historical and relational definition of cultural texts while redefining, in Toni Morrison's terms, how "knowledge, however mundane and utilitarian, plays about in linguistic images and forms cultural practices."[40] Needless to say, this position challenges Roger Kimball's claim that "popular culture is a tradition essential to uneducated Americans."[41] Of course, what is at stake are not only important questions about how knowledge is produced and taken up, but what it means to provide the conditions for students to become competent and critically versed in a variety of literacies while at the same time expanding the conditions and options for the roles they might play as cultural producers (as opposed to simply teaching them to be critical readers).

Although it is central for university teachers to enlarge the curriculum to reflect the richness and diversity of the students they actually teach; they also need to decenter the curriculum. That is, as Stanley Aronowitz points out, students should be actively involved in governance, "including setting learning goals, selecting courses, and having their own, autonomous organizations, including a free press."[42] Not only does the distribution of power among teachers, students, and administrators provide the conditions for students to become agents in their learning process; it also provides the basis for collective learning, civic action, and ethical responsibility. Moreover, student agency emerges from a pedagogy of lived experience and struggle, not from mere formalistic mastery of an academic subject.

I have suggested that educators need to become provocateurs. They need to take a stand while refusing to be involved in either a cynical relativism or doctrinaire politics. This suggests that central to intellectual life is the pedagogical and political imperative that academics engage in rigorous social criticism while becoming a stubborn force that can challenge false prophets, fight against the imposed silence of normalized power, "refuse to allow conscience to look away or fall asleep,"[43] and critically engage all those social relations that promote material and symbolic violence. At the same time, such intellectuals must be deeply critical of their own authority and how it structures classroom relations and cultural practices. In this way, the authority they legitimate in the classroom (as well as in other public spheres) would become both an object of self-critique and a critical referent for expressing a more "fundamental dispute with authority itself."[44]

Central to my argument is the need for educators to define themselves less as narrow specialists, classroom managers, or mouthpieces for corporate culture than as engaged public intellectuals willing to address those economic, political, and social problems that must be overcome if both young people and adults are going to take seriously a future that opens up rather than closes down the promises of a viable and substantive democracy. There is a lot of talk among social theorists about the death of politics and the inability of human beings to imagine a more equitable and just world in order to make it better. I would hope that, of all groups, educators would be the most vocal and militant in challenging this assumption by making it clear that at the heart of any form of critical education is the assumption that learning should be used to expand the public good and promote democratic social change, especially for young people. Public and higher education may be one of the few spheres left where the promise of youth can be linked to the promise of democracy. Education in this instance becomes both an ethical and political referent in that it not only furnishes an opportunity for adults to provide the conditions for young people to become critically engaged social agents, but also offers the symbols of a future in which democracy creates the conditions for each generation of youth to struggle anew to sustain the promise of a democracy that has no end point and must be continuously expanded into a world of new possibilities and opportunities for keeping justice and hope alive.

In conclusion, I want to suggest that struggles over how we view, represent, and treat young people must be understood as part of a larger public dialogue about how to imagine a future linked to the creation of a strong inclusive democracy while simultaneously articulating a new vocabulary, a set of theoretical tools, and social possibilities for envisioning civic engagement and political transformation. We have entered a period in which the war against youth, especially poor youth of color, offers no apologies because it is too arrogant and ruthless to imagine any resistance. But the collective need and potential struggle for justice should never be underestimated even in the darkest of times. And, of course, the stakes for the existing and future generations of young people are much too crucial both for them and for the fate of democracy to ignore.

Notes

1. Francis Fox Ivan, *The War at Home: The Domestic Costs of Bush's Militarism* (New York: The New Press, 2004).

2. I analyze neoliberalism in great detail in Henry Giroux, *The Terror of Neoliberalism* (Boulder, CO: Paradigm, 2004).

3. Stanley Aronowitz, "The Retreat to Postmodern Politics," *Situations* 1, no. 1 (April 2005): 32.

4. Lawrence Grossberg, "Why Does Neo-Liberalism Hate Kids? The War on Youth and the Culture of Politics," *The Review of Education, Pedagogy & Cultural Studies* 23, no. 2 (2001): 133.

5. Lt. Col. Dave Grossman and Gloria DeGaentano, *Stop Teaching Our Kids to Kill* (New York: Crown, 1999).

6. "The State of America's Children 2004," *Children's Defense Fund,* press release, July 13, 2004, http://www.childrensdefense.org/pressreleases/040713.asp.

7. Ellen Willis, "Historical Analysis," *Dissent,* Winter 2005, 113.

8. Jeffrey Selingo, "Bush Budget Takes Aim at Student Aid and Research," *Chronicle of Higher Education,* February 18, 2005, A5, A21–A24.

9. Paul Ford, "Weekly Review," *Harper's Online,* February 22, 2005, http://www.harpers.org/WeeklyReview.html.

10. Anne E. Kornblut, "Bush Urges Rigorous High School Testing," *New York Times,* January 13, 2005, 26.

11. I have taken up this critique in great detail in Henry A. Giroux, *The Abandoned Generation* (New York: Palgrave, 2004).

12. Laura Flanders, "Bush's Hit List: Teens and Kids," *Common Dreams News Center,* February 13, 2005, http://www.commondreams.org/views05/0213-11.htm.

13. Mike Allen and Peter Baker, "$2.5 Trillion Budget Plan Cuts Many Programs," *Washington Post,* February 7, 2005, A01.

14. Paul Krugman, "Bush's Class-War Budget," *New York Times,* February 11, 2005, A23.

15. Ibid.

16. Ginger McCall, "Secretary of Ed.'s Attack on Cartoon Spells Trouble," *Pitt News,* February 2, 2005, 1.

17. Frank Rich, "The Year of Living Indecently," *New York Times,* February 6, 2005, AR1.

18. Earl Ofari Hutchinson, "Crips, Bloods and Laura Bush," *Black America Today,* February 7, 2005, http://www.blackamericatoday.com/article.cfm?ArticleID=745.

19. Noreena Hertz, *The Silent Takeover: Global Capitalism and the Death of Democracy* (New York: The Free Press, 2001), 11.

20. Pierre Bourdieu, *Acts of Resistance: Against the Tyranny of the Market* (New York: The New Press, 1998); Pierre Bourdieu et al., *The Weight of the World: Social Suffering in Contemporary Society* (Stanford: Stanford University Press, 1999).

21. Zygmunt Bauman, *In Search of Politics* (Stanford: Stanford University Press, 1999), 2.

22. Naomi Klein, *No Logo* (New York: Picador, 1999), 177.

23. Grossberg, "Why Does Neo-Liberalism Hate Kids?" 133.

24. Jean Comaroff and John L. Comaroff, "Millennial Capitalism: First Thoughts on a Second Coming," *Public Culture* 12, no. 2 (2000): 305–306.

25. Peter Beilharz, *Zygmunt Bauman: Dialectic of Modernity* (London: Sage, 2000), 160.

26. Comaroff and Comaroff, "Millennial Capitalism," 332.

27. Cited in Roger Simon, "The University: A Place to Think?" in *Beyond the Corporate University,* ed. Henry A. Giroux and Kostas Myrsiades (Lanham, MD: Rowman and Littlefield, 2001), 47–48.

28. Cited in Frank Hearn, *Reason and Freedom in Sociological Thought* (Boston: Unwin Hyman, 1985), 175. The classic statements by Dewey on this subject can be found in John Dewey, *Democracy and Education* (1916; repr., New York: The Free Press, 1997); see also John Dewey, *The Public and Its Problems* (Columbus: Ohio University Press, 1954).

29. C. Wright Mills, *Power, Politics, and People,* ed. Irving Louis Horowitz (New York: Oxford University Press, 1963).

30. Cornelius Castoriadis, "The Nature and Value of Equity," in *Philosophy, Politics, Autonomy: Essays in Political Philosophy* (New York: Oxford University Press, 1991), 140.

31. Jerome Bind, "Toward an Ethic of the Future," *Public Culture* 12, no. 1 (2000): 52.

32. Cornelius Castoriadis, "The Greek Polis and the Creation of Democracy," in *Philosophy, Politics, Autonomy,* 112.

33. Arundhati Roy, *Power Politics* (Cambridge, MA: South End, 2001), 6.

34. Edward Said, *Representations of the Intellectual* (New York: Pantheon, 1994), 11.

35. Vaclav Havel, "The Responsibility of Intellectuals," *New York Review of Books,* June 22, 1995, 37.

36. Greg Toppo, "U.S. Students Say Press Freedoms Go Too Far," *USA Today,* January 30, 2005, http://www.usatoday.com/news/education/2005-01-30-students-press_x.htm.

37. I am indebted to Perry Nodelman for this insight about the wider pedagogical influences our students can have on younger students.

38. Said, *Representations,* 52–53.

39. Edward Said, "Scholarship and Commitment: An Introduction," *Profession* (2000): 7.

40. Toni Morrison, *Playing in the Dark: Whiteness and the Literary Imagination* (Cambridge: Harvard University Press, 1992), 49–50.

41. Kimball cited in Lawrence W. Levine, *The Opening of the American Mind* (Boston: Beacon, 1996), 19.

42. Stanley Aronowitz, "A Different Perspective on Educational Equality," *The Review of Education, Pedagogy and Cultural Studies* 16, no. 2 (1994): 24.

43. All of these ideas and the quotation itself are taken from Edward Said, *Humanism and Democratic Criticism* (New York: Columbia, 2004), 142.

44. R. Radhakrishnan, "Canonicity and Theory: Toward a Poststructuralist Pedagogy," in *Theory/Pedagogy/Politics,* ed. Donald Morton and Mas'ud Zavarzadeh (Urbana: University of Illinois Press, 1991), 112–135.

CHAPTER 10

Being Caught Otherwise

Mario Di Paolantonio

> The destiny of an annotation is to be always bad.
>
> *Jacques Derrida*

In her *Ethics of Remembering* (1998) Edith Wyschogrod spells out the particular paradox that entangles us when we work to transmit the past. Wyschogrod notes that because the historian works with the texts of an other who cannot speak for herself, the historian must pledge a *promise* that she will remain loyal to her words, that she will in a gesture of pure *affiliation* restore the past in its own terms, guarding its summons against any present condensation or reduction. Yet, Wyschogrod admits to the impossibility of ever fully realizing this promise and affiliation. She writes, "The historian is placed in a Catch-22. Obligated by her vow to restore the past in its actuality, she nevertheless recognizes the impossibility of doing so" (1998:xii).

Admittedly, if the historian's pledge to the past merely transmits a negative protocol for policing our fidelity to the text it surely falls short of registering a "living narration" that can evoke, in this present and in subsequent generations, the task of giving countenance, of meeting, responding, and passing on the past. Moreover there is a risk of this pledge to fidelity's becoming a relentlessly insistent and restrictive demand, perhaps even a form of necrophilia, which would foreclose the creativity required by those in the present to reanimate the past as one of "our" concerns. In the narrow confines of such a restrictive injunction for historical transmission, what could possibly motivate and engage us to grapple with the words of an absent other, with an alien way of speaking? For in order to engage with this task, in order to meet with and so feel obligated to stories from other times and places, do we not need to begin our response in our immediate discursive reality? Surely we cannot become obligated to represent/engage with the past through an unmediated form. Unquestionably then, the past requires a "contact point," an "annotation," a thorough reworking through our present modes of reception and dissemination in order for it to be re-presentable and meaningful to us. But once this past becomes expressed as one of our concerns, through our present forms of mediation and terms, what preserves its difference from being wholly subsumed? What prevents its otherness from being compressed and revised within the exigencies of the moment, within a form that fits the present model of circulation? What guards the past from becoming a mere footnote that authorizes our terms and legitimizes our desires? How can it be annotated, brought into our present terms, so that it engages and motivates us to honor its words, so that we may respect and respond to its difference?

This conundrum, which inevitably plagues historiography, has been a concern that Gadamerian hermeneutics attempts to address. As a process that seeks to transmit the past into the present in order to preserve the difference of the past while simultaneously generating an understanding that conforms and expands our present vocabulary, hermeneutics appears to offer a thorough lesson and means of resolving the paradox of historical transmission. But the hermeneutical response—as I will unfold—is ultimately concerned with transmitting the past (the other, the one who cannot speak for herself) into the present so that a shared understanding, a particular tradition, can be continued and expanded. What are the ethical consequences of this hermeneutical way of working with the past? Engaging the double binds that Jacques Derrida sets up in his essay "This Is Not an Oral Footnote" (1991), and also drawing on Walter Benjamin's "The Task of the Translator" (1923/1968), I will trace the indelible entanglements and limits of the hermeneutical endeavor to transmit what is other to our present terms. This will allow me to expose the ethical necessity of recognizing an exterior point that is beyond meaning, understanding, or communication. The discussion is divided into three sections. First, I provide a consideration of what it means to link onto or make a comment upon texts that oblige us to think beyond our present understanding. Second, I unfold an account of what hermeneutics (via Gadamer 1975) proposes to the task of annotation, that is, to the task of inheriting and reworking the past into our present terms. Finally, I consider what the implications might be for the annotator who comes before the double bind of an interdiction and an injunction that commands and defers beyond our settled terms.

In order to walk somewhat less perplexed into the mire of historical transmission, I will utilize the model of the annotation as the metaphor for engaging these issues. Conceivably this model will allow me to stress and explore the paradoxical issues of linking and transmitting the past into the present. For the annotation as a process of writing, stitching, glossing, while simultaneously extending, renewing, and perpetuating the text (which is always in the past and so other to the present), appears to be an apt image for underscoring what is at stake in the task of facing and reworking what is other to the present. I am here following the gesture of Derrida (1991), who recognizes that inasmuch as the model of the annotation always already implies its "secondary position," its dependence on an other text, its reliance on citing and cutting from a larger and previous piece, it allows us to keep in mind the inevitable limits that catch, entangle, and ultimately subject any act of inheritance and transmission.

Part One: The Stakes in Historical Transmission

> The woman was testifying not to the number of the chimneys blown up but something else, the reality of an unimaginable occurrence. One chimney blown up in Auschwitz was as incredible as four. The number mattered less than the fact of the occurrence. The woman testified to an event that broke the frame of Auschwitz, where Jewish armed revolts just didn't happen, and had no place. She testified to the breakage of a framework. That was historical truth.... Knowledge in testimony is not simply a factual given that is reproduced and replicated by the testifier, but a genuine advent, an event in its own right. (Laub 1992:60, 62)

Right away let us forefront the stakes in historical transmission by engaging with words that do not appear to tell us the "truth" as we know it, words that gesture us to something that escapes our terms, that not only point to our epistemological blind spots but also unsettle our terms. Let us begin by considering how testimonies of historical trauma put us at a loss. For often through their very ambivalence such testimonies *ask* us to have "faith" in what is not present, in that which is unseen and exceeds our understanding. Because such testimonies speak about that which has not been, or cannot be, adequately understood or referred to, it would be unjust if we were to link onto their claims in order to evaluate the extent to which they satisfy "truth conditions." For any attempt to make them subject to a process of verification before a "tribunal of knowledge," which admits only descriptive sentences of cognitive value, would subsume the particular request made by such testimonies: ignoring or forgetting a testimony's implicit injunction to think beyond our present understanding. The temptation for the present to take hold of itself again by understanding what unsettles it, by demanding an explanation, by linking questions of "reality" and "truth" with that which speaks in an other way is, according to Lyotard, always a "possible inevitable temptation"[1] that is available to the addressees (to those that hear the testimony and attempt to link or comment on it). But this possible commentary "cannot annul the event, only tame it and master it, thereby disregarding [*forgetting*] the other" (1988:163–164). The event (the testimony) remains, of course, but the "inevitable temptation" for the addressee to close its vulnerability to the other by turning the testimony into an object of/for knowledge accomplishes to efface not the testimony, but the injunction to think beyond our present understanding. Hence a testimony is forgotten, not necessarily because its content does not get heard or represented, but because a linking (or a commentary) forms, in which the "scandal of the other," that which obliges the addressee to think beyond itself, to make itself vulnerable to difference, comes to be contained in a cognitive set of "qualities" which the addressee "grasps" in order to call itself back to itself (the same).

Obviously then, concerning ourselves with how we comment or link onto testimonies is a serious ethical activity that allows us to question the ways in which "meanings" are created or contained in the complex social process of historical transmission. This is an urgent task when we consider, as the problematic unfolded above suggests, that there is an "inevitable temptation" to mend the ruptures of our "traditional interpretive instruments" by reconciling the plea of the other, which asks us to think beyond the present, within a commentary or a linking that demands a cognitive presentation (a presentation within the same). What is at stake here is how to resist this "inevitable temptation," how to respect the disjunction between our present understanding and that which continually points to our own inability to decipher or determine any "graspable" meaning within our terms. What this suggests, of course, is that our endeavor in linking, commenting, or (more to the point for this discussion) annotating testimonies should avoid those attempts to fill or patch up the holes in our frames of understanding and interpretation, and instead heed the retrieval of difference, which, in always already deferring the present (understanding), comes to provide the condition for the possibility of transmitting an other history. But how can we link onto that which continually calls out our limits and stages our epistemological blind spots? What would it mean to annotate or comment on that which exposes our lack in understanding and interpretation? Does not the possibility of the annotation break down at this point? For does not the annotation necessarily assume the will to define, maintain, understand and hence transmit an event/text as knowledge?

Part Two: Annotating Through the Hermeneutical Loom

Although wanting to talk about the possibility of annotating as a potential ethical endeavor, as a linking that respects the words of the other beyond our present frames of understanding, I realize that this gesture toward a differential (as opposed to assimilative) transmission comes before the law. In wanting to posit the possibility of an annotation that attempts to resist the "inevitable temptation" to link the other within the same, I inevitably bump against the genre (the laws) of the annotation. Although I want to talk about the annotation in another way, I must first note the present fact that the annotation is a historical institution brought into being and governed by the laws of its genre (Derrida 1991:196).

The genre, as a set of laws for transmitting knowledge or information, inevitably relates to many of the dominant traditions/institutions (laws) of interpretation. Its function, at one level, is economic: by transmitting/posting a reading/writing within the institutional borders, it seeks to stabilize the possibilities of interpretation. In this sense, the genre binds the annotation to the text in terms of a "tradition": that is, in terms of a historically mediated form of understanding that shapes and constrains the possible protocols for determining meaning. Although the annotator may certainly revamp and alter textual meanings, he does so only within the genre of an already mediated protocol that enables his re-visioning to be understood. Meaning is thus always situated within a genre: a historically constituted and transmitted institution that is actually a tradition of commentators and annotators.

Notice here that the genre, as an institution for interpreting or transmitting texts, is not based on a timeless and unmediated (prediscursive) form. On the contrary, because the genre is reproduced within a tradition of commentators and annotators who stand in history and speak in language, it is historical and linguistic. Rather than being the foundation for meaning, the genre is a function of tradition, which itself is conditioned on the possibility of transmitting and fusing past commentaries with the present. So inasmuch as the genre binds and conditions the annotator, at one level, the annotator rebinds and reconditions the genre at another. For the annotation is not a "passive," "benign mediation," but an "active transmission" that constantly renews the works of the past as present.[2] The annotator thus reproduces the genre by linking past and present meanings: by the "activation" of past and present presumptions into the fusion of a shared understanding. In this way, "the annotator ... presents a reading that create(s) the acceptable range of conversation within the group he supposedly serves" (Hanna 1991:184). The work of the annotator then makes the continuity and self-understanding of a tradition possible while at the same time fusing the text within the "present living actuality." For the text is not transmitted just to be historically footnoted but to be concretized through interpretation in its current validity.

I have, of course, been reworking the genre of the annotation within a hermeneutical scheme that simultaneously acknowledges the constrained nature and creative character of interpretation/transmission. As a process of interpretation and transmission that works for the preservation and generation of meaning, hermeneutics promises much to the annotator. Indeed its concerns with the possibility of continuity and understanding seem to reflect and conform to the laws of annotation: namely, to define, maintain and transmit an event/text. By following a sketch of some of the claims of hermeneutics (as proposed by Gadamer 1975),[3] I wish to point out the inevitable limits that the annotator will face as he interprets and transmits the meaning of texts hermeneutically, that is, within the generating and constrained laws of the genre.

According to Gadamer, "everything written is in fact in a special way, the object of hermeneutics" (TM:336). Even that which is intended as little more than a gloss on, or a concise reordering of the rhetorical divisions and figures of a text, is guided by a genre that works within the past and present presuppositions of "our" tradition ("our historicality"). Whereas historicism makes its claims to objectivity by proposing to raise itself from the presuppositions of the past and present, hermeneutics regards these presuppositions as continuous: as bridged by tradition, as making possible the fusion of understanding. Because the interpreter cannot occupy some neutral point outside of his linguistically mediated understandings and presuppositions, Gadamer claims that "there can be no such thing as a direct approach to the historical object that would objectively reveal its historical value" or meaning (TM:292). There is no Archimedian point from which human reason (the interpretive method of historicism) can order or recover the past as "objective knowledge" for the present. He goes on, "The truth is that there is always contained in historical understanding the idea that the tradition [transmitted to] us speaks into the present and must be understood in this mediation—indeed, as this mediation" (TM:293; brackets mine). For Gadamer, then, we can only understand from within our present mediation (within our linguistic-historical presuppositions) and so cannot claim to recover some supposed meaning of the historical object apart from our present reconstruction of it. Gadamer attempts to avoid the problematics that would result from such a claim, namely, that of a self-enclosed present, by proposing that our present presuppositions are not hermetically sealed, but rather are "enabling prejudices" that "open up" to the reflective application of one's tradition (TM:258–267).

The fact that the interpreter reads through a specific medium of presuppositions that selects, accents, suppresses, and orders certain aspects of the text creates not the obstacle for grasping the meaning of the text but its enabling condition. Because a text is always at a distance from the present we need to overcome that distance by making sense of it, by drawing out its significance for our time. But the text in order to be understood requires a contact point with the present. For without this contact point, without a medium that is intelligible to the present, the text will not be understood, and so will remain at a distance and perhaps be forgotten. According to this scheme the contact point is to be found in the interpreter's presuppositions ("prejudices"), which constitute the initial directedness of his ability to approach and eventually grasp the text. As the interpreter projects or transfers the language-world he already understands onto the text, he comes to provide a contact with the text that renders it intelligible in the present. Like the translator who works within the language-world of his audience in order to make the text meaningful to it, the interpreter brings into play his presuppositions (which are the forejudgments of the present) and so manages to translate the text's distance into the meaningful terms of the present.

Since the interpreter's present world is projected onto the text, it is evident that there will be no recovery or transmission of the text in its pristine state. In fact the text will be, at all times, selected, ordered, and accented in different ways by different presents. Gadamer sees this as a "productive endeavour," but this translation into the present "does not, of course, mean that [the interpreter/translator] is at liberty to falsify the meaning of what the other person says. Rather, the meaning must be preserved, but since it must be understood within a new linguistic world, it must be expressed within a new way." (TM:346; brackets mine). So the interpreter/translator must simultaneously "respect the character of his own language, into which he is translating, while still recognizing the value of the alien, even antagonistic character of the text and its expression" (TM:349). It is all too evident that in order to avoid the critique that hermeneutics is *only* concerned with how the present (interpreter) appropriates and subsumes the past (text) into its presuppositions Gadamer must provide a reciprocating (circular) explanation of understanding. That is, hermeneutics must account for how the present and the past modify and act on each other so that they fuse and give rise to understanding. Understanding then is not to be conceived as a unilateral process, but as a reciprocal application of the past to the present and the present to the past. Allow me to unfold the workings of this proposal.

Although the interpreter always already starts from his present presuppositions, his desire in wanting to overcome the distance or otherness of the text, by understanding it, means that the text still escapes his full understanding (his presuppositions). This "effort of understanding which is found wherever there is no immediate understanding" sets in motion a process where the interpreter's presuppositions are gradually worked out (legitimated or delegitimated) in his encounter with the text. In other words, because the text resists the imposition of the interpreter's presuppositions, the interpreter must (if he wishes to interpret/understand the text) filter out his legitimate presuppositions from the illegitimate ones. In this process the interpreter's presuppositions will have to prove adequate to the text: that is, they will have to allow for understanding, or they will have to be modified or discarded. Hence, the process of interpretation is a matter not of avoiding our presuppositions but of testing them against the text. As Gadamer writes:

> [The] hermeneutically trained mind must be, from the start, sensitive to the text's newness. But this kind of sensitivity involves neither "neutrality" in the matter of the object nor the extinction of one's self, but the conscious assimilation of one's own fore-meanings and prejudices. The important thing is to be aware of one's own bias, so that the text may present itself in all its newness and thus be able to assert its own truth against one's own fore-meanings. (TM:238)

Because interpretation allows us to examine and modify the legitimacy of our presuppositions, we cannot conceive of the interpretive act as merely something that we do to a text; for in this process something also "happens to us over and above our wanting and doing" (TM:xvi). This reciprocal instance can be treated as analogous to a "successful dialogue": where participants enter into a conversation with their particular view points, but as the dialogue unfolds their presuppositions change since "both are concerned with an object that is placed before them" (TM:341).

> Just as one person seeks to reach agreement with his partner concerning an object, so the interpreter understands the object of which the text speaks ... if successful they both come under the influence of the truth of the object and are thus bound to one another in a new community ... in which we do not remain what we were. (TM:341)

In a "successful dialogue" each participant arrives at a resolution that, thanks to the observations made by each during the discussion, has transformed his or her original presuppositions into a "richer understanding." But this convergence of insight is not the result or the property of either participant; rather it results from a reciprocal relationship that creates a common third.

Something like this convergence of insight also takes place when an interpreter grasps the meaning of a text. As the interpreter encounters the text in its otherness (in its absence from the realm of understanding), he reexamines his presuppositions while also paying attention to what the text seems to be saying. His success in "overcoming the otherness" of the text will, of course, depend on whether he has discovered a way of reconciling some of his present presuppositions (which have undergone reexamination) with what the text seems to be claiming. This process "not only [allows] those prejudices that are of a particular and limited nature to die away, but causes those that bring about genuine understanding to emerge clearly as such" (TM:264). Simultaneously we have here not the recovery of an original text, but rather the application of the text into the meaningful terms of the present. Being able to grasp the meaning of the text allows for a "rising to a higher universality that overcomes not only our own particularity but also that of the other." A "higher universality" develops as understanding renders the presuppositions/particularities of both interpreter and text into a "fusion" that overcomes their parochialism with the common grounds of the tradition. This is "the full realization of conversation, in which something is expressed that is not only mine or my author's, but [a] common [tradition]" (TM:350; brackets mine).

Because a text understood creates a common language, because it creates a "fusion of horizons" that widens the particularities of the present while translating the text into our present circumstances, no past or present horizon (presumption) can be seen as a self-enclosed totality that is fully determined. For each horizon modifies and acts on the other so that they intersect. *Yet* within a given horizon (within the given linguistic-historical presuppositions) a certain order can be detected; and this order, however minimal, comes to govern the ways in which present and past horizontal intersections occur. According to Gadamer our desire to understand a text from the past is not to be thought of so much as an action of one's present subjectivity but as the placing of oneself within a process of tradition (TM:258). For a tradition has always established an order toward any text. Thus, in addition to his presuppositions the interpreter begins his reading/writing of a text with what has already been previously ordered and handed down to him as an "effect" of the text. Since a text is transmitted in time it comes to compile "effects" that will impact upon (constrain) the interpreter's reading/writing. The ways in which the text has been previously discussed, analyzed, questioned, and annotated in books and other media necessarily affect the interpreter's understanding of the text and subsequently transmit the tradition into the present. Here both the "effects" of the text (the old interpretations) and the present understanding to be achieved are the (pro-)creators of the tradition.

The concentric circles that I have been sketching seem to provide the annotator with a model that takes into account his concerns to define, maintain, understand, and hence transmit the text into the present. For the hermeneutical laws, which see understanding as a reciprocal transference between past and present, seem to provide a way for the annotator to understand and transmit something other than himself and his present, and yet define this other in a way that contributes to and expands not only his present understanding but the continuity of understanding in the tradition. The annotator who works within the laws of hermeneutics would not assume that the text's horizon is identical with his present horizon; however, the annotator's *will to* transmit and understand can "only [be] something laid over a *continuing tradition,* and hence it immediately recombines what it has distinguished in order, in the unity of the historical horizon that it thus acquires, to become one with itself" (TM:273; emphasis mine). This circular (self-contradictory) proposal, which moves from difference to identity and back, is what allows the annotator to simultaneously avoid the naïveté of historicism (the claim that the interpreter can objectively recover some supposed meaning of the text outside his own time) and the problematics of a self-enclosed present (the belief in no other time outside the present). But this circular scheme is concentric precisely because its laws lead to and depend upon an all-encompassing and inescapable tradition. For notice that the movement from difference to identity and back is initiated in order to bring about a fusion of horizons that allows us to more fully understand not only the text's intertextuality but also ultimately our tradition. In this way understanding takes place in one direction: toward the common and continuous grounds of our tradition. "Something *distant* has to be brought close, a strangeness overcome, a bridge built between the once and now" in order to ensure an understanding that allows for the continuity of the tradition (Gadamer, cited in Ormiston and Schrift 1990:33). Here the tradition forms the evolving matrix through which all signs must pass on their way to understanding. For Gadamer then, "The truth of the tradition is never put in question, only the dynamics of its communications, extension, renewal, and constant revivification" (Caputo 1987:112).

Although the complex scheme of hermeneutics has attempted to avoid the interpretive constraints of an authorial intention, it ends up replacing it with the constraints of the conventions of the interpretive tradition. While the fusion of horizons claims to allow us to understand the text both in its identity with the present and its difference from it, the scheme remains subservient to the continuity of the tradition "whose being consists in the return to itself from what is other" (TM:15). The hermeneutical project then is ultimately concerned with transmitting and understanding the text in the present in order to "seek one's own in the alien, to become at home in it, [so as to establish] the basic movement of [the tradition]" (TM:15; brackets mine). The reappropriation of the alien into the folds of the finite (historically determined) but indefinitely evolving tradition makes possible "new" meanings, but only within the traditional form (the previous "effects") of understanding that shape and constrain the possible protocols for determining meaning. We are thus assured that behind the different finite expressions there will always be "something" that will allow us to return (grasp) back to the tradition (home). Hence, hermeneutics "gives us comfort in the face of the flux, ... [it] reassure[s] us that all is well, that beneath the surface of historical transition an unchanging, infinite spirit labors" (Caputo 1987:112; brackets mine).

The interpretive community is obviously an important aspect in the continuity of a tradition. For, as hermeneutics argues, it permits the retelling of the text into the present circumstances, allowing creative transformation while still maintaining the predominant sense of what is "true" and "valuable" about the tradition. Here both textual predecessors and present interpreters form a fabric of intertextuality that weaves texts to other texts and contexts. Reading and retelling within the interpretive community, we come to recognize and utilize normative and literary allusions that help us to understand our sense of self and our traditions more fully.

Part Three: Annotating Otherwise

But what happens when we come upon that which does not provide us with any information or understanding? What value do we attribute to that which cannot be told as a retelling, to that which does not make allusions to the generic conventions of our tradition? Reading and retelling within the interpretive community seems ethically suspect when we consider these questions. For if understanding requires the reconciliation of the interpreter's present presumptions with the text and its mediated "effects" we can only be affected by that which has already been presently or previously understood within the tradition. In other words, understanding is a matter of weaving and retelling those presumptions that cohere with the already established allusions of a tradition. The intertextual weavings, in this sense, would mummify the singularity and surprise of the strangeness of the other within the familiar. As Nietzsche reminds us, this "familiar means what we are used to so that we no longer marvel at it, our everyday, some *rule* in which we are stuck, anything at all in which we feel at home. Look, isn't our need for knowledge precisely this need for the familiar, the will to uncover under everything strange, unusual, and questionable something that no longer disturbs us?" (cited in Ormiston and Schrift 1990:14).

What happens when a retelling is a telling that *disturbs* the frames of the familiar? Are we responsible for retelling it so that we can come to understand it? Are we to understand it so that we can repair the tears of our tradition? By again considering these self-questioning questions alongside the hermeneutical will to fuse the past and the present into a horizon that enriches and continues the tradition, we, at this point, must explicitly take note of the limits of the very motor of hermeneutics: the will to understand, to overcome, to grasp the other within the genre of an already mediated protocol for determining meaning. For hermeneutics views the continual expansion of the tradition, and I would add of Being, as fundamentally grounded on the will to understand. Early in *Truth and Method* Gadamer writes, "The ability to understand is the fundamental endowment of man, one that sustains his communal life with others" (TM:21). Through understanding we have coherences, contexts, correspondences, and thus the fundamental predicate of human existence. In this sense, all attempts at linking or commenting with an other (our "communal life with others") are inevitably weaved within the laws for transmitting knowledge or information. Clearly then, hermeneutics shows itself to be an ontological project that expels all that overflows understanding. The juridical implication of hermeneutics mimics the Occidental interpretive practice of reconciling the difference of the other within the assumed Identity of the tradition. Like Plato's strategic footnoting of Homer's texts within the binding of his Republic, or the Church patriarchs' exegetical reworkings of the disruptive texts of the Old Testament into the "New" institutionalized encasement, the annotator who works hermeneutically becomes part of a tradition that can be characterized by a "supervisory" law of interpretation and transmission. This is a law that, despite the always already dispersing Identity of the text, attempts to domesticate or exclude the contradictions or disturbances that might undermine the fusion of understanding or the identity of the tradition.

The annotator who seeks to transmit the meaning of a text comes before a set of laws that simultaneously constrain and recreate the prevailing relations between texts, contexts, normative, and literary allusions that exist within the self-enlarging totality of the tradition. If we want to avoid the ethically bankrupt claim that maintains the priority of a self-enlarging totality over that which disrupts it, we would have to breach all laws that threaten the exteriority of the other. In other words, our annotations would have to more or less cease concerning themselves with the will to transmit/relate meaning and instead attempt to secure the alterity that overflows understanding. This would put the annotator before the law in a fundamentally different way (Derrida 1991:201).

Concerned with preserving the exteriority of the other, the annotator comes before the limits of those laws that constrain and recreate how texts are related to other texts and how meaning is to be preserved and transmitted within this relationship. Because the other is to be absolutely exterior, the other cannot be grasped in terms of any cognitive relation. If the other is to be beyond any totality it must rupture and baffle the prevailing intertextual relations of the tradition. Hence, the inaccessible relation to the other puts the annotator before the Law of law, before what must not and cannot be reconciled within the prevailing relations of the interpretive system.

But what would this coming before the Law of law actually imply for the annotation? What results when our annotations are obliged before that which cannot be grasped as a relation? Of course, these questions, which are always about grasping the meaning of that which is beyond meaning, cannot be considered without the direct risk of *meaning* nothing. Of course, then these questions should not be approached directly; so allow me to further entangle this discussion by unraveling the threads of a double bind. In the essay entitled "This Is Not an Oral Footnote," Derrida proposes that the annotator comes before the "prescriptive double bind of an interdiction and an injunction":

> [W]e see how this law text, which makes the law, produces at the same time a double bind: it says to the reader or auditor, "Be quiet, all has been said, you have nothing to say, obey in silence," while at the same time it implores, it cries out, it says, "Read me and respond: if you want to read me and hear me, you must understand me, know me, interpret me, translate me, and hence, in responding to me and speaking to me, you must begin to speak in my place, to enter a rivalry with me. (1991:201–202)

If we want to transmit the meaning of a text we come before an injunction that compels us to *read and respond* and so *create* relations (a restitution) between the text and the interpretive system. Implicitly or explicitly we will create these relations by selecting and reframing the text so that it points to and stands for our present concerns; in other words, our retellings for the present will displace and rival the text as it *speaks in its place*. Having worked through Gadamer's circular proposal, that simultaneously acknowledges the creative character and constrained nature of transmission, we recognize the setting here and perhaps anticipate that this injunction (*to create*) will be insufficient/problematic without an equally commanding opposite (*a constraint*). Thus, in what appears to be a hermeneutical gesture Derrida binds before this injunction an interdiction that obliges us to *be quiet*, to humble ourselves so as to respect and consider the claims and "effects" of the text: *all that has been said* before. In Gadamer's hermeneutical scheme the apparent conundrum between the injunction and the interdiction is overcome by the will to understand. For the will to understand sets in motion a reciprocating (circular) process where the interpreter's present presumptions are gradually worked out with the constraints of the text's claims and "effects," in order to produce a fusion of understanding—a fusion that, to remind ourselves, leads to the continuity and enrichment of the tradition. But notice that in Derrida's scheme the relation between the injunction and the interdiction does not produce any circular or reciprocating movement that would lead to some gradual integration, or an emerging totality, or any ongoing continuity. The relationship between the injunction and the interdiction is unmoving, static, rigid: it is precisely a *double bind*.

Doubly bound to the constraints of the text and the creative act of interpretation the annotator, according to Derrida, is *caught* (1991:192, 201). Equally caught and compelled before an injunction and an interdiction the annotator attempts to wander back and forth, but his circular movements in truth go nowhere: "I cannot or should not speak, but I promised that I would do so. I must and cannot; in truth, I should and should not keep my promise" (Derrida 1991:201). In truth, the annotator says nothing definite and presents no identifiable relations between texts except for an endless deferral: *I must and cannot; I should and should not.* Caught between the possibility and impossibility, between the necessity and prohibition of interpretation, the annotator cannot really transmit the meaning of the text and so "puts off until 'later' what is presently denied, the possible that is presently impossible" (Derrida, cited in Behler 1991:71). Has the annotator broken his promise (at least one of them)? Or does he despite it all keep the Promise of his promise?

It is true here that the annotator does not fulfill his postal function of receiving and sending meaning, but in the preface to the paradoxical binding of the annotator Derrida has already warned us that "*the destiny of an annotation is to be always bad*" (1991:102). Fated to always break or garble the chain (destiny) of messages between the proper senders and the proper addressee, for recall that he is caught between an unavoidable and impossible task (his promise to respect the injunction and an interdiction), the annotator can only remain true to the Promise of his promise. This Promise is not the promise to transmit/fulfill meaning (later), but the Promise within every promise that can *never* be now nor have ever a present time: a time when one can simultaneously (and absurdly) say, "I promise you now" and "I have delivered my Promise to you now." The annotator's concern then is with a lack, an irrecuperable beyond, with a tense state that is never (and never will be) here and now, with an infinitely deferred future perfect: that Promises the promise.

This promissory aspect gestures the annotator toward a point of exteriority that cannot be recovered or contained by any reading or retelling (weaving) within the interpretive community. Unlike the hermeneutical gesture, the concern here is not to preserve and recreate the intertextual laws that exist within the self-enlarging tradition but rather to bring these laws before the Law. Before the Law of law the annotator no longer recollects or weaves the threads of the text into the intertextual fabric of the tradition; instead he unravels the threads and so tears the fabric, exposing the once seamless web of meaning to the very construction and limits of its material. This unraveling that concerns itself with the promissory aspect of that which will never be present in any present exposes the law (that which guides the synchronous succession of past and present texts within the folds of the tradition) to the Law (to that which lies beyond all fusion, all totality). This unraveling and tearing unveil the violence in the law: the violence of every interpretation, of every meaning, of every intertextual relation that inevitably excludes in its will to represent. Before the Law of law the annotator would keep reminding the law of what remains from its inevitable violence. Before this ethical critique of law, the annotator, apart from anything else, would have to attempt to allow the other to (somehow) reappear both as the point of exteriority (as the beyond/possible to every present/totality) and as the excluded other.

But by this point the "what" question, which has commissioned this discussion and hence undoubtedly retains itself at the back of our minds, must be explicitly posed: what would this annotator (who works before the Law of law) annotate if not meaning, if not relations, if not the application of the text? What type of annotation would this *be*? Although concerned with that which is always already lacking, the annotator surely in the very presence of writing his annotation risks *meaning* nothing: risks turning what is beyond meaning into *meaning*. But perhaps we can think of a residual activity in language that will always exceed or interrupt the immanence of the Same, the recuperating weaving of meaning; Derrida certainly sees the activity of "nothingness" in this way when he speaks of a critical "space" that allows us to ask the question, "(what is) meaning to say?"

> [I]t is necessary in such a space, and guided by such a question, that writing literally mean nothing. Not that it is absurd in the way that absurdity has always been in solidarity with metaphysical meaning. It simply tempts itself, tenders itself, attempts to keep itself at the point of the exhaustion of meaning. To risk meaning nothing is to start to play, and first to enter into the play of *différance* which prevents any word, any concept, any major enunciation from coming to summarize and to govern from the theological presence of a center the movement and textual spacing of differences. Whence ... the chain of substitutions ... which is not simply a metonymical operation that would leave intact the conceptual identities, the signified idealities, that the chain would be happy just to translate to put in circulation.... To be entangled in hundreds of pages of a writing simultaneously insistent and elliptical, imprinting, as you saw, even its erasures, carrying off each concept into an interminable chain of differences, surrounding or confusing itself with so many precautions, references, notes, citations, collages, supplements—this "meaning-to-say-nothing" is not, you will agree, the most assured of exercises. (1981:14)

Because what is said is always lacking or exceeding the sense that it gestures toward, tracing the limits of meaning will not lead us into silence but will involve and entangle us in the unrelenting task of unraveling the *undecidability* encountered each time we face a text. While following the play of *différance* may expose the heddles that grasp the threads of meaning, there are no ontological resonances—no attempt to mean anything—within this process of clarification/unraveling. Being neither a word nor a concept, the play of *différance* (the play of nothingness/deferral) mobilizes/traces an exclusively "negative activity." But this is truly a *strange* "negative activity," for *différance* marks the space of the neither/nor that *is nothing*—that which resists predication. In this sense, we cannot speak of *différance* as something that could be meaningful or unmeaningful, that is present or absent, that could be recoverable or lost, that is or is not: it has no end, no telos, no origin, no whole that will ever be present.[4] Neither being nor nonbeing *différance* offers us a "negativity" that tempts, strains, and exhausts the already existing positive and negative (binary) register; it offers us the nondialectical and nonsynthetic *activity* (infinite deferral) of language.

Do we not again come upon a point of exteriority that cannot be recovered or contained within any relation or totality? This discussion seems to be *caught* up with this point. But the question was (and impossibly insists), "what" would the annotator annotate if not meaning? Although I risk meaning nothing (risk turning this "nothing" into meaning), the suggestion that keeps apprehending the discussion seems to imply that the task of the annotator is not only to unravel that which has been excluded and remains unrepresentable (the differences that take place inside the text, and between texts/context), but also to transmit/release—through the performative play of *différance* that takes place in every present/time—the impossible yet urgent aspiration of what Benjamin calls "pure language."

Before we dismiss the latter claim as at best leading to another negative theology (ontology) or at worst to some quasi-mystical time, I want to give force to the reading that Benjamin's "pure language" is *nothing really* but an urgent aspiration to what is beyond us. Why should the transmission/release of this urgent yet impossible aspiration concern the annotator? Benjamin's essay "The Task of the Translator" concerns itself with the provocative and enigmatic attempt at interpreting and transmitting otherwise than meaning. He claims:

> The traditional concepts in any discussion of translations are fidelity and license—the freedom of faithful reproductions and, in its service, fidelity to the word. These ideas seem to be no longer serviceable to a theory that looks for other things in a translation than reproduction of meaning.... For this very reason translation must in large measure refrain from wanting to communicate something, from rendering sense. (1968:77–78)

Much like Derrida's performative engagement with the annotation, Benjamin's working through the possibility of translation recognizes the hermeneutical conundrum between the poles of fidelity (the constraint of the text) and license (the injunction to create/relate the text within our present concerns), and in a somewhat similar gesture proposes not the reconciliation between these two poles, but an exterior point that escapes the register of communication (understanding). For Benjamin a translation fails when it limits itself to transmit information (meaning) since information is the least essential part of a text (1968:69–70). Hence the task of the translator is not to communicate something but to release the more or less veiled, yet nonetheless urgent aspiration that remains within all language: the impossible possibility for a "pure language" beyond the *function* of meaning.

The release of this breath (which is *really nothing*) actually cracks the universal empire of the Same, which claims to guarantee all translations by the presence of shared signifieds (meaning) among all languages. Because the aspiration of a "pure language" is beyond meaning we do not seek an original meaning that then comes to be translated: an identity on the level of the signified that can be interchanged on the level of the signifier. Brushing his language against the grain of an other language, the translator reveals that *we cannot understand what we do not understand until we see that our understanding fails,* that our language lacks the Same. Translating this aspiration which is beyond meaning—beyond any identifiable signified that functions between each language or context—actually exposes the translator's own language to what cannot be interchanged, to what remains outside any relation. In this way the translator becomes aware of the previously unacknowledged limits of *his own* language. The translator thus "realizes in his own language that pure language which is under the spell of another . . . For the sake of pure language he breaks through decayed barriers of his own language" (Benjamin 1968:80). A translation that aspires to the limits of meaning (a "pure language") provides language with the possibility to distance itself from itself in a self-reflexive (self-alienating) act that welcomes the strange and retranslates/reworks/reinvents *itself* through the reader.

The seductive appeal of hermeneutics is in its complex justification for *what* we understand. It plays on our "inevitable temptation" to gather all the loose threads within the comfort of home. Dissolving the ossified poles that form the basis of the hermeneutical loom will bring us into a place of uncertainty and *undecidability* that certainly will be haunted by texts that have no "resting point," by words that go nowhere finally—toward no predefined end/destiny/home. Benjamin's aspiration for a "pure language" is not an otherworldly denial of *what* we understand/communicate, but an urgent gasp for *how* we might open our symbolic realm to what is *otherwise* than *what* we understand/communicate. This aspiration seeks to correct "the basic error of the translator . . . that preserves the state in which his own language happens to be instead of allowing his language to be powerfully affected by the foreign tongue" (Benjamin 1968:81). Benjamin's translator, and Derrida's entanglement with the annotation, thus offers us not a formula or rule for transmission and interpretation but an aspiration that seeks to resuscitate and so release the breath and possibility in language. One does not, properly speaking, perceive this breath; nor can one in perpetuity cling or grasp onto its impossible possibility.[5]

Both Benjamin and Derrida respectively ensnare us through *double binds* (between the poles of fidelity and license, between the injunction and the interdiction), not as a hermeneutical prop or rehearsal, but so that we may come to grapple with that *moment* of *undecidability* that presents us with the task and (im)possibility of transmitting the words of the other into the present. The paradoxical bind between fidelity and license thus does not impose paralysis; rather it is in fact the very condition of a *responsible approach,* of a responsible *decision* to texts from other times and places. The moment of *undecidability* invoked through the tension and entanglement between the poles of fidelity and license is precisely an *aporetic* moment, that is, a moment where the rules with how to proceed, with exactly how much authority should be given to the words of the other or how much license to take in order to reanimate them so that they can become significant for us, are in contradiction, tangled, not insured, or not known in advance. It is a moment that recognizes that for responsibility to be possible at all an instance of *undecidability* must face us and bind our attention; otherwise the responsibility for reception and transmission would merely deteriorate into a programmatic or formulaic application of rules.

Undecidability thus gives the annotator a task; it is an instance of *obligation* where she must *face* her decisions between fidelity and license without recourse to any preset schemata that would ensure the resolution to a conflict or would justify an answer through a rule. In this way it obliges and subjects the annotator as a reader—as an inheritor of texts, as one who simultaneously aspires to transmit, change, betray, and preserve the words of the other—to pay close *attention,* to take and think her time, to carefully attend to how the words of the other face her here, now, and beyond. This calls the annotator to a particular accountability for *how* her encounter and transmission proceeds through the interminable questions, tensions, and double binds that issue from her reading practices, from being faced by the words of an absent other who demands fidelity and yet needs her to take license. The gesture to accountability is not to establish any final resolution or reconciliation, but rather to preserve and engage the tensions, tangles, and double binds thus described.[6]

Notes

1. It is worth noting the full force of Lyotard's ethical point here:

> An addressor appears whose addressee I am, and whom I know nothing, except that he or she situates me upon the addressee instance. The violence of the revelation is in the ego's expulsion from the addressor instance, from which it managed its work of enjoyment, power, and cognition. It is the scandal of an I displaced onto the you instance. The I turned you tries to repossess itself through the understanding of what dispossesses it. Another phrase is formed, in which the I returns in the addressor's situation, in order to legitimate or to reject—it doesn't matter which—the scandal of the other's phrase and of its own dispossession. *This new phrase is always possible, like an inevitable temptation. But it cannot annul the event, it can only tame and master it, thereby disregarding [forgetting] the transcendence of the other.* (Lyotard 1988: 110–111; emphasis mine)

2. Ralph Hanna III takes issue with those rhetorical rules that require the annotator to avoid interpretation or the imposition of his being onto the text. He claims that these rules consequently give way to the dismemberment of the annotator from the annotation: "Twentieth-century annotators are completely removed from the text page (reduced merely to textual evidence) and are required to fragment their activities into tasks presented as rhetorically discrete, so that they can never appear whole consciousness in touch with the text. But . . . this rhetorical prescription seems to me merely an expression of guilty knowledge, a way of allowing annotation to proceed as a form of benign mediation, a service profession, which it is not" (1991:180–181).

3. G. Gadamer, *Truth and Method,* G. Barden and J. Cumming (trans. and eds.) (New York: Seabury Press, 1975). Henceforth cited as: (TM: followed by page number).

4. One of the "nondescriptions" that Derrida provides of *différance* claims:

> Already we have to delineate *that différance is not*, does not exist, is not a present-being in any form; and we will be led to delineate also everything *that* it *is not,* that is, *everything*; and consequently that it has neither existence nor essence. It derives from no category of being, whether present or absent ... *Différance* is not only irreducible to any ontological or theological onto-theological reappropriation, but as the very opening of the space in which ontotheology—philosophy—produces its system and its history, it includes ontotheology, inscribing it and exceeding it without return. (1992:110

5. In an evocative/performative reading that explores the citation through Derrida's spectral logic, Julian Wolfreys gestures us to consider the myriad of ways in which the citation (thought of as an authorial mark that arrives from another time and place, as a mark that is inherently iterable, hence annotation-able, translatable, etc.) haunts all reading and writing. As a means of considering the *impossible possibility* that the citation unleashes (as challenge/task/limit) in language he asks, "Is it ever possible (or indeed inescapable) to cite resonance, atmosphere, or to put it more crudely, tone, style?" (2002:23).

6. Extending from Derrida's suggestion I want to note that the tension between 1) the *interdiction* that obliges us to guard the particularity of the referent/text, and 2) the *injunction* that equally obliges us to transmit the text so that it makes a contact point with our present terms is what makes possible the conception of a dissemination that does not efface the singularity of the address while passing it on. The tension thus exists as an *ethical force* that interrupts the immanence of any injunction or interdiction that excludes its relation to another imperative or temporal modality that contradicts or points to the lack of its own self-sufficiency.

References

Behler, Ernst. *Confrontations: Derrida/Heidegger/Nietzsche*, Steven Taubeneck (trans.). Stanford: Stanford University Press, 1991.

Benjamin, Walter. "The Task of the Translator." In *Illuminations*, Hannah Arendt (ed.); Hanry Zohn (trans.), pp. 69–82. New York: Schocken Books, 1923/1968.

Caputo, John. *Radical Hermeneutics: Repetition, Deconstruction and the Hermeneutic Project*. Bloomington and Indianapolis: Indiana University Press, 1987.

Derrida, Jacques. "Implications: Interview with Henri Ronse." In *Positions*, Alan Bass (trans.), pp. 1–14. Chicago: Chicago University Press, 1981.

———. "This Is Not an Oral Footnote." In *Annotation and Its Texts*, Stephen A. Barney (ed.), pp. 192–205. New York: Oxford University Press, 1991.

———. "Differance." In *A Critical and Cultural Theory Reader*, 1st ed. Antony Easthope and Kate McGowan (eds.), pp. 101–132. Toronto and Buffalo: University of Toronto Press, 1992.

Gadamer, Hans-Georg. *Truth and Method*, G. Barden and J. Cummings (trans. and eds.). New York: Seabury Press, 1975.

Hanna, Ralph III. "Annotation as Social Practice." In *Annotation and Its Texts*, Stephen A. Barney (ed.), pp. 178–184. New York: Oxford University Press, 1991.

Laub, Dori. "Bearing Witness or the Vicissitudes of Listening." In *Testimony: Crisis of Witnessing in Literature, Psychoanalysis and History*, Shoshana Felman and Dori Laub (eds.), pp. 57–74. New York: Routledge, 1992.

Lyotard, Jean-François. *The Differend: Phrases in Dispute*, G. Van Den (trans.). Minneapolis: University of Minnesota Press, 1988.

Ormiston, Gayle L., and Alan Schrift, eds. *Transforming the Hermeneutic Context: From Nietzsche to Nancy*. Albany: State University of New York Press, 1990.

Wolfreys, Julian. "Citation's Haunt: Specters of Derrida," *Mosaic* 35 (1 March, 2002): 21–34.

Wyschogrod, Edith. *An Ethics of Remembering: History, Heterology, and the Nameless Others*. Chicago, London: University of Chicago Press, 1998.

CHAPTER 11

Moving Beyond the Modernist/Postmodernist Knowledge Binary

Toward a Cosmopolitical Pedagogy and a New Academic Responsibility

Gregory O'Leary and Peter Pericles Trifonas

Introduction

Many who write in the field of education, especially when articulating a conception of knowledge for schooling, shy away from labels like *modernist* or *postmodernist*. This is none too surprising given that a lot is projected onto either term. The former is sometimes equated with epistemological realism, empiricism, or positivism, regardless of the particularity of the position. Linkage to absolute truth and epistemic certainty in schooling and curriculum development is quite often assumed. A similarly restrictive set of connotations accompany the latter term. Everything from complete nihilism to radical relativism is arbitrarily attached. Some think all postmodernist educators unilaterally reject all claims to knowledge. While closer inspection usually reveals that few theorists fit so neatly into such classifications, the impact of such entrenchment on the field of education has been nonetheless profound.

Because we have lived within the conceptual locations that divide so-called modernist and postmodernist perspectives for so long, we have constructed paradigms of exclusion with respect to understanding how to overcome difference within pedagogical formations and what it means to know. There is a current need to readdress the conceptual grounds of the divide, to clarify some of the ideological presuppositions, and to reach a synthesis between paradigmatic positions in terms of where curriculum theory currently stands.

Within this chapter, we historically trace the reintroduction of a modernist view of education through a seminal article written by Paul Hirst some forty years ago. As a corrective to overly generalized depictions of modernist educational theory, which sometimes reduce all modernist pedagogy to a series of vague all-inclusive descriptors, we decided to start with a specific and "famous" article on liberal education from the academic right (Martin, 1981: 98). By juxtaposing Hirst's conception of a liberal education (which is both situated within and differentiated from the classical principles that preceded it) with some of the postmodern and poststructural ideas around education and knowledge that have since followed, we hope to get to a place where we can begin to map out future trajectories and pathways for education and curriculum theory. To simply ask what knowledge is of the most worth is no longer enough. It reveals the limitations of a pseudo-, unproductive schism that has stunted the growth and progress of educational thinking. Rather than providing yet another tug in a war of positions, it is time to direct our efforts toward responsibly engaging others in education. It is time for a new ethical "turn" in educational thinking and our conception of academic responsibility.

Paul Hirst—Liberal Education and the Nature of Knowledge

From the start of his essay "Liberal Education and the Nature of Knowledge," Hirst (1965) argues that the phrase "liberal education" takes on many different meanings depending on the author and the context in which it is used. In fact, he argues that liberal education, unfortunately, is usually defined by what it is not. Hirst wants to rectify this negative tendency by giving liberal education an explicit positive content, so that it can be of use in the serious business of educational planning. His contention is that a *liberal education,* regardless of the vagaries characterizing the use of the term, is "an education based fairly and squarely on the nature of knowledge itself, a concept central to the discussion of education at any level" (LE:1).[1]

Classical Conceptions—A Greek Notion of Liberal Education

Hirst starts his analysis by looking back to a Greek notion of liberal education. In this classical conception, education was rooted in two philosophical doctrines. The first involved the doctrine that it was the mind's very nature to pursue knowledge. Thus, in doing so, humanity was thought to be pursuing the good of the mind and the good life generally. The achievement of knowledge was the means to this end. Second, it was thought that the mind, in the right use of reason, could know the essential nature of things. Thus, human life was actually given shape by what was thought to be true, knowledge that corresponded with reality. The whole of human understanding was hierarchically structured, and justified, by forms of knowledge that were "ultimately real and immutable" (LE:2).

The implication of these two doctrines is threefold. Through a process of education concerned simply and directly with the pursuit of knowledge, corresponding to objective reality, the Greeks based education on what was thought to be true (*aletheia*), as opposed to passing values or fleeting opinions (*doxa*). Second, because this knowledge was thought to be a virtue, education had value as the fulfillment of the mind, and was not motivated by some purely vocational consideration. And, third, given the significance of knowledge for the good life, liberal education had a prescriptive quality, essential to human understanding of how we ought to live. Education was liberal because it freed the mind to function according to its true nature. It freed reason from error and conduct from wrong. For the Greeks, education was freedom, generally.

Hirst notes that this Greek ideal has had a prominent place throughout history. In fact, he asserts that the final ground, for the values that should determine education, has "ever since the Greeks been repeatedly located in man's conception of the diverse forms of knowledge he has achieved" (LE:3). Hirst, as he stated clearly at the outset of his essay, also agrees that any truly liberal education system must involve an introduction to and pursuit of the forms of knowledge. The definition and justification of liberal education must be based "on the nature and significance of knowledge itself, and not on the predilections of pupils, the demands of society, or the whims of politicians" (LE:3).

Educating "Outside" the Forms of Knowledge

Failure to base schooling in the forms of knowledge leads to problems of a serious nature for Hirst. This is evident in his analysis of a well-known report released by Harvard that, in his opinion, privileged mental abilities in the characterization of liberal education. In *General Education in a Free Society: Report of the Harvard Committee,* liberal education is defined through both "the qualities of mind it ought to produce and the forms of knowledge with which it ought to be concerned" (LE:5). But, according to Hirst, the relationship between the two is never made clear. Describing education is said to be "at one time looking to the good man in society and at another time as dictated by the nature of knowledge itself" (*General Education in a Free Society,* 1946: 58). But, again, in Hirst's opinion, the latter is never given precedence in the report, as what is being aimed at is clearly "the cultivation of certain aptitudes and attitudes of the mind" (ibid.). These mental abilities are: to think effectively, to communicate thought, to make relevant judgments, and to discriminate among values. According to the report, these are characteristics of the mind "so important as to prescribe how general education should be carried out" (ibid., 65).

But how these aims of education are to be carried out, other than the vague notion that these abilities must be "consciously developed in all studies and generalized as far as possible" is never fully explicated (LE:6). Worse yet for Hirst is the distinct impression given in the report that "liberal education can be characterized in terms of mental abilities and independently of fully specifying the forms of knowledge" (LE:6). For Hirst, terms like "effective thinking" are used as labels for mental activities that result in an achievement within a form of knowledge, such as the solving of a mathematical problem. Thus, the criteria for effective thinking is peculiar to the particular area of knowledge concerned; otherwise it has no significant application. For Hirst, it is "only when all the abilities are fully divided out into the various domains and we see what they refer to in public terms that it is at all clear what is involved in developing them" (LE:7). No adequate account of a liberal education can be premised on supposedly general unitary abilities that rest outside the forms of knowledge and, hence, the particular criteria for their application.

The Seeds of Separation

Hirst separates his particular conception of knowledge from the significance the basic Greek doctrines give to the notion that knowledge is developed through "a unified picture of the mind in its relation to reality" (LE:4). Hirst was keenly aware of the difference between arguing that knowledge is grounded in reality and arguing that knowledge involves the growth of "ever clearer and finer distinctions in our experience" (LE:23). He is also well aware of the fact that the Greek notion of liberal education in the pursuit of knowledge is "seeking the development of the mind according to what is quite external to it, the structure and pattern of reality" (LE:4). If the justification of the whole Greek position is heavily predicated on the truth and value of coming to know the essential nature of things, what happens if knowledge is no longer thought to be rooted in some reality? If any doubt is cast on the nature of knowledge, and knowledge is no longer seen as the understanding of reality, the whole harmonious Greek structure defining the nature of the relationship between mind, knowledge, and reality is "liable to disintegrate" (LE:4). Thus, Hirst asks "whether those who do not hold the doctrines of metaphysical and epistemological realism can legitimately subscribe to a concept of education of this kind" (LE:3). This is surely one of the main reasons for his present reassertion and reinterpretation of Greek principles predicated on a somewhat different understanding of the forms and nature of knowledge.

Reasserting and Reinterpreting the Basis of Classical Schooling

It is clear that Hirst's conception of a liberal education, like that of his Greek predecessors, is determined in scope and content by knowledge itself. Hirst even says that his idea of a liberal education has "significance parallel to that of the original Greek concept. It is [still] an education concerned directly with the development of the mind in rational knowledge, whatever form that freely takes" (LE:14). But this is "no longer supported by epistemological and metaphysical doctrines that result in a hierarchical organization of the various forms of knowledge ... the doctrines of classical realism based on the ultimacy of knowledge as ordered and determined by reality" (LE:12). Hirst's present reformulation of the Greek conception of liberal education is, thus, not based in metaphysical realism and not to be "confused with attempts to mold the mind to some external reality (Bailey, 1984: 69).

Hirst's Conception of Liberal Education—The Forms "Reformulated"

For Hirst a consistent conception of a liberal education must be worked out fully in terms of the forms of knowledge. And, for Hirst, a developed form of knowledge is thought to have four distinguishing features. First, the developed form contains central concepts that are peculiar in character to the form, such as figurative language in literature. Second, the form has a distinctive logical structure and, thus, a network of possible relations in which experience can be understood. Third, the form is testable against experience in accordance with particular criteria that are peculiar to the form. And, fourth, the form has developed particular techniques and skills for exploring experience and testing distinct expressions, the result of which has been the "amassing of all the symbolically expressed knowledge that we have in the arts and the sciences" (LE:16). Though the forms are distinguishable in these ways, this is not to say that "acquiring knowledge of any form is simply a matter of solitary study of the symbolic expressions of knowledge" (LE:16). Hirst is clear that all knowledge also involves some measure of making judgments and using symbols in ways that can only be learned in a tradition. Rather than base his conception of the forms on knowledge that are thought to correspond to what is ultimately real, Hirst defines the forms of knowledge as "the complex ways of understanding experience which man has achieved, which are publicly specifiable and gained through learning" (LE:9). For this reason, a liberal education must concern itself with "developing a person's ways of understanding experience" (LE:19).

For Hirst, it is the disciplines that constitute the range of unique ways we have of understanding experience. Thus, in order to be able to interpret experience comprehensively, certain disciplinary skills must be acquired. Although Hirst goes to some lengths in his later writings to deny that these forms are themselves intellectual disciplines, it is safe to conclude that his liberally educated person will acquire the conceptual schemes and cognitive perspectives they are supposed to have through a study of mathematics, physical sciences, human sciences, history, religion, literature and the fine arts, and philosophy (Martin, 1981: 99). These forms essentially represent the classification of knowledge into distinguishable and definable conceptual frameworks through publicly denoted criteria and publicly recognizable sets of operating symbols. These are, for Hirst, the "basic articulations whereby the whole of experience has become intelligible to man" (LE:11).

It would appear to follow that Hirst is in no way precluding integrated study of the forms of knowledge. The disciplines "will not necessarily be studied separately" and may even borrow from one another (Martin, 1981: 99). But, as was evident in Hirst's rendering of the Harvard Report, this is not to be confused with advocating that the development of a mental ability in one discipline will necessarily result in the existence of the same ability in another domain of knowledge. According to Hirst, such a "facile view is seen to be quite untenable if it is once understood how these abilities are defined and how any one form of knowledge is related to them" (LE:8). Hirst purports that this "unfortunate desire to use unifying concepts is a relic of the time when all the forms of knowledge were thought to be similar" (LE:7). But the extent to which this is true "is a matter for empirical investigation into the transfer of training" (LE:7). Furthermore, there is the "danger of looking for transfer of skills where none is discernible" (LE:8). It is "much more plausible and much more common to relate directly the study of particular subjects" (LE:8).

In summary, Hirst's conception of liberal education is concerned with the comprehensive development of the mind in acquiring knowledge. Schooling, then, is determined in scope and content by knowledge itself, grounded in our experience of the "common world of persons and things we all share" and structured through a framework of disciplines (LE:23). The aim of the study of a discipline is to develop a student's way of understanding experience and the "distinct way in which our experience becomes structured round the use of accepted public symbols" (LE:15). It is "to come to have experience articulated by means of various conceptual schemas" (LE:12). The student is, thus, schooled in the lessons of human experience over given content areas and disciplines that form the mind. And, thus, the mind, in Hirst's re-interpretation, is not thought to take on the pattern of, or conform to, some external reality. But this is not to diminish the "objectivity" of education for Hirst. Public criteria are still thought to provide objectivity to the forms of knowledge. Coming to understand a form of knowledge involves satisfying "the meaningful and valid ways in which its terms and criteria are used ... the publicly accepted framework of knowledge" (LE:21). Over time these become "objectified and progressively developed," establishing criteria through which disciplines develop and human experience can be understood. To be liberally educated, one must be initiated into these distinguishable forms of knowledge.

Some Implications of Hirst's Model

Hirst does not delve too deeply into the implications of his theory for the practical conduct of liberal education. He only makes "certain very general comments about the characteristic features" of schooling within his conception of a liberal education, as a more "detailed treatment would involve psychological and other considerations that are quite beyond the scope of [his] paper" (LE:18). Still, it is not too difficult to envision the type of schooling that Hirst is advocating here.

According to Hirst, liberal education is concerned with the comprehensive development of the mind in acquiring knowledge. And this acquisition of knowledge should come via critical training and discipline. For Hirst, the student should acquire facts, conceptual schemes and techniques for different types of reasoning. Curricula must be constructed to introduce students to each of the several disciplines and "must be constructed to cover at least in some measure the range of knowledge as a whole" (LE:18).

A liberal education is not concerned with the technician's knowledge of the detailed application of the disciplines in practical and theoretical fields. According to Hirst, what is being sought is "sufficient immersion in the discipline for a person to know the distinctive way it works ... and then sufficient generalization over the whole range of the discipline so that his experience begins to be widely structured in this distinctive manner" (LE:19). What is being aimed for, according to Hirst, is that students come to look at things in a certain way. Liberal education is more about being able to recognize empirical assertions or aesthetic judgments for what they are, as opposed to knowing all the details that can in fact be discerned. To this Hirst adds that students should have and know an outline of the major achievements in each area. This provides "some grasp of the range and scope of experience that has thus become intelligible" (LE:19).

Hirst extends this line of thinking when he advocates that a liberal education should be composed of study of at least the paradigm examples of all of the various forms of knowledge in the disciplines. This study is to be "sufficiently detailed and sustained to give genuine insight so that pupils come to think in these terms" (LE:20). Hirst wants liberal education to provide students with the means to use concepts and criteria accurately in different domains. The implication of this, of course, is that there is an accurate way and, by extension, a wrong or inaccurate way. The aim of a liberal education is, after all, the understanding of experience in a "unique way" for Hirst (LE:20).

Certain branches or sections of a discipline are more satisfactory than others in terms of setting up the curriculum of a liberal education. Hirst argues that "many sections of physics are probably more comprehensive and clear in logical character, more typical of the well developed physical sciences than, say, botany" (LE:20). According to this paradigm principle, some sections are better than others as an introduction to scientific knowledge. The same can be said in other disciplines where, according to Hirst, "many would favor a course in literature to any one other" (LE:20). It is not too difficult to see where all this is going. All things are not in fact equal (LE:21).

For Hirst, it is not problematic to claim to have a publicly accepted framework of knowledge. The logic of the form of knowledge shows the valid ways in which its terms and criteria are used. The logic is publicly expressed. It consists of the general and formal principles to which the terms "must conform in knowledge" (LE:21). If there is to be knowledge at all for Hirst, it is "simply that the framework lays down all the general formal relations of the concepts" (LE:21).

Responses to Modern Schooling: Sources for a "Post" Modern Pedagogy

Hirst's conception of a liberal education appears to have many attractive elements, possibly even to one of a postfoundational persuasion. At first blush, an education system built on public consensus and publicly agreed-upon operating symbols has a particular appeal. Surely, the principle of reason and the pursuit of knowledge are both important in and of themselves. Rationality is said to be something that leads to the productive good of the whole. And a community of consensus, gesturing toward inclusion, has to be a good thing. For a young teacher entering the profession, these appear to be reasonable and rational principles to build a practice upon.

But the foundational logic that has traditionally informed the curricular content of pedagogy and the institution of education has been challenged in the "post" modern era. Through poststructural theory, postmodernism questions the belief in the possibility of describing the determinate rules and systems of reality a posteriori perception. Doubt and skepticism cloud the depiction of truth as a generalizable universal of experience independent of bias, prejudice, or the ideological attributes of tradition and history (Harvey, 1990; Lyotard, 1984). Many of the French philosophers of the postmodern age, in particular, have questioned some of the assumptions of Western epistemology. Jacques Derrida, Michel Foucault, Jean-François Lyotard, and Jean Baudrillard have addressed the ethical implications of the Enlightenment mentality-morality of modernism for the institution of education and critically gauged the complex problems of knowledge, power, and language in relation to the construction of discipline and disciplinarity.

Hirst's conception of liberal education is based on pursuit of the forms of knowledge found in separate and definable disciplines. Moreover, the knowledge that is archived into such disciplines is thought to be achieved through public consensus. The notion of community here is one predicated on the Habermasian notion of a clear and unfettered exchange of communication as rational, public discourse. It is as if, through dialogue, our society comes to reasonable and rational conceptions of knowledge over time that lead to the productive good of the whole. But for the postmodernist theorist, community does not actually work this way. To start, a community is actually an institution based on "exclusion," as opposed to inclusion, or a taking up of arms (munitions) against others. And it is certainly not an institution capable of consensus—more like dissensus. We do not have equal representations or, even, the means for equal representation within a community because society is stratified according to arbitrary markers like class, gender, sexuality, or ethnicity. Nor are there a set of transcendent or transcendental values that appeal to everyone within a community. From the postmodernist perspective, the notion that a community is made up of equal voices masks the true nature of human associations within political structures that privilege some voices over others.

This "masking" of the true nature of human associations within political structures applies to the formation of disciplines. For the postmodernist, the knowledge archived into traditional disciplines does not develop naturally or come through a community of equal voices or a process of public consensus. The hierarchical schemata of densely prescriptive knowledge structures that are the basis for educational practices and curricular formations are supported by an exemplar of epistemology as transmissive knowledge in the modernist ideal. It is grounded on an empirical research base that is an immutable archive of science and its laws. What is officially recognized as "knowledge" ***orders*** and ***is likewise ordered by*** the institutional formation of the disciplines

(Apple, 1992). The system of valuations/devaluation is based in the immediate contingencies of a binary logic. As we saw with Hirst, some things get characterized within a form of knowledge as "accurate," others "inaccurate." This opposition forms the Western foundation and certainty of knowledge. It is a way of thinking whose effects are congealed within the totalizing medians of an easily transferable logic of culture and science. Truth becomes the effect of a discourse supported by the prevailing structures of power. Some topics are worthy of an introduction to scientific knowledge or literary knowledge. Others less so. Physics in, botany out. Literature takes precedence over, say, fine arts. Claiming public consensus, or public acceptance, is an ideal of discipline formation that covers and simultaneously justifies the cultural politics of knowledge and reinforces an illusion of equity that naturalizes the ideological basis of sociohistorical meaning constructions.

Along these lines of theoretical demarcation, Foucault (1980) conducted remarkable genealogical researches into the archaeology of the discursive ordering of meaning and sense within the human sciences. The historicity of Western episteme is illuminated throughout his work as the synchronic and diachronic structuring of language usage and form that constitutes a nexus of power/knowledge relations. Foucault identifies how discourse is codified by the cultural expropriations of language, via its production and its reception. Power is instituted through linguistic means as a theory of praxis to be performed. In short, for Foucault an "ethics of knowledge" is born of discourse practices. From the ordering of vague concepts in the mind to the surreptitious workings of language upon the culture of society, the discursive nature of human existence is analyzed by Foucault through an architectonic mode of conceptual reconstructions. His archaeology is a method for defining the expanding regions of an array of belief systems that function to inform subjectivity through the disciplining of the subject. In this context of its usage, the word "discipline" specifically refers to the active process of training or educating the body for docile subservience (e.g., a master and a disciple), a meaning that is brought out in the Latinate origins of its root. Foucault (1980) tried to reveal the operative features of this cruel force of institutional domination by analyzing how the surveillance techniques used in schools and prisons (taking exemplary form in the model for the Panopticon developed by Jeremy Bentham) are internalized by a willful subject functionally capable of dissent. The linguistic essence of the representation of subjective identity subsumes the difference between being and milieu, humanity and socius. The desire to "respect such differences, and even try to grasp them in their specificity" (Foucault, 1973: xii) of construction is what fascinated Foucault. Even more to the point was the question of why a subject would seek to be dominated, which is an important theme running through his work. This line of inquiry enabled him to reflect upon the obvious ideological inconsistencies within the macrology of institutionalized systems of thought and how readings of subjectivity may be conducted from the microscopy of an intense questioning of attitudes toward language.

Even more radically antifoundationalist in scope than the de-archiving methods of Foucault, Derrida (1976) has theorized a conception of difference that is an ironic reversal of the laws of speculative idealism governing Western philosophy from the ancient Greek thinking to Hegel and afterward. Even in deconstruction, difference is an epistemological benchmark of "the Other." But Derrida moves beyond the idealization of identity to signify the (non)ended of absolute knowledge or the self-effacement of dialectical totalities that can never be resolved (Derrida, 1981, 1976). He extends the Hegelian imperative for a strict negativity to the quasi semantics of meaning deferrals that suspend closure. This is an iterability articulated by the affective differences of the trace of repetition displacements, or *différance.* What Foucault (1980) and Derrida (1992) have both clarified are the dangers of liberal humanist arguments for the "singularity" and "particularity" of subjective identity. It is their contention that projects intending to regularize the cognitive, the affective, and even the bodily behaviors of individuals within the field of a society or culture can no longer be condoned by promoting "the truth" of knowledge through a dialectical symmetrization of subjective identity as either positive or negative in nature. To suggest that there can be such an equationing of subjectivity through interventive means is a very troubling hypothesis. There is difference in similarity, similarity in difference. There are differences within subjectivities correlating to differences within perception that must be taken into account. Valorizing the fragmentation of subjectivity or acknowledging the openness of difference warrants an appreciation for the plurality of discourses or alternative configurations of legitimate meaning sources that embrace the contexts of society and culture. Foucault suggests that "we must not imagine a world of discourse divided between accepted discourse and excluded discourse ... but as multiplicity of discursive elements that can come into play in various strategies" (cited in Martusewicz 1992: 147). In identifying the need to be open to a plethora of subject positions, what postmodern theorizing forthrightly discourages is the recuperation of "otherness," an objectification of identity leading either to a rejection or an "exoticization" of the other (see McLaren, 1994). Such a differentiation of subjectivities reconstitutes a stereotypical metaphor of "cultural authenticity" and ignores the reality of individuals as existing within communities of difference.

Knowledge claims that grant primacy to Western epistemological edicts, while suppressing the capacity to reinforce the ideological differences of marginalized group identities in relation to the historicity of "Reason," are exclusionary. Especially, insofar as a reliance upon an introspective normativity is entrenched within a monodimensional view of subjective consciousness. Poststructuralism provides the critical means for facilitating a hermeneutic shift in the discursive means for upholding regimes of power/knowledge and that critical act of resistance would offer much needed respect to the dissonance of voices kept at the border lines of a "general culture" (Giroux 1988). Jencks (1992: 36) elucidates the ethical ramifications of perpetuating the logic of a one-sided epistemological background characteristic of the dominance of one culture by another to illustrate how the prospective effects of this myopia can be opposed with what a postmodern education expects of its participants:

> It is crucially important that free communication be safeguarded and a good education provided for everyone. Otherwise, it is quite certain we will create more vicious divides within society and between cultures, and deepen the shame of a post-industrial society—the permanent underclass. Such moral points are not out of place ... since every post-modern discourse emphasizes the interconnectedness of things.

In explaining the purpose of recognizing varying viewpoints to consolidate an aura of community, Jencks converges upon the unifying aspect of postmodernism that would foster an appreciation for otherness and difference through concentrating upon the contextual dependency of human understandings relative to the multivariate nature of experience (Giroux 1990). A noncoercive environment in which to initiate genuinely intersubjective dialogues between perspectives is crucial to the familiarization of differences for the enrichment of society overall. Acceding to differences of alternative domains within the communicative substrata of "Culture" could lead to a sublimation of the axiomatics for upholding a hierarchy of privilege by defusing the institutionalized logic of an enforced unity of identity through either visible or invisible means of discipline, training, and correction designed to "normalize" subjectivity. What entitles the subalterned or disenfranchised to a voice denies the reification of subjectivity that a general culture depends upon. Its radical ethics protects the inherent differences of subjective identity against the consensus and consistency of a dominant discourse (Spivak, 1992).

A corollary effect of establishing a semiosphere of cultural communication is the psychological necessity of coping with the effects of a lack of determinacy in meaning-making. Or, what is the aftermath of a fissuring of rigid moral orders of discourse arising from approbation of otherness or of difference. This relativistic type of social bonding requires a more "open" than "closed" interpretative matrix through which to renegotiate the cultural politics of a critical awareness and subjective differences. Within postmodernism, poststructural theories of signification proffer such flexible critical tools for analyzing the cybernetics of institutional knowledge constructions in order to reveal how the ideological presuppositions within the textualized forms of a discursive expression of content mediate to systemically neutralize the freedom of subjective conclusions by a reconstruction of the conceptual conditions of "truth" through writing (see Kellner, 1988). Sometimes described as needlessly cynical or just "playful," poststructuralism suspends the finality of an idiosyncratic reading by resisting the terminating values of signification within a text. Meaning is taken to a subjective plateau of situationally viable, but potentially variable interpretative choices that cannot appeal to objective measures or standards for a verification of "truthfulness" (Derrida, 1976). Poststructuralism destabilizes the disinterestedness of knowledge. It grounds texts firmly within the literary contexts or the situations of their constructions to expand the intersubjectivity of world to the variegated dimensions of "possible worlds" (Eco, 1979). Poststructuralism denies objectivity within perception. It places perception within the affectivity of discourse so as to account for the effectuation of consciousness from linguistic contexts and practices. The validity of arguments is shown not to be self-evident in language, but contiguous to a presentation of contextually discerned phenomena that are both faithful and unfaithful to the constructions of their own logic (Derrida, 1976).

Jean-François Lyotard (1984) and Jean Baudrillard (1981) align the postmodern arena of information exchange to the spectacle of computer-simulated graphics and the images of techno-pseudo presentation that are multiplying within the symbolic field of cultural production. The effects of these "new" visual-based media fetishize the sense of otherness or of difference within community. They implode and fix the conceptual limits of identity in a ready-made format for a globally disseminated, intersubjective networking of fictional realities. According to Baudrillard, the swift metastasization of available technologies for modeling simulations of real-world phenomena have so permeated contemporary society through the proliferation of "virtual media" (e.g., television, video, computers, etc.) that the boundaries separating "the real" from "the fabricated" are no longer distinguishable. Just disguised in the glossy formulaic alternatives of an idyllic *hyperreality* (Baudrillard, 1981). These *simulacra* of the real transgress the subjective experience of the world as real. Having been refurbished and recoded, the essential qualities of reality consequently shape the subjective understanding and knowledge in a newly self-conscious way. A more intricate and sophisticated system of information de-archiving is now required by the discerning subject (see Baudrillard, 1981). Baudrillard identifies parody as the critical lens. Seeking the existence of a transcendental referent or signified in technological dissimulations of the real is no longer possible. There are no limits to what can or should be thought in the parameters of simulated realities because there are no limits to what can be produced. It is because the generic or normative archetypes of fictionalizations of phenomena are fed back into the real that "truth" therefore loses all plausibility within the infinite permutations of meaning-making propagated through the cross-mediality of a visual semiotics of cultural literacy. Lyotard echoes the postmodern stance Baudrillard puts forward an apropos representation by refuting the commensurability of meaning across incompatible ideologies or competing epistemologies and modernist metanarratives from postmodern discourses:

> Consensus does violence to the heterogeneity of language games. And invention is always born of dissension. Postmodern knowledge is not simply a tool of the authorities; it refines our sensitivity to differences and reinforces our ability to tolerate the incommensurable. (1984, p. 75)

The application of the Wittgenstein phrase "language games" to discourse refers to, at least, a partial incommensurability of understandings among subjects or a nonpractical consensus of intersubjectivity. The reconcilability of meaning-making emanates less from genuine agreement than from the pragmatic suppression of differing ideological orientations maintained relative to individual belief systems. What Lyotard would seem to suggest is that claims to knowledge can only be approached through a self-critical consciousness, whereby dissent is the questioning of the difference of concepts in a constantly malleable state of flux. It is a prototype of reading for broadening a subjective acquaintance of the likelihood of alternative semantico-stylistic prospects within expression. Scrutinizing the astructural "depths" of the interplay of these discursive potentialities fuses the interpretability of content with "textualizations" of experience by harnessing the critical power of the subject to unearth the ideological undertones that influence the recording of a perspective and the means to attempt to comprehend it.

All of these theorists are concerned in some way with recognizing the heterogeneity of perspectives within contemporary societies. And each is well aware that this is difficult to attain whenever a dominant ideology, metanarrative, or systemized tradition is accepted as natural, neutral, necessary, or given. In such cases, what happens to those voices in society that deviate from the so-called norm? That fall outside the apparent publicly agreed-upon principles that undergird education and society? The distressing signs of the historical legacy of modernism are to be found in the material domain of discriminatory social practices instituted by the cultural politics of an exclusionary agenda in the name of neoliberal conceptions of an autonomous subject. This difference or deviation from the accepted "norms of being" has been accorded a pejorative connotation in relation to highly arbitrary criteria of judgment based on the ever-so-problematic categories of race, ethnicity, class, gender, and sexuality. This conscious disenfranchisement of alternate subjectivities or "otherness" is in effect the empirical ground of marginalization within the social sphere of community. It is the material result of the societal production of the meaning of representation that rationalizes the social value placed on acts of inclusion and exclusion. Difference therefore comes to be measured practicably in relation to the acceptable configuration of cultural ordinances of aspect—being like others means being acceptable to a closed conception of community as the taking up of arms against the radicality of difference. Any deviation from standardized images of "normality" is figuratively conceived in terms of narrowly defined criteria and the fixed, qualitative scaling of personal or group characteristics. Marginalization ensues. Consequently, the question of difference has come to be elided with the question of the effects of dominant ideologies upon what are the identity politics of the representation of selfhood within community.

Postmodern Education?

The break of postmodern theorizing with representational foundationalism has been much celebrated. But where this "epistemological rupture" leads remains a highly contested issue. On the one side, the more apophatic factions within the postmodern debate envision the presently confused critical condition as the result of an apocalyptic resignation looking forward in space and time to the end of history: all options will soon be exhausted in toto, leaving no "tangible" future from which to realize the human progression of a history of meaning (Kellner, 1988; see also Best and Kellner, 1991). On the other side, more optimistic factions view the current condition of the postmodern critical collage as an extension of interpretative differences denied modernism and portray the alterity of the re-representation of ideas by a linking of the cultural sphere of knowledge to an intertwining of discourses exhibiting an endless intertextuality of expressive forms (Hutcheon, 1992; see also Bennington, 1986). Linda Hutcheon (1992), for example, points out that the fractured pluralism of our times has given rise to the need for a revitalization of theorizing and of expression. She posits a metafictive antigenre of writing that might successfully cohabitate with the ideological vicissitudes of a postmodernist politics of knowledge. The critical subtlety of a postmodern consciousness engenders an acceptance, if only a relative one, of the very belief systems it attempts to subjugate and to problematize by incorporating them within the boundless textuality of its pliant corpus. In this fashion, perspectival standards are immanently assessed so as to permit for "aesthetic forms and social formations to be problematized by critical reflection" (Hutcheon, 1992: 77). Relating the postmodern dilemma of difference more specifically to the growing discipline of cultural studies, Stuart Hall (1986) believes individuals can no longer subscribe to critical absolutes within such a magnitude of contradictory understandings of reality that is pervading societies. Systematized traditions can offer insights for a critical consumption of their relative value as discourses of difference or examples of otherness so as to change the force of "old arguments" in light of more original and more radically open perspectives. Whereas theoretical absolutism has offered a "series of uneven developments that have emerged out of conflicts between traditional economic models and new cultural formations and modes of criticism" (Giroux, 1988: 10–11), a postmodern perspective would, more often than not, embrace an acceptance of plurality and of difference within hermeneutic frameworks through a self-critical analysis of the discursive structuring of the conceptual layout of arguments related in order to bring to the surface any "blind spots" (i.e., contradictions of position, ideological hierarchies, etc.). Such a "deconstructive reading" would play the language or themes of a text against itself to test the solidity of the logic of its conceptual foundations (Derrida, 1976). Deconstruction reveals the argumentative means of organizing the authority of a subject position taken up in a text by evaluating the preoccupations of discourse that follow the linguistic structuring of a perceived reality. Derrida (interviewed in Kearns and Newton, 1980: 21) warns of the dangers of instrumental uses of deconstruction to unilaterally reject all claims to knowledge:

> I would never say that every interpretation is equal . . . The hierarchy is between forces and not between true and false. . . . I would not say that some interpretations are truer than others. I would say that some are more powerful than others. The hierarchy is between forces and not between true and false. There are interpretations which account for more meaning and this is the criterion.

The external and internal interaction of the "system of forces" acting to generate meaning-making potential (to which Derrida has often referred as the outcome of the cumulative effects of psychologically motivated factors) is never identical for any two individuals (see Derrida, 1976, 1981). Every individual brings to an act of reading the mental differences of a subjective identity drawn from experiences that have inculcated the (un)conscious formation of a personalized psychic reality. Derrida (also from Kearns and Newton, 1980; 21–22) comments further upon the role of the difference of subjectivity in deconstruction:

> No-one is free to read as he or she wants. The reader does not interpret freely, taking into account only his own reading, excluding the author, the historical period in which the text appeared and so on. . . . I think that one cannot read without trying to reconstruct the historical context but history is not the last work, the final key, of reading.

Derrida's explanation, at odds with the hyperrelativism attributed to deconstruction by its critics, leaves open a hermeneutical space or "gap" in which to explore the significance of the intentionality of meaning (re)constructions to be derived from the reading, while simultaneously suggesting that such considerations are to be seen as but a single agent coloring the discursive mediation of experience resulting in the textualization of "reality." Perspectives may not be consciously "selected," but differences within the discursive conditions of experience forefront a variety of subject stances that therefore concede a surplus of positional definitions.

Postmodern theoretical discourses, via the tenets of poststructuralism, engage in criticism removed from nurturing the isolation of personal meaning-making by constantly searching for "the possible" in "the unlikely" or "the improbable." And the iconoclastic experimentalism of this epistemological adventurousness is valorized by the gravity of Jencks's (1992: 11) postmetaphysical observations: "The uncontested dominance of the modern world view has definitely ended. Like it or not the West has become a plurality of competing subcultures where no one ideology and episteme dominates for long." Rather than helping to create an adversely competitive environment that would deny "subcultures" the right to be heard over the monologue of dominant metanarratives, accepting the heterogeneity of perspectives within contemporary societies requires legitimating the postmodern interplay among a variety of differing voices (Lyotard, 1984).

The Ethical Turn: The Debt and Duty of New Academic Responsibility

Has the uncontested dominance of the modern worldview definitely ended? Has the West become a plurality of competing cultures and subcultures where no one ideology or episteme dominates for long? When directed toward the field of education, the answer to these questions is not altogether clear. We have definitely had a reconceptualization of curriculum in the academy. The influx of postcolonial theory, critical pedagogy, neo-Marxism, feminist theory, and the new sociology of education has certainly been felt. But how that has trickled down to teacher training and, more specifically, the school system generally is altogether another matter. Some argue that despite massive changes in the nature of society over the last forty years the prevalent conception of what constitutes worthwhile knowledge in liberal education is still very much like the one that Hirst details here (Quin, 2000). To garner some sense of how this impacts at the level of school policy, consider how one school commission articulated its definition of highly valued knowledge more than twenty years after Hirst published his article:

> Knowledge is the province exclusively of the mind; divided by its own logic into the boundaries of disciplines, represented by subjects in the school curriculum and by faculties in school organization; having an existence independent of the knower: the preserve of a select few, for whose membership there must

> be competition; acquired by instruction, its acquisition assessed by norm-referenced testing. (Commonwealth Schools Commission, 1987: 20)

Today, another twenty years removed from this foundational definition of knowledge, thousands of American educators and schools have even renewed calls for a "core knowledge movement" based on the premise that a grade-by-grade core of common learning is necessary to ensure a sound and fair education. Founded by E. D. Hirsh, Jr., the core knowledge movement is said to be based on a large body of cognitive psychology, as well as careful examination of several of the world's most effective school systems. Interestingly, when considered in relation to the applicability of Hirst's conception of liberal education today, the core knowledge Web site claims that "schooling should provide a solid, specific, shared core curriculum in order to help children establish strong foundations of knowledge" (http://www.coreknowledge.org, 2007). It all sounds a little too familiar. Who gets to decide what knowledge is of most worth, what knowledge is "core" for everyone?

The question of a stable core of knowledge is beside the point entirely. Educational possibility does not involve definitively determining whether the educated person today is still, even if partially, one "who has had—and profited from—a liberal education of the kind outlined by Hirst in his famous essay" (Martin, 1981: 98). Nor is it about deciphering just how far critical theories and critical pedagogies have seeped into mainstream educational thinking to protect the paradigmatic and ideological boundaries of the disciplines. The goal is no longer to simply ask "What knowledge is of the most worth?" or to attempt to assign a relative value to the pertinence of specific modernist or postmodernist theories of knowledge or curriculum development. Now, more than ever, there is a different obligation: an obligation to recognize the presence of the infinite possibilities and multiple horizons of alterity that destabilize the grounding of subjectivity and our knowledge about what it means to be human, which in turn expands the boundaries of disciplinarity. This newly arisen responsibility highlights the problem of opening or creating locations welcoming otherness within academic institutions and the architecture of its disciplinarity. But the irony is that schools and universities occupy the colonized space of traditional knowledge archives and are at the same time alterior to the logic of the status quo simply by producing new forms of knowledge and blazing trails of discovery that change the disciplines.[2] New locations of responsibility are enacted within academic institutions. The ethical problem of who *can, should be*, or *is* capable of determining the propriety of knowledge claims—the space and place of the cultural-institutional indexicality marking the public paths of the disciplines and what it means to know, its entrances and exits—is a flash point of conflict. Pedagogical institutions put in motion the academic machinery for the cultural reproduction of knowledge and its testability as forms of practice. Teaching is always already implicated in the perennial question of democracy and discipline, knowledge, difference, otherness, social justice, and the right to education for each and every subject and citizen. In "The Future of the Profession or the Unconditional University," Jacques Derrida invokes the urgency of the need to recognize new tasks for pedagogy after the cosmopolitical orientations of globalization that directly address the academic responsibility of educational institutions and by extension those who teach, work, and live *in* and, perhaps, *for* them, as the teaching body (*le corps enseignant*).[3] What does this mean exactly to the future of the "professor" of knowledge? To say that pedagogical institutions, and those who are a part of it, are it, possess total and unabiding and, hence, *irresponsible and unaccountable* control of the intellectual domain they survey is to surmise a legacy of exclusion. There is no space left to welcome other possibilities and conditions of knowledge that are not sanctioned. It becomes a question of unconditional affinity and openness toward embracing the epistemological difference of the other without giving way to hesitance or reservation, empirical qualification and moral judgment, let alone indignation.

The question of a "proper domain" of knowledge is a question of rights, of institutions, of community and difference, of humanity and what is proper to the study of humanity—of propriety and domination, appropriation, expropriation, of property, participation, ownership and fairness, and therefore of law, ethics, and ultimately, of social justice. In the end, the question of knowledge brings us back to the connections between culture and knowledge within educational institutions. It extends the problem of democracy and *democraticity*, governance and governmentality, of the responsibilities and principles relating to the formation and formativity of a system of a "public education" on an international scale. Derrida alludes to an unconditional responsibility toward otherness via the cosmopolitical as "mondialization" or "worldwide-ization" within the disciplines rooted in the enigmas of disciplinarity or "epistemism" and subjective experience that inflect knowledge. It is a matter of locating the axiomatic difference of these terms and their interrelatability—a hospitable space and place that only an open concept of community and education can entreat them to because there is difference.

An academic community must welcome the production of different knowledges and efface the traditional boundaries of knowledge and research that build walls around the disciplines and what it means to know. A genealogy of difference essentially exposes alterity within formations of thought constructed as logical and rational. What is thought to be common sense without self-interest requires an ethical expansion of thought and thinking. A *moving beyond* limitations or borders without conditional limits to knowledge protected by the ideological beacon of the discourse of "enlightened thinking." An unconditional academic responsibility would safeguard freedom of thought: the principle right to say everything and anything. The academic responsibility Derrida has wished to "awaken or resituate"[4] is a *double gesture that bridges the ungrounded space of the conditions of possibility over which positions on ethics and responsibility, reason and rationality are thought-out and taken.* The difficulty of this "new academic responsibility" is the fact that it actively opposes the "prohibiting limitations"[5]: "The unacceptability of a discourse, the non-certification of a research project, the illegitimacy of a course offering are declared by evaluative actions: studying such evaluations is . . . one of the tasks most indispensable to the exercise of academic responsibility, most urgent for the maintenance of its dignity."[6] To intervene decisively in the business of education is to appeal (to) reason, to ask for the concession of reasons out of which to judge judgments made in the name of truth and the imperative for gaining knowledge and teaching it as such.

This antinomic responsibility can be characterized as "the experience and experiment of the *aporia*"[7] enacted within the general domain as a hypothetical "community of thought,"[8] a community that is committed to the "sounding [of] a call to practice it."[9] Nurturing a "community of the question"[10] is a chance for safekeeping the possibility of an academic responsibility that is proto-ethical. How would it function? Derrida explains as follows:

> Such a community would interrogate the essence of reason and of the principle of reason, the values of the basic, of the principle, of radicality, of the *arkhe* in general, and it would attempt to draw out all the possible consequences of this questioning. It is not certain that such a thinking can bring together a community or found an institution in the traditional sense of these words. What is meant by community and institution must be rethought. This thinking must also unmask—an infinite task—all the ruses of end-orienting reason, the paths by which apparently disinterested research can find itself indirectly reappropriated, reinvested by programs of all sorts. That does not mean that "orientation" is bad in itself and that it must be combated, far from it. Rather, I am defining the necessity for a new way of educating students that will prepare them to undertake new analyses in order to evaluate these ends and choose, when possible, among them all.[11]

After the affirmative ethics of deconstruction, this means a "going-beyond that is both an acceptance and a deepening"[12] of reflection on the concepts of ethics, education, and responsibility and a resignation to rethink them if necessary.[13] And thus, to effectuate a change in the thinking of academic responsibility and of our roles as researchers, teachers, and intellectuals.

Derrida asserts, "'Thought' requires *both* the principle of reason *and* what is beyond the principle of reason, the *arkhè* and an-archy."[14] The creation of a chance for the future occurs by keeping the memory of the past alive. There must be an archive, a body of knowledge, to work from, for, and against. It is at the interspaces of old and new knowledge constructions beyond the grasp of "meaning" or "reason" that risks are taken to move beyond what we already know by endeavoring to put the systematicity of what may appear to be grounded or static into motion, play, ***kinesis***. The institutional meeting place of a new academic responsibility, its ethics and politics, would engage the undecidability of interpretative links where a new academic responsibility could be forged between those disciplines that speak a constative (theoretical) language and others that make performative (interventive) statements, like a bridge across an abyss of reason. It "risks" reenvisioning the education after the cosmopolitical condition: a hypothetical situation of geoglobal interconnectivity or "mondialization" having an "inter-national or inter-state dimension"[15] and related to the question of the *emanation* and diaspora of the *polis* and *politeia as a way of life and a way of knowing*. The idea of the cosmopolitical solidifies the problem of a universal history or "the link among the cities, the *poleis* of the world, as nations, as people, or as States."[16] However, we cannot in good conscience subscribe to the constellations of a panoptic vision of an "abstract universalism"[17] that strangles difference in the name of a general culture of homogeneous communities, permanent archives, and exclusionary institutions. Kant postulated the cosmopolitical as an organic global synthesis of cultures and subjects upon which a template for writing the blueprint of any and all institutions *to come* can exist. In many ways, the vision still guides us and the pedagogical imperatives of today's educational and social institutions.

Interrogating the modality of this desire for sameness demands a rethinking of the future of thinking and works toward illuminating and transforming rather than dismissing or deriding the historicity of "philosophical acts and archives."[18] In questioning the ground of institutions and the reason of their institutionality with respect to the formation of subjectivity, we engage the real-world effects produced by the performative force of epistemological discourses and their responsibility as instances of founding and therefore of foundation that forces us to rethink the nature of what it means to be sovereign, to have rights, to be human, and to know. The notion of the cosmopolitical arises from an antiutopian thrust, contrary to the ideal of a natural universalism of thought and action uniting thinking and subjectivity in the image of the global citizen. It enables us to link the problem of human rights and difference with the Derridean conception of the cosmopolitical point of view in a positive rather than a negative way via the notion of mondialization. We must remember that knowledge and knowing are articulated by the continual reaggregation of the logic of the letter, the terms of its reading as production and reproduction, and the domain of its archive. The problem of how to go about securing both private and public "access to this language and culture, first and foremost by means of education,"[19] involves, more or less, the working out of the problems of subjectivity, community, and difference central to answering the question of academic privilege (who has the right to knowledge?) and the power of location (how? and why?).

The pedagogical onus on an affable (simple, crude, vulgar) modality of cultural production and reproduction without the complexity of resistance or complications of difference fixes the parameters of an institutional ethic of response and responsibility on the conditional boundaries of knowledge and limits the horizons of new forms of thinking and research. But this reduction of the frame of reference to categorical imperatives that willfully ignore the limitations and boundaries of a project of repeating the historicity of Western education occurs only if and when the cosmopolitical nature of difference as a source for new professions of faith is not taken into account. It would be wrong to ignore the diversity within the composition of what we call knowledges and to cull a universal thinking without a diversity of knowledge. The emanation of the cosmopolitical view is a gathering of multiplicity in knowledge communities that articulate the ethical terms of a responsibility to acknowledge the profundity of differences within the same archive of knowledge and thinking, the unimaginable manifestation of many of its parts and partners, nations, states, and peoples whose materiality comprises and cannot but exceed the conceptual totality of its essence. These aspects are not unrelated insofar as such ethico-qualitative judgments require an identification of who would have the privilege and opportunity of participation regarding curricular decisions about the future of the right to education, and why. The global diaspora of what it means to know is the open ground of a *democracy-to-come,* with a *pedagogy-to-come,* and the potentially diverging paths of its filiations, friendships, what is held close, in affinity, to the spirit and the heart, not the mind. *On the one hand,* the demise of the autotelic subject—a subject defined *in, of,* and *by* itself—is fueled by a global vision of a shared community running rampant today. *On the other hand,* the idea of global citizenship as the seat of human hybridity nurtures the impetus toward a communal proclivity of the autotelic Subject as a shared identity and produces the call for a leveling of difference, quite ironically, through what Jacques Derrida has called the cosmopolitical point of view. The world vision of a new humanity privileges both particularity and therefore uniqueness while at the same time creating the conditions for essentialism and the universalization of difference that effaces differences in a mass sharing of an amorphous "global culture."

The productive effect of alterity marks itself on subjectivity as a reflectivity characterized by alienation and growth in relation to the articulation of differences across the signs of culture, language, and the archives of knowledge manipulated and guarded by communications technologies. But the rapid proliferation of new systems, *technes,* and means of representation have hastened the call for a new *humanitas* (that is cosmopolitically friendly) whereby communities of difference are conjoined in new affiliations that render their uniqueness in the difference of themselves as a common feature of a world picture molded by the forces of globalization. **Otherness is present, yes, but with a debt and duty to the historicity of what has gone before.** The concept of the cosmopolitical defines human heterogeneity and similarity through the necessity of marking the interior and exterior limits of culture through language and the rise of other technologies of representation that seek to transfix the world picture of the socioeconomic and ethico-political future of global citizens. The logic of the cosmopolitical within the notion of a global subject, *what it means to know,* and the inauguration of a new academic responsibility broaches the question of human rights and education. It asks us to rethink the certainty of knowledge as a philosophical project of genealogical excavation in relation to social justice and educational equity.

Notes

1. Paul H. Hirst, "Liberal education and the nature of knowledge," in *Philosophical Analysis and Education*, ed. R. D. Archambault (London: Routledge and Kegan Paul, 1965). Henceforth cited as: (LE: followed by page number).
2. Jacques Derrida, "Des humanités et de la discipline philosophiques"/"Of the Humanities and Philosophical Disciplines," in *Surfaces* VI.108 (v.1.0A-16/08/1996): 1. The page references are from the Website version of the text (http://tornade.ere.umontreal.ca/guedon/Surfaces/vol6/derrida.html).
3. See Derrida, "Où commence et comment finit un corps enseignant," 111–153.
4. Ibid., 14.
5. Ibid., 13.
6. Ibid.
7. Derrida, *The Other Heading: Reflections of Today's Europe,* 41.
8. Derrida, "The Principle of Reason," 16.
9. Ibid., 16.
10. Derrida, "Violence and Metaphysics: An Essay on the Thought of Emmanuel Levinas," 80.
11. Derrida, "The Principle of Reason," 16.
12. Gianni Vattimo, *The End of Modernity: Nihilism and Hermeneutics in Postmodern Culture,* trans. Jon R. Snyder (Baltimore: Johns Hopkins University Press, 1988), 172.
13. See Rodolphe Gasché, *Inventions of Difference: On Jacques Derrida* (Cambridge, MA: Harvard University Press, 1994).
14. Derrida, "The Principle of Reason," 18–19.
15. Derrida, "Of the Humanities and Philosophical Disciplines," 2.
16. Ibid.
17. Ibid.
18. Ibid.
19. Ibid.

References

Althusser, L. (1971) *Lenin and Philosophy and Other Essays*, trans. B. Brewster. London: New Left Books.

Apple, M. W. (1992) Education, culture, and class power: Basil Bernstein and the neo-Marxist sociology of education. *Educational Theory* 42(2): 1–27.

Bailey, Charles. (1984) "The challenge of relativism, ideology, and the state." In *Beyond the Present and the Particular: A Theory of Liberal Education*. Boston: Routledge and Kegan Paul.

Baudrillard, J. (1981) *Simulcres et Simulation*. Paris: Galilée.

Bennington, G. (1986) "Postmodernism." In L. Appignanesi (ed.), *Postmodernism*. London: Institute of Contemporary Arts, 5.

Best, S., and Kellner, D. (1991) *Postmodern Theory*. New York: Guilford.

Commonwealth Schools Commission. (1987) The National Policy for the Education of Girls in Australian Schools. Canberra: Commonwealth Schools Commission.

Derrida, J. (1976) *Of Grammatology*, trans. G. C. Spivak. Baltimore: Johns Hopkins University Press.

———. (1978) "Violence and Metaphysics: An Essay on the Thought of Emmanuel Levinas." In *Writing and Difference*, trans. Alan Bass. Chicago: University of Chicago Press, 80.

———. (1981) *Dissemination*, trans. B. Johnson. Chicago: University of Chicago Press.

———. (1983) "The Principle of Reason: The University in the Eyes of Its Pupils," *Diacritics*, Fall, 3–20.

———. (1990) "Où commence et comment finit un corps enseignant," in *Du droit à la philosophie*. Paris: Galilée, 111–153.

———. (1992) *The Other Heading: Reflections of Today's Europe*, trans. Pascale-Anne Brault and Michael Naas. Bloomington: Indiana University Press, 41.

Eco, U. (1979) *The Role of the Reader: Explorations in the Semiotics of Text*. Bloomington: University of Indiana Press.

Foucault, M. (1973) *The Order of Things*. New York: Vintage Books.

———. (1980) *Knowledge/Power*, trans. C. Gordon. New York: Pantheon Books.

General Education in a Free Society: Report of the Harvard Committee. (1946) Cambridge, MA: Harvard University Press.

Giroux, H. A. (1988) "Border pedagogy in the age of postmodernism." *Journal of Education* 170(3): 162–181.

———. (1990) "The politics of postmodernism." *Journal of Urban and Cultural Studies* 1(1): 5–38.

Hall, S. (1986) "On Postmodernism and articulation: An interview." *Journal of Communication Inquiry* 10(2): 45–60.

Harvey, D. (1990) *The Condition of Postmodernity*. Cambridge, MA: Blackwell.

Hirst, Paul H. (1965) "Liberal education and the nature of knowledge." In R. D. Archambault (ed.), *Philosophical Analysis and Education*. London: Routledge and Kegan Paul.

Hutcheon, L. (1992) "Theorizing the postmodern." In C. Jencks (ed.), *The Post-Modern Reader*. New York: St. Martin's, 76–93.

Jencks, C. (1992) "The postmodern agenda." In C. Jencks (ed.), *The Post-Modern Reader.* New York: St. Martin's, 10–39.

Kearns, J., and Newton, K. (1980) "An interview with Jacques Derrida." *Literary Review* 14: 21–22.

Kellner, D. (1988) Reading images critically: Toward a postmodern pedagogy. *Journal of Education* 170(3): 31–52.

Lyotard, J. F. (1984) *The Postmodern Condition: A Report on Knowledge*, trans. G. Bennington and B. Massumi. Minneapolis: University of Minnesota Press.

Martin, Jane Roland. (1981) "The ideal of the educated person." *Educational Theory* 31(2), 97–109.

Martusewicz, R. A. (1992) "Mapping the terrain of the post-modern subject: Post-structuralism and the educated woman." In W. F. Pinar and Reynolds (eds.), *Understanding Curriculum as Phenomenological and Deconstructed Text.* New York: Teachers College Press, 131-158.

McLaren, P. (1994) "Critical pedagogy, political agency, and the pragmatics of justice: The case of Lyotard." *Educational Theory* 44(3): 319–340.

Quin, Robyn. (2000) "A socio-historical study of the construction of knowledge in secondary media education in Western Australia: Whose knowledge?" Ph.D. diss., Edith Cowan University, 2000.

Spivak, G. C. (1992) "Acting bits/identity talk." *Critical Inquiry* 18(4): 770–803.

About the Contributors

Michael W. Apple is the John Bascom Professor of Curriculum and Instruction and Educational Policy Studies at the University of Wisconsin–Madison. He has written extensively on the relationship between differential power and educational policy and practice. Among his recent books are *Educating the "Right" Way: Markets, Standards, God, and Inequality*; *The State and the Politics of Knowledge*; and the 25th anniversary, 3rd edition of *Ideology and Curriculum*.

Jonathan Arendt is a doctoral candidate at the Ontario Institute of Education at the University of Toronto. His areas of interest include poststructuralism and curriculum theory. His work engages narratives of race and ethnicity as well as the politics of education and cultural studies.

Mario Di Paolantonio is assistant professor at York University. His research examines the formation and pedagogical implications of public memory in post-traumatic societies. He is also a research associate and member of the Testimony and Historical Memory Project at the Ontario Institute for Studies in Education.

Paulo Ghiraldelli, Jr., is a professor of philosophy and education at the Universidade Federal de Peranà, Brazil. He is the editor of *Contemporary Pragmatism* and the *Encyclopaedia of Philosophy of Education*. He is also visiting professor in philosophy at Oklahoma State University and has lectured widely in Europe and North America.

Henry A. Giroux is global television network chair in Communication Studies at McMaster University. He is the author of numerous articles and books including *Channel Surfing, Counternarratives* and *The Mouse That Roared: Disney and the End of Innocence* (Rowman and Littlefield).

Neil Harrison is a lecturer in education at the University of New England, Armidale, Australia. He has worked in indigenous education since 1978 as a primary, secondary, and VET teacher, and is currently teaching preservice teachers to include indigenous perspectives in their classrooms. His forthcoming book is titled *Teaching in Indigenous Education*.

Douglas Kellner is the George F. Kneller Chair in the Philosophy of Education at UCLA and is the author of many books on social theory, politics, history, and culture including *Jean Baudrillard: From Marxism to Postmodernism and Beyond* and *Herbert Marcuse and the Crisis of Marxism*. He has also written many works in cultural studies such as *Media Culture* and *Media Spectacle*; a trilogy of books on postmodern theory with Steve Best; a trilogy of books on the Bush administration, including *Grand Theft 2000* and his latest book, *Media Spectacle and the Crisis of Democracy*.

Peter McLaren is a professor in the Division of Urban Schooling, Graduate School of Education and Information Studies, University of California–Los Angeles. He is the author and editor of more than 35 books on topics ranging from critical ethnography and the sociology of education to critical social theory and critical pedagogy. His most recent books include *Che Guevara, Paulo Freire, and the Pedagogy of Revolution* (Rowman and Littlefield, 2000); *Life in Schools* (4th ed.) (Allyn and Bacon, 2002); and *Marxism Against Postmodernism in Educational Theory* (edited with D. Hill, M. Cole, and G. Rikowski) (Lexington Books, 2002). Professor McLaren lectures worldwide on the politics of liberation. His works have been translated into 17 languages.

Gregory O'Leary is a doctoral candidate at the Ontario Institute for Studies in Education at the University of Toronto. Gregory's primary writing involves historically and theoretically shifting conceptions of English and literacy. He has received two prestigious national awards for his work, both the Doctoral and Master's Canada Graduate Scholarships. His work has most recently appeared in *JCT*, and he is currently working on another article entitled "After Literacy: Towards a New Ethics of Curriculum."

Valerie Scatamburlo-D'Annibale is an associate professor in the Department of Communication Studies at the University of Windsor in Ontario, Canada. Her work on social theory, critical pedagogy, and media analysis has been published in various venues including *Cultural Studies/Critical Methodologies*, the *Journal of Educational Philosophy and Theory*, *Current Perspectives in Social Theory*, and in edited book collections including *Filtering the News: Essays on Herman and Chomsky's Propaganda Model* and *Bound by Power: Intended Consequences*.

Lisa Taylor is associate professor at Bishops University in teacher education. She works with postcolonial and feminist perspectives. Her research involves ethnographic projects on critical multiculturalism, multiliteracies, as well as literature education.

Peter Pericles Trifonas teaches at the Ontario Institute for Studies in Education at the University of Toronto. He has taught at schools and universities in North America and Europe. His books include *The Ethics of Writing: Derrida, Deconstruction, and Pedagogy, Revolutionary Pedagogies, Pedagogies of Difference*; *Ethics, Institutions, and the Right to Philosophy* with Jacques Derrida; *Communities of Difference*; and *Good Taste*.

Brenda Trofanenko is an assistant professor of Education at the University of Illinois at Urbana-Champaign. Her research interests include identity and representation; public institutions and historical understanding; and the relationship among academic, popular, and school history in both digital and nondigital media.